Hiking
Georgia

Donald W. Pfitzer

FALCON®

GUILFORD, CONNECTICUT
AN IMPRINT OF THE GLOBE PEQUOT PRESS

FALCONGUIDES

Library of Congress Cataloging-in-Publication Data
Pfitzer, Donald W.
    Hiking Georgia / by Don Pfitzer. — Rev. & expanded.
        p. cm.
    Rev. ed. of: The hiker's guide to Georgia. c1993.
    Includes bibliographical references (p.) and index.
    ISBN 1-56044-717-6
    1. Hiking—Georgia—Guidebooks.   2. Family recreation—Georgia—Guidebooks.   3. Backpacking—Georgia—Guidebooks.   4. Georgia—Guidebooks.   I. Pfitzer, Donald W.   Hiker's Guide to Georgia. II. Title.
GV199.42.G46P46 1999
796.51'09758--dc21   99-14075
                                                                              CIP

Manufactured in the United States of America
Second Edition / Fifth Printing

CAUTION
Outdoor recreational activities are by their very nature potentially hazardous. All participants in such activities must assume the responsibility for their own actions and safety. The information contained in this guidebook cannot replace sound judgment and good decision-making skills, which help reduce risk exposure, nor does the scope of this book allow for disclosure of all the potential hazards and risks involved in such activities.

Learn as much as possible about the outdoor recreational activities in which you participate, prepare for the unexpected, and be cautious. The reward will be a safer and more enjoyable experience.

♻ Text pages printed on recycled paper.

Contents

National Park Service Trails

Northeast Georgia: Blue Ridge Mountains
National Forest Trails

State Park and Wildlife Management Area Trails

Middle Georgia: Piedmont and Fall Line Area

National Forest Trails

State Park Trails

National Park Service Trails

National Wildlife Refuge Trails

Metro Atlanta Area State Park Trails

National Park Service Trails

Chattahoochee River National Recreation Area

Augusta City Area

Southwest Georgia: Coastal Plain State Park Trails

Southeast Georgia: Coastal Plain and Atlantic Coast
State Park and Wildlife Management Area Trails

National Park Service Trails

National Wildlife Refuge Trails

Long Trails

for
Christian Morgan Pfitzer

Acknowledgments

Many people helped make this book possible. Thanks to the Department of Natural Resources, both the Parks and Historic Sites Division and Wildlife Resources Division. Lonice Barrett and David Waller, directors of the two agencies gave me much support and encouragement. I also appreciate the help that came from the U.S. Forest Service, National Park Service, and U.S. Fish and Wildlife Service.

I am especially grateful to Henry Chambers, Trails Coordinator for the State Parks and Historic Sites Division, who helped in deciding which trails to include, walked with me on many trails, and reviewed the descriptions of most of the trails. Without his help the project could not have been completed in a timely manner. Harvey Young, Executive Assistant, Wildlife Resources Division, was especially helpful with maps and natural history research. LeRoy Powell was of great editorial help and as a hiking companion. Thanks to Dr. M. Virginia Tuggle and Annette Loudermilk who graciously reviewed the sections dealing with personal health and safety.

Thanks also to those who were so generous in providing information and assistance: from the U.S. Forest Service Bruce Jewell, Jim Kidd, Larry Thomas, Mike Davis, and Afton Martin; from the National Park Service Jim Howard, Newton Sikes, Richard Hanks, and Mike Webb; from the State Parks and Historic Sites Division; Madelyn Foard, David Foot, Wally Woods, Bob Slack, Gae Stovall, Sonie Shams, Herman Channell, Charles Parkman, and Glenn Agor; from the State Wildlife Resources Division; Dottic Head, Carroll Allen, Noel Holcomb, Allen Padgett, Don Wofford, and Chuck Hand; from the U.S. Fish and Wildlife Service; Jerry Lord.

Special thanks to the Georgia Appalachian Trail Club, the Benton MacKaye Trail Association, and the Pine Mountain Trail Association whose members volunteered thousands of hours working on trails and see to it that they are kept in good shape. If it were not for them many miles of trails would never be completed.

Thanks to the ethical and considerate hikers and campers who spend time in the wilderness and leave it without leaving a trace.

Finally, I am most grateful and appreciative of the help and encouragement from Billie Pfitzer who put up with all the hiking trips and my periodic frustration and who spent many hours editing copy.

Map Legend

MAP LEGEND

Interstate	(00)	Swamp	
U.S. Highway	(00)	Marsh	
State or Other Principle Road	(00)		
Forest Road	[000]	Mountain/Elevation	✕ 0000'
Interstate	⟹	Waterfall	//
Primary Road	⟹	Dam	▬
Secondary Road	⟹	Spring	⌒
Unpaved Road	=====⟹	Mound	▲
Trailhead/Parking	○ ⓟ	Campground	⋀
Main Trail(s)	-------	Trail Shelter	△
Alternate/ Secondary Trail(s)	·········	Picnic Area	⊼
Boardwalk		Gate	•—•
Canal		Bridge	)(
Creek	∼	Footbridge	目
River	∼	Church	⚲
Lake		Cemetery	†
Power Line	•-•-•-•	Gazebo	●
Railroad	+-+-+-+	Cabins/Cottages	■
		Buildings	▬
		Park Entrance	↑
		Overlook/Observation	⊡
		Point of Interest	▨
		Photo Blind	☐

National Forest/Wilderness/ State Park Boundary

State Boundary

Divide

N

0 ———— 1
Miles

Location of Hikes

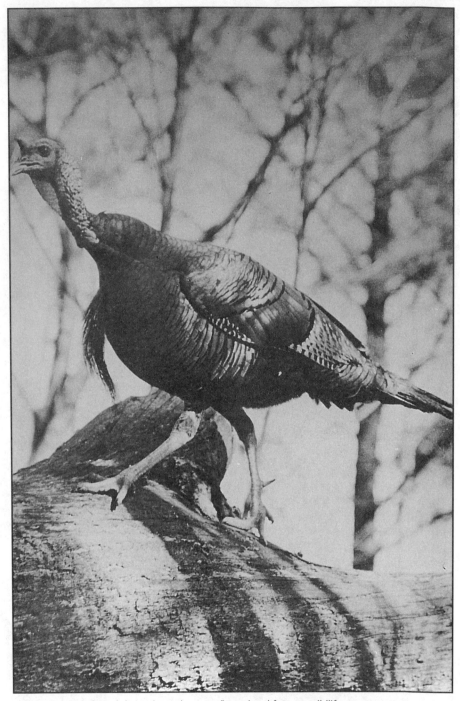

Wild turkeys are found throughout the state (in national forests, wildlife management areas, state parks, and national wildlife refuges). They can be heard gobbling in spring.

Introduction

Georgia has everything to delight the hiker. The largest state east of the Mississippi beckons to you with nearly 1,000 miles of trails. You can walk along wild mountain streams, through rolling foothills, or among the towering pines of the coastal plain. There are hundreds of species of animals and thousands of species of plants to be discovered along the trails of Georgia.

Trails vary in length and difficulty from an easy one-hour walk along a quiet nature trail in a state park to an eighty-mile trek on the Appalachian National Scenic Trail; or from a stroll along a sandy beach of an undeveloped island to hikes among the sheer sandstone cliffs in Cloudland Canyon. Because many of the trails in Georgia are short, less than five miles, and Georgia's temperate weather permits hiking year-round, you can enjoy repeating the hike on these shorter trails throughout the year as each season exhibits its own special charm.

Of the more than 800 miles of trails discussed in this guide, all trails are on public land and most are in the mountains and hills of north Georgia. However, there are many interesting and challenging hikes in central and south Georgia.

Hiking is truly an activity for all ages and physical abilities. Men and women seventy or more years old have hiked the Appalachian Trail. Wide-eyed children with their parents have watched a doe and her fawn cross their path in a quiet woodland of a state park. There are trails for people with special needs from sight impaired to wheelchair dependent.

Physicians, cardiologists, and others tell us that walking briskly for thirty minutes three times a week will do great things for the heart, and that walking is the best form of exercise for more people than any other. Hiking in natural areas is more than physical therapy. Seeing a flower in bloom, glimpsing a squirrel scamper up a tree, watching a deer bound away only to look back inquisitively, listening to a bird stake his claim for nesting territory, or pausing and absorbing the beauty of grand mountain scenery or the closeness of a cypress swamp is therapy for the mind.

Georgia's trails lead to areas rich in botanical, zoological, and geological lore, to cold mountain trout streams, or peaceful warm-water lakes. Trails in national forests and state wildlife management areas may lead to secluded and remote hunting grounds. Whatever your interest may be, there is probably a trail on Georgia public lands that will help you find your point of interest.

PHYSIOGRAPHIC REGIONS AND NATURAL HISTORY

Five major physiographic provinces span Georgia from south to north—Coastal Plain, Piedmont, Blue Ridge, Ridge and Valley, and Cumberland

Plateau. The most extensive of these is the Coastal Plain. It extends from numerous subtropical barrier islands of the Atlantic Coast north to the very irregular "fall line," which crosses the state from Augusta through Milledgeville and Macon to Columbus. Lying north of the fall line is the Piedmont Plateau, rolling foothills that rise gradually from 500 feet to about 1,700 feet where they meet the mountains about fifty miles north of Atlanta. Three smaller regions lie north of the Piedmont: the Blue Ridge, the Cumberland Plateau, and the Ridge and Valley. The largest is the Blue Ridge in the northeast, a part of the Appalachian mountain system, considered to be among the oldest mountains in the world. The mountains here rise to the greatest height in the state, 4,783 feet at Brasstown Bald. The Cumberland Plateau is in the extreme northwest corner of the state. It is part of the Allegheny mountain system and is represented by Lookout and Sand mountains, which reach to 2,000 feet. Between these two regions lies the Ridge and Valley, which extends from the Georgia-Tennessee line southwest seventy-five miles toward Cedartown.

The coastal islands, bathed by the warm flows of the Gulf Current, have many subtropical affinities. The mountains that are more than 4,000 feet have strong affinities to Canadian forests. Georgia spans the continent in climate and plant and animal forms, giving you an almost unlimited range of experiences from which to choose.

Plant and animal diversity in the Blue Ridge is world renowned. More than 150 species of trees and 400 species of shrubs and vines grow in the state. Add an almost countless number of flowering herbaceous plants, ferns, mosses, liverworts, lichens, mushrooms and other fungi, and the sum equals a plant community as diverse as anywhere in the country. Also known to occur in Georgia are more than 65 species of mammals, more than 75 species of snakes and lizards, and more than 120 species of salamanders, toads, frogs, and turtles.

A number of good field guides are available to satisfy your desire to know what plant or animal you see on the trail. *Native Trees of Georgia* printed by the Georgia Forestry Commission, *Wildflowers of the Southeastern States* by Duncan and Foote and any one of the Peterson Field Guide series will help. See Appendix C, Information Sources, for a more comprehensive list.

ARCHAEOLOGY AND HISTORY

The mark of man on Georgia extends from Ice-Age paleo-Indian culture predating 9000 B.C. through gatherers, mound builders, and more permanent villages of farmers who settled here in the early 1500s when DeSoto traveled the full length of Georgia in search of gold. Colonial history in Georgia predates the Revolutionary War, and the Civil War of the 1860s is recorded throughout the state. One of the earliest true trail blazers in the state was the botanist, William Bartram. He traveled through Georgia extensively during the mid-1770s; the Bartram Trail bears his name today. In 1838, the U.S. Government forced the strong democratic society of the

Cherokee Indian Nation of north Georgia to resettle on a reservation west of the Mississippi River. Much of Georgia's history is found along the many miles of trails that lace the state.

CLOTHING AND EQUIPMENT

Comfortable clothes and footwear will do more to make a hike pleasant than almost any other thing. The great variety of hiking and walking situations make it impossible to cover all personal needs, but here are a few suggestions. Dress in layers. The first is a light, inner layer made of material that will wick away moisture from the skin; next is a warmer porous layer that can be removed if necessary; and over that wear an outside layer that is wind and/or rain proof. This permits you to regulate your temperature easily by putting on or taking off layers as the weather and exertion dictates. A good poncho or rain coat should be standard backpacking equipment. Rain in Georgia is frequent and unpredictable.

Everyone seems to have a different idea about what type of footwear to use. It becomes a personal preference, but it should be sturdy and supportive. Many people still wear good leather boots for serious hiking, while others prefer lighter weight boots with breathable, water resistant fabrics. The best advice for the beginner is to visit a good outfitter of outdoor sports equipment and try on several styles before finally deciding.

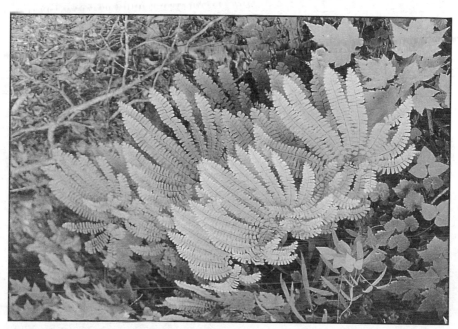

Northern maidenhair ferns are found in the mountains.

Since some stores rent equipment, this is a great way to find out what type of tent, backpack, or other camping equipment is best suited for you. Several good books on the subject are mentioned in Appendix C. Most are available in libraries. One of the best is Colin Fletcher's *The Complete Walker III*. Others are available in the better outdoor sporting goods stores.

Walking is one of the most popular forms of exercise and recreation in the country today. When I was growing up, walking was a way of life. My family walked to the streetcar line, a distance of about a mile along a gravel road lined with mixed woods and fields. We gave no thought to walking as recreation or exercise. But as a very young person with an interest in natural things, I remember these walks were more pleasant rather than being a chore.

PACK IT IN, PACK IT OUT

Few things are more irritating or distasteful than finding aluminum cans, candy wrappers, and other litter along the trail. "Pack it in - pack it out" should be the working motto of every hiker. This is true for short day hikes just as much as for the wilderness backpacker. Get in the habit of taking an extra garbage bag on hikes just to pick up litter left by those unthinking people who use the trail. A clean trail is less inviting to litter.

Modern, lightweight camp stoves and lanterns eliminate the need for campfires and the unsightly stone fire rings left behind. Backpack stoves are ideal for wilderness camp cooking. If you must build a fire on the trail, use a shallow pit instead of a stone fire ring, and when you leave the campsite be sure the fire is completely out and covered over with soil.

The Fun of Hiking Safely

PLANNING THE HIKE

Hiking should be fun even if you hike just to cover ground or for the benefits of physical fitness. Plan hikes that are within your physical ability. Do not attempt hikes or backpacking segments that are more than you can safely accomplish in daylight. Know the terrain. Use USGS 7.5-minute quad maps or talk to someone who has been there. Hiking after dark is not only uncomfortable it is dangerous, especially if you are not familiar with the topography and trail conditions.

Always leave an itinerary of the hike with someone before you leave. It should include where you will be hiking, where you will park, your estimated time of completing the trip, and who to contact if necessary. Listed under each trail description is a section "**For More Information.**" This can be used to contact personnel in state parks, national forests, and other public lands where trails are located should emergencies arise. There are registers on the Appalachian Trail at the trailhead on Springer Mountain and at many of the shelters. It is a good idea to leave pertinent information at these points. For some hikes such as the Appalachian Trail, it is necessary to register with the land managing agencies. The Coosa Backcountry Trail, which originates at Vogel State Park, Tallulah Gorge State Park, and the Pine Mountain Trail at F. D. Roosevelt State Park are other trails requiring registration to obtain a free permit to camp along these trails.

Many of the trails are in national forests where hunting is permitted in season. State records indicate that there is little risk in hiking during the hunting season. However, during the hunting season it is a good idea to wear a bright, preferably blaze orange, outer garment like a jacket, vest, or cap. Don't flash a white handkerchief during deer season or a red or blue one during turkey season. Since hunting is not permitted in state parks, this leaves hundreds of miles of excellent trails for hikers to use all through the hunting season.

Hiking and walking seem so simple it lulls the walker into being careless at times. No hike, whether a day hike or a weeklong backpacking hike, should begin without the basic essentials of a first-aid kit and simple survival items. Think of it like fastening your seat belt before driving to the corner store or on a 500-mile interstate trip. The first-aid kit is a very personal item and its contents will depend on the hiker's personal needs and concerns for a particular hike. However, the kit can be very small and light and should contain at least Band-aids, roll of gauze and/or gauze compresses, a roll of adhesive tape, Ace or other elastic wraparound bandage, aspirin or other headache tablets, a tube of antibacterial ointment, a patch of Mole Skin, needles, scissors, or a Swiss Army knife with scissors. This can all go in a small Ziplock bag. Longer backpacking hikes for more than

5

one night should contain these same items as well as such things as Benadryl for allergic response, a small packet of meat tenderizer for insect stings, a mild laxative, something to combat diarrhea, and other personal items may be added. A good, compact snake-bite kit that includes an efficient suction device can also be added if the hiker is so inclined.

Survival kits can and should be simple and efficient; a compact space blanket or large garbage bag, a whistle, waterproof matches and/or a reliable cigarette lighter, compass, high energy food bar, ten or twenty feet of light nylon rope, and a small flashlight. These items are essentials and are recommended to be with you at all times, especially when on side trips away from your backpack or campsite.

SHOULD I DRINK FROM THAT SPRING?

In Georgia the answer is no, unless the water has been treated by boiling, filtered with a reliable filter/purifier, or treated with an effective chemical purifier.

There is no real shortage of water in Georgia from the mountains to the sea. However, water quality can be a problem. For this reason it is almost always advisable for day hikers to take water from home for drinking unless drinking water is known to be available. All state parks and most U.S. Forest Service campgrounds and recreation areas will have potable running water. Only occasionally will you find yourself several miles from surface water either from a spring, stream, or lake. On the long trails, like the Appalachian Trail, water sources are frequently marked both by signs and on maps of the trails. Again, this water should be treated before it is considered bacteriologically safe to drink.

Giardiasis is the most common water-borne epidemic disease in Georgia. It is estimated that four percent of the population harbors the protozoan parasite, *Giardia lamblia*. The disease is usually caused by drinking water or eating food contaminated with the protozoa. The parasites colonize in the upper small intestine, resulting in millions of them being excreted daily in stools. Cysts containing many dormant giardia protozoa are passed in the stools of many small mammals like the raccoon and beaver. Larger mammals, including the black bear, deer, wild pigs, cattle, horses, and dogs can also be disseminators. Of course, people can and do spread the parasite to water sources when improperly disposing of feces.

It is easy to steer clear of this hiking hazard by, first, not drinking water directly from streams, no matter how clean, pure, and remote they seem to be. If it is necessary to use water from springs and streams while making long hikes, treat the water first. Making the water safe to use is quite simple, even if time consuming. The simplest method is to boil the water for three or four minutes. Dr. William McKell, medical advisor for Southeastern Outdoor Press Association, recommends that water must be boiled or treated with saturated potassium iodide or tetraglycine hydroperiodate (Globaline). Contaminated water used to wash fruits, vegetables or drinking utensils can also be a source of infection. It should be treated just like drinking water.

Symptoms caused by giardiasis include watery diarrhea, abdominal bloating, flatulence, abdominal tenderness, cramping pain, and weight loss. McKell says, "Unlike bacterial causes of traveler's diarrhea, giardiasis is not likely to spoil your vacation. It may, nevertheless, be an unpleasant souvenir, occurring one to two weeks following cyst ingestion." On the contrary, if the hike is for a week or more on one of the long trails the symptoms can spoil the trip and cause severe dehydration, which can be serious if not treated quickly. In diagnosis the physician should be made aware of the possibility of exposure. The two most commonly used drugs today are quinacrine (Atabrine) and metronidazole (Flayl). Both are obtained by prescription only. The physician will inform the patient of the dosage and potential drug side-effects, which may be unpleasant.

Considerate and ethical hikers will dispose of wastes using proper sanitary methods. The U.S. Forest Service recommends that feces be buried at least eight inches below the surface and at least 100 yards from natural waters. This means that a small shovel or spade should be a standard part of any camper's equipment. I have an old World War I trenching trowel about 11 inches long, including the handle, that fits in a sheath and is ingeniously made to be used as a hatchet, spade, and even a modified hammer. It only weighs eleven ounces and has served well for more than forty years of insect collecting and camping.

Very practical water filters are available today for long hikes and even for base-camp hiking where day hikes are made from a common campsite. Water filters should be capable of filtering *Giardia* along with bacteria and suspended clays and other particles. Change the filter cartridge regularly.

WEATHER

Hiking in Georgia is a year-round activity. There are about as many good hiking days in winter as in summer or spring. Snow and cold or freezing rain in the mountains, and spring and summer showers and thunderstorms throughout the state are about the only weather conditions that hamper your comfort on the trail. Fall weather is best, and September through November is the most popular time to hike.

You must be aware of changing weather conditions. If thunderstorms are in the forecast, recognize that lightning in forest cover can be dangerous. Do not hike along ridgetops and on mountain crests with large exposed rock formations during electrical storms, especially with metal frame backpacks.

Georgia weather is such that winter hiking can be pleasant. It is fun and beautiful to hike in the limited snow that falls in the mountains. Plans for snow hiking should include adequate footwear and clothing to tolerate the cold, wet conditions in case an emergency occurs. Being wet and cold invites hypothermia, a life threatening condition.

Weather in the mountains can change rapidly from pleasant temperatures and clear skies to stormy, wet, and cold conditions in a matter of a few hours. The mountains receive an annual rainfall of sixty to eighty inches. The rest of the state is in the fifty inches per year range. Snowfall

Sonie Shams, who hiked the entire Appalachian Trail alone, talks about backpacking and long hikes at Amicalola Falls State Park.

occurs in the mountains every year, while in south Georgia snowfall is rare. Frequent rains are the most common weather-caused inconvenience to hikers.

BLAZES AND OTHER TRAIL MARKERS

All but a very few trails described here are marked in some fashion. A paint mark (blaze) on a tree is the most used trail marker. One trail will be marked or blazed throughout with one color paint. In a state park with several different trails, a different color may be used for each trail. A few trails are marked with a white, three- or four-inch, diamond-shaped piece of metal nailed to trees and posts along the trail instead of paint blazes. The Chattooga River Trail is marked this way. A new type marker, a flat fiberglass post about four inches wide and four or five feet tall, is being used to mark some trailheads and occasionally along some trails. These are less vulnerable to vandalism and are marked with decals designating trail use and activities not permitted on the trail. In the Oconee National Forest, the U.S. Forest Service has placed numbers on the posts to indicate the trail number.

It has become standard to mark sudden changes in direction of a trail with two blaze marks, one above the other on the same tree. Otherwise most trails are marked so that you should not travel more than a quarter mile without seeing a blaze. The state park and many U.S. Forest Service trails are marked with paint blazes much more frequently than this.

Where two trails occasionally join for a distance, two colors or types of blazes will be used together until the trails separate again.

Hazards in the Backcountry

HYPOTHERMIA

This has been called the number one killer of all outdoor injuries. Hypothermia is the lowering of internal body temperature from exposure to cold, wind, rain, or from being immersed in cold water. Hypothermia can occur when outdoor temperatures are not very cold. It is more common in states like Georgia with moderate climates than in very cold climates. Learn to recognize the symptoms and know that injuries increase the risk of hypothermia. First signs include shivering, followed by no shivering and becoming disoriented and confused. Later the person may appear apathetic and moody. As hypothermia becomes more advanced, the person may lapse into a coma.

The first step in treatment of hypothermia, after making all possible arrangements to get the person to expert medical attention, is to reduce heat loss; get out of the wind and into dry clothes and/or a windproof shell like a space blanket. Pay special attention to covering the head and back of the neck. A cap, hat, or anything windproof and warm should cover the head where a great amount of heat loss occurs. Next try to produce heat in the body core. It is the core that must be reheated. If the victim can drink give them hot, sweet fluids, *not alcohol.*

After applying dry clothes and a windproof outer covering get the patient walking, with support if necessary. Exercise is the best way to improve internal organ heat. If you are alone and recognize hypothermia, drink hot fluids like sweet hot chocolate, get into dry clothes, protect yourself from the wind, and keep moving. Exercise is the most important. Obviously the condition must be recognized before one becomes disoriented or confused.

Sonie Shams, a young woman who hiked the entire 2,100 miles of the Appalachian Trail in 1988, survived a harrowing experience with hypothermia. In her seventh day out from Springer Mountain, the early April weather changed from balmy and clear to soft rain. The next day brought mixed rain and sleet. With an injury to her knee and carrying a heavy pack, she began to experience the symptoms of hypothermia without realizing it. Instead of staying at the shelter near Jacks Knob she managed to reach Unicoi Gap in a confused and disoriented condition. To her good fortune she got the attention of a lady motorist who had stopped in the parking area at Unicoi Gap. The lady recognized Sonie's condition immediately and took her to Helen, Georgia, about ten miles down the mountain. After recuperating for two

Alligator, found in most south Georgia rivers and swamps—Okefenokee Swamp, state parks in southeast and southwest areas, and Cumberland Island.

days in Helen, Sonie was able to take up where she left off and eventually reached Mount Katahdin in Maine.

INSECTS, SNAKES, AND OTHER CRITTERS

Georgia has a great variety of insects—including bees, wasps, hornets, and fire ants—as well as spiders, chiggers, and ticks, snakes, and mammals—including black bears, wild pigs, skunks, and the like. But for the hiker very few of these critters, except for stinging and biting bugs, are of any real concern. The chances of encountering a wasp nest along a trail is much greater than a poisonous snake. Bear encounters are almost nonexistent, except at campsites where garbage has been allowed to accumulate. At some shelters along the Appalachian Trail where hundreds of campers a year spend the night, bears may come at night looking for food. To virtually eliminate all bear problems, hang all your food high in a tree and don't sleep with food in the tent or beside the sleeping bag. You will seldom if ever see black bears while walking trails. They are very timid and will usually run before you get close enough to see them.

The greatest and most frequently encountered danger can come from **stinging insects**. This is true throughout the state where wasps build nests on bridge hand rails or under benches along the trail. Running the hand against a wasp nest or brushing against a nest hanging on low vegetation can cause stings that are fortunately only temporarily painful for most people. Most agencies make every effort to remove these dangers along trails that are used regularly, especially on trails used by children. However, for those few who are allergic to bee and wasp stings, the problem can be life threatening. The physicians' advice is for you to know your condition and prepare for it. Preparation includes knowing what to do and having appropriate medication in the first-aid kit to use immediately if stung. Prescribed antihistamines or other medication should be with anyone who is known to be allergic to bee stings.

Chigger or red bugs, mosquitoes, other biting flies and non-biting gnats are common throughout the state. They are most annoying during the warmer months and during twilight and nighttime hours. Fortunately, there are very effective repellents that reduce this annoyance. An all-around repellent will contain at least thirty percent DEET. This along with other ingredients will repel insects and protect against red bugs and more importantly against ticks. Another tick repellent that also kills ticks is PERMANONE. It should not be applied directly to the skin but is very effective when applied to clothes and footwear before going into areas where ticks may be encountered.

In Georgia there are two tick-borne diseases that are noteworthy, Lyme disease and Rocky Mountain spotted fever. Lyme disease occurs throughout Georgia but is most prevalent in the southern two thirds. It is transmitted by the deer tick or black-legged tick. This tick is much smaller than the wood or dog tick which can transmit spotted fever. A few spotted fever cases are reported each year. Lyme disease has become much more frequent.

The safest way to avoid ticks on the trail is to use the repellents before the hike and examine yourself carefully immediately after a day hike and once a day or more on longer hikes. The deer tick nymphs are very tiny and are the most active carrier of the Lyme disease spirochete and may be picked up even during mild winter months in middle and south Georgia.

Once a tick has become attached, its removal in the first eight or ten hours is important. To remove the tick, forceps should be used to grasp the tick as close to the skin as possible and gently, but firmly, pull the tick away trying not to leave the tick's mouthparts in the skin. If the tick's body is squeezed it can act like a syringe forcing the tick's body fluids with the spirochetes into your body. This can only enhance the potential for Lyme disease. A new device called the Pro-tick Remedy is about the handiest instrument I have used to remove an attached tick. It is available in outdoor sporting goods stores. It is made by SCS LTD, Stony Point, NY. Once the tick is removed, the bite should be cleaned with alcohol or other antibiotic and observed for several days. In about half the cases of Lyme disease, a redness occurs around the bite and may take on a bulls eye appearance called erythema migrans. This should be reported to a doctor as soon as possible. If treated early, Lyme disease can be quickly cured.

The best defense against Lyme disease is to protect yourself with repellents, keep pant legs tucked into footwear, and examine yourself frequently when in tick habitat.

Poisonous snakes in Georgia run the full range from the small secretive coral snake to the Eastern diamondback rattlesnake, our largest North American snake. The timber rattlesnake occurs throughout the state from the mountains through the Coastal Plain. It may be called the canebrake rattlesnake in the southern part of the state. Rattlesnakes are uncommon and seldom seem. Both the northern and southern copperheads occur in Georgia. The larger southern copperhead is found throughout the Piedmont, along the fall line and in the Coastal Plain. The northern copperhead is generally found in the Piedmont and all of the mountain regions. The cottonmouth is found from the fall line south throughout the Coastal Plain along streams, river swamps, and marshes.

Most hikers seem to fear the snakes more than other hazards along the trail, and snake-bite kits are carried with little knowledge of how to use them. Most of these kits have blades to cut the fang puncture, a tourniquet, disinfectant, and other things—none of which are practical first aid for a poisonous snake bite.

If a snake-bite kit is taken, it should be the type with a good syringe. Sawyers kits are equipped with syringes and are very light and easy to use. The use of the syringe is only a first-aid effort while getting to professional medical attention. The syringe is also very useful to relieve the effects of insect stings.

Anole, a common lizard seen on thick vegetation in middle and south Georgia.

If you are within an hour of help, a hospital or doctor's office, try to remain calm and get to medical attention quickly.

Be cautious stepping over logs. Keep hands and feet out of cavities around boulders. Carry and use a flashlight if it is necessary to walk around the campsite or on trails at night during warm weather.

Poison ivy is present on many trails in Georgia. It is most obvious in late spring and throughout the summer months. Learn to recognize it and avoid it. Washing exposed skin as soon as possible after exposure is the best way to prevent irritation. Just because you are not allergic to poison ivy today does not mean that you may not be later. The best protection is to learn to recognize it and avoid rubbing against it while walking or sitting.

Using This Guide

EASY, MODERATE, STRENUOUS

These degrees of difficulty are based on the grade or incline of the trail. A flat trail with very little elevation change is designated easy even if it is a half mile or five miles long. A moderate hike will have a moderately steep grade for extended distances, while a strenuous trail may have steep grades for a half mile or more. Degree of difficulty may be expressed with two or three ratings, as easy to moderate or moderate with strenuous stretches. Where a trail is uneven and footing is more difficult because of boulders or other obstacles, this will be discussed in the description of the hike.

What one person in excellent physical condition may call moderate may be strenuous to another in poor condition. Thus, the ratings are not precise. They are only intended to provide a simple method of planning a hike based on the terrain.

MAPS

There are good maps for almost all of Georgia. Most United States Geological Survey quadrangle (USGS quads) maps are up-to-date. These 7.5-minute topographic maps are excellent for planning the hike and for keeping up with your position on the trail. They are especially useful in case you get disoriented or just plain lost. Places where these maps can be purchased are listed in Appendix D.

The U.S. Forest Service has excellent maps of the Chattahoochee and Oconee National Forests. The Forest Service also has maps of the Appalachian National Scenic Trail, the Cohutta Wilderness Area, and the Chattooga Wild and Scenic River. Most state parks have trail maps small enough to place in a pocket. Some may not be to scale, but they will keep you oriented. If studied carefully before the hike they can be beneficial not only in orientation but in taking advantage of all the special natural and historical points of interest along the way. Trails maps also are available for the National Park Service lands. Trails on Kennesaw Mountain National Battlefield are well mapped. Even with all the historical markers and information signs on the trail, the map adds tremendously to the hiking experience. The same is true for the Chattahoochee River National Recreation Area, Chickamauga Battlefield National Military Park, and Ocmulgee National Monument.

Maps are included with each of the trail discussions. These are of necessity small scale and are designed to provide basic information in finding the trailhead and planning the hike. The larger scale USGS quads are ideal for planning any extended hike and knowing in advance what the topography is like, where water sources are, and keeping oriented on the trail. Learn to use them.

A family on a day hike in the mountains.

Family Hiking

HIKING WITH CHILDREN

With the birth of a child, some new parents might think their hiking and backpacking days are over, at least until Junior is old enough to walk several miles and carry a pack. But parents who forego hiking trips during a child's formative years are not only missing out on some of the most rewarding and memorable experiences to be enjoyed as a family, but the kids also will miss a tremendous learning experience in which they will gain confidence and a growing awareness of the world around them.

Kids can enjoy the backcountry as much as their parents, but they see the world from a different perspective. It's the little things adults barely notice that are so special to children: bugs scampering across the trail, spider webs dripping with morning dew, lizards doing push-ups on a trailside boulder, splashing rocks into a lake, watching sticks run the rapids of a mountain stream, exploring animal tracks in the sand—these are but a few of the natural wonders kids will enjoy while hiking backcountry trails.

To make the trip fun for the kids let the young ones set the pace. Until they get older and are able to keep up with their parents, forget about that thirty-mile trek to your favorite backcountry campsite. Instead, plan a destination that is only a mile or two from the trailhead. Kids tire quickly and become easily sidetracked, so don't be surprised if you don't make it to your destination. Plan alternative campsites en route to your final camp.

Help children enjoy the hike and to learn about what they see. Always point out special things along the trail. Help them to anticipate what is around the next bend—perhaps a waterfall, or a pond filled with wriggling tadpoles. Make the hike fun and interesting, and kids will keep going.

Careful planning that stresses safety will help make your outing an enjoyable one. Young skin is very sensitive to the sun, so always carry a strong sunscreen and apply it to your kids before and during your hike. A good bug repellent, preferably a natural product, should be a standard part of the first-aid kit. Also, consider a product that helps take the itch and sting out of bug bites. A hat helps keep the sun out of sensitive young eyes. And rain gear is also an important consideration. Kids seem to have less tolerance to cold than adults, so ample clothing is important. If your camp will be next to a lake or large stream, consider bringing a life vest for your child.

Parents with young children must, of course, carry plenty of diapers, and be sure to pack them out when they leave. Some children can get wet at night so extra sleeping clothes are a must. A waterproof pad between the child and the sleeping bag should keep the bag dry, an important consideration if you stay out more than one night.

Allow older children, who are able to walk a mile or two, to carry their own packs. Some kids will want to bring favorite toys or books along. These special things they can carry themselves, thus learning at an early age the advantages of packing light.

Kids may become bored more easily once you arrive in camp, so a little extra effort may be required to keep them occupied. Imaginative games and special foods they don't see at home can make the camping trip a new and fun experience for kids and parents alike.

Parents with very young children can find an alternative to baby food in jars to alleviate extra weight. There are lightweight and inexpensive dry baby foods available, and all you do is add water.

Children learn from their parents by example. Hiking and camping trips are excellent opportunities to teach young ones to tread lightly and minimize their imprint upon the environment.

There are many good camping and hiking areas in the state where children can experience the fun of seeing a beautiful flower, butterfly, babbling brook, or watch a bluebird bring food to its young in an easy-to-see nest box. To see a deer bounding away in a woodland setting can be very exciting for child or parent. Many state parks have excellent camping and nature trails ideal for beginning hikes. Interpretive programs are conducted by well-trained park naturalists and program specialists. Some parks have backpacking, camping, and hiking programs that teach techniques. These hands-on programs teach how to camp and hike and how to do it with minimum impact on the trails and natural areas. Amicalola Falls State Park has a program for wilderness camping and hiking. This also includes long hikes like the Appalachian Trail.

Careful planning that stresses safety will help make your trip an enjoyable one. Biting insects—mosquitoes, gnats, and flies, can destroy a trip. Be prepared with an effective repellent that you have tried on the kids ahead of time. It is too late when you are on the trail to find out that the repellent is more irritating than the bugs. DEET is the effective ingredient in most repellents. However, prolonged overuse of thirty percent DEET can cause some reactions in children. To ease parents' concern with the stronger repellent, two products have been introduced, one called Skedaddle and the other Skintastic, have 6.5 percent and 7.5 percent DEET respectively. Although not quite as effective as stronger DEET concentrations they are useful and less irritating to children.

Poison ivy is ever present on many trails. Children should be made aware of what it looks like and to not touch it. Long pants and sleeves will help prevent contact with this pesky plant. Wash with soap as soon as possible after exposure to help prevent skin rashes. Be especially watchful for stinging insects—wasps, hornets, and bees. The first-aid kit should contain an effective topical ointment to relieve the pain of stings. Examine children carefully and often for ticks. If a tick has become attached remove it as described in the section dealing with ticks.

It is also important to have comfortable clothes suitable for the season. Be aware that children can be more sensitive to cold than adults and prepare for it. Properly fitting shoes will help prevent blisters on young, tender feet.

Set up a tent at home and consider spending a night or two in it so your child can grow accustomed to your backcountry shelter. A flashlight can help with temporary fear of the dark. Kids seem to prefer rectangular sleeping bags that allow freedom of movement. Don't forget a knit cap for the child to wear in the sleeping bag on cool nights. It will help greatly to keep the young one warm.

All or part of the following hikes are suitable for family day hikes or backpacks. Carefully read each description and prepare for any hazards that may be present. After the number and name of each hike, you will find suggestions for destinations.

State parks are great places for family hiking with the added advantage of campgrounds with fully equipped comfort stations and trailer and tent camping. Some parks have walk-in primitive camping sites for more privacy and off-the-road experience. The trails in or associated with state parks are mostly shorter day hikes; however, some like **Vogel State Park** in the mountains has the 12.5-mile **Coosa Backcountry Trail** for more strenuous backpacking trips. A free permit is required for this wilderness hike.

National Park Service areas in Georgia have especially good trails for family day hiking without camping. The **Chattahoochee River National Recreation Area** has more than forty miles of trails in the shadow of metropolitan Atlanta. Most are short trails that can be completed in two or three hours. The battlefield parks, **Kennesaw Mountain** and **Chickamauga,** provide not only outdoor and natural history experiences but unparalleled walks interpreting history of state and country. The **Ocmulgee National Monument** is an outstanding archaeological and historical site. It has six miles of easy trails, a picnic area, a fine museum, and visitor center. Situated on the edge of Macon it is ideal for family outings.

The great value of shorter trails within an hour or two of home is that they can be visited year-round. Each season presents an entirely new experience on the same trail. The seasonal cycle brings spring flowers with migrating and nesting birds, summer with young wildlife and more flowers, fall colors and southward migrating birds, and completing the cycle with an occasional winter snow. In winter, the woods are more open and provide better vistas of forested areas.

The U.S. Forest Service, like the state parks, have developed and undeveloped recreation areas in both the **Chattahoochee** and **Oconee national forests.** These are well suited for family camping and day hiking on the many trails that lead from the campgrounds into the mountains or surrounding forests. Many are close to scenic waterfalls, wilderness areas, and other scenic locations. Most of the Forest Service recreation areas are open for camping from late spring to early fall. The trails are open for hiking year-round. A young family with two very small children in "off-road" strollers hiked the **Andrews Cove Trail (Hike 24)** in January. This is a two-mile trail

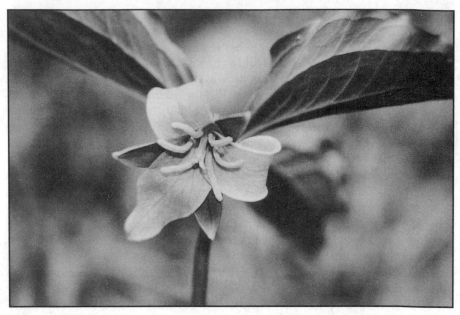

Nodding Trillium.

one way. When asked how the strollers worked on the trail, they said it was exceptionally easy. The children were obviously enjoying the experience.

Paved trails at **Anna Ruby Falls (Hike 22)** and **Red Top Mountain State Park (Hike 47)** are well suited for conventional strollers. They are used extensively by parents with very small children. **Ocmulgee National Monument** in Macon also has some paved trails.

Many trails provide access to good fishing and hunting areas, ideal places for outings. This is especially true in the national forests and state wildlife management areas. Many of the trails in the mountains of north Georgia lead to trout streams. They are ideal for one-day trips. A hike in for a mile or more will get you away from the crowd, then fish during the day and hike out the same day.

To recap, important considerations to keep in mind when hiking with children are careful planning, stress safety, and making the trip fun and interesting. There may be extra hassles involved with family hiking trips, but the dividends are immeasurable. Parents will gain a rejuvenated perspective of nature, seen through the eyes of a child, that will reward them each time they venture out on the trail.

Trails for Hikers with Special Needs

State and federal land managing agencies in Georgia are putting much effort into making their facilities accessible for visitors, including hikers, with special needs. Many state parks in the flat Coastal Plain or southern region of the state have trails that can be used by parents with children in strollers and by wheelchairs with some assistance. This is because the land is relatively level and the sandy-loam soil will support the wheels with wide tires. Many visitors to George T. Bagby State Park in southwest Georgia have used wheelchairs with specially equipped balloon-type tires. They have found most of the three-mile trail and the wildlife viewing gazebo accessible. At Okefenokee National Wildlife Refuge the entire length of the 4,000-foot boardwalk and its two photographic blinds can be traveled by wheelchair. There are no railings, making it possible for the wheelchair or walking visitor to feel much closer to the swamp. Ocmulgee National Monument near Macon has about 1,200 feet of paved trail. In the Piedmont and mountain parks there are several short, paved trails and one specially designed trail for sight-impaired visitors.

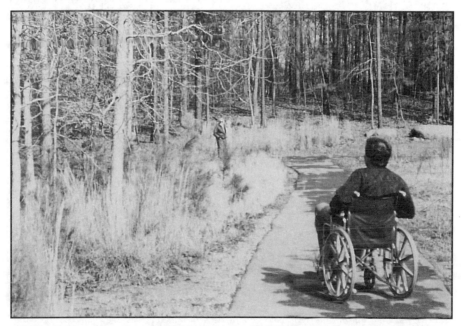

Wildlife plantings along the paved 0.75-mile trail at Red Top Mountain State Park attract birds, deer, squirrels, rabbits, and other animals for the delight of the hikers.

Lion's Eye Nature Trail at Anna Ruby Falls parking lot is designed for visually impaired hikers and includes Braille interpretive signs.

Woodchuck; a common inhabitant of the northern part of the state.

Typical of what is happening to make it easier for disabled persons to enjoy the outdoor facilities of state and national lands is a cooperative effort of the U.S. Fish and Wildlife Service and the Department of Labor's Office of Job Corps. John Turner, the director of the U.S. Fish and Wildlife Service, said, "This partnership is a good deal for everyone. The students in the Job Corps' Vocational Skills Training Program will learn valuable vocational skills, while USFWS facilities receive much needed attention." This same attitude and effort is happening with all land managing agencies.

Georgia has a number of opportunities for the hiker with special needs who wants to get into the outdoors. Many of the state parks and all national parks have restrooms and/or visitor centers that are wheelchair accessible.

Places where some trails have been made accessible or accessible with assistance are the following:

Georgia Parks and Historic Sites: Hike 4 - Cloudland Canyon State Park; Hike 31 - Amicalola Falls State Park; Hike 40 - Victoria Bryant State Park; Hike 47 - Red Top Mountain State Park; Hike 48 - Fort Yargo State Park; Hike 69 - Providence Canyon State Park; Hike 70 - Reed Bingham State Park.

National Parks: Hike 7 - Chickamauga Battlefield National Military Park; Hike 56 - Ocmulgee National Monument; Hike 60 - Kennesaw Mountain National Battlefield Park; Hike 63 - Cochran Shoals; Hike 66 - Medlock Bridge; Hike 81- Cumberland Island National Seashore.

U.S. Forest Service: Hike 22 - Anna Ruby Falls and Lion's Eye Nature Trails; Hike 25 - Dukes Creek.

U.S. Fish and Wildlife Service: Hike 83 - Okefenokee National Wildlife Refuge.

There is some variation in the interpretation of *accessible*. This depends on the degree of affliction and the type of equipment used. As mentioned the wide tires on some types of wheelchairs makes many trails accessible that would not be for conventional narrow tires. In the list of trails above there are some that are not paved but have been used successfully by hikers in wheelchairs with balloon tires.

In each description of the hikes mentioned above are listings for the land management offices, with addresses and phone numbers, that can be contacted for more information about the current conditions of the trails.

Volunteering

Georgia is home to several hiking clubs and conservation organizations that are involved in hiking. Some devote a large amount of their time to trail maintenance. The Georgia Appalachian Trail Club, Benton MacKaye Trail Club, and the Pine Mountain Trail Association plan regular outings to work on these trails. There is also ample opportunity to volunteer with the Georgia Department of Natural Resources, U.S. Forest Service, National Park Service, and U.S. Fish and Wildlife Service to help maintain trails. These agencies welcome volunteers who are willing to help maintain and mark trails. The U.S. Forest Service's "Adopt-A-Trail" program is especially suited to volunteer efforts. Information for contacting these agencies is in Appendix B.

Georgia Appalachian Trail Club members take a lunch break from trail maintenance work on the Appalachian Trail at Hog Pen Gap.

1 Chickamauga Creek Trail

General description: It is a pleasant 6.2-mile hike with enough length and diversity to make a nice day or overnight hike. There are no grand views but there is plenty of wildlife, wildflowers, and a diversity of forest types.

General location: Chickamauga Creek Trail is in the northwest corner of the state, about nine miles east of La Fayette in the Armuchee Ranger District of the Chattahoochee National Forest. The trail can be reached at two points, both off Georgia Highway 136.

Maps: Trail Guide to the Chattahoochee-Oconee national forests; Catlett USGS quad.

Degree of difficulty: Moderate.

Length: 6.2-mile loop trail.

Elevations: The lowest elevation on the trail is at the lower point on Chickamauga Creek, 950 feet. The Ponder Branch trailhead is 1,017 feet and the highest point is 1,615 feet on Dick Ridge at the Tennessee Valley Divide.

Special attractions: Well managed second growth hardwood forest as well as plentiful wildlife—including deer, turkeys, squirrels, foxes, bobcats, and skunks—wildflowers, and a very good birding area.

Best season: Open all year; the best times being spring, fall, and winter. During deer and turkey season, you should stay on the trail, hike from late morning to early afternoon, and wear a blaze orange cap or vest. Deer season is open from October through December. Turkey season is March 20 to May 15.

For more information: U.S. Forest Service, Armuchee Ranger District, 805 East Villanow Street, P.O. Box 465, La Fayette, GA 30728; (706)638-1085.

Finding the trailhead: Go east from La Fayette on Georgia Highway 136 about seven miles to the crest of Taylor Ridge at Maddox Gap. Here, Forest Road 250, an unpaved road, turns north. Follow this road for 1.8 miles to Forest Road 250A. This is the point where the trail crosses over the Tennessee Valley Divide. You can park off to the side of the road here and begin hiking the trail in either direction. It is recommended to hike in a counterclockwise direction.

To get to the other trailhead continue east on Georgia Highway 136 for another 1.5 miles to Ponder Creek Road. Turn north or left and go about 0.6 mile on this paved road to Forest Road 219, which is unpaved. Go 1.7 miles to the end of the road. You will ford the small Ponder Branch on the way. The trailhead is toward the stream, cross a footbridge and pick up the loop trail near the powerline right-of-way.

The Forest Road 219 trailhead is at the road's end, has a nice turnaround and camping area with water. The stream here is called Ponder Branch and the area is called Baker Hollow. The Forest Road 250 trailhead on Taylor Ridge has limited parking space.

The hike: The ridges and valleys of this area run generally in a northeast to southwest direction. In this southern end of the province the valleys are usually very wide and the ridges relatively far apart. For this trail, however,

Chickamauga Creek Trail

East Chickamauga Creek

250A

TAYLOR RIDGE

250

To GA 136
Maddox Gap

TENNESSEE

DICK RIDGE

VALLEY DIVIDE

1614'

POWER LINE

ROCKY RIDGE

219

N

0   1
Miles

Ponder Creek

Ponder Creek Rd.

To
Villanow

To
Lafayette

136

a unique geographical condition exists. Taylor Ridge and Dick Ridge are not only close together, they are connected by a short lateral ridge that forms the divide between Tennessee River Valley and the Alabama River Valley. The Chickamauga Creek Trail goes into both drainages and on both ridges. Ponder Branch flows south through several creeks to the Coosa River. East Chickamauga Creek flows north into several of the other Chickamauga Creek branches before emptying into the Tennessee River. Both are small, permanent streams with protected watersheds lying completely in the national forest.

The Chickamauga Creek loop trail can be hiked in either direction and from two access points. It is best to hike around the loop in a counterclockwise direction to avoid the steeper climb from East Chickamauga Creek to the crest of Dick Ridge.

A short trail leads from the parking area across Ponder Branch on a footbridge to the loop trail. The powerline right-of-way crosses the trail near this point. Turn to the right and begin the gentle climb up the side of Rocky Ridge through a mountain laurel thicket. Wildflowers, trailing arbutus, trilliums, azaleas, dogwoods, redbuds, dwarf crested iris, cardinal flowers, wild geraniums, Solomon's seals, violets, phlox, and fire-pinks, are abundant all along the trail. Hardwoods are dominant for most of the trail. Along the moist slopes yellow-poplar, white oak, maple, and hickory trees are most numerous. On the ridgetops Chestnut oaks, black oaks, and hickories are dominant. Large loblolly pines are scattered throughout the forest. Pine thickets occur on a few well drained, dry slopes.

The trail continues up the ridge switching back and forth from one cove to the next until you reach the ridge crest. This crest is followed until you cross under the powerline. All trees have been cleared from under the transmission lines. This open area is very attractive to deer. After the powerline, the path goes along the east side of the ridge in a much more open forest. The trail intercepts a dirt road, follows it up to the crest, and continues to the drainage divide, which is the highest point on the trail. From here the trail begins the descent to East Chickamauga Creek. A long stretch of exposed sandstone formations are along the path.

The path then drops quickly through several switchbacks until you reach another old roadbed that is the trail to the creek. At East Chickamauga Creek you follow the old road upstream. This is a very attractive small stream flowing through limestone rocks. The water is clear, and many snails, called periwinkles, can be seen attached to the stones. Wildflowers are abundant along the creek. The path crosses over the stream several times as you climb up to the Tennessee Valley Divide and Forest Road 250 to the other trailhead.

At the forest road, the trail drops immediately back into the woods and goes down the Ponder Branch watershed to Baker Hollow. This is another very attractive hardwood forest with many large trees, especially the American beech trees growing on the stream bank. The branch is crossed several times in the course of dropping down to the flat area with mountain laurel and many wildflowers. You will cross under the powerline right-of-way just before you come to the end of the loop at the spur trail that leads back to the parking area.

The streams, hardwood forests mixed with pine and laurel thickets, ridgetops, and valleys make this trail an exceptionally good birding area. It is also a fine small game, deer, and turkey hunting area.

2   Johns Mountain and Keown Falls Trails

General description: These two trails are connected at the Keown Falls observation deck above the falls—Johns Mountain is a 3.5-mile loop, and Keown Falls Trail is a 1.8-mile loop.

General location: The trails are in the Armuchee Ranger District in the northwest corner of the state, a part of the Chattahoochee National Forest near Villanow.

Maps: Chattahoochee National Forest Map; Sugar Valley USGS quad.

Degree of difficulty: Moderate with short stretches of steep grades. The stone steps to the Keown Falls Overlook are steep but protected by railings.

Length: Johns Mountain Trail is 3.5 miles; Keown Falls Trail is 1.8 miles. Both are loop trails.

Elevations: The elevation at Keown Falls Recreation Area is about 985 feet; Johns Mountain Overlook is 1,885 feet. Elevation at the top of Keown Falls is 1,400 feet.

Special attractions: Keown Falls, a fifty-foot-straight drop over a protruding rock ledge, can be spectacular during the wet season. This is a unique part of the Ridge and Valley area with grand scenic views from two observation decks. The Johns Mountain overlook deck is wheelchair accessible. Excellent wildflower displays occur in spring and leaf colors in the fall.

Best season: This is a year-round hike. You should pay close attention to spring and summer thunderstorms and winter snows. The access road to Keown Falls Recreation Area is closed from November 1 until April 1. This adds 0.7 mile one way to the hike up to the falls.

For more information: U.S. Forest Service, Armuchee Ranger District, 805 East Villanow Street, P.O. Box 465, La Fayette, GA 30728; (706)638-1085. Georgia Wildlife Resources Division, Game Management, 2592 Floyd Springs Road, Armuchee, GA 30105; (706)295-6041.

Finding the trailheads: To get to Johns Mountain Overlook from La Fayette take Georgia Highway 136 east thirteen miles to Villanow. One-half mile past Villanow turn right (south) on Pocket Road. Go four miles south to Forest Road 208, a gated and graveled road. It leads to the parking area for the Johns Mountain Overlook. The trailhead for this loop trail is at the overlook parking area.

The directions for Keown Falls Trail are the same except that the entrance to the Keown Falls Recreation Area and trailhead is two miles farther south on Pocket Road at Forest Road 702, a gated road open from May 1 to October 31. The trailhead is at the parking and picnic area at the end of this 0.7-mile unpaved road.

The hikes: The hike to the falls gives you a good look at the changing habitats from the moist coves on the east side of Johns Mountain to the beginning of the drier, better drained ridgetop and sandstone brow. The Johns Mountain Trail remains higher on the ridge side and top and provides pleasant views of the surrounding mountains, especially from the Johns Mountain Overlook. Johns Mountain is also a state wildlife management area.

The ideal day hike here is from the Keown Falls Recreation Area to the falls going counterclockwise on the loop. At the falls overlook deck, the Johns Mountain Trail begins. Walk this trail clockwise, that is start to the left at the trail sign for Johns Mountain Overlook. It is 2.5 miles to the overlook. Drop back down the mountain one mile to the falls and take the trail that leads under the falls, around to the smaller falls under the sandstone cliffs, and down the mountain to the recreation area trailhead.

The trail from the Keown Falls Recreation Area begins at the parking area and passes under a large A-frame on a graveled path with a hand-placed rock border. This continues until the loop segment begins at the sign with arrows pointing in both directions. For this description we will go to the right or directly to the falls. Hiking up to the falls you will go through a pleasant cove forest with many spring flowers and in the fall beautiful leaf colors. The trail parallels the stream until it reaches the steeper part of the climb. The path crosses the stream and enters an area of massive boulders. Ferns and wildflowers are at their best in this east-facing cove in early spring. Trillium, toothwort, windflower, giant chickweed, azalea, mayapple, dwarf crested iris, Solomon's seal and false Solomon's seal bloom in spring along with many others. Flowering trees are just as colorful. They include yellow-poplar, dogwood, redbud, and serviceberry just to name a few.

You now begin the climb to the falls as the path switches back and forth at a moderate grade until the sandstone cliffs are approached. Mountain laurel and Virginia pines form thickets through which the trail passes to the stone steps that lead up to the observation deck. It is 0.7 mile to the deck. The elevation is 1,400 feet and you have climbed 415 feet.

When there is a good water flow, the falls are quite impressive as the stream drops fifty feet over the rock overhang. An uncommon fern called the woolly lip fern grows on the rock cliffs. It is found only in a few very specific sites in the state.

Along the stream above the falls, the pinkster azalea blooms in April and the mountain laurel in May. Here the sign for the Johns Mountain Overlook and trail directs you to either the left or right. To the left, it is 2.5 miles to the overlook, to the right is one mile. The trail is a much more gradual climb to the left, which is to the south. The forest near the top of

Johns Mountain, Keown Falls, and Pocket Recreation Area Trails

To Villanow

John's Mt.
Observation
Deck

208

Keown Falls
Recreation
Area

Keown
Falls

702

John's Mountain Trail

Keowon Falls Trail

John's Creek

Pocket Road

Pocket Trail

N

Pocket
Recreation
Area

To
156

0   1

Miles

the mountain is made up of white oaks, chestnut oaks, black oaks, post oaks, hickories, and shortleaf and Virginia pines as dominant species. The path climbs gradually up and along the sheer sandstone cliffs on the east. Near the top, the trail turns to the west across the flat plateau of the mountain through a park-like forest of smaller trees. On the west side just before you reach the steep cliffs, the path turns north to follow the crest of the mountain over large boulders and among twisted oaks, pines, and a few hickories. Occasional breaks in the forest give peeks of what you will see at the overlook.

Near the highest point, you pass a radio relay tower, and in a few yards you are at the overlook and parking area. Great sunsets and sunrises are common from this splendid observation deck. The view extends to Taylors Ridge, Pigeon, and Lookout mountains in the west and the Armuchee Valley. To the east is Furnace Valley and Horn Mountain. People in wheelchairs can come to the parking area by vehicle and roll onto the observation deck.

This parking area also is the trailhead for the Johns Mountain Loop Trail. From here, it is one mile down to Keown Falls. The path follows an old roadbed through the oak-hickory-pine woods. The cove through which the stream flows to the falls is on the right. The trail then parallels the eastern bluffs and back to the falls.

Go back down the stone steps and turn to the trail under the falls. If there is a good flow of water, this is a rare opportunity to actually walk between the falling water and the rock overhang. The path follows at the

Keown Falls from overlook. Johns Mountain Trail meets the Keown Falls Trail here.

base of the bluff and is quite wet during the rainy season. The smaller falls comes through a cleft in the cliff. You must step over the small branch flow below the falls and among large boulders. Very shortly the boulder field is passed and the trail makes a couple of switchbacks down to more level walking and the end of the trail.

Johns Mountain Wildlife Management Area is open for deer, turkey, and small game hunting during the fall and early winter months. When walking the trails at this time, stay on the trails and wear blaze orange clothing such as a cap or jacket. Most hunting is done in early morning and late afternoon. It is best to hike in the middle of the day, from about 9 A.M. to 3 P.M.

3 The Pocket Recreation Area Trail

General description: A 2.6-mile loop trail in the Armuchee District of the Chattahoochee National Forest and an area geologically and botanically unique.
General location: The Pocket is in the northwest corner of the state east of La Fayette.
Maps: Chattahoochee National Forest Map; Sugar Valley USGS quad.
Degree of difficulty: Easy.
Length: A 2.6 mile loop.
Elevations: The trail varies from about 885 feet at the campground to about 1,000 feet along the low ridges.
Special attractions: An interlacing of large spring branches through the valley floor. Outstanding patches of pink lady's-slipper orchids blooming in late April. Boardwalks over the broad wet areas associated with the springs.
Best season: The campground is closed from November 1 until April 1, however, the trail can be hiked year-round. Spring is best for the many wildflowers and fall for the leaf color.
For more information: U.S. Forest Service, Armuchee Ranger District, 805 East Villanow Street, P.O. Box 465, La Fayette, GA 30728; (706)638-1085.

Finding the trailhead: From La Fayette take Georgia Highway 136 east about thirteen miles to Pocket Road, one-half mile past Villanow. Turn south (right) on Pocket Road and go eight miles to the recreation area. One trailhead is across the road and the spring branch from the comfort station. The other is near campsite 15. The trail is hiked in either direction.

The hike: The area known as The Pocket is a valley surrounded by the horseshoe shaped formation of Mill and Horn mountains. The loop trail begins and ends in the well-managed campground in the Pocket Recreation Area. Several large springs well up on the colluvial floor of this north facing valley. This delightful hike passes through pine woods, hardwoods, and across spring runs on convenient boardwalks. At about halfway around the loop in a dominantly Virginia pine area, a large patch of pink lady's

Forest Service cleans up Pocket Recreation Area Trail after the Blizzard of 1993. More than 200 trees fell.

slipper orchids begin blooming about April 20. If you look closely, you will see others among the pines at different places on the trail. Many other wildflowers are blooming here in spring and throughout summer and fall. Toothworts, trilliums, mayapples, violets, bluets, and many, many others. In spring, crystal clear brooks flow and wet bogs appear. Some of the bogs have thick mats of sphagnum, a moss that grows only in very wet areas. Boardwalks are used to cross some of the more permanently boggy areas.

The trail moves from the wet areas to dry ridge sides where oaks, hickories, and pines dominate with dogwoods, sourwoods, low and high blueberry bushes, and wildflowers covering the forest floor.

This area suffered extensively from the Blizzard of 1993. Great numbers of very large Virginia and loblolly pines and some hardwood trees fell throughout the forest. Many fell across the trail and Forest Service personnel spent many hours of back-breaking labor clearing the trail.

One of the main springs in the campground flows an estimated 12,000 gallons an hour. It flows from a concrete housing built many years ago when the area was a Civilian Conservation Corps camp. The flow of some of the other springs in the area is almost equal to this.

An amphitheater is planned to be built on a quiet wooded slope near the end of the trail. This open-air facility will be wheelchair accessible. The path to the amphitheater will pass through a wooded area of large yellow-poplars, maples, buckeyes, and other forest species along a pretty spring brook so those in wheelchairs can enjoy a part of the Pocket Trail.

Cloudland Canyon State Park Trails

4 Cloudland Canyon State Park Trails

Overview: Cloudland Canyon is a unique geological feature in Georgia only because so little of the Cumberland Plateau Physiographic Province touches the state. The canyons and waterfalls are beautiful and awesome. The flatter tops of the mountains are in sharp contrast to the sheer canyon walls. All of this is softened by an almost complete cover of trees and shrubs that add color to the ancient sandstone cliffs. In spring, the shades of green as the different species of trees begin to leaf out is just as striking as the multicolor fall display when the same species of trees take on their individual hues before the leaves fall. In winter, the leafless trees expose the gray gulf walls for a fresh and different look. Throughout the Cumberland Plateau, canyons with the great sandstone bluffs are called gulfs or gulches.

General description: A paved trail 0.25 mile long goes along the rim overlooking the canyon that is completely wheelchair accessible. Two other major trails, the 5.2-mile West Rim Trail and the 6.2-mile Backcountry Trail, form the main trail system here.

General location: Cloudland Canyon State Park is in the extreme northwestern corner of the state. It is on the western edge of Lookout Mountain about eight miles east of Trenton and eighteen miles west of La Fayette on Georgia Highway 136.

Maps: A page-size map is available in the park office; Durham USGS quad.

Degree of difficulty: The West Rim Trail is moderate with a few steep, rocky places. The trails down to the falls are short but strenuous. The Backcountry Trail is moderate to strenuous.

Length: The West Rim Trail is a 5.2 mile loop; the Backcountry Trail, a 6.2 mile loop. The trail to the first falls is 0.3 mile; to the second falls is 0.5 mile one way, most of which is wooden steps.

Elevations: The highest point on the West Rim Trail is about 1,800 feet; the lowest point crossing Daniel Creek just above the first falls is about 1,600 feet. The highest point on the Backcountry Trail is 1,960 feet; the lowest crossing Bear Creek is about 1,450 feet. From the rim down to the lowest falls is a drop in elevation of about 500 feet. Sitton Gulch Creek falls another 500 feet before it leaves the gulf.

Special attractions: Rugged geology and beautiful scenery, waterfalls and cascading streams, wildlife watching, birding, wildflowers, fall colors, and camping.

Best season: Year-round.

For more information: Cloudland Canyon State Park, 122 Cloudland Canyon Park Road, Rising Fawn, GA 30738; (706)657-4050.

Finding the trailheads: The trailhead for the West Rim Trail is at the Overlook parking area. The trailhead for the Backcountry Trail is at the Group Camp parking area.

The hikes: From the **West Rim Trail,** a spur trail leads down to the two major waterfalls. This way to the falls is mostly wooden steps carefully and strategically built down the bluff to permit access to this grand area without undue damage to the rich, yet fragile, plant communities. The trails are designed to provide excellent vantage points to enjoy the rugged and beautiful vistas.

The trail for both the waterfalls and the West Rim begins in the parking lot for the overlook and picnic area. The path is paved and wheelchair accessible. The trailhead is well marked. The West Rim Trail is blazed with white, and the falls trail with yellow. You are cautioned to stay on the trail and not climb on rocks or around the waterfalls. The rocks can be very slippery and dangerous. Caution is also advised for people with heart problems and those in poor physical condition.

The trail goes behind several cabins and begins the descent to Daniel Creek, which forms the waterfalls and drops into Sitton Gulf. In a short distance, the trail to the falls turns off to the right in a series of wooden steps. The West Rim Trail continues on and reaches a picturesque footbridge over fast-flowing and cascading Daniel Creek. Catawba rhododendron and mountain laurel thickets interspersed with sourwood, dogwood, and larger oaks, hickories, hemlocks, and maples shade the trail. After crossing the bridge, which is only about thirty or forty yards above the highest falls, you begin climbing up to the plateau top. Mosses, ferns, and many wildflowers line the trail. You go through an area of large sandstone boulders and rock overhangs that form natural shelters. After some switchbacks and about one mile into the trail, you will walk along the rim of the gulf. From here you can see down from carefully selected overlooks.

You leave the canyon rim and come to the Whiteoak Spring branch. A bridge crosses the branch and marks the point where the loop trail comes back. Going around in a clockwise direction cross over a portion of the plateau through the oak-hickory forest of the Cumberland Plateau. There is very little change in elevation for the next mile. Blueberries, dogwood, and sourwoods are some of the plants found under the larger trees. Dwarf iris, pipsissewa, spring beauties, phlox, bird-foot violets, and many other wildflowers grow in the well drained sandy soil and along the small stream drainages. Two paths lead off the trail giving access to the tent and trailer campgrounds. The paved park road is crossed at about 2.5 miles. From here you approach the western escarpment of Lookout Mountain where you can look down on the town of Trenton and Lookout Valley, a drop of more than 1,200 feet. The path goes north along this rim to stone steps and a spectacular rocky point overlook. On a clear day you can see to the Tennessee River, where it forms the famous Moccasin Bend.

Climb back up the rocky steps and continue back toward the western rim of Sitton Gulf. The path leads to several beautiful overlooks along the way. Almost anytime during the day you will see hawks or vultures soaring on the wind currents along the steep escarpments. The path returns to the bridge where the loop ends and backtracks across Daniel Creek and the trailhead. Along the way you will pass other spur paths that lead to cabins. There is much to see along this rim.

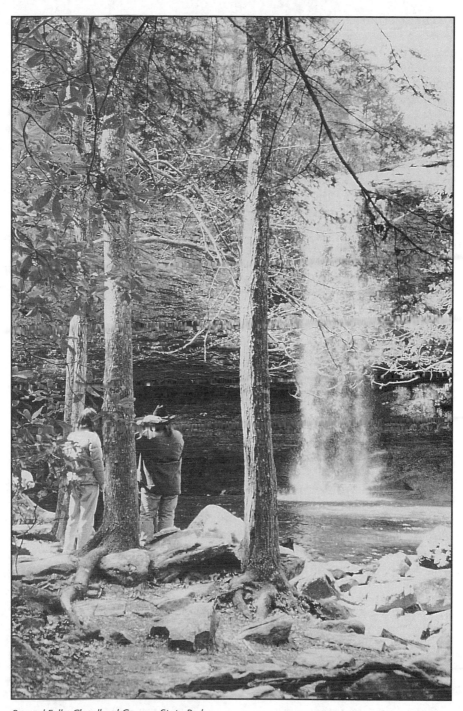

Second Falls, Cloudland Canyon State Park.

The trail down to the falls is off the West Rim Trail and is a series of wooden steps and boardwalks. The flowers growing on the steep side of the canyon face are outstanding. Jack-in-the-pulpit, windflower, hydrangea, foam flower, Solomon's seal, long-spurred violet, dwarf crested iris, bellwort, and great patches of trillium are only a few of the flowers blooming in spring. Several species of ferns, including maidenhair and marginal ferns, are among all the other lush vegetation. Magnificent yellow-poplars, hemlocks, and buckeyes are growing on the lower levels of the gulch. The quantity of water over the falls varies greatly from season to season. The water falls into large splash pools and then continues to cascade down over the boulder strewn streambed. Each of the falls has its own distinctive beauty, making the hike down and back over the face of the canyon wall on the well-built steps worth the trip.

The **Backcountry Trail** begins at the parking area for the group camp. This red blazed trail is designed for backpacking and camping. Two primitive campsites are along the trail.

Follow the path that drops gently down toward Bear Creek. Bear Creek joins Daniel Creek in Sitton Gulf and becomes Sitton Gulch Creek. The same interesting geology and plant communities are here as along the West Rim Trail. Soon, however, the steep descent begins down the side of the canyon, which is also the way out. The trail does several switchbacks that keep the grade reasonable. Once on the floor of the valley, hike through tall hemlocks and yellow-poplars going upstream to one of the most attractive stream crossings in the state. The footbridge spans Bear Creek under a massive rock cliff overhang in a beautiful pristine setting.

From Bear Creek climb up through laurel and rhododendron thickets, past rock outcrops, and along a small stream. This segment of the trail can be very wet in the winter and spring. Exceptionally large patches of long-spurred violets grow beside the trail and the brook.

Along this brook you come to a double blaze mark on a tree, indicating that the trail makes a significant turn. It is here that the loop portion of the trail begins. Continue straight ahead or cross the branch and follow an old, obscure logging road and go around the loop clockwise. This description continues straight ahead where the trail flattens and goes through wooded areas more open than on the plateau. The first primitive campsite is marked with a white blaze. It is easily recognized by the fire ring and the more open brush-free area. A spring is nearby. From here the topography is much less steep and easy to hike.

The forest has been cut over several times in the past but is now in a fine stand of hardwoods mixed with a few pines. Blueberries are all along the trail and would be a welcome snack in summer when they are ripe. The dominant trees are white oak, chestnut oak, black oak, hickory, a few maples, sourwood, and dogwood.

The second primitive campsite is on the highest point along this trail. It is also marked with white blazes and has a fire ring. It is at 3.1 miles, which is almost exactly halfway.

The trail then swings back around to the south and along the eastern edge of the Bear Creek gulf. With the leaves off the trees you can see the point overlooking Sitton Gulf. An old roadbed becomes the path and is an easy descent toward the end of the loop. Cross the creek and turn to the right going downstream and you are headed back to Bear Creek and to the trailhead. The climb out after you cross Bear Creek is steep and strenuous.

Sitton Gulf overlook, on a wheelchair-accessible section of trail in Cloudland Canyon State Park.

5 Crockford–Pigeon Mountain Wildlife Management Area Trails

Overview: Pigeon Mountain is a spur off the east side of Lookout Mountain, a part of the Cumberland Plateau. It has all the same characteristics of the plateau that rises from the limestone formations of the valleys through shale layers to the sandstone bluffs of the plateau escarpments. The two trails described here span that geological formation.

Most of Pigeon Mountain is in the Crockford–Pigeon Mountain Wildlife Management Area under the supervision of the Department of Natural Resources, Wildlife Resources Division. The name comes from the now extinct passenger pigeon which once roosted here in great numbers and for Jack Crockford, former Director of the Wildlife Resources Division. The mountain is noted for its many extensive caves that honeycomb the limestone formations under the plateau. The best known of the caves is Ellison Cave, with exceptionally deep pits.

The **South Pocket Trail** is on the west side of the mountain and begins in the valley and ends 1,000 feet higher on the plateau. The area is steeped in natural and human history. The **Rocktown Trail** goes to an interesting series of sandstone rock formations covering more than 100 acres near the middle of Pigeon Mountain.

Deer hunting season in the wildlife management area is in November and December for several days each month. Turkey season is from March 20 to May 15. It is advisable to wear blaze-orange, either a cap or vest or both, while you arc hiking during these times.

General description: The South Pocket Trail is a three-mile, one-way day hike, and the Rocktown Trail is a flat, easy one-mile hike.

General location: Pigeon Mountain is in the northwest corner of the state in Walker County about ten miles west of La Fayette. The South Pocket Trail is on the west side of the mountain. The Rocktown Trail is about nine miles west of La Fayette and about 2.5 miles south of the mountaintop end of the South Pocket Trail as the crow flies. It is best reached from the east side of the mountain driving up from the check station.

Maps: A small page-size map is available at the check station or from Department of Natural Resources; Cedar Grove and La Fayette USGS quads.

Degree of difficulty: South Pocket Trail is moderate. Rocktown Trail is easy.

Length: South Pocket Trail is three miles one way, beginning at the lower parking area. Rocktown Trail is 1.1 mile one way. To walk among the interesting rock formations may be another half mile.

Elevations: South Pocket Trail begins at about 920 feet and ends at about 1,960 feet. Rocktown Trail is relatively level and is at about 1,850 feet.

Special attractions: South Pocket Trail includes unique geological formation of limestone and shale with a picturesque waterfall along with wildflowers, some very rare; wide range of geological formations; wildlife; excellent birding area, and fine scenery. The special feature at Rocktown is the unique sandstone formations along with wildflowers, birding, and other wildlife watching.

Crockford–Pigeon Mountain WMA Trails

To (193) and Davis Crossroads

Church

Hogjowl Road

Pocket Road

To McLemore Cove

Pocket Branch

N

0   1
Miles

Pocket Falls

To McCutchen Spring Road and South Pocket Trail

South Pocket Trail

High Point 2330'

To Rape Gap

To Check Station

West Brow Trail

Gated

McCutchens Spring Road

Rocktown Trail

To Rocktown

Rocktown

Best season: Year-round. Spring and fall are the best times for spring wildflowers, fall leaf colors, and songbird and raptor migrations.

For more information: Regional Supervisor, Department of Natural Resources, Wildlife Resources Division, 2592 Floyd Springs Road, Armuchee, GA 30105; (706)295-6041. Department of Natural Resources, Wildlife Resources Division, 2070 U.S. 278 Southeast, Social Circle, GA 30279; (770)918-6416.

Finding the trailheads: South Pocket Trail: Go west from La Fayette on Georgia Highway 193 for about 5.5 miles to Hog Jowl Road. Turn south on Hog Jowl Road about 2.5 miles to Pocket Road. This turn is difficult to see. It is at the top of a rise just past the Mount Herman Baptist Church. Pocket Road is a dead end. It is paved for about 0.5 mile and gravel for the next 0.8 mile. After fording a small branch, you come to a gravel parking area on the left. It is best to park here and walk the 0.4 mile on the jeep road to the waterfall area, although the trailhead is frequently listed as being at the falls. This road may be gated.

Rocktown Trail: Take Georgia Highway 193 west from La Fayette for about 2.5 miles to Chamberlain Road. Turn south or left and go 3.3 miles to the Crockford–Pigeon Mountain Wildlife Management Area Check Station sign. Turn right into the management area on gravel road. The check station is on the left. It is a good idea to stop here and check the maps on the information board. Continue on the road past the check station, up the mountain for 4.6 miles to the Rocktown Road. This is a gravel road that ends in about 0.75 mile at a gravel parking area and turnaround. An information board here gives some of the history of the area. The trailhead is at this sign.

The hikes: South Pocket and Rocktown trails are the only trails in this wildlife management area that are designated foot travel only. All other trails are combined with horseback and/or bicycle riding. Trail marking on the other trails can be misleading. It is recommended that when you hike trails other than South Pocket and Rocktown you have and use the current USGS 7.5 minute Cedar Grove and La Fayette quadrangle maps. There are many miles of unmarked trails and old logging and jeep roads on and around the mountain. They make for interesting hiking, but it is easy to get lost on Pigeon Mountain if you are not careful. At the time of this writing, there are six blazed trails for hiking, horseback riding, and bicycling. Blazes and some of the names have been changed. The Pocket Trail was blue blazed at one time. It is now blazed with pink and called the South Pocket Trail. Some of the old blue blazes are still visible. The Wildlife Resources Division is developing new trail-use regulations and more uniform trail designations and blazing.

To get the full benefit of the **South Pocket Trail**, begin at the gravel parking area and hike up the rough, jeep road to the falls where the trail crosses over Pocket Branch.

The hike up the jeep road takes you beside and above one of the most unique botanical areas in the state. *The Georgia Conservancy's Guide to the North Georgia Mountains* states that "Several rare and uncommon plant species have been recorded here, making it one of the most remarkable botanical areas in northwest Georgia. There are at least eleven significant species found almost nowhere else in Georgia which are present in the small mesic hardwood forest below the wet-weather falls. These include celandine poppy, Ohio buckeye, bent trillium, nodding spurge, lance-leaf trillium, wild hyacinth, log fern, harbinger of spring, Virginia bluebell, hairy mock-orange, and blue ash. When the plants are in bloom the forest below the waterfall near the start of the trail is truly remarkable, with some species occurring in thick beds."

The Georgia Department of Natural Resources, assisted with funds from the Turner Foundation, has installed an 800-foot boardwalk with a loop that passes through the area of greatest plant diversity along Pocket Branch. It is the **Shirley Miller Wildflower Trail,** named for the wife of former governor Zell Miller, both of whom were very instrumental in preserving natural areas in the state. Interpretive signs enhance the educational experience for hikers. This boardwalk, which is wheelchair accessible, was dedicated in 1999 and is a fine addition to this unique area.

The 0.4-mile jeep road ends at a clearing near the falls and the trail crosses Pocket Branch. From here to the plateau rim at the top of the mountain is about 2.6 miles. You pass through a hardwood forest of oaks, hickories, red cedars, yellow-poplars, buckeyes, mulberries, and a variety of other large trees. The undergrowth is dogwoods, redbuds, sourwoods, and lower shrubs—including mountain laurel, sweet shrub, wild hydrangea, spice bush, blueberry, and azalea. There are no steep grades, in fact there are several flat and some downhill stretches. Switchbacks keep the climb moderate although more than 1,000 feet of elevation is gained. You pass interesting rock outcrops with wet seeps supporting many flowers and ferns. At the top, you intercept the West Brow Trail marked with white blazes. If you hike south along this wide path on an old roadbed, you come to a dirt road, McCutchens Spring Road. In the clearing beside the road is an exceptionally large redbud tree. Any one of its three stems is much larger than most redbuds.

Backtracking along the West Rim Trail, you can drop back down South Pocket Trail again or follow the West Rim Trail to High Point, the highest point on Pigeon Mountain at 2,330 feet. This path has white blazes and wends among the unusual rock formations of the brow. This trail continues along the brow passing sandstone spires precariously perched on the very edge of the rim. The blue blazed North Pocket Trail intercepts the West Brow Trail about 1.5 miles east of High Point. Following this trail back to The Pocket closes a loop of about 6.5 miles. Sections of the North Pocket Trail are very steep. The West Brow and North Pocket trails are for horses and bicycles. It is not recommended that you hike this loop without the aid of the quad maps. The signing and blazes can be confusing, especially with the many unmarked side trails.

The **Rocktown Trail** is easy, flat, and begins at the well-developed gravel parking area. It crosses the headwater branch of Allen Creek and goes through a mixed forest of Virginia pines, oaks and hickories. A few large boulders are passed before you reach the area of huge boulders. Do not let the one-mile trail lead you to think you should take only a few minutes to make the hike. You can easily spend a day among the rock formations and not see it all. The brownish-red color of the rocks is caused by iron ore deposits. Iron ore mining was extensive at one time around Pigeon Mountain.

6 Arrowhead Wildlife Interpretive Trail

General description: An easy and pleasant two-mile hike and one of the most unique short trails in the state.
General location: About ten miles north of Rome in the northwestern corner of the state, this trail is located on the grounds with the Georgia Wildlife Resources Division's Northwest Regional Office and at the Arrowhead Public Fishing Lake.
Maps: The Wildlife Resources Division trail map available in the headquarters office; Armuchee USGS quad.
Degree of difficulty: Easy.
Length: A pleasant 2.2 miles.
Elevations: There is little change in elevation throughout the trail.
Special attractions: Wildlife watching and photography; Canada geese nesting in spring and goose families in late winter; wintering waterfowl; resident wood ducks; active beaver lodges and dam; songbirds; wading birds; wildflowers in spring, summer, and fall; explanations of habitat management for wildlife and fishing.
Best season: There is much activity among the wildlife species throughout the year. This is truly a year-round hike.
For more information: Regional Supervisor, Georgia Wildlife Resources Division, Game Management Section, 2592 Floyd Springs Road, Armuchee, GA 30105; (706)295-6041. Department of Natural Resources, Wildlife Resources Division, 2070 U.S. Highway 278 Southeast, Social Circle, GA 30279; (770)918-6400.

Finding the trailhead: From Rome go north about ten miles on U.S. Highway 27 to Georgia Highway 156. Turn east and go 2.3 miles to Floyd Springs Road. Then turn left or north and go two miles to the DNR Wildlife Resources Division Northwest Regional Game Management Headquarters. The trailhead is in the gravel parking area at a large sign with a map of the trail and orientation information.

The hike: This is one of the most unique short trails in the state. It is a short course in wildlife management for both non-game and game animals. It includes open fields, forest, forest edge, and aquatic habitats. Interpretive signs strategically placed along the path explain what has been done to improve the diversity of animals and plants. The trail winds among

Arrowhead Wildlife Interpretive Trail

the ponds of the old fish hatchery providing excellent aquatic habitat. Wildflowers, birds, mammals, insects, and other living things make this an interest-packed walk. It is short enough for a quick morning or evening walk and has enough variety for a day spent watching and photographing.

The wide, easy-to-follow path begins at the corner of the parking area. You can look down on one of the old fish hatchery ponds as you begin walking through open field to the first interpretive sign with information about waterfowl and wading birds—the Canada geese nest in April. The next stop is at a platform overlooking a small pond. A wood duck nest box is mounted on a post in the willow- and alder-lined pool. A sign tells about this duck and the habitat it needs.

You pass a pole with martin gourds for nest boxes and into the wooded area where the trail is marked with blue blazes. At first it is an almost pure pine stand where the dwarf iris blooms beside the path in April. This tract of land has a good whitetail deer population that is described at the next

45

Wood duck nest box in pond on the Arrowhead Wildlife Interpretive Trail.

sign. The trees have changed now to an almost pure hardwood forest. You walk along a dirt roadbed cut for a fire-break. The importance of dead and hollow trees is described at the next sign followed by the discussion of the red oak and pignut hickory as forest trees. Forestry management practices are described. Blueberries are abundant where prescribed burns have encouraged their growth. The trail now passes through a small field of grasses, clover, and a few small shrubs. This is a planned wildlife opening in the forest to provide food for a number of different animals. The edge of the opening is important to many birds not otherwise found in the woods, and many other animals take advantage of these grassy openings.

The trail goes back into the woods, through a wet area, and to the sign discussing an important practice called "prescribed burning."

Another open field with an attractive rectangular pond is next. Nest boxes are located here for wood ducks. The bluebird also thrives in these old open fields. This is described on the next sign with a nest box nearby. Walking toward the larger ponds of the old hatchery you pass a sign telling about the naturalized Japanese honeysuckle that is now used by many species of wildlife.

The trail crosses the dikes between the ponds. Watch for nesting platforms for Canada geese in most of the ponds. The geese readily adapt to them and also nest on the banks of the ponds right on the ground. Red-wing blackbirds nest in the willows and alders at the pond edge. Beyond the ponds the trail follows along the spring creek that supplies water for the ponds. Here beavers have built a large dam. Their lodges can be seen in the backwater. Many other animals, both aquatic and terrestrial, use the beaver pond and its edges.

The trail markers lead you back to the south side of the ponds and back to the trailhead. There is much wildlife to be seen along these ponds, and the species vary much from season to season. Reptiles and amphibians are abundant by the water's edge. An alligator has taken up residence in the old pools. The careful hiker can see and photograph many kinds of plants and animals on this trail.

7 Chickamauga Battlefield National Military Park Trails

Overview: In 1890, Congress authorized the creation of Chickamauga and Chattanooga National Military Park, the first of four such parks— Shiloh, Gettysburg, and Vicksburg—before the decade was out. Chickamauga Battlefield is in Georgia just across the state line from Chattanooga, Tennessee. The trails in this park are designed to interpret the battles fought here. Chickamauga was one of the bloodiest battles of the Civil War with the loss of more than 18,000 of the 66,000 Confederate troops and 16,000 of the 58,000 Federal troops were lost. The battlefield was dense woods and thick underbrush unlike other Civil War battles fought in open fields. The forest conditions you see today are much the same as the soldiers saw them in September 1863. There are about forty miles in seven trails, each color blazed to follow a specific theme of the historical battles. The terrain is low rolling hills, none of which are steep or difficult. During wet weather some of the trails will have shallow standing water from the many small branches that flow through the area. There is an abundance of wildlife, and the park is a great place to see birds and wildflowers. The trails are for day-use only. There are no campsites in the park area.

General description: Moderate trails of varying lengths from five to twenty miles long.

General location: In the northwest corner of Georgia about five miles south of the Tennessee-Georgia state line on U.S. Highway 27. Park headquarters and visitor center is located at the north entrance on U.S. Highway 27.

Maps: The National Park Service has maps of the trails, color-coded by blaze colors; Fort Oglethorpe and East Ridge USGS quads.

Degree of difficulty: Moderate: There is very little change in elevation throughout the battlefield, but the length of most of the trails increases the difficulty.

Length: There are seventy-eight miles of trails if each trail is hiked separately. With much overlap among the trails, there is actually forty miles of marked trails. The Perimeter Trail is twenty miles. Historical and Cannon trails are fourteen miles each. Memorial Trail is twelve miles and General Bragg, Confederate Line, and Nature trails are seven, six, and five miles respectively.

Elevations: Topography in the battlefield area ranges from about 900 feet in the northwest section near Snodgrass Hill down to West Chickamauga Creek at about 700 feet.

Chickamauga Battlefield Trails

TRAIL: BLAZE
Perimeter: Blue
Historical: Pink
Cannon: Yellow
Memorial: White
General Bragg: Red
Confederate Line: Orange
Nature: Green

Special attractions: Study of Civil War history; birding and wildlife viewing; wildflowers.

Best season: The park is open year-round. Hiking is best in fall, winter, and spring. Summer weather can be hot and sultry. Spring wildflowers are abundant and fall colors of the many hardwood trees can be spectacular.

For more information: Superintendent, Chickamauga and Chattanooga National Military Park, P.O. Box 2128, Fort Oglethorpe, GA 30742; (706)866-2512. For information on the Kiwanis Club youth trail program write: Rossville Kiwanis Club, P.O. Box 488, Rossville, GA 30741.

Finding the trailheads: The trailheads for the Perimeter and Historical trails are at the visitor center; for Cannon, Memorial, and General Bragg trails are at South Post Gate; for Confederate Line Trail is at the Texas Monument on Battle Line Road; and for the Nature Trail is on U.S. Highway 27 near Viniard-Alexander Road.

The hikes: These trails provide a unique and enjoyable way to study Civil War history in a natural setting. The visitor center has outstanding exhibits and an extensive gun collection. You have an almost hourly account of the battles described on plaques, interpretive signs, and great monuments along the trails. The great diversity of open fields, deep forests, dense undercover, and waterways make excellent birding and wildlife watching opportunities. The wildflowers that dominate in spring and leaf colors in fall add beauty to the trails.

The **Perimeter Trail** is the longest of the seven marked trails. It leaves from the visitor center and follows south on U.S. Highway 27 to the Florida Monument. The blue trail marker is here and encompasses most of the 5,500 acre Chickamauga Battlefield. The hike goes south along the western side of the park both on roads and in woods and fields. The trail crosses Vittatoe Road, Dyer Road, and to Glenn-Kelly Road. Follow this road for a short distance and then along Glenn-Viniard Road to U.S. Highway 27, the La Fayette Road. Along this west side, the Perimeter Trail is joined by the pink marked Historical Trail, the yellow Cannon Trail, and the white Memorial Trail. After crossing U.S. Highway 27 the blue Perimeter Trail joins the green marked Nature Trail. West Chickamauga Creek forms the park boundary at the southeast corner of the park where Perimeter and Nature trails track together. The Perimeter Trail leaves the Nature Trail and continues north and crosses Viniard-Alexander Road, Alexander's Bridge Road, and follows Jays Mill Road to Brotherton Road. There it joins the red General Bragg Trail, the white Memorial Trail, and the yellow Cannon Trail and continues through wood and fields back to U.S. Highway 27 and the visitor center.

Remember that there is no drinkable water on the park trails. You must carry water with you. During the summer, it is a good idea take along insect repellent for mosquitoes and biting flies.

The **Historical Trail,** with pink blazes and markers, is designed to interpret the varied Confederate assaults on the strong Union line, Longstreet's fierce charge, the Confederate breakthrough, and the strong

50

and heroic stands of generals Wilder and Thomas. At Snodgrass Hill, General George Thomas became known as the "Rock of Chickamauga." The log cabin on the hill belonged to the Snodgrass family and was used as a hospital for both Confederate and Union wounded soldiers at the same time.

This trail goes east of U.S. Highway 27 at the Florida Monument past Polk's Headquarters Monument. Farther east, the trail goes toward the Bragg Headquarters Monument and Brotherton Road. Going west on Brotherton Road, it passes Winfrey Field, Brook Field, the Ohio Monument, and goes on to U.S. Highway 27. Across the highway is the Brotherton Cabin. Hike south on the west side of U.S. Highway 27 to the Glenn-Viniard Road.

The Historical Trail leaves the highway and goes west for a short distance then turns north through woods and fields and back to the west to Wilder Tower. Here it stays with the white Memorial Trail and yellow Cannon Trail and shortly picks up the Perimeter Trail, which heads north to Snodgrass Cabin and Hill. Go west along roads and through a wooded area to U.S. Highway 27 and the Kelly House. Follow U.S. Highway 27 south to Poe Road and continue along Poe Road to where it comes back to U.S. Highway 27. Cross the highway and turn back north to Battle Line Road and on north to Alexander's Bridge Road and to the visitor center.

The **Cannon Trail** is designed to see the artillery batteries, referred to as the "long arm of the Army." These batteries may be seen as the trail passes one cannon group after another. Each cannon group is situated and placed as they were during the battles.

The yellow blazed Cannon Trail begins at the South Post Gate. Hike north to U.S. Highway 27 and the Florida Monument. The trail then joins three other trails to the east—the blue Perimeter Trail, the red General Bragg Trail, and the white Memorial Trail. These four trails run together to Jays Mill Road. There turn back to the west and follow beside Brotherton Road across Alexander's Bridge Road to U.S. Highway 27 and south where the trail parallels the highway to Glenn-Viniard Road. From the Brotherton Cabin, three trails track together to Wilder Tower and soon pick up the Perimeter Trail going north to the vicinity of Snodgrass Field. Turn east there, and the Cannon and Memorial trails become one trail to Glenn-Kelly Road and the trailhead.

The **Memorial Trail,** with its white blazes, is for the eight brigade commanders who lost their lives at Chickamauga. Monuments dedicated to them and the stories of their feats are told along this trail. Pyramids of cannon balls are located at the site where each commander was fatally wounded.

The Memorial Trail follows the same route as the Cannon Trail with the exception of a deviation at Brotherton and Alexander's Bridge Road. The Memorial Trail goes north along the Alexander's Bridge Road to Battle Line Road. Turn south on Battle Line Road to the Alabama Monument where it connects with the pink Historical Trail, crosses U.S. Highway 27 to Dyer Road and the Brotherton Cabin. There the Memorial and Historical trails join the Cannon Trail and proceed together to the trailhead.

The seven-mile **General Bragg Trail** is identified with red markers and blazes. It was developed to tell the story of Confederate General Braxton Bragg, a man of strong will and ability; a very complex southern leader.

This trail starts at South Post Gate on Glenn-Kelly Road. It is marked by yellow and white blazes to the Florida Monument and follows the same path with three other trails to Jays Mill Road. These trails with the Bragg Trail turn back to the west on Brotherton Road, across Alexander's Bridge Road where it turns north, joining the Confederate Line Trail to Battle Line Road. Go north on Battle Line Road to Alexander's Bridge Road and continue past the Georgia Monuments back to the Florida Monument and the completion of the loop. If you parked at South Post Gate you must backtrack across U.S. Highway 27 and back south to the trailhead.

The **Confederate Line Trail** follows the dense southern forest and tangled undergrowth that became the soldier's nightmare. The Confederate battle line was to the east of the Union forces. The vegetation here is much like it was during the time of the battles.

The orange blazed trail begins at the Texas Monument on Battle Line Road and goes southeast through the heavily wooded area to and across Brotherton Road. Continue hiking south, crossing a creek and on to Robertson's Brigade plaque, passing Bledsoe's Battery plaque and to Viniard-Alexander Road. Follow this road a short distance beyond Hood's Division tablet. Here the trail turns north into the woods and continues on north, crossing Brotherton Road and on to the Alabama Monument. It is now only a short distance to the trailhead at the Texas Monument.

Cannons and interpretive plaques along the Nature Trail at Chickamauga National Battlefield Park.

The **Nature Trail** is in the southeast section of the park and gives you a different look at some of the creek bottom habitat. The trailhead is on U.S. Highway 27 about 100 yards south of Glenn-Viniard Road. Two loops, one beyond the other, make a five-mile path with green blazes.

Beavers building dams on the water courses along this trail have flooded enough of the path so that it will be necessary for the Park Service personnel to relocate and redesign the route. Only portions of the trail can be hiked now. It is recommended to begin at Buckner's Corps descriptive plaque 0.6 mile east of U.S. Highway 27. Walk down the gated road through woods with thick stands of cedar. On the right, a trail post with the stick-man symbol and number 237 marks the green blazed trail that leads through a cedar thicket to a cannon battery and the point where the two loops of the Nature Trail join. From here, the path leads to the fields along West Chickamauga Creek. This area was on the mail route between Nashville, Tennessee, and Atlanta and Augusta, Georgia. The route crossed the creek at a place called Dalton's Ford.

The path loops around with the Perimeter Trail for a short distance and then comes back to the gravel road and back to the parking area. A large field along the road is frequently used by deer and other wildlife.

The Rossville, Georgia, Kiwanis Club has developed a Chickamauga Battlefield trails program for Boy Scouts, Girl Scouts, and other youth groups. Scouts can earn award medals and patches by hiking and completing questionnaires for each of the seven hikes.

8 Lake Conasauga Recreation Area Trails

Overview: The Conasauga Recreation Area is located in the Cohutta Mountains and provides hikers with a wide variety of opportunities. The elevation remains above 3,000 feet, making this a relatively cool place in summer. Campgrounds, picnic areas, boat launching ramp, and beautiful mountain forests make this a popular get-away place.

General description: Three trails vary from a quiet walk around the nineteen-acre Conasauga Lake, the highest in Georgia, or an easy hike through a songbird management area to a moderate hike up to Grassy Mountain fire tower with views of the largest of the Chattahoochee Forest wilderness areas.

General location: The recreation area is about ten air miles northeast of Chatsworth, in the Chattahoochee National Forest very near the Tennessee state line. By road it is a twisting twenty-mile climb, mostly on unpaved roads, into the Cohutta Mountains.

Maps: A page-size map of the Songbird and Lake trails with the beginning of the Tower Trail is available from the campground host; Crandall USGS quad.

Degree of difficulty: Easy to moderate.

Length: The Songbird Trail is a 1.7-mile loop; the Lake Trail is a one-mile loop; and the Tower Trail is 2.1 miles one way.

Elevations: The lowest point is 3,140 feet, and the highest is at the fire tower on Grassy Mountain, 3,692 feet.

Special attractions: Exceptional birding, wildflowers, mountain scenery, wildlife, lake and stream fishing, hunting in nearby Cohutta Wildlife Management Area, tent and trailer camping, and closeness to the Cohutta Wilderness make this a great place for both the novice hiker and experienced backpacker.

Best season: Spring and fall bird migrations, flowers, leaf color and camping attract the most people; however, winter brings siskins, red crossbills, grosbeaks, and other interesting winter birds. Summer offers cool evenings and many wildflowers and animals.

For more information: U.S. Forest Service, Cohutta Ranger District, 401 G. I. Maddox Parkway, Chatsworth, GA 30705; (706) 695-6736.

Finding the trailheads: From Chatsworth go north on U.S. Highway 411 four miles to Eton. Turn right (east) at the only traffic light and follow the paved CCC Camp Road until the pavement ends. At this point, the road becomes Forest Road 18. Follow on this gravel road to Forest Road 68. Turn left and go about ten miles to the end of FR 68 at the recreation area. On the way you will pass the Holly Creek Check Station and the large Cohutta Wildlife Management Area sign. This is a steep climb with some scenic overlooks. At the top of the mountain, FR 68 turns left and FR 64 turns right. These dirt roads are the boundary of the Cohutta Wilderness Area. Follow the signs to Lake Conasauga Recreation Area.

Footbridge at beaver pond on the Songbird Trail, an excellent birding area in Lake Conasauga Recreation Area.

Lake Conasauga Recreation Area Trails

From Ellijay go west on Georgia Highway 52 for nine miles to the Lake Conasauga Recreation Area and the Wildlife Management Area signs. Turn right on a paved road. This becomes Forest Road 18 in about one mile. The road forks at the pavement end. Take the left fork, Forest Road 18, about two miles to Forest Road 68. Turn right and follow the directions above.

The trailhead for the Songbird and Tower trails is on Forest Road 49 (an extension of FR 68) across from the camping overflow area. A gravel parking area is provided. The Lake Trail can be accessed from several points around the lake—the campground, picnic areas, and boat launching ramp. Campers can start the Tower Trail and walk down to the Songbird Trail from the dam.

The hikes: The **Songbird Trail** passes through the 120-acre songbird management tract developed cooperatively by the U.S. Forest Service and the Georgia Wildlife Resources Division's Nongame–Endangered Species Program. Clearings in the forest kept in grass/shrub stands, a beaver pond, rhododendron thickets, and mature forests provide habitat diversity attractive to a wide range of bird species. Experienced birders have recorded 125 bird species present at some time of the year. These include such birds as migrating sandhill cranes and red crossbills, nesting rosebreasted grosbeaks, scarlet tanagers, and chestnut-sided warblers.

From the trailhead on Forest Road 49, it is possible to hike either the Songbird or Tower trails. Cross the road and go past the wheelchair-accessible toilets and down a gravel roadway that has been blocked to vehicular traffic. This cove drains into the stream on which the beavers have built a dam creating a ten-acre pond. A clearing is on the right with forest on the left. Watch for deer, pig, or black bear tracks in the soft ground along this road. Rhododendron and mountain laurel line the pathway to the pond. Bat boxes have been placed along the trail.

At the pond you may see wood ducks that use the cavities in the dead trees or the artificial nest boxes that have been placed on poles in the pond. Belted kingfishers use this area along with many other birds and mammals. An observation platform on the side of the pond affords an excellent place to sit and watch quietly. The beaver's lodge and dam are visible. The trail continues to an information sign. The trail that leads down from the dam and campground intercepts the trail at this point. Continuing on along the beaver pond you cross the branch on a footbridge and begin the climb through thick rhododendron for about 100 yards where the Tower Trail takes off to the right. From here to the fire tower on Grassy Mountain is 1.7 miles.

The **Songbird Trail** continues on through thick rhododendron, laurel, dog-hobble, and other shrub growth and white pine, hemlock, yellow-poplar, buckeye, and other tall forest trees. Pass another opening and expect to see towhees, cardinals, catbirds, brown thrashers, indigo buntings, and other open habitat species. Benches at strategic places along the trail afford excellent, quiet viewing places. Besides birds and mammals, the pond attracts many reptiles and amphibians (turtles, salamanders, frogs, and toads), insects (dragonflies, damselflies, crane flies, butterflies, and gnats), all of which can be seen while taking advantage of the benches. The trail crosses the upper end of the beaver pond and back to the wider, old roadbed. Turn to the right and go back to the trailhead.

The **Tower Trail** leaves the Songbird Trail and climbs at a moderate grade through a rhododendron thicket and then opens into a beautiful mixed hardwood forest with large fern glades of New York fern, wood fern, and others. Large clumps of Christmas ferns are scattered about the east and north facing slopes. This section of the trail is an exceptional wildflower area. Lady's slippers, showy orchids, rattlesnake plantain, and other orchids are present at different times of the spring and summer. Solomon's seals, false Solomon's seals, false lily-of-the-valleys, bellworts, wood-lilies, several trilliums, mayapples, wild geraniums, azaleas, violets, squaw-root, one flowered cancer-root, and a host of other flowers bloom in spring. At this elevation the blooming season is two or three weeks behind lower areas in the mountains.

The trail reaches the road to the fire tower (Forest Road 49) near the crest of Grassy Mountain; walk the road to the tower, about 0.75 mile. Here the forest is made up of smaller, somewhat stunted southern red and other oaks. Blackberries grow abundantly along the road in the open sun, along with many other plants, especially daisies, asters, Queen-Anne's-lace, and other sun tolerant flowers. At the fire tower you can climb to the first landing and have a grand view of the mountains to the northeast in the Cohutta Wilderness, the Ridge and Valley Province to the west, and south to Fort Mountain and Fort Mountain State Park. This is a great place to watch for migrating hawks in the fall and on clear days in spring and fall for migrating sandhill cranes.

At the first switchback down the road, take one of two choices for the return to the trailhead. Either go back down the trail and around the Songbird Trail or continue down the forest service road. The distance is about the same. Birders may wish to take the road for a greater variety of habitats. In early July, the blackberries are ripe.

The **Lake Trail** can be walked from several places in the campground, picnic areas, and boat ramp. It is a level, quiet walk with views of the lake all the way around. The lake is usually crystal clear and in late spring and early summer watch for bluegills building spawning beds on the lake bottom. Great patches of dog-tooth-violets or trout lilies grow under the rhododendron and hemlocks. Ferns are all along the trail. Look for wild ginger or heart-leaf and maybe even a pink lady's slipper that has been missed by campers who unthinkingly pick wildflowers. Rhododendron and mountain laurel bloom during the summer. The lake and fish in it attract belted kingfishers that perch on exposed limbs over the water and dive into the water to catch a meal of fish. The one-mile walk is ideal morning or evening exercise for campers as well as a fine birding walk.

9   DeSoto Falls Trail

General description: Three falls, or cascades, are on the 2.5 miles of trail that range from easy to strenuous.

General location: It is in the Chestatee Ranger District of Chattahoochee National Forest, and about fifteen miles north on U.S. Highways 19/129 from Cleveland to the DeSoto Falls Recreation Area sign.

Maps: U.S. Forest Service map of Chattahoochee National Forest; Neels Gap USGS quad.

Degree of difficulty: The two lower falls are reached by easy to moderate hikes. The last mile of the upper falls is strenuous.

Length: To the lower series of falls is a one-mile loop. From the trailhead to the upper falls is 2.0 miles one way. The middle falls on the same trail is 0.75 mile from the trailhead.

Elevations: From the campground at 2,040 feet the trail climbs to 3,000 feet at the overlook for the upper falls.

DeSoto Falls Trail

Special attractions: Cascading streams with attractive waterfalls, wildlife, wildflowers, trout fishing, and camping in a well-managed campground.
Best season: Year-round hiking; heaviest water flows are in late winter and spring making the falls more impressive; camping in spring, summer, and fall; spring for wildflowers and spectacular leaf colors in the fall; trout fishing from April through October.
For more information: U.S. Forest Service, Brasstown Ranger District, 1881 Highway 515, Blairsville, GA 30512; (706)745-6928.

Finding the trailhead: The trailhead is at the bridge across Frogtown Creek in the campground. The hike also can be reached from the day-use parking area, following the arrows through a picnic area to the paved road or from the campground.

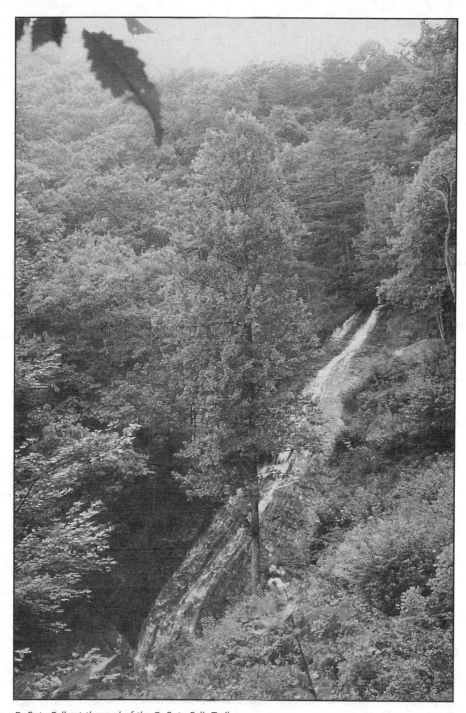

DeSoto Falls at the end of the DeSoto Falls Trail.

The hike: The trail begins at a picturesque footbridge across Frogtown Creek at the DeSoto Falls Scenic Recreation Area and campground in the Chattahoochee National Forest. After crossing the bridge a large wooden sign welcomes the hiker to DeSoto Falls Scenic Area. The falls got their name from a legend that tells of finding a piece of armor near the falls, and it was believed that it belonged to Hernando de Soto or one of his men. A sign directs visitors to the left for the lower falls in 0.5 miles and to the right for the middle and upper falls in 0.75 and 2.0 miles respectively.

Turning left, downstream on the west side of Frogtown Creek, the well-traveled trail leads to a lower series of cascades on a tributary to the main creek. An upper and lower trail make this a loop of about one mile. An observation platform provides a good view of the small but attractive falls.

Returning to the bridge, the trail continues upstream for 0.75 mile to the middle falls, also on a tributary to Frogtown Creek. A platform has been constructed at the end of a short spur trail for viewing the falls and surrounding area. This is a picturesque area rich in wildflowers during spring. Return to the main trail and continue upstream. The path leads uphill in a series of switchbacks that begin the more strenuous part of the hike. The end of the trail is along a rock outcrop with a railing and observation point about the same level as the top of the falls. Since this falls is very near the crest of one of the ridge spurs off Blood Mountain, there is very little water flowing over the 150-foot, sloping rock face during dry periods of the year. The waterfall is much more dramatic in late winter and spring, but the mountain sides exhibit grand color during the fall. Fine spring flower displays begin as early as March and continue with colorful displays of shrubs and trees like dog-hobble, silverbell, serviceberry, yellow-poplar, other deciduous magnolias, mountain laurel, rhododendron, sourwood, and others from April through August.

10 Cooper Creek Wildlife Management Area Trails

Overview: This Management Area has three trails that originate from the Cooper Creek Recreation Area. They follow old logging trails and new footpaths through a variety of hardwoods, mixed pine and hardwoods, and white pine and hemlock forests. They cross ridges and small trout streams. Other spur trails branch off from the main trails.

Cooper Creek Scenic Area is one of the more interesting forest areas in the Chattahoochee National Forest. Old timber stands remain untouched except for a few trees removed many years ago. Trout fishing in Cooper Creek and its tributaries, wildflowers, wildlife, and camping add to the hiking opportunities. **General description:** These trails are interconnected for a total of 5.5 miles of easy to moderate hiking.

Cooper Creek WMA Trails

General location: The recreation area is near Suches in the Cooper Creek Wildlife Management Area in the Chestatee Ranger District of the Chattahoochee National Forest.

Maps: U.S. Forest Service Chattahoochee National Forest Map; Mulky Gap USGS quad.

Degree of difficulty: Easy to moderate; there are a few short, steep grades.

Length: The Millshoal Creek Trail is 2.4 miles; Yellow Mountain 3.6 miles, and Cooper Creek, a connector between the other two, is 0.4 mile.

Elevations: The 2,160 foot contour runs through the Cooper Creek Recreation Area campground. From there the highest elevation on the Yellow Mountain Trail is 2,963 feet, a climb of 800 feet.

Foot log on the Yellow Mountain Trail in Cooper Creek WMA.

Special attractions: Old-growth timber stands, trout fishing, wildflower and wildlife viewing, camping, and hiking.

Best season: Year-round, with spring and fall best for flowers and leaf color and summer for fishing. The Cooper Creek Wildlife Management Area is open for hunting during specific dates in fall and winter.

For more information: For marked trails in the Cooper Creek Scenic Area: Chattahoochee National Forest, Brasstown Ranger District, 1881 Highway 515, Blairsville, GA 30512; (706)745-6928. For camping in Cooper Creek Recreation Area: Chattahoochee National Forest, Toccoa Ranger District, East Main Street, Suite 5, Owenby Bldg., Blue Ridge, GA 30513; (706)632-3031.

Finding the trailheads: From Dahlonega take Georgia Highway 60, through Suches, north, twenty-two miles to Forest Road 4 and the sign for Cooper Creek Wildlife Management Area. The Cooper Creek Recreation Area is at the junction of Forest Roads 4 and 236. The trailheads for Yellow Mountain and Millshoal Creek trails are on Forest Road 236 across from the campground.

The hikes: The trailhead for **Yellow Mountain Trail** is about 300 yards up the gravel Forest Road 236 from the Cooper Creek Recreation Area. This is the best marked and most used of the trails out of this campground. The path leads up a gentle ridge slope through a fine stand of white pines and into a hardwood cove with several large yellow-poplar and white oak trees. As the trail works to the south side of the ridge above Cooper Creek it enters an area of mountain laurel thickets with some large flame azalea plants. Trailing arbutus and galax grows abundantly where the path is carved out of the steep south-facing slope. At about one mile, the Yellow Mountain Trail is joined by the short spur trail called the **Cooper Creek Trail**. This can be used as a loop trail back to the Millshoal Creek Trail and down to the campground, a distance of about one mile. Continuing on the Yellow Mountain Trail along the ridge another spur trail leads off to the north and reaches Duncan Ridge Road (FR 39) in slightly less than a mile. Again this could be a loop hike by taking this spur to Duncan Ridge Road and hiking down the road to either the Millshoal Trail or continuing on to Mulky Gap Road, turning left, and on to the campground.

Staying on the Yellow Mountain Trail the highest point along the trail is reached very quickly. Here Yellow Mountain is about 3,000 feet high and in winter when the leaves are off offers a grand view of the surrounding valleys and mountains. This trail is the northern boundary of the Cooper Creek Scenic Area. The path continues down the ridge crest into a stand of large hemlocks and white pines, switching back and forth until it reaches Bryant Creek and dense growths of rhododendron, dog-hobble, and laurel. Bryant Creek is crossed on a log, and the path climbs the ridge past a clear-cut area and to Addie Gap at Forest Road 33A. To the south on this road is Cooper Creek and to the north is Duncan Ridge Road. There is ample parking should you begin the hike here.

From the Cooper Creek Recreation Area, the **Millshoal Creek Trail** begins across the gravel Forest Road 236. A wooden sign barely visible from the road marks the trailhead. Marked by a yellow blaze the trail starts a steady climb through white pines and hardwoods with small patches of trailing arbutus and galax at the path's edge. Old chestnut logs and new sprouts from old stumps remind the hiker of the importance of this great tree that was once dominant on these ridges. The path switches back and forth up a steep ridge with patches of mountain laurel, white pines, chestnut oaks, and several species of ferns. At about 0.6 mile the trail forks. A signpost gives directions to the campground and the **Cooper Creek Trail** connector between Millshoal Creek Trail and Yellow Mountain Trail. The left fork continues the Millshoal Creek Trail. It drops down along a north facing slope with wood ferns, New York ferns, and many spring flowers. The trail follows a logging road on a gentle grade. After about 0.5 mile the old road passes by a clearcut area where a new logging road has been cut. Staying on the logging road the trail crosses Millshoal Creek and reaches the Duncan Ridge Road (FR 39).

This trail is poorly marked and would be best attempted as an orienteering exercise rather than a marked hiking trail. About 0.2 mile up Duncan Ridge Road, the trail enters the woods to the north and climbs up to the gap below Hickory Knob. This portion of the trail is not well marked.

A loop hike can be made by walking back down Duncan Ridge Road to Mulky Gap Road (FR 4) and back to the campground. This would require a 1.5-mile walk on the road.

---

11 Arkaquah and Brasstown Bald Trails

Overview: The highest point in the state, 4,788 feet, is Brasstown Bald. A steep, paved trail leads from the parking area to the summit. For those who do not want to hike to the summit, a concessioner operates a shuttle bus from the parking area to visitor center for a fee. The Arkaquah Trail begins at the parking lot and follows west along a high ridge until it drops rapidly to Track Rock Gap. Both trails are in the Brasstown Wilderness providing spectacular views in a pristine setting.

General description: The 0.5-mile summit trail is moderate, and the 5.5-mile Arkaquah Trail is more strenuous.

General location: Brasstown Bald is near the center of the North Georgia mountains, about twenty miles from Blairsville and about twenty-five miles from Helen.

Maps: Chattahoochee National Forest map; Jacks Gap, Hiawassee, and Blairsville USGS quads.

Degree of difficulty: Moderate and strenuous, depending on the direction hiked.

Length: The paved Summit Access Trail is 0.5 mile one way. Arkaquah Trail is 5.5 miles one way.

Arkaquah and Brasstown Bald Trails

To Jacks Gap and (180)

Brasstown Bald 4788'

Jacks Knob Trail

4287'

4222'

Chimneytop Mountain 4303'

Arkaquah Trail

Low Gap

3410' Cove Gap

3640'

Track Rock Gap

Track Rock Gap Rd.

To Blairsville

0   1
Miles

Elevations: The parking area is at 4,320 feet. The summit of Brasstown Bald is 4,788 feet. The Arkaquah Trail remains near 4,000 feet for about 2.5 miles. The last 1.5 miles drops rapidly to Track Rock Gap at about 2,200 feet.

Special attractions: Grand scenery and spectacular wildflower displays in spring and early summer along with fall leaf color makes this one of the most popular areas in the mountains. The roads are clear during much of the winter; however, an occasional snow makes the road from Georgia Highway 180 to the Brasstown parking area impassible. Birders find this area especially rewarding during the spring and fall migrations as well as for resident species during the summer.

Best season: Spring, summer, and fall are the best. The visitor center is open every day from Memorial Day through October and on weekends in early spring, depending on the weather. The trails are open year-round, however, it is not advisable to hike the Arkaquah Trail in heavy snow.

For more information: U.S. Forest Service, Brasstown Ranger District, 1881 Highway 515, Blairsville, GA 30512; (706)745-6928. Brasstown Bald visitor center, (706)896-2556. Brasstown Heritage Association Bookstore at the parking area, (706)896-3471.

Finding the trailheads: From Blairsville go south on U.S. Highway 19/129 for eight miles to Georgia Highway 180. Turn east on Highway 180 for nine miles to Jacks Gap and the Highway 180 Spur. Turn north for three miles to the parking area. This is a very steep drive, gaining almost 1,500 feet in three miles. From Helen go north fourteen miles on Georgia Highway 75 to Highway 180. Turn west or left and go six miles to Jacks Gap and the road to the parking area. Trailheads for both trails are in the parking area.

The Arkaquah trailhead is at the northwest corner of the Brasstown parking area. The west end trailhead is at Track Rock Road and the parking area for the Track Rock Archaeological Area.

The hikes: The **Brasstown Bald Trail** to the summit and visitor center is paved. It is steep, climbing almost 500 feet in the half-mile walk. You walk through thick rhododendron and mountain laurel along with stunted hardwoods. During the late spring and early summer this can be a mass of flowering color. In fall, the leaf colors are spectacular. The visitor center exhibits tell of "Man and the Mountain" and other features unique to this highest point in Georgia. The visitor center stands above the trees and affords a 360-degree view of the surrounding wilderness and distant villages. On a clear day four states can be seen from here.

Arkaquah Trail from Brasstown Bald parking area is a moderate 5.5 miles. The path is through thick rhododendron and laurel along a southwest facing slope. Look for pink lady's slippers, bluets, Solomon's seals, toothworts, trilliums, galax, squaw-root, and other spring flowers blooming beside the trail in May along with many ferns. As you reach the crest of the ridge gnarled and stunted yellow birch and oak trees are festooned with "old man's beard," a lichen that gives the forest an elfin atmosphere. This is especially true on many days when the clouds shroud the mountain. You stay on the ridge crest past Chimney Top Mountain and on along

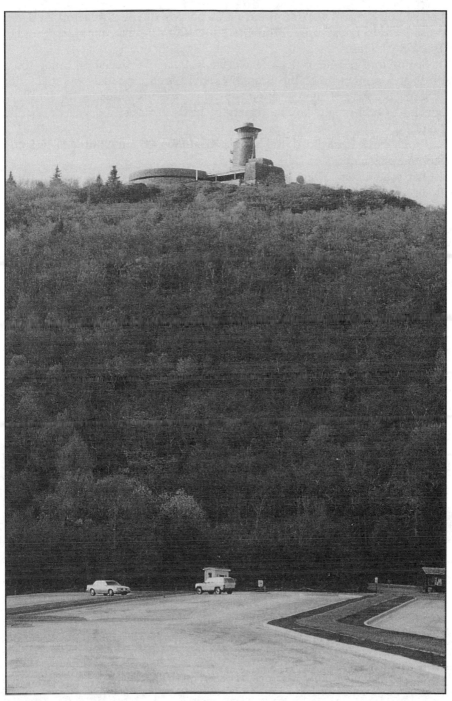

Brasstown Bald Visitor Center and Observation Deck on Brasstown Bald, highest point in the state (4,788 feet above sea level).

Locust Log Ridge. The path goes from one gap to the next ridgetop until you cross Buzzard Roost Ridge. From there the path descends at a steep grade to Track Rock Gap.

Spring and fall migrations of warblers, tanagers, thrushes, other songbirds and raptors make the Brasstown Bald area especially popular with birders. Because of the elevation, northern species mingle with southern species to add greatly to the variety of birds. This is just as true for the plants.

From Track Rock Road, the hike is strenuous as you climb nearly 2,000 feet to eastern end.

The road distance between the two trailheads, Brasstown Bald and Track Rock parking areas, is about twenty-five miles. There is no drinking water along the trail.

12 Wagon Train Trail

General description: This is the third trail that leads from the popular Brasstown Bald. This one is the roadbed of what was to become Georgia Route 66. Construction was carried out during the 1950s, but was never finished as the road it was intended to be. The paved road up the other side of the mountain from Jacks Gap was completed and is now called Georgia Highway 180 Spur. The Wagon Train Trail passes through the Brasstown Wilderness down to the campus of Young Harris College. The name for the trail comes from the custom of dozens of local families who formed wagon trains to travel the winding roadbed from Young Harris to camp and socialize on the Bald. Only foot and horseback travel are permitted today in the wilderness area.
General location: Brasstown Bald and the parking area is at the end of Georgia Highway 180 Spur off Georgia Highway 180 about twenty miles from Hiawassee. The town of Young Harris is seven miles west of Hiawassee on U.S. Highway 76.
Maps: U.S. Forest Service map of Chattahoochee National Forest and the Trail Guide to the Chattahoochee and Oconee national forests; Hiawassee and Jacks Gap USGS quads.
Degree of difficulty: Moderate or strenuous. If hiked from the Brasstown Bald parking area to Young Harris or from Young Harris to the Brasstown parking area in one day, it is considered moderate. If hiked from the Brasstown Bald parking area to the Chattahoochee Forest boundary line, one mile from the Young Harris College campus, and back to the parking area in one day, it is strenuous. The same is true if hiked from Young Harris to the top and back in the same day.
Length: From the Brasstown Bald parking area to Young Harris this trail is seven miles. The last mile before Young Harris is over a steep, rough road on private property. Respect it as such.
Elevations: The trailhead at Brasstown Bald is about 4,625 feet above sea level. The Chattahoochee Forest boundary line near Young Harris is about 2,400 feet and the gate at the Young Harris College campus is about 2,000 feet.
Special attractions: The historical significance of the trail; hiking through a wilderness area; the change in elevation resulting in a great variety of plant and

Wagon Train Trail

To Hiawassee

Young Harris
Young Harris
College Campus

Sharp Hill
2320'

76

To
Blairsville

NATIONAL FOREST BOUNDARY

Granny Knob
× 2840'

Carrol Gap

× Double Knob
1000'

CHATTAHOOCHEE
NATIONAL
FOREST

×
Rattlesnake Knob
2760'

TOWNS COUNTY
UNION COUNTY

CHATTAHOOCHEE
NATIONAL
FOREST

BUCK RIDGE

× Chimney Top
4200'

Brasstown Creek

BRASSTOWN
WILDERNESS

BRASSTOWN
WILDERNESS

× Little Bald Mountain
4400'

N

Brasstown Bald ×
4788'

P

Fodder Creek

180

0   1
Miles

To 180
and Jacks Gap

Hoe Creek

69

animal species; outstanding wildflower displays from spring through fall, and fall leaf colors all make this a great hike.

Best season: Spring, summer, and fall are best. Although there are days in winter when the weather would make hiking impractical, there are many pleasant winter days suitable for hiking.

For more information: Brasstown Ranger District, 1881 Highway 515, P.O. Box 9, Blairsville, GA 30512; (706)745-6928.

Finding the trailhead: From the Brasstown Bald parking area walk up the paved trail between the gift shop and the concession building. This is the trail to the summit. At about 100 yards you come to an unpaved service road. A sign here refers to the Wagon Train Trail. Turn right and follow this road which becomes the narrower trail. At the Young Harris College campus a private road marked by a red gate is the beginning of the road on private property that leads to the national forest boundary. It is necessary to get permission from the college to park and to begin at this end. There is no other access to the national forest boundary.

The hike: From the Brasstown Bald parking area this hike starts on the paved summit trail between the log cabin gift shop and the concession building. About 100 yards up this trail is an opening in the dense rhododendron. This is the two-track, grassy road that is the upper end of the Wagon Train Trail. Turn right and follow it to the gated section of the trail that enters the Brasstown Wilderness. Here the trail loses the two-track character. The path follows under the Bald as it winds along the most appropriate contour for a roadbed. Because this was surveyed as a vehicle road the grade is never very steep for hiking. Much rock had to be blasted out to make the road. These rock surfaces, now almost fifty years old, have healed with many lichens and mosses growing on them. Most notable are the large, draping patches of sphagnum moss, which usually thrives only in very wet bogs, growing here because it is regularly bathed in moisture in the form of clouds, fog, and rain. Many times throughout the year the upper stretch of the trail is shrouded in clouds that seem to hang in the trees. The slightest breeze will cause the trees to release the droplets of water that hang from each leaf.

The rock tripe, the most obvious lichen, covers the rock walls with large dinner plate–sized, loose, leathery patches. Many other lichens, including old man's beard, hanging from the trees and clumps of reindeer-moss on the ground, are along the trail. The moss species are just as abundant.

Spring comes slowly at this elevation but also lasts longer because you can follow it up the mountain. It brings on a profusion of flowering trees, shrubs, and herbs. Among the trees are silverbells, serviceberries, dogwoods, yellow-poplars, buckeyes, and sourwoods. Catawba and rosebay rhododendron, mountain laurel, dog-hobble, azalea, highbush and lowbush blueberry, sweet shrub, wild hydrangea, raspberry, and a host of other shrubs are here. Buttercups, large clumps of bluets, robin's plantains and pussy-toes, Solomon's seals and false Solomon's seals, toothworts, foam flowers, white and blue violets, yellow violets, mayapples, several species of trilliums, and pink and yellow lady's slippers only begin the list of flowering plants along the trail.

Steep slopes opposite the blasted-out rock walls afford grand views of the mountains in winter and early spring on clear days. The trail passes along the north-facing slopes through quiet and majestic cove hardwood forests with large yellow-poplars, hemlocks, silverbells, yellow birches, basswoods, buckeyes, and maples. On the points and western and southern slopes the tree canopy becomes the oaks, hickories, sourwoods, black gums, and pines under which may be rhododendron and mountain laurel or one or more kinds of huckleberry bushes.

This trail has the greatest change in elevation of all the short trails in the state. At this latitude there is about two or three degrees temperature change per 1,000 feet of elevation change. This means that at the top it may be as much as six to ten degrees cooler than at the bottom. This is significant while hiking.

The slope, either hiking down or up the trail, is never very steep while in the wilderness area. Some stretches are actually quite flat. The road on private land at the lower end is eroded and quite steep in places so that walking is less pleasant. Only in a few areas has the trail been so eroded that walking is difficult because of exposed stones.

To avoid parking at the Young Harris end the best hike would be from the top down to the gate at the national forest boundary and back up to the top. Primitive camping is permitted in the national forest; however, it is advised to take water or water purification supplies. There are few springs along the way. You will notice several fire rings at wide places along the trail. These would be appropriate places to camp. Good wilderness camping ethics suggest that a campfire not be used, rather take a suitable backpack stove for cooking.

Summer view from Wagon Train Trail.

13   Jacks Knob Trail

General description: From two to five miles of moderately strenuous hiking through diverse terrain and plant communities.

General location: Brasstown Bald is in the heart of the Chattahoochee National Forest in Towns and Union counties, the north-central part of the state. The Jacks Knob Trail is crossed by Georgia Highway 180 between U.S. Highway 129 and Georgia Highway 75, about fifteen miles southeast of Blairsville.

Maps: Chattahoochee National Forest map; Jacks Gap USGS quad.

Degree of difficulty: Moderate to strenuous.

Length: From Brasstown Bald Scenic area to Chattahoochee Gap and the Appalachian Trail it is five miles. From Georgia Highway 180 to Chattahoochee Gap two miles, both one way.

Elevations: 4,320 feet at the north end to 2,964 feet at Jacks Gap and back to 3,540 feet at Brookshire Top and 3,520 feet at the Chattahoochee Gap and the Appalachian Trail.

Special attractions: Spectacular views from the high points and a challenging hike along the higher ridges and into the gaps makes this an interesting one-way trail. Wildflowers from many spring herbaceous plants to the grand display of mountain laurel and rhododendron. Fall leaf colors can be dazzling. Birds of the higher mountains like ravens, hawks, and warblers make this a good birding and wildlife watching trail.

Best season: This can be a year-round trail with spring, summer, and fall the best. There are many winter days suitable for a hike at this elevation.

For more information: U.S. Forest Service, Brasstown Ranger District, 1881 Highway 515, P.O. Box 9, Blairsville, GA 30512; (706)745-6928.

Finding the trailhead: One trailhead is at the south end of Brasstown Bald parking area. The other is about the middle of the trail on Georgia Highway 180 at Jack's Gap.

The hike: This trail follows the ridge crest from the highest mountain in Georgia to Chattahoochee Gap where the Chattahoochee, Georgia's most famous river, has its origin. Its lowest point is where it crosses Georgia Highway 180 at Jack's Gap. In the five miles, there are north, east, south, and west facing slopes each with somewhat different plant communities. There are no streams to cross. You are apt to see deer, turkeys, ruffed grouse, squirrels, and a variety of birds, including the raven, the large crow of the high mountains. This blue blazed trail begins at the south end of the parking area for Brasstown Bald visitor center. You enter a rhododendron thicket and continue south on Wolfpen Ridge, climbing steadily to the highest point on the trail at 4,561 feet. From here the path leads down steadily and rather steeply, losing more than 1,500 feet to Jacks Gap and Georgia Highway 180. Cross the highway and begin a climb up Hiwassee Ridge. Go around the southwest side of Henry Knob more or less on a contour through a mature hardwood forest with large rock outcrops above the path. Spring seeps keep selected rocky areas very moist and support marginal and Christmas ferns, mosses, and wild hydrangeas along with a

Jacks Knob Trail

Brasstown
Bald
4788'

P

WOLFPEN

RIDGE

4564' 180
SPUR

Rocky
Mountain
4191'

Soapstone Creek

180

Jacks Gap P

Otter Branch

Henry Knob
3520'

3638' Brookshire
Top

HIWASSEE RIDGE

N

0   1
Miles

Jacks Knob

Chattahoochee
Gap

Appalachian Trail

number of other moisture tolerant plants. Passing through a young stand of white pines, you enter a sweeping north facing cove of mature hardwoods. Stepping stones have been placed in the only running stream on this path. The trees of this cove produce great amounts of food for wildlife. Turkeys, deer, bears, bobcats, foxes, and an array of small mammals and birds take advantage of the nuts fallen from trees, while bobcats, foxes, hawks, and owls prey on the small animals.

The trail continues around to the east side of Brookshire Top and drops down into another of the several gaps. From here the path is the crest of Hiwassee Ridge, the Towns and Union county line. From the gap south of Eagle Knob just before starting up Jacks Knob, the trail goes around the west side and drops down to Chattahoochee Gap and the Appalachian Trail. Chattahoochee Spring, headwater for the Chattahoochee River, is just below this gap about 120 yards.

The Jacks Gap USGS quad shows the trail splitting just north of Jacks Knob with both prongs ending at the Appalachian Trail at Chattahoochee Gap and near Red Clay Gap. The left fork is not blazed with blue blazes like the right prong of the trail. The trail to the left or southeast has been used so infrequently it is imperceptible. It is not advisable to walk it unless you have the current Jacks Gap USGS quad and are experienced in orienteering.

From the south end of Jacks Knob Trail at the Appalachian Trail, it is possible to return to Georgia Highway 180 or hike east on the Appalachian Trail to the Blue Mountain shelter, 2.25 miles, or to Unicoi Gap (GA 75), an additional 2.2 miles. If you hike southwest on the Appalachian Trail, you will go past the Low Gap shelter, 5.0 miles, or an additional 4.2 miles to Hog Pen Gap on the Richard B. Russell Scenic Highway (GA 348).

14 Lake Winfield Scott Recreation Area Trails

Overview: Three fine trails in the vicinity of and around the beautiful Lake Winfield Scott Recreation Area give the hiker several interesting options. The Lake Trail encircles the lake and is an easy loop. Jarrard Gap Trail is a comfortable hike from Lake Winfield Scott to Jarrard Gap on the Appalachian Trail. The Slaughter Creek Trail, with the same trailhead as Jarrard Gap Trail, also leads to the Appalachian Trail. These two trails with the 2.3-mile hike on the Appalachian Trail makes an interesting day loop hike of slightly more than six miles.

The Lake Winfield Scott Recreation Area offers good fishing for trout in the eighteen-acre lake. Hardwood coves are excellent spring flower areas. These trails lead to the Appalachian Trail and to Blood Mountain, the highest point on the Appalachian Trail in Georgia. This is a particularly good birding area and has pleasant camping facilities.

General description: About four miles of easy to moderate hiking trails.
General location: The entrance to Lake Winfield Scott Recreation Area is 4.5 miles east of Suches on Georgia Highway 180 and seven miles from U.S. Highway 19/129 near Vogel State Park. The lake is in the Brasstown Ranger District of the Chattahoochee National Forest.
Maps: Chattahoochee National Forest map; Neels Gap USGS quad.
Degree of difficulty: The Lake Loop Trail is easy, following the contour of the lake. Both Jarrard Gap and Slaughter Creek trails are easy to moderate. The section of the Appalachian Trail from Jarrard Gap to Slaughter Gap is also moderate.
Length: Lake Trail, 0.4 mile; Jarrard Gap Trail, 1.2; Slaughter Creek Trail, 2.7.
Elevations: Lake Winfield Scott is at 2,870 feet. The trailhead begins at the headwater of the lake and climbs to 3,290 feet at Jarrard Gap and 3,920 feet at Slaughter Gap.
Special attractions: Good fishing, wildflower and bird viewing, and camping.
Best season: Spring and fall are best times for hiking because of the cooler weather and spring flowers and fall colors; however, the trails are open year-round and only inaccessible during periods of heavy snow.
For more information: Chattahoochee National Forest, Brasstown Ranger District, 1881 Highway 515, P.O. Box 9, Blairsville, GA 30512; (706)745-6928.

Finding the trailheads: The trailhead for Jarrard Gap and Slaughter Creek trails is at the information sign and parking area on the east side of the lake. The Lake Loop Trail can be approached at several places giving good access to fishing.

The hikes: The **Lake Loop Trail** is a 0.4 mile walking path around the small but beautiful clear lake. Jarrard Gap and Slaughter Creek trails follow the same wide path beside Slaughter Creek near where it flows into the lake. Just before the footbridge crossing over the creek, the trail turns left and enters a wooded area marked plainly with a blue blaze. The sign refers to both trails. After a short walk along the creek, the path crosses it on a log and comes out onto a gravel road. Turn right on the gravel road and follow the blue blazes to the sign for the Slaughter Creek Trail that leaves the road to the left. The **Jarrard Gap Trail** continues on the road for a few yards and enters the woods at a sign indicating the direction and 0.7 miles to Jarrard Gap. The blue blaze is on a large boulder in the middle of the trail, which continues on through a pleasant cove hardwood forest up Lance Branch in a gentle grade to the gap and the Appalachian Trail at elevation 3,290 feet. A spring is located just below the intersection with the Appalachian Trail.

Slaughter Creek Trail passes through a similar cove hardwood forest. The path is 2.7 miles of moderate climbing that follows an old logging road for much of its distance. From Slaughter Gap, the hiker can continue on to Blood Mountain (4,458 feet) on the Appalachian Trail or follow the Appalachian Trail to Jarrard Gap and return to Lake Winfield Scott. Blood Mountain has large areas of catawba rhododendron blooming in June and July and sweeping vistas of surrounding mountains.

The Slaughter Creek and Lance Branch coves are excellent spring wildflower habitat—bloodroot, lady's slipper orchid, Clinton-lily, Solomon's seal

Lake Winfield Scott Recreation Area Trails

and false Solomon's seal, dwarf crested iris, foam flower, toothwort, and many other blooming plants. Large fern glades of New York ferns interspersed with Christmas and maidenhair ferns occur along the trail. Except for very short stretches of roadway the trails pass through fine examples of second growth cove hardwood forests.

15 Sosebee Cove Trail

General description: The hike consists of three easy loop trails that total about 0.5 mile in this scenic park.
General location: In the north-central portion of the state near Blairsville in the Chattahoochee National Forest.
Maps: Chattahoochee National Forest map; Coosa Bald USGS quad.
Degree of difficulty: Easy.
Length: 0.6 mile in three loop trails.
Elevations: The trail begins at about 3,200 feet and drops only about fifty feet.
Special attractions: One of the finest stands of second-growth hardwoods, especially yellow-poplar trees, and an outstanding array of wildflowers in spring and summer on the forest floor. One of the largest yellow buckeye trees in the state is right beside the trail.
Best season: Early spring before the leaves shade the forest floor for a fine show of wildflowers.
For more information: Chattahoochee National Forest, Brasstown Ranger District, 1881 Highway 515, P.O. Box 9, Blairsville, GA 30512; (706)745-6928.

Finding the trailhead: From Blairsville, take U.S. Highway 129 south nine miles to Georgia Highway 180; turn right and go three miles to Sosebee Cove parking area with space for about three or four vehicles. The trailhead is at the parking area on Georgia Highway 180.

The hike: The trail provides access to the 175-acre Sosebee Cove Scenic Area of great trees and wildflowers typical of the southern Appalachian cove hardwood forests. The Sosebee Cove Scenic Area is a memorial to Arthur Woody, who served as forest ranger from 1911 to 1945. The trail leads from Georgia Highway 180 down into this beautiful hardwood forest in three successive loops, each a little deeper than the preceding one. A sign at the beginning of the trail tells of the memorial to Ranger Woody and the plant life in the cove. You are very quickly greeted by one of the largest buckeye trees (about seventeen feet in circumference) in the state and by many large yellow-poplars, also called tulip trees. As with many high-elevation southern Appalachian streams the small branch flowing through the cove is preferred habitat for many salamanders. Lady's slippers, Solomon's seal, false Solomon's seal, mayapples, hepaticas, several species of trilliums, and many other spring wildflowers grow in great

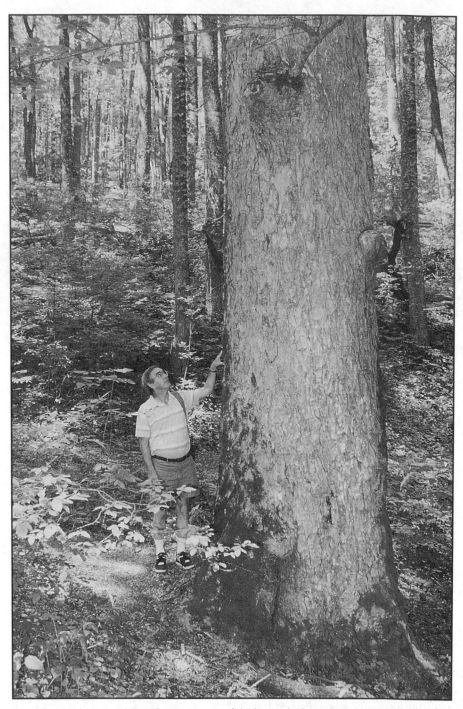

Big yellow buckeye tree in Sosebee Cove, one of the largest in the state.

abundance along the trail. This trail is a must for anyone interested in wildflowers, especially for photography. It is possible to photograph a dozen or two species in one day during late April and May. There are no steep sections that would prevent anyone with limited disability from walking the shortest loop.

Sosebee Cove Trail

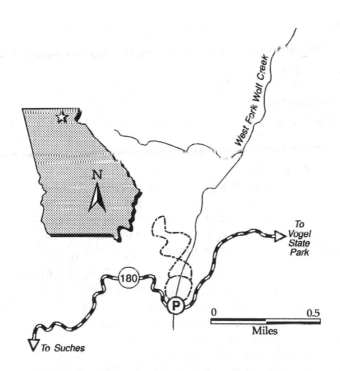

16 High Shoals Scenic Area and Falls Trail

General description: About 1.5 miles of easy to moderate trails. There are five waterfalls, only two of which are reached easily by the trail.

General location: High Shoals Scenic Area is in the Brasstown Ranger District on the Tennessee Valley side of the Blue Ridge.

Maps: Chattahoochee National Forest Map, Trail Guide to the Chattahoochee-Oconee national forests; Tray Mountain USGS quad.

Degree of difficulty: Easy to moderate.

Length: 1.3 miles one way. One mile to Blue Hole Falls and an additional 0.3 mile to High Shoals Falls observation deck.

Elevations: The elevation at the parking area is 2,880 feet. The trail drops to about 2,400 feet at the base of the lower falls.

Special attractions: Beautiful waterfalls, wildlife, wildflowers, trout fishing, and birding.

Best season: Year-round with spring through fall offering the best display of wildflowers, including mountain laurel and rhododendron. During the winter, freezing weather and high water can make the trail more difficult to reach and to hike. The falls are more dramatic in winter and spring.

For more information: Chattahoochee National Forest, Brasstown Ranger District, 1881 Highway 515, P.O. Box 9, Blairsville, GA 30512; (706)745-6928.

Finding the trailhead: The trailhead is reached from Georgia Highway 75 11.4 miles north of Helen. Turn right on Forest Road 283 and go for 1.5 miles up a steep grade to the High Shoals sign. A short distance after leaving the paved road this road fords the upper reaches of the Hiawassee River, which can be a problem for low clearance vehicles during wet, rainy seasons, especially winter and early spring. FR 283 continues on to Indian Grave Gap and the Appalachian Trail. The trailhead is near the High Shoals Falls sign at a small, unpaved parking area on FR Road 283 where there is space for three or four vehicles to park.

The hike: High Shoals Creek originates on Tray Mountain, one of the summits on the Appalachian Trail that is more than 4,000 feet in elevation. The moderately steep trail leads the hiker into another one of the beautiful coves and cascading mountain streams so typical of the north Georgia highlands. The trail ends at two waterfalls.

The trail begins with steps going down from the parking area. Blue blazes mark the path throughout its length. The trail descends the steep-sided cove. A number of switchbacks keeps the grade moderate for the descent and climb back out. A big oak tree with cavities large enough to have accommodated a hibernating bear in times past stands beside the path before the first switchback. Hardwood trees in the cove give way to large white pines and hemlocks as the trail nears High Shoals Creek. Several spring seeps cross the path that are easily stepped across even during wet weather. The cascading water of the creek can be heard well before the trail reaches the stream. At the creek the trail abruptly flattens out and follows an old roadbed to the first bridge on the trail. It crosses High Shoals Creek in a beautiful level area in the cove that has been used for many seasons as a primitive campsite. Thick rhododendron covers the stream as the path follows downstream. Three footbridges span brooks and spring seeps that cross the path. The cascading creek can be heard but not seen because of the thick rhododendron. The large rock outcrops along the trail indicate the same formations that form the falls. The first turnout in the trail at about one mile leads quickly to Blue Hole Falls. This thirty-foot falls spills into a deep catch pool in front of the wooden platform installed by the Forest Service. A sign on the trail leading to this falls warns about the dangers of leaving the trail and climbing on the rocks. The smart hiker will heed these warnings.

Returning to the main trail again, the path descends quickly to the next turn to the left and to the dramatic High Shoals Falls and another observation platform. The creek falls more than 100 feet, splashing grandly down the steep rock face. Many moisture tolerant plants, including liverworts, mosses, and flowering plants add to the beauty of falls. The massive rhododendrons on either side of the stream, large hemlocks, white pines, and hardwood trees complete the enchantment of the site.

The path is all downhill coming to the falls. It is all uphill going back to the trailhead.

High Shoals Scenic Area and Falls Trail

17 Holcomb Creek Trail

General description: A pleasant 4.5 miles of hiking to waterfalls on trails through a diversified forest.

General location: This trail is on the Tullulah Ranger District of the Chattahoochee National Forest east of Rabun Bald in Rabun County.

Maps: Chattahoochee National Forest maps; Rabun Bald USGS quad.

Degree of difficulty: Easy to moderate.

Length: About one mile to Holcomb Creek Falls and 0.5 mile more to Ammons Creek Falls. Returning to Hales Ridge Road without going by Holcomb Falls, add another mile. The total hike including the walk down Hales Ridge Road to the original trailhead is about three miles.

Elevations: The trailhead is at 2,553 feet and the trail comes back out on the road at 2,791 feet. The falls are at about 2,600 feet.

Special attractions: Two waterfalls in a typical rhododendron-lined mountain stream setting. The rhododendron along with mountain laurel put on a fine display of color from late spring through the summer. Spring flowers and fall leaf color adds to the fine birding area. Holcomb Creek is a good trout stream.

Best season: Year-round with best waterfall conditions in winter and spring. Spring and fall for flowers, leaf color, and passerine bird migrations.

For more information: Chattahoochee National Forest, Tallulah Ranger District, 809 Highway 441, P.O. Box 438, Clayton, GA 30525; (706)782-3320.

Finding the trailhead: From Clayton take Warwoman Road east about ten miles to its crossing of West Fork. Turn left onto Overflow Creek Road and go nine miles to where it intersects with Hales Ridge Road, Forest Road 7. The trailhead is at this junction with a sign designating Holcomb Creek Falls. There is space for two or three vehicles to park.

The hike: There are a number of trails in the north Georgia mountains that lead to waterfalls. This one not only leads to two falls, but the trail itself is pleasant and diversified. It leads through rhododendron tunnels and under excellent stands of hemlocks, white pines, and stately hardwoods. Holcomb and Ammons creeks are both rapidly cascading streams visible in places throughout the hike. The trail begins where Overflow Creek Road ends at a sharp, hairpin curve in Hales Ridge Road. A Forest Service sign and a post with the hiker symbol directs the hiker to Holcomb Creek Falls. The trail drops quickly down a steep cove lined with rhododendron, mountain laurel, hemlock, white pine, and a wide assortment of hardwoods. Switchbacks keep the grade at a moderate rate of descent. In places, the trail is completely covered over with the rosebay, or great white rhododendron. These bloom from late May through the summer after the mountain laurel blooms. These two large shrubs add much color and pleasant shade to the walk during the warmer months. The rather narrow path follows along a steep slope before the trail begins to level out and gently climb up to the falls. The noise of the water can be heard well before the cascade is in sight.

Holcomb Creek Falls is one of the more attractive waterfalls in the Georgia mountains. It falls in a succession of drops for about 120 feet. Standing at the bottom where a bridge crosses the creek, it is hard to see the full length of the cascading water. Crossing the stream the path follows downstream for a short distance before turning up through a very beautiful cove. Large yellow-poplars, buckeyes, and other hardwoods form a dense canopy over silverbells and dogwoods. Many ferns, partridge berries, and, in the spring, early blooming wildflowers enhance this grand forest. A

Holcomb Creek Trail

large hemlock fell across the trail, and a section of the log was sawed out to permit the trail to go through. Someone made a seat in one end of the log, which makes a welcome rest stop in this section of the trail. Just before reaching the falls, a trail sign points back to Hales Ridge Road.

At Ammons Creek an observation deck provides a good view of the falls and the creek as it plummets down under the deck through narrow rock crevices. Turning back, the trail bends around the ridge above Holcomb Creek and parallels the creek back to the road. This portion of the trail leads through a more open forest. It passes a very impressive cascade above Holcomb Creek Falls. Large patches of trailing arbutus, some more than four feet across, grow along the right or uphill side of the trail. These will bloom with a most pleasant odor as early as late February and into early April. Foam flowers, bloodroots, jack-in-the-pulpits, wood anemones, several species of trilliums and violets, and other spring flowers will make the hike colorful from March to early June. In late fall, the gentians and numerous composites add color to the forest floor. The trail ends at Hales Ridge Road where it crosses Holcomb Creek. An easy 0.6 mile walk back to the starting point completes the loop.

18 Ellicott Rock Wilderness Trail

General description: The Ellicott Rock Trail is actually an extension of the longer Chattooga River Trail described in Hike 87. The Ellicott Rock section is added here even though it is in South Carolina. The Chattooga River is the state line between Georgia and South Carolina and it is closer to larger populations in Georgia than South Carolina. The trail follows the river from Burrells Ford Bridge to the North Carolina state line and the Ellicott Rock. One of the parking areas for the trail is on the Georgia side of the river.

General location: Ellicott Rock is the exact northeastern corner of Georgia. It is where Georgia, North Carolina, and South Carolina join in the northwestern corner of Ellicott Rock Wilderness. The trailhead is very near Burrells Ford Bridge, which is about twenty-three miles from Clayton, Georgia.

The point was established as a result of a dispute over the boundary between South Carolina and Georgia. This point is midway in the Chattooga River at latitude 35 degrees north. The surveyor, Andrew Ellicott, established this point in 1813 for the boundary between North Carolina and South Carolina where he engraved "LAT 35°, A D 1813, NC + SC" on a boulder that forms part of the massive stone bank of the river. In 1996 South Carolina embedded a survey marker in another rock in the Chattooga River at latitude 35 degrees north, which is now called the Chattooga Rock.

Maps: U.S. Forest Service map of the Chattooga National Wild and Scenic River; Tamassee USGS quad.

Degree of difficulty: Moderate.

Length: Two trailheads give this trail two different lengths. If walked from the entrance to the Burrells Ford parking area or campground it is 3.8 miles. If

Ellicott Rock Wilderness Trail

NORTH CAROLINA
GEORGIA

SOUTH CAROLINA

Ellicott Rock

Bad Creek

ELLICOTT
ROCK
WILDERNESS

GEORGIA

SOUTH CAROLINA

Chattooga River

East Fork

To
Walhalla
Fish
Hatchery

Harden Creek

Burrells Ford
Bridge

Spoon
Auger
Falls

To
Clayton

646

Burrells Ford
Campground

708

N

0   0.5

Miles

walked from the parking areas at Burrells Ford Bridge it is 3.3 miles.

Elevations: Burrells Ford Bridge is about 2,080 feet above sea level; Ellicott Rock is about 2,180 feet. Since the trail follows the river closely there is only about 100 feet total change in trail elevation; however, there are short steep grades in the trail as it goes over bluffs and other features along the river.

Special attractions: The Ellicott Rock Wilderness Area; historic mark for three states by surveyor Andrew Ellicott in 1813; scenic views of the Chattooga River; Spoon Auger Falls; wildflowers from late winter to late fall, fall leaf color, and unusual plants; and trout fishing are but a few attractions of this trail.

Best season: Spring and fall are the best times for wildflowers and leaf color. The trail is shaded for its entire length making it pleasant in summer and there are many winter days suitable for hiking. Snowfall in this section of the mountains may be as much as twenty days from November to March.

For more information: U.S. Forest Service, Tallulah Ranger District, 809 Highway 441 South, Clayton, GA 30525; (706)782-3320. U.S. Forest Service, Andrew Pickens Ranger District, 112 Andrew Pickens Circle, Mountain Rest, SC 29664; (803)638-9568.

Finding the trailheads: Burrells Ford on the Chattooga River is twenty-three miles from U.S. Highway 441 and Warwoman Road in Clayton. Take Warwoman Road to Georgia Highway 28. Turn right and go 1.7 miles to Forest Road 646. A Burrells Ford sign is here. This is a winding, gravel road for seven miles to the Chattooga River and Burrells Ford Bridge, the Georgia/South Carolina line. There is a parking area on the Georgia side and the South Carolina side. There are two points near the Burrells Ford Bridge, both on the South Carolina side, from which you can hike this trail. The trailhead closest to the bridge is about 50 yards on the left. It is marked with a fiberglass post with the hiking icon. The other is about one-half mile farther up the road across the road from the parking area for the Burrells Ford Campground. This path is similarly marked.

The hike: If you begin this trail near the Burrells Ford Bridge the trailhead is about fifty yards up the road on the left side. It is marked with the standard Forest Service trail post with the hiker icon. At first the path is wide and relatively flat through a pleasant stand of hemlock, white pine, yellow-poplar, and a few white oak trees. Although closer to the streambank than the Forest Service permits camping many people camp here because it is so level and shady and the forest floor is open. The Chattooga River is a popular trout stream, managed jointly by both Georgia and South Carolina wildlife agencies and the U.S. Forest Service. A creel census box is near the beginning and a sign encourages catch-and-release fishing. Very soon the trail enters the Ellicott Rock Wilderness Area and remains in it for the rest of the hike.

The most common of the low bushes along the path is bear-huckleberry and dog-hobble. In spring there will be a wide variety of flowering plants including Solomon's seals, sessiles and Vacey's trilliums, foam flowers, toothworts, jack-in-the-pulpits, pink lady's slippers, and others. The prominent ferns in later spring and through the summer are New York and Christmas ferns.

Very shortly you come to the first small stream to cross. This is the branch that forms Spoon Auger Falls only about 200 yards up the side trail with several switchbacks to negotiate the steep slope. If you climb this path do not be misled by the several pretty but small four- or five-foot waterfalls. The real falls is much more impressive, and in wet weather is exceptionally picturesque.

At a half mile the trail along the river joins the trail that starts near the Burrells Ford Campground parking area and the Foothills Trail that goes up the mountain into South Carolina and past the Walhalla Fish Hatchery.

The path now hugs the riverbank, departing from it only where steep rock walls make it impossible to stay close to the water. At many of these places the trail goes through virtual tunnels of rhododendron, mountain laurel, and dog-hobble. Where the trailside vegetation is more open the spring flowers are more numerous. Several orchids grow here. Rattlesnake plantain with its green leaves with white veins, and cranefly orchids with green leaves on one side and deep red on the underside are more obvious than the flowers. Pink lady's slipper may be found sparsely along the way.

At about one mile there is a wide sandy beach on the trail side of the river. This may be a good place to stop for a picnic or just rest and watch the river go by.

April, May, and June are the prime months for blooming plants. Rhododendron, mountain laurel, dog-hobble, silverbell, buckeye, yellow-poplar, Fraser magnolia, cucumber tree, dogwood, and redbud are among the shrubs and trees.

At about 1.5 miles you reach the East Fork, the creek that flows down from the Walhalla Fish Hatchery. Here you can camp under a great stand of hemlocks, white pines, yellow-poplars, and other large trees. The mouth of the East Fork at Chattooga River is also a very popular trout fishing place. It is worthwhile to stop as you cross the East Fork to examine the uniquely constructed footbridge. It is made entirely of large and small logs. Even the footings are large logs fitted together to make end columns on both sides of the stream. On the north side of the bridge is the 2.5-mile trail to Walhalla Fish Hatchery. The sign here also reads that Burrells Ford is 1.5 miles and Ellicott Rock is 1.7 miles on ahead.

From here on the trail is much less used than below the East Fork. The trail changes elevation very little even though it passes around a very steep mountain slope. There is more rhododendron, mountain laurel, and dog-hobble.

About a half mile from the East Fork you cross Bad Creek. There is no bridge but most of the time the flow is such that you can rock-hop across it. Across Bad Creek there are several old trails that may be old logging roads. Ignore them and stay on the well-used path continuing along the river.

All along the way is excellent birding for warblers, thrushes, nuthatches, woodpeckers, and others. The belted kingfisher uses the river and is frequently seen.

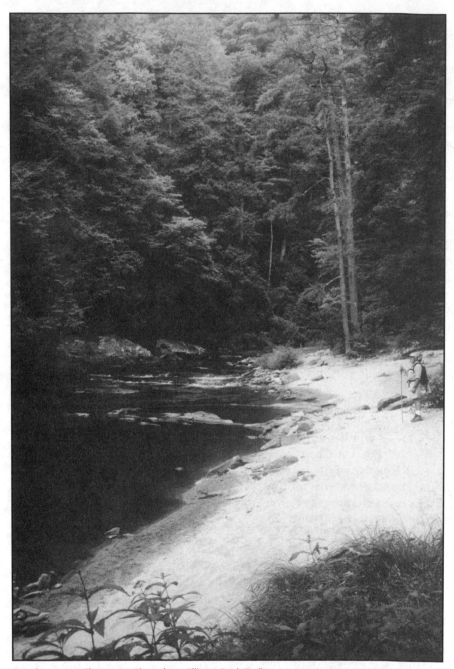

Beach area on Chattooga River along Ellicott Rock Trail.

Some of the more unusual plants along the way are Dutchman's pipe vine, rough-leaf dogwood, running groundpine, shining clubmoss, and Clinton's lily.

Less than a quarter mile from Ellicott Rock and the North Carolina line you cross a small footbridge over an unnamed branch and enter a nice open area above the river. There is no obvious sign or evidence that you are at the state line. A large hemlock has a black rectangular blaze with a red bar below and a black square above. Ellicott Rock is along the streambank below. There, if you look carefully, you may find "LAT 35° / A D 1813 / N C + S C" engraved in the rock. Out in the river are two large boulders. On one is a new survey control mark set by South Carolina in 1996, labeled Chattooga Rock, Geodetic Survey. This point in the river is where Georgia, North Carolina, and South Carolina meet.

For a longer hike you can continue on into North Carolina on the Ellicott Rock Trail where it forks—one trail going to the Forest Road 441 parking area while the other fork goes to a parking area on a forest service road off Bull Pen Road (North Carolina Highway 1100).

19 Rabun Beach Recreation Area/ Angel Falls Trail

General description: A pleasant walk slightly more than a mile along a small cascading stream ending in a couple of short switchbacks up a steep rhododendron covered path to Panther and Angel falls.

General location: In the Tallulah Ranger district of the Chattahoochee National Forest at the Rabun Beach Recreation Area.

Maps: Chattahoochee National Forest map; Tiger USGS quad.

Degree of difficulty: Easy to moderate.

Length: 1.3 miles one way.

Elevations: The trail begins at 1,780 feet and climbs to about 2,500 feet at Angel Falls.

Special attractions: Panther and Angel falls on Joe Branch. Late spring and summer rhododendron flowering displays along with other flowering plants. Good birding. Well-kept campground.

Best season: Year round with best waterfall conditions in winter and spring. Flowering plants from early April through the summer.

For more information: Chattahoochee National Forest, Tallulah Ranger District, 809 Highway 441, P.O. Box 438, Clayton, GA 30525; (706)782-3320.

Finding the trailhead: From U.S. Highway 441, go three miles north of Tallulah Falls or 9.6 miles south of Clayton and turn west at the Rabun Beach Recreation Area sign on Old 441 Road. Go about 2.5 miles and turn left onto Lake Rabun Road and to Rabun Beach Recreation Area. The trailhead for the hike to Angel and Panther falls begins at the north end of the recreation area campground 2. A gravel parking area is provided for vehicles.

The hike: Joe Creek, the tumbling stream with the falls, is crossed on a small bridge and the trail continues up the left side of the branch. Small cascades of two- to three-foot drops greet you and portend the nature of the stream all the way to the falls. Dog-hobble, rhododendron, mountain laurel and American holly grow under the taller hemlock and white pine that shade the path for the first 200 or so yards. The trail then passes through more open canopies of yellow-poplars, maples, buckeyes, deciduous magnolias, oaks, and other hardwoods until it reaches the dense laurel and rhododendron thickets that add so much enchantment to these pleasant short hikes in the mountains.

In spring, before the hardwood trees leaf out, the early blooming flowers put on a nice show along either side of the path. Several species of ferns and a large patch of clubmoss, a fern relative, add variety to the floral show.

Rabun Beach Recreation Area/Angel Falls Trail

Panther Falls is the first of the two falls on the trail. Joe Creek here drops about fifty feet in a series of steps down a stratified rock formation. The sign here points to Angel Falls, another 600 yards upstream. The trail switchbacks up to the more open and pretty falls. The material for the observation platform was air-dropped in place by helicopter below the falls. This provides an excellent view of the fifty-foot cascade over similar rock formations of Panther Falls below. The moist rocks alongside and at the foot of the falls supports a wide variety of plants specific to this habitat type. Michaux's or mountain saxifrage, ragwort, alumroot, ferns, mosses, and liverworts are among many others thriving here. The trail crosses Joe Creek at the platform and loops back downstream through the great stands of rhododendron, crossing the stream several times on small bridges. An exceptionally large hemlock is on the side of the trail below Angel Falls. It is about four feet in diameter and along with other evergreens provides shade for the nice walk back to the trailhead.

Lower section of Angel Falls Trail, Rabun Beach Recreation Area.

20 Warwoman Dell Nature Trail and Becky Branch Falls Trail

Overview: Warwoman Dell is more well-known for its historical significance than for its trails, which are short and easily covered in about an hour of leisurely walking. Becky Branch Falls has carved a secluded grotto in the rock only a quarter of a mile from the parking area in the Warwoman Dell Recreation Area. A nature trail and history of the pre-Civil War Black Mountain Railroad are located here.

Picnic shelters, running water, and clean restrooms make this a very pleasant break in a visit to this northeastern Georgia area.

General description: A couple of short, easy to moderate trails in a beautiful area steeped in history.

General location: Three miles east of Clayton on Warwoman Road in the Tallulah Ranger District of Chattahoochee National Forest.

Maps: Chattahoochee National Forest map; Rabun Bald USGS quad.

Degree of difficulty: To Becky Branch Falls moderate but short; Warwoman Dell Nature Trail, easy.

Length: Nature Trail 0.4 mile; Becky Branch Falls, 0.25.

Elevations: At the recreation area the elevation is 1,884 feet. The walk to the falls climbs 160 feet.

Special attractions: Attractive, small waterfalls; interpreted nature trail, including rare ferns; picnicking; pre-Civil War and early 1930s history, including old remnant trout holding facilities.

Warwoman Dell/Becky Branch Falls Trail

Best season: Year-round, with spring best for wildflowers and waterfalls; beautiful fall foliage.

For more information: Chattahoochee National Forest, Tallulah Ranger District, 809 Highway 441, P.O. Box 438, Clayton, GA 30525; (706)782-3320.

Finding the trailheads: The trailhead for both the nature trail and Becky Branch Falls is in the Warwoman Dell parking area.

The hikes: The **Becky Branch Falls Trail** begins at the parking area and goes up steps to Warwoman Road. Cross the road and go up the right side of Becky Branch. The path is well worn and contains a switchback or two before reaching the wooden footbridge below the pretty, twenty-foot cascade that tumbles over granite ledges down through a rhododendron thicket. Flowers are abundant in spring from March through May along with a showy display of laurel and rhododendron. Cross the bridge and walk down the opposite side of the branch. A spring house is on the right side of the trail, which leads back to the road. The trail system here can be confusing because the Bartram Trail crosses Warwoman Road at the same place. A metal historic marker on the roadside describes the significance of the Bartram Trail.

The **Warwoman Dell Nature Trail** begins at the west end of the parking area. It was built by a volunteer youth group from the Rabun Gap/Nachoochee School at Dillard. About twenty-five numbered stations identify plants and habitat relationships. The path is easy and passes through the unique fern- and moss-shrouded habitat of the Dell.

21 Three Forks Trail

General description: A easy to moderate mile-long trail that follows the contours of the land with only a gentle descent through oak/hickory forest with the occasional rhododendron and mountain laurel to the confluence of three creeks that form West Fork of Chattooga River.

General location: This trail is in the Chattooga National Wild and Scenic River area in the extreme northeast corner of the state.

Maps: Chattooga National Wild and Scenic River map available from the U.S. Forest Service; Satolah USGS quad.

Degree of difficulty: Easy to moderate with steep descents and return climbs at the river.

Length: From John Teague Gap to Holcomb Creek, just above Three Forks is about 1.2 miles one way.

Elevations: From 2,360 feet at John Teague Gap to 1,800 feet just below the Three Forks junction.

Special attractions: Excellent river gorge scenery, fall colors, wildflowers including a fine patch of pink lady's slippers, and trout fishing.

Best season: Spring and fall for flowers and leaf color; spring, summer, and fall for scenery and trout fishing. This area is moderately used during squirrel, deer, and grouse hunting seasons.

Three Forks Trail

For more information: Chattahoochee National Forest, Tallulah Ranger District, 809 Highway 441, P.O. Box 438, Clayton, GA 30525; (706)782-3320.

Finding the trailhead: Go sixteen miles east of Clayton on Warwoman Road to West Fork of Chattooga River and four miles north on Overflow Creek Road (Forest Road 86) to John Teague Gap. The Three Forks sign at John Teague Gap is frequently broken, with only part of the letters readable. The trailhead is at the small, unpaved parking area on the right or northeast side of the road. The parking area has room for three or four vehicles.

The hike: Three Forks Trail has one of its trailheads on Rabun Bald. For our purposes here only the section from John Teague Gap on the Overflow Creek road will be described.

From the parking area, the trail follows the north face of the ridge. It goes through a pine-oak-hickory forest and an occasional thicket of catawba rhododendron, losing elevation on a gentle slope. The blaze marks are white diamonds, however, there are very few marks. This is no problem since the trail is well worn and there is very little chance of getting off on a wrong path.

About halfway a single blue blaze designates the boundary of Chattooga National Wild and Scenic River area, which encompasses much of the watersheds of the three creeks that form West Fork. At about one mile, the trail intercepts an old jeep road. Stay to the left, following the old roadbed. Several earthen barriers to stop off-road vehicles have been scraped into the trail and must be sidestepped during wet weather. The trail ends at a wide bedrock area at Holcomb Creek. Here you can see one of nature's greatest works as the full volume of the creek swirls down through a narrow crevice eroded into the rock. If the creek is swollen by recent rains the sight is awesome.

Three Forks is a great place to explore the many natural history features of the area or to trout fish. The overhanging rock cliffs and river gorge habitat holds interesting plants and animals. The nests of the rare wood rat can be found under the rock shelters along the steep-sided river gorge. Dutchman's pipe vines climb over the alders along the river.

A 0.7 mile trail branches off the Three Forks Trail where it intercepts the old jeep road. It leads in a southeasterly direction down to the West Fork below the junction of the three creeks. It ends with a steep descent into the river gorge and to a primitive campsite with fire rings. From Three Forks for about a mile downstream, the river cascades in grand fashion from one low waterfall and pool to another. This is truly a wild and beautiful mountain

Fishing on the West Fork of the Chattooga River on the Three Forks Trail.

stream. Climb under the laurel and rhododendron upstream for about 0.25 mile to see the three streams—Holcomb, Overflow, and Big creeks—become the West Fork of the Chattooga River. A fine waterfall just upstream on Holcomb Creek is visible too.

Another trail called Three Forks Trail on the Satolah USGS quad map winds its way along old jeep roads from Georgia Highway 28 near a place called Satolah. It approaches Three Forks from the northeast, roughly paralleling Big Creek. This trail is much longer and not well enough marked to describe here. But it would be an excellent trail for orienteering enthusiasts.

22 Anna Ruby Falls and Lion's Eye Nature Trails

Overview: Anna Ruby Falls is the most popular waterfall in the north Georgia mountains. The Lion's Eye Nature Trail begins at the parking area, is designed for sight-impaired hikers, and is wheelchair accessible.

General description: A short paved trail, with a moderate grade that follows picturesque Smith Creek to the twin Anna Ruby Falls.

General location: About 2.5 miles from Helen, adjoining Unicoi State Park.

Maps: Trail Guide to the Chattahoochee National Forest, Unicoi State Park Trails map; Tray Mountain USGS quad.

Degree of difficulty: Moderate.

Length: 0.4 mile one way.

Elevations: The hiker climbs about 170 feet from the visitor center to the falls observation deck which is at about 2,150 feet.

Special attractions: Beautiful view of the twin falls of York and Curtis creeks. Wildflowers are abundant during the spring, as many as thirty to forty species in bloom at one time during April and May. U.S. Forest Service visitor center and special trail for visually impaired hikers at the beginning of the trail.

Best season: This is a year-round trail. The only time the trail may be closed is during heavy snowfall.

For more information: Chattahoochee National Forest, Chattooga Ranger District, 200 Highway 197 N, Clarksville, GA 30523; (706)754-6221.

Finding the trailheads: Take Georgia Highway 75 north from Helen for one mile. Turn right on Georgia Highway 356 for 1.5 miles; then go left on Forest Road 242, the entrance road to the Anna Ruby Falls. The trailheads are at the visitor center and parking area.

The hikes: A paved 0.4-mile trail from the parking area and visitor center extends along Smith Creek to Anna Ruby Falls. The hike is easy to moderate with benches along the way providing comfortable resting places for those who need to take it easy. An observation bridge and deck and a second deck at the end of the trail provides great views of the twin falls.

Anna Ruby Falls, Lion's Eye, and Smith Creek Trails

York Creek

Anna Ruby Falls

Anna Ruby Falls Trail (paved)

Visitor Center and Sight-Impaired Trail

P

HICKORYNUT RIDGE

242

Smith Creek Trail

Cottages

Smith Creek

Gate

Campgrounds

Unicoi Lake

P

Cottages

356

Lodge

To Helen

UNICOI STATE PARK

To Lake Burton

0   1

Miles

N

The trail can be slippery when wet or with snow, so walking shoes are recommended. This is a good trail to take children hiking. The pavement is safe and the grade, although moderate, is not too difficult even with children in strollers. A complete canopy of hardwood trees shades the trail during the warm months.

Spring flowers and the beautiful tumbling Smith Creek are the foremost attractions of this trail. Forest Service and Unicoi State Park employees feature guided walks along the trail in spring to help visitors and hikers recognize and identify the dozens of flower species. There may be as many as thirty or forty species in bloom at one time. The large boulders along Smith Creek support some of the largest colonies of rockcap ferns in the state. Large tulip trees, buckeye, and maple trees line the stream along with silverbells, rhododendron, mountain laurel, dog-hobble, and many species of flowering shrubs. Yellow root used by mountain people to relieve sore throat grows abundantly along the stream and trail. Squaw-root and the rare one-flowered cancer-root, both parasitic plants, grow right

Anna Ruby Falls,, where York and Curtis creeks come together to form Smith Creek. One end of Smith Creek Trail is here.

along the paved trail. The stream tumbles in cascades over the boulder-strewn creek bed in a series of falls and pools. This section of the stream is closed to trout fishing and large trout can be seen in the pool below the observation deck of the visitor center.

The **Lion's Eye Nature Trail,** for the visually impaired, begins at the parking area near Smith Creek and goes along the creek. This short loop with Braille interpretive signs and guide rail describes the sounds, smells, and texture of the forest. The trail is paved and easily traveled by wheelchair. It was installed by the White County and Clermont Lion's clubs in cooperation with the Forest Service.

23 Smith Creek Trail

See map on page 97

General description: A pleasant five-mile day hike that is a good practice or exercise trail for longer hikes.

General location: Near Helen in the Chattahoochee National Forest and Unicoi State Park.

Maps: Chattahoochee National Forest map; Unicoi State Park map; Tray Mountain and Helen USGS quads.

Degree of difficulty: Moderate.

Length: From Anna Ruby Falls to Little Creek campground is 4.6 miles one way. To reach the trailhead at Anna Ruby Falls requires a 0.4 mile walk.

Elevations: The Observation bridge at Anna Ruby Falls is 2,150 feet. The trail goes up to about 2,600 feet on Hickory Nut Ridge and back to 1,760 feet at the campground.

Special attractions: Attractive patches of rhododendron, mountain laurel, wildflowers, and ferns. Wildlife in the area includes deer, turkey, squirrels, and other small mammals. A good birding trail.

Best season: Year-round, with spring and fall being the most pleasant. It is completely shaded by evergreen and hardwood trees in summer.

For more information: Chattahoochee National Forest, Chattooga Ranger District, 200 Highway 197 N, Clarkesville, GA 30523; (706)754-6221. Unicoi State Park, 943 Anna Ruby Falls Road, Helen, GA 30545; (706) 878-3983.

Finding the trailhead: From Helen, go one mile north on Georgia Highway 17/75 and turn right on Georgia Highway 356. Travel 1.5 miles to the entrance to Unicoi State Park. Follow the signs to Anna Ruby Falls or to Unicoi State Park campground. The trailhead is marked on the paved road to the campgrounds, just beyond the cottage area; or the hike can begin at the Anna Ruby Falls parking area and visitor center. The trailhead sign on the road reads: "Smith Creek Trail, Anna Ruby Falls 5 Miles, estimated walking time one way 3 hours."

The hike: This trail could be considered a part of the Unicoi State Park trail system. One end of the trail is at Little Creek campground in the park, the other at Anna Ruby Falls. It is a high trail that passes along the west side of

Hickory Nut Ridge. It does not follow along Smith Creek. This is a pleasant five-mile hike one way. It is well used and is marked with blue blazes.

It is easiest to hike from Anna Ruby Falls down to the Unicoi campground or plan an all day hike from the campground up to the falls and back. From the falls the path climbs gradually along the side of Hickory Nut Ridge through an open hardwood cove and dense patches of rhododendron and mountain laurel. During the winter and early spring when the leaves are off the trees, there are excellent views of the surrounding mountains. At one point high on the ridge, there is a good view to the northwest of Steep Creek Falls. Several spring brooks cross the trail, all of which can be stepped over easily. Wooden timber steps have been installed in places where short, steep banks are encountered. Old American chestnut logs that died in the mid-1930s are still visible on dry southwestern slopes.

The path dips in and out of the coves between ridge spurs. Rhododendron thickets along the steep side of the ridge add pleasant variety to the walk, which generally follows a contour as the northwest slope of the ridge is traveled. At about midway in, the hike passes through an area of very large boulders.

The trail reaches the crest of Hickory Nut Ridge and passes close to a jeep road visible to the east and south. On this crest, the forest is mostly short leaf pine that has been damaged by southern pine beetles. Many of the trees fell across the path and have been sawed to permit easier passage. The steepest segments of the path are negotiated by switchbacks that keep the grade only moderately steep. The trail parallels and then crosses a pretty brook before it reaches the jeep road on Hickory Nut Ridge. Staying just above the paved service road to the campgrounds, the trail ends or starts at the Little Brook campground entrance and a few yards from a kiosk and parking turnout in the road.

24 Andrews Cove Recreation Area Trail

General description: An easy to moderate two-mile hike.
General location: The recreation area entrance is 6.5 miles north of Helen on Georgia Highway 17/75.
Maps: Chattahoochee National Forest Map; Tray Mountain USGS quad.
Degree of difficulty: Easy to moderate.
Length: Two miles one way.
Elevations: The recreation area is about 2,600 feet. The trail ends at Indian Grave Gap at 3,120 feet.
Special attractions: Excellent wildflower display in spring, wild turkeys, deer, squirrels and other small mammals, trout fishing, good birding, camping and a notable natural area.
Best season: Year-round hiking; however, the recreation area camping is closed during the winter months.

Andrews Cove Trail

For more information: U.S. Forest Service, Chattahoochee National Forest, Chattooga Ranger District, 200 Highway 197 N, Clarkesville, GA 30523; (706)754-6221.

Finding the trailhead: The trailhead begins near campsite 6. The trail begins just beyond campsite 6 and is designated by a wooden sign "Andrews Cove Trail - Appalachian Trail 2 Miles."

The hike: The Andrews Cove Recreation Area is situated in a picturesque cove hardwood forest. The trail leads to Indian Grave Gap and the Appalachian Trail. Along the trail, you'll find evidence of former living in the cove by mountain homesteaders and gold mining during the late 1800s. The recreation area has excellent campsites, comfort station, and drinking water from a hand pump. The large trees and rhododendron provide seclusion even though the area is within earshot of the heavily traveled mountain highway.

Marked with a blue blaze the path climbs easily but steadily in the beautiful hardwood cove with maples, oaks, yellow-poplars, buckeyes, white pine, hemlock, and undergrowth of dogwoods and other flowering shrubs. Andrews Creek is a beautiful, tumbling trout stream on the left side of the trail as it proceeds to the Indian Grave Gap. The path leads around a spring that emerges from beneath a massive boulder where it flows to the creek. Rock piles indicate former home sites. Rock fields along the side of Tray Mountain to the right or southeast side of the trail are resplendent with wildflowers and provide habitat for several species of small mammals, especially shrews.

The trail becomes progressively steeper as the end of the cove is reached, and the path begins the ascent to the gap. The cove hardwood forest gives way to a drier, better-drained forest of chestnut, black and southern red oaks. The Andrews Cove Trail ends at the Appalachian Trail. From here, the Appalachian Trail can be hiked in either direction. To the right, or northeast, is Tray Mountain, which reaches to 4,000 feet. To the left, or southwest, leads to Unicoi Gap and Georgia Highway 17/75.

25 Dukes Creek Trail

General description: A pleasant one-mile walk down a steep-sided gorge to a tumbling mountain creek.
General location: Approximately 6.5 miles northwest of Helen.
Degree of difficulty: Easy to moderate. The first segment of the trail is wheelchair accessible.
Length: One mile.
Maps: Chattahoochee National Forest map; Cowrock USGS quad.
Elevation: At the trailhead the elevation is 2,120 feet. The trail drops 340 feet to Dukes Creek at 1,780.

Dukes Creek and Raven Cliff Falls Trails

Special attractions: Waterfalls and scenic stream cascades and rapids in the gorge with wildflowers along the trail and fall colors. An ideal birding walk in spring during warbler migration.

Best season: Spring and fall. Waterfall is most impressive during the spring flows; however, the trail is open all year except during heavy snow when the Richard Russell Scenic Highway may be closed.

Finding the trailhead: The trailhead is on the Richard Russell Scenic Highway (GA 348), approximately two miles from Georgia Highway 356. The trail begins at the south end of the paved parking area.

The Hike: Dukes Creek Trail descends in several hairpin turns down into Dukes Creek Gorge, ending at the creek across from Dukes Creek Falls. Dukes Creek Falls is actually on Davis Creek and falls about 250 feet in a very scenic spray. The beginning of the trail is completely wheelchair accessible. The remainder of the trail is an easy walk into the gorge. A restroom, benches, and picnic tables are available at the parking area.

Where the gorge slope is especially steep, a beautifully engineered board-walk has been installed. The paved walkway at the beginning of the trail has turnouts permitting wheelchairs to pass without danger of touching. At the best observation point for seeing the waterfalls, a wide platform overlook with a clear view of the falls and the gorge has been constructed. The platform is equipped with benches. This is the limit for wheelchair accessibility.

After the paved stretch, the trail surface is fine gravel or natural loamy soil. It is usable in all weather conditions. During wet, ice, or snow conditions, the footing may be slippery. Wide wooden steps have been installed at two or three of the steep switchbacks in the trail. Between these steep descents the path is relatively flat and at no point except at the creek's edge is the grade more than a gentle slope. The trail passes through dense rhododendron thickets growing on the very steep gorge slope. About half-way down, the forest changes to the typical cove hardwood trees and on some of the drier sites oaks, hickory, and Virginia pine dominate. As with

Unpaved section of trail in Dukes Creek Gorge, Dukes Creek Trail.

many trails in the mountains, spring migrating warblers can be heard as they pass through on their northern journey.

Once at the bottom, you can reach the water's edge only with some difficulty. Dukes Creek is a series of beautiful cascades, rapids, and pools. Because of the thick cover of rhododendron, mountain laurel, dog-hobble, and other woody vegetation, it is very difficult to walk along the stream's edge either upstream or down. But this is a fine trout stream, and if fishermen want to expend the energy they can be rewarded with some fine catches of rainbow and brown trout.

26 Raven Cliff Falls Trails

See map on page 103

General description: A 2.5-mile path that follows a relatively gentle grade to the cliffs through which the creek flows to make the falls.
General location: In the Chattahoochee National Forest about 6.5 miles from Helen.
Maps: U.S. Forest Service map for Chattahoochee National Forest in Georgia; Cowrock USGS quad.
Degree of difficulty: Moderate.
Length: 2.5 miles one way
Elevations: From 2,040 feet at the parking area to 2,600 feet at the base of the Raven Cliff Falls. The climb up around Raven Cliff is another 100 feet or more.
Special attractions: Dodd Creek with several significant cataracts and low waterfalls; a variety of flowers, trees and other plants; unique cliff formation; camping and trout fishing make this a very popular trail.
Best season: Year-round, however, spring and fall are best for flowers and leaf colors. Water flow in Dodd Creek is best in spring.
For more information: U.S. Forest Service, Chattahoochee National Forest, Chattooga Ranger District, 200 Highway 197 N, Clarkesville, GA 30523; (706)754-6221.

Finding the trailhead: Take Georgia Highway 75 north out of Helen for 1.5 miles to Georgia Highway 365 and travel 2.3 miles to the Richard B. Russell Scenic Highway (GA 348); turn right and drive 2.8 miles to the gravel, unmarked parking area where Bear Den Creek crosses. The trailhead is at the parking area.

The hike: This trail is in the newly designated Raven Cliffs Wilderness Area and follows the beautifully cascading Dodd Creek. The trail begins at the parking area where Bear Den Creek crosses to join Dodd Creek. The two creeks become Dukes Creek. The trail is on the edge of the 9,649 acre Raven Cliffs Wilderness Area, established in 1986. At first, the trail is a wide roadbed for about 100 yards, with short spurs that lead to primitive campsites along the heavily used trout streams. Leaving the white pine and hemlock flat area, the path leads along cascading Dodd Creek in a northwesterly direction to the cliffs.

Blue blazes mark the trail throughout its course. The trail is easy to follow because of the marked blue blazes and its heavy use. In the first quarter mile, the hiker sees the first of several falls and cascades before reaching Raven Cliff Falls at the end of the cove. The trail alternately brushes up against the stream and above the water level thirty to fifty feet when the steep-sided valley makes it necessary. The trail follows a gentle grade with only an occasional short, steep climb. It passes through rhododendron and mountain laurel thickets that form pleasant passageways of thick overhead cover. A number of logs have fallen across the trail but are easily stepped across or walked around. Spring seeps and small brooks cross the trail, making wet places that can be crossed on conveniently placed stepping stones. During rainy weather, portions of the trail are quite wet and slippery.

This is a narrow, eastern exposed cove and is rich in plant species. Large hemlock and white pines, yellow-poplars, deciduous magnolias, hickories, oaks, maples, buckeyes, and many other trees are along the moist valley sides and floor. Under this canopy a resplendent array of flowering plants bloom throughout early spring, summer, and into late fall. Hepaticas, dwarf irises, trout lilies, Jack-in-the-pulpits, Solomon's seals, trilliums, foam flowers, parasitic squaw-root, and one-flowered cancer-root, as well as many other spring flowers that make their show beginning in early March. Later in the year, wild geraniums, saxifrages, asters, white snakeroot, mountain mint, and other flowers finish out the year. A number of ferns are along the trail. Christmas fern and spleenworts in bunches; large glades of New York fern; beech, maidenhair, and rockcap ferns near the cliffs; and a sharp eye will find others.

The trail ends at the massive cliff face through which Dodd Creek flows as Raven Cliff Falls. The stream flows through a narrow cleft in the rock wall and comes out at the bottom in a series of falls and cascades. A side trail leads up and around the cliff for access to the top and views of Dodd Creek valley, 3,620-foot Adams Bald, Wildcat Mountain, and Piney Ridge.

This is a heavily used trail for both day hiking and overnight camping. It is easy to get to and a pleasant trail with a variety of interesting things. It is an ideal trail for a leisurely day hike, exploring the cliff area and the several old roads, now overgrown, that are intercepted by the trail along its way to Raven Cliffs. This is an fine trail for family hiking.

27 Ladyslipper Trail/Lake Russell Recreation Area

General description: This six-mile loop trail offers glimpses of different forest management practices and offers good wildlife viewing opportunities.

General location: Lake Russell Recreation Area is in the Chattooga Ranger District in the northeast corner of the state, approximately two miles north of Cornelia.

Maps: Chattahoochee National Forest Map; Ayersville and Lake Russell USGS quads.

Degree of difficulty: Moderate, with a few short steep grades and some wet, muddy areas along the trail where horse travel has caused water to stand at spring seeps crossing the trail. These are no more than a few yards across.

Length: The loop is 6.2 miles, including about one mile of retracing along the same path at the beginning and end of the trail.

Elevations: The trailhead is about 1,050 feet and the trail crosses Red Root Mountain once at about 1,300 feet and later in the loop at 1,402 feet.

Special attractions: A number of forestry management practices, many wildflowers, fall leaf color, wildlife, excellent birding, trout fishing in Nancy Town Lake and Creek, camping, hunting, and scenic views.

Best season: This a year-round hiking area, however, the recreation area is open only from Memorial Day to Labor Day. The trails, boat ramps, and lakes are open all year.

For more information: U.S. Forest Service, Chattooga Ranger District, 200 Highway 197 N, Clarkesville, GA 305234; (706)754-6221. Georgia Wildlife Resources Division, Game management, 2150 Dawsonville Highway, Gainesville, GA 30501; (770) 535-5700.

Finding the trailhead: From I-985/GA-365 take the Cornelia Exit and go to Cornelia. Take Georgia Highway 123 north toward Taccoa for about two miles to the unincorporated town of Mount Airy. Turn onto the Lake Russell Road, which also is Forest Road 59, and go about 2.5 miles to the Nancy Town Lake and group camping sign. The parking area is at the Nancy Town Lake dam. The trailhead is at the group campground on Nancy Town Creek at the head of the lake. The road to this area is gated and you must park at the dam and make the 0.3 mile walk to the trailhead, which is in the parking area for the group camp.

The hike: The trail is both a horse trail and hiking trail. It leads through forests of varied management practices, including an area where trees were cut to stem the damage caused by the southern pine beetle. This part of the Chattahoochee National Forest is also the Lake Russell Wildlife Management Area managed by the Georgia Wildlife Resources Division. You will pass several wildlife openings—areas planted to grasses and other wildlife foods to enhance the wildlife populations. Located on the edge of the Piedmont and Blue Ridge provinces, species from both physiographic areas are present, adding variety to the hike. This is especially true for the many

Ladyslipper and Sourwood Trails

wildflowers and flowering shrubs and trees you will see during the spring and summer months.

The hike actually begins at the parking area at Nancy Town Lake dam, because the road to the group camp is gated. It is about 0.3 mile along a pleasant paved road looking down on Nancy Town Lake to the parking area at the group camp. You will pass a rustic picnic shelter and picnic tables and cross the creek on a footbridge to get to the sign designating Ladyslipper Trail. Blue blazes mark the way throughout the trail.

Cross another bridge over Nancy Town Creek and begin the hike along the east side of the lake. After passing another picnic shelter, the trail gradually climbs through mixed pine-hardwoods with low blueberry bushes, dogwoods, sourwoods, and other shrubs growing under the larger trees. As you go higher up the side of Red Root Mountain, actually a ridge, the hardwoods give way to a more pure pine forest of shortleaf and Virginia pines.

108

At the crest of this ridge the trail turns onto a gravel road. A post with the word "Trail" and an arrow directs you down the road in a northerly direction. Follow the road for about a quarter mile to another signpost with an arrow pointing to the right. All the signposts along this trail have the blue paint blaze like the blazes on the trees. The loop portion of the trail begins here. In about 4.5 miles you will come back to this road, which runs along the crest of Red Root Mountain.

As you turn to a southeast course, the trail enters a young pine thicket and drops down a steep-sided ravine at a moderate grade. Horse use of the trail is evident now. An erosion gully in the middle of the narrow trail and very wet muddy areas where spring seeps cross the path make foot travel a little more difficult. However, the trail is easy to follow and provides a pleasant way through this interesting area. When hikers encounter horse riders on the trail, the hiker should step to the side of the path and let the horse go by.

Look for pink lady's slipper orchids growing along the path where there is a mixture of mature pines and hardwoods. This showy flower is also called the moccasin-flower and gives the trail its name. It blooms in late April and May along with many other spring wildflowers for which this trail is noted.

For the two or three miles, you will pass over several low ridges and into valleys with intermittent and permanent streams. All are either crossed with footbridges or are easily stepped over. At one point the southern pine beetle has so severely damaged a pure pine stand, it was necessary for the

Nancytown Lake near trailhead for Ladyslipper, Sourwood, and Lake Russell trails.

Forest Service to cut a large number of pine trees to stop the spread of the beetles.

You will notice other forestry management practices such as old clear-cuts that are in various stages of reforestation, current practices where timber is harvested by leaving selected seed trees standing, shelterwood, group selection, and single tree species selection. Each of these practices is designed to harvest timber in the best possible way for each forest site and condition.

You will also pass open fields that have been planted to grasses and other wildlife food plants. These areas are developed by the Georgia Wildlife Resources Division specifically to add variety to the habitat types for wildlife. Deer and turkeys are the most obvious species, their tracks and droppings are evident. However, these areas also add great variety to the habitat and support many nongame species. Songbirds, rabbits, squirrels, wood and field mice, hawks, owls, and a great variety of other species benefitted by the openings in the forest. The trail passes through one of the plantings near the middle of the loop.

At the end of the field, the blue blazes lead to the service road and a wildlife opening, crosses a stream, and turns to the right. Here the trail follows the road about a half mile and again turns into the woods to the left at a post trail-marker with an arrow. Another footbridge is crossed before the path intercepts another old roadbed. This road has also been eroded where horse hooves have broken the soil. The path remains on this road, climbing at a moderate rate to Forest Road 92 (Red Root Road). Here the trail parallels Red Root Road, climbing more until it reaches the rounded, almost flat crest of Red Root Mountain, the highest point on the hike at 1,402 feet.

On the left or south side of the path is a thicket of young pines, on the right a mature mixed woods. You drop down to the west and to the dirt road. This is the first road encountered on the trail. Turn left and in a short distance you come to the end of the loop. Continue on the road, retracing the first part of the hike, to the south and southwest to the post trail-marker. Turn to the right into the woods and down the path to Nancy Town Lake and the trailhead.

28 Sourwood Trail/Lake Russell Recreation Area

See map on page 108

General description: A pleasant walk of nearly three miles to a small waterfall and beaver ponds.

General location: In northeast Georgia east of Cornelia in the Chattahoochee National Forest.

Maps: Small page-size maps available from the Chattooga District Ranger office in Clarksville; Ayersville USGS quad.

Degree of difficulty: Easy to moderate.

Length: 2.7 miles.

Elevations: The trailhead is at 1,064 feet and the highest elevation along the trail is about 1,300 feet.

Special attractions: Nancy Town Falls; an active beaver pond; excellent wildflower variety; wildlife—including wild turkeys, deer, squirrels—and a good birding area.

Best season: Year-round.

For more information: Chattahoochee National Forest, Chattooga Ranger District, 200 Highway 197 N, Clarksville, GA 30523, (706)754-6221.

Finding the trailhead: From Cornelia take U.S. Highway 123 about three miles to Mount Airy, turn right or east on Forest Road 59, Lake Russell Road, at Lake Russell Recreation Area sign. Go 2.5 miles and turn left at the group camp entrance. A sign designates trail-use parking. The trailhead is on Red Root Road at the bridge at the head of Nancy Town Lake.

The hike: It is a loop trail with a variety of forest habitats from clearcuts and new pine plantations to maturing hardwood coves with large yellow-poplars, oaks, hickories, and pines. There also is a variety of wildflowers and other herbaceous plants along the path.

The trail begins at the bridge across a small branch flowing into Nancy Town Lake. A trail sign marked "SOURWOOD TRAIL, A 2.7 MILE LOOP TRAIL, NANCY TOWN FALLS 1.5 MILES" is beside the road. Blue blazes mark the trail that follows an old roadbed for about 200 yards along a steep hillside with a noticeable stand of Christmas ferns and mountain laurel. After crossing the branch on a footbridge, the path leads up a gentle slope through loblolly pines planted in a clearcut area. Along the stream and into the pine planting, the bird life will be quite different from the more mature forest, which the trail follows thereafter. Deer tracks will almost always be present in the exposed clay soil of the path. The trail crosses Nancy Town Road at about the highest point on this hike. Here enter a hardwood forest, very open and composed of white oaks, chestnut oaks, black and southern red oaks, along with scattered hickories and other nut producing trees.

Look for places in the leaves where turkeys have been scratching in search of acorns and other food. Expect to see squirrels and a variety of forest songbirds. In fall and winter, cranefly orchid leaves, green on top side and blood red beneath, and the green heartleaf or wild ginger leaves are in contrast to the brown leaves of the forest floor.

After crossing two branches on footbridges and crossing over low ridges, the grasses of the shallow beaver pond on Nancy Town Creek make a large opening in the woods. The path comes down to the small stream at the head of the pond. A sign points to Nancy Town Falls upstream. The main trail continues downstream along the edge of the beaver pond. The falls is a short distance up the small rocky stream. It is a pretty falls cascading over a rock ledge about twenty feet high.

In November, the blue soapwort gentian blooms at the water's edge. Grape ferns, Christmas ferns, brownstemmed spleenwort grow along the trail where it passes by the side of the beaver pond. Wood duck nest boxes have been placed on poles in the beaver pond. A pause here in winter or during the spring nesting season may be rewarded by seeing a beautifully colored wood duck. The beaver dam is across the creek where the valley narrows, and the path joins an old roadbed again and goes through thickets of mountain laurel with the creek, free-flowing now, on the left. A very large patch of ground pine is on the right of the trail under and near a stand of shortleaf pine. The ground pine, one of the clubmosses related to ferns, is in full fruiting stage in November.

The pathway, following close to the creek, crosses over a metal footbridge and goes down the left bank through laurel and rhododendron. The creek cascades over rock ledges just before the hike ends at Red Root Road and turns right for a 0.4-mile walk on the road back to the trailhead. At the only Y in the road stay to the left.

29 Panther Creek Trail

General description: This 5.5-mile trail is an excellent day hike that follows a beautiful tumbling, cascading stream through a steep-sided valley with rocky cliffs.

General location: Ten miles north of Clarksville in the Chattooga Ranger District of Chattahoochee National Forest.

Maps: U.S. Forest Service map of the Chattahoochee National Forest; Tallulah Falls and Tugaloo Lake USGS quads.

Degree of difficulty: Easy to moderate with very short, more difficult places, negotiating rock ledges.

Length: 5.5 miles to Davidson Creek one way. Panther Creek Falls is 3.6 miles from the recreation area at U.S. Highway 441.

Elevations: The trail begins at 1,500 feet and drops down to about 1,150 feet below Panther Creek Falls and 770 feet at Davidson Creek.

Special attractions: Geological uniqueness, waterfalls and numerous cascades, botanical diversity, fishing, fall leaf color.

Best season: Year-round with spring best for wildflowers, fall color in October and November, and trout fishing April through October.

For more information: Chattahoochee National Forest, Chattooga Ranger District, 200 Highway 197 N, Clarksville, GA 30523; (706)754-6221.

Finding the trailhead: Take U.S. Highway 23/441 nine miles north from Clarksville or three miles south from Tallulah Falls to the Panther Creek Recreation Area. The trailhead is across the highway from the recreation area. The eastern end of the trail can be reached by taking Yonah Dam Road from Yonah Lake to the mouth of Davidson Creek.

The hike: Panther Creek crosses old U.S. Highway 23/441 after leaving the Panther Creek Recreation Area in the Chattahoochee National Forest. Panther Creek Falls is reached after about 3.6 miles. The trail terminates at an unpaved road near the junction of Davidson Creek and Panther Creek and can be hiked from either end.

The trail begins on the opposite side of old US 441 from the Panther Creek Recreation Area and paved parking area. Look for a trailhead sign. Blue blazes mark the trail to Davidson Creek. It then goes under new US 23/441 bridge that crosses Panther Creek. You soon enter a mixed forest of oaks, hickories, yellow-poplars, and pines. Trailing arbutus grows abundantly along the first half mile. One patch is right at the trailhead and large patches of the earth-hugging, sweet-smelling plant occur regularly along

Footbridge across Panther Creek, Panther Creek Trail.

Panther Creek Trail

To Yonah Dam

Davidson Creek

Panther Creek Falls

Mill Shoals

Panther Creek

To Tallulah Falls
and Clayton

23

441

Panther
Creek
Recreation
Area

To Hollywood
and Clarkesville

N

0   Miles   1

the south- and west-facing sections of the trail. Mountain laurel thickets border the pathway and bloom en masse in May, followed in June and July by the great white rhododendron growing along the stream.

The trail then goes down the left side of Panther Creek and cascading water can be seen or heard throughout much of the hike. Two rock overhangs only a few yards apart are encountered at about 0.8 mile into the hike. If you do not pay attention to the two blazes on a white oak at the second cliff overhang, it is easy to pass by the sharp left turn the trail takes up through the rocks for several feet to gain access to the earth path above the thick laurel and rhododendron. If this turn is missed, as it is obvious that many have done, the worn path *without* blue blazes follows close to the creek and you must climb over, under, and through the stems of the shrubs for almost a quarter mile. It eventually comes out again on the blazed trail in a stand of hemlock and white pine at a level primitive campsite and fire ring. If the blazed section of the trail is followed, it takes the hiker above the laurel thicket on a relatively easy grade.

From here, the trail crosses Panther Creek on a well made footbridge and is now in a very peaceful level area going down the right or west bank. Little Panther Creek enters the main stream from the east about 100 yards below the bridge. This level area is rich in wildflowers, ferns, ground pine, and other plants thriving in the rich alluvial soil. Several small tributaries are crossed either on footbridges or by stepping stones.

The creek again enters a steep-sided rock cliff area where two steel wire guard fences have been installed to prevent mishaps. The Forest Service recommends that hikers with heavy packs use extra caution walking under the rocky overhangs. Panther Creek picks up speed again here and dashes over several beautiful cascades before reaching the largest and most precipitous falls. Panther Creek Falls is three separate cascades, each with its own pool. The trail leads out onto a large rock overlook for the upper and middle section of the falls. The path to the lower cascade takes you below the falls and to the edge of a large pool. This is one of the more visible and showy of the north Georgia falls.

From the falls, the trail remains on the south and east side of the creek to the junction with Davidson Creek. This section of the trail is designated by the Forest Service as a Protected Botanical Area because of the richness and diversity of the plant life. It is in the Brevard Fault Zone, which is characterized by a narrow band of limestone that supports vegetation not commonly found in north Georgia. The rare and pretty flower called gaywings grows along the Panther Creek Gorge.

Panther Creek Trail is a good day hike from the recreation area to the falls and back, or for a one-way hike all the way to Davidson Creek with arrangements for transportation there. Since the water along the trail is not safe for drinking, it is not recommended for overnight camping. Panther Creek and most of its tributaries flow out of farm or residential land.

30 Fort Mountain State Park Trails

Overview: Fort Mountain State Park offers an interesting assortment of natural and human history. It lies on the southwestern edge of the Southern Appalachian range and melds into the Ridge and Valley Province giving it a wide variety of habitat types and geological diversity. Old gold mines and active talc mines are in the vicinity.

The trails vary from a short walk along the ancient stone wall, from which the mountain got its name, to the 8.2-mile Gahuti Backcountry Trail with campsites for backpackers. Five trails are well marked, interesting, and easy to follow.

General description: About fourteen miles of trails that vary in length and difficulty.

General location: The park is located seven miles east of Chatsworth on Georgia Highway 52 in Murray County.

Maps: The park office has a page-size map showing all the trails, lengths, and blaze colors; Crandall USGS quad.

Degree of difficulty: Easy to moderate with some strenuous stretches on the Gahuti Trail.

Length: Old Fort Loop and Stone Wall trails 1.6 miles; Big Rock Nature Trail, 0.7 mile; Lake Loop Trail, 1.1 miles; Gahuti Backcountry Trail, 8.2 miles; Gold Mine Creek Trail, 2.3 miles.

Elevations: From 2,000 feet to 2,845 feet throughout the park.

Special attractions: Historically and geologically the ancient stone wall or "fort" is the most unique feature of the area; outstanding vistas of the surrounding mountains, and natural history.

Best season: The park is open year-round and is limited only during heavy snowfall. Spring wildflowers and fall foliage colors along with bird migrations favor these times.

For more information: Fort Mountain State Park, 181 Fort Mountain Park Road, Chatsworth, GA 30705; (706)695-2621.

Finding the trailheads: The trailhead for the Old Fort Loop Trail is at the Old Fort parking area on the north end of the park. The trailhead for the Gahuti Backcountry Trail is at the Cold Springs Overlook parking area. Other trailheads are at various points around the small lake.

The hikes: The most popular trail is the **Old Fort Loop Trail** that leads to the ancient stone wall. At the beginning of the trail, a large metal plaque prepared in 1968 by Georgia Department of State Parks tells of the mystery and legends of the stone wall and the mountain. The trail to the north leads to the mysterious and prehistoric wall of rocks from which Fort Mountain takes its name. Many generations of explorers, archaeologists, geologists, historians, and sightseers have wondered about the identity of the unknown builders and the purpose of their handiwork. From the brink of the cliff on the east side of the mountain, the wall extends 855 feet to another precipice on the west side. Its highest part measures about 700 feet, but generally it rises to a height of two or three feet. There are twenty-nine pits scattered fairly regularly along the wall with the wings of a gate-

Fort Mountain State Park Trails

Fort Mountain State Park.

way at one point. Speculation regarding the builders and their purpose covers a wide field. It includes references to sun worship and last ditch defense by prehistoric white people, bloody warfare between rival Indian tribes, defense fortification by Spanish conquistadors hunting gold, and honeymoon havens for Cherokee Indian newlyweds. Nobody knows which of the many legends and theories is true or false. The true answer still lies buried somewhere in antiquity and may never be unearthed.

From the sign, the trail with the yellow blaze leads to the stone wall where there are two more plaques that tell of additional mysteries of the interesting arrangement of the stones. Beyond the wall about 200 yards the trail reaches the stone tower built in the 1930s by the Civilian Conservation Corps on the summit of Fort Mountain. The trail along the stone wall is marked by a blue blaze. The access trail to the Chatsworth Overlook extends a short distance from the Fort Mountain Loop Trail and is marked with a red blaze. The trees on the mountain summit show the weathering of wind, rain, ice, and snow and are much older than they look. During spring migration of warblers and other birds, this trail offers the birder a unique opportunity to see at close range and not just hear many species in a short time.

Gahuti Backcountry Trail is an 8.2-mile loop that travels around the crest of Fort Mountain. The trail is marked by an orange blaze and can be hiked in either direction. A grand view of the Cohutta mountains and

Wilderness Area greets you at the very beginning. Especially during late fall, winter, and early spring the colors and vistas are exceptional. For the most part, the trail is easy to moderate; however, there are some short steep climbs and descents as the trail leads through the ravines and around the ridge crests. These can be slippery when wet or when covered with snow. Three campsites are strategically located along the trail for back-packers. Permits obtained from the park office are necessary for use of these campsites. No permit is necessary for day use of the trail.

Big Rock Nature Trail begins at the sign along the park road a few yards south of the dam on Gold Mine Creek. This 0.7-mile path is marked by a yellow blaze and is the jewel of the park. After walking under a powerline, the trail leads through a stand of small Virginia pines and then into a more dominantly deciduous hardwood forest of oaks, maples, sour-woods, black gums, and yellow-poplars. The undergrowth is thick with sweet shrub and spice bush along with mountain laurel as the trail dips into a wet area. Dropping sharply to the bluff line, it intercepts the Gahuti Backcountry Trail, turns to the right and follows the rocky bluff line. The view from here is spectacular.

Catawba rhododendron is in bloom during May and June, along with mountain laurel and many species of spring wildflowers. Rockcap fern is abundant on the large rocks near the wooden steps and short boardwalk that leads to an overlook and down to the falls of Gold Mine Creek.

The orange blaze continues on along the bluff line, while the Big Rock Nature Trail turns upstream beside the picturesque cascades as the creek pours over the rock ledges. Above the tumbling water, the creek and trail become flatter until the base of the dam is reached. Then the trail ascends steeply to the road.

The **Lake Loop Trail** is an easy, flat path around the lake marked in blue blazes for a distance of 1.1 miles. It can be accessed at one of several places from the dam around to the swimming area and campgrounds on the north side. On the north side, several wet areas provide the hiker with opportunities to see such wildlife as frogs, salamanders, and other aquatic and semiaquatic animals. Patches of large cinnamon ferns grow in these wet glades along with aquatic plants like lizard-tail, arrowhead, and the semiaquatic smartweeds. The trail passes cabins, picnic areas, swimming area, fishing dock, and campgrounds. Boardwalks cross some of the wet areas. On the east end and south side of the lake, mountain laurel and rhododendron form a canopy over the trail. This is an excellent birding trail with both water birds and forest species present. A day-use parking area with picnic shelters is on the south end of the dam.

All access trails in this park are marked with a red blaze. One of these trails takes off from the Lake Loop Trail on the southeast end of the lake and connects with the Gold Mine Creek Trail. This loop trail begins at a low gap where it also intercepts the Gahuti Backcountry Trail. The white blazed **Gold Mine Creek Trail** is easy to follow as it goes along an old roadbed up a gentle slope to the ridgetop and then turns down the watershed of Gold Mine Creek. At this point the access trail to the Gold Mine camping

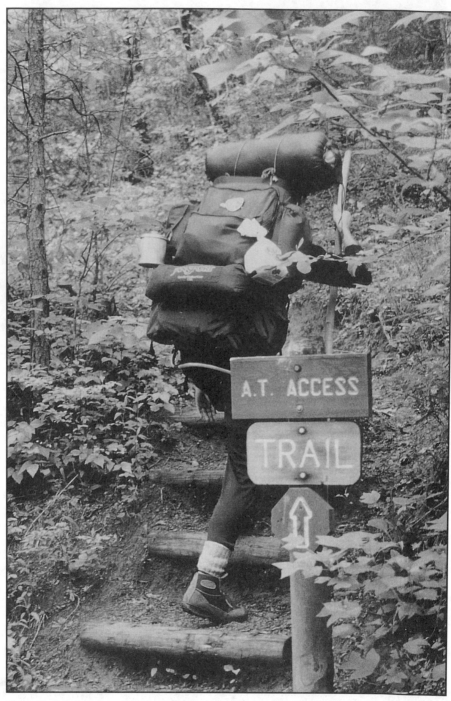

The Amicalola Falls Access Trail to Springer Mountain. The southern terminus of the Appalachian Trail is eight miles away.

area takes off to the right and the orange blaze of the Gahuti Backcountry Trail continues on.

Dropping down through the cove to the creek, hemlock and other streamside plants begin to show up again. The stream is so small at this point that crossings are of no consequence. After following the water course for about 0.2 mile, the trail leaves the stream and passes through a beautiful glade of New York ferns under an open, second-growth, hardwood forest to connect again with the access trail down to the lake.

31   Amicalola Falls State Park Trails

Overview: Amicalola Falls State Park offers hikers a great variety of outdoor choices. The trails are well marked and carefully maintained.

Amicalola is a Cherokee word meaning "tumbling waters." The falls, formed by Little Amicalola Creek, plunge 729 feet in several cascades; it is the highest waterfall east of the Mississippi River.

Amicalola Creek is managed as a trout stream and is open to fishing from the last Saturday in March through the end of October. Campground and hotel accommodations in the lodge are available. Cafeteria style meals are served at the lodge. Hikers may be fortunate enough to experience an occasional winter snow with accumulations of from two to ten inches that may last for a week or more.

General description: About 3.5 miles of easy to moderate hikes in three trails and the approach to the famous, 2,160-mile Appalachian Trail.

General location: About twenty miles east of Ellijay and fourteen miles west of Dahlonega on Georgia Highway 52.

Maps: Amicalola Falls State Park detailed trails map, U.S. Forest Service map of Chattahoochee National Forest and Georgia section of Appalachian Trail; Amicalola USGS Quad.

Degree of difficulty: Easy to moderate.

Length: Base of the Falls Trail, 0.4 mile; East Ridge Spring Trail, 1.3 miles; West Ridge Spring Trail, 1.7 miles.

Elevations: 1,700 to 2,700 feet.

Special attractions: Amicalola Falls, spring flowers growing in a cove hardwood forest, dogwood, mountain laurel, rhododendron, and many other shrubs and trees bloom in profusion. Fall offers brilliant colors from the sourwoods, maples, oaks, and many other species of hardwood trees; fishing.

Best season: Spring and fall are best; however, the trails are open all year and can be exceptionally beautiful in winter with snow. The hiker should be aware that the trails can be very slippery when leaves are wet or during periods of ice or snow.

For more information: Amicalola Falls State Park and Lodge, 240 Amicalola Falls Park Road, Dawsonville, GA 30534; (706)265-4703 or Lodge (706)265-8888.

Finding the trailheads: All trailheads are at or near the visitor center near the foot of the falls. The hikes can also be started from the lodge.

Amicalola Falls State Park Trails

The hikes: The **Base of the Falls Trail** is an easy to moderate paved trail, 0.4 mile long one way. It begins at the reflection pool that follows Little Amicalola Creek as it tumbles through a fine stand of yellow-poplar trees in a typical southern Appalachian cove hardwood forest. Spring flowers abound along this trail from March through May. Two observation platforms along the path have benches for resting and watching for wildlife. The trail ends in a steeper climb at the second observation platform near the base of the falls.

The trail is markedly different during each season. In spring there is a show of wildflowers; bloodroot, several species of trilliums, Virginia cowslips, trout lilies, foam flowers, jack-in-the-pulpits, and blue and yellow violets just to name a few. Some of the shrubs and trees blooming early in spring are dogwood, redbud, maple, serviceberry, and yellow-poplar. Because of the popularity of the falls and fishing for trout in the reflection pool and Little Amicalola Creek this is a very heavily used trail.

East Ridge Spring Trail, about 1.3 miles one way, begins behind the visitor center. It is a blue-blaze trail that climbs about 1,000 feet to the Falls Overlook. It starts with a gentle grade through hardwood forest for about 100 yards and then becomes a steep grade with several switchbacks for another quarter mile through a laurel thicket, or as the mountain people call it, an "ivy slick." The trail breaks out onto an old logging/service road with a moderately steep grade until it reaches the Amicalola Falls Lodge. It continues just behind the lodge to the trail for the Falls Overlook, a grand view of the surrounding mountains from the short wooden bridge. The trail then continues as the Appalachian Approach Trail and proceeds for about 7.5 miles to Springer Mountain, the southern terminus of the Appalachian National Scenic Trail.

From the Falls Overlook, you can continue back down the mountain to the visitor center by way of the West Ridge Spring Trail or return down the same East Ridge Spring Trail.

The **West Ridge Spring Trail** is broken into several loops all of which are well marked and identified with appropriate blazes. From the beginning of the trail, across the road from the visitor center, there are "Nature Trail" signs that lead eventually to the West Ridge Spring on the paved road to the Lodge. Because of the many switchbacks this trail is easy to moderate and travels through lush cove hardwood forest and open, dry, pine, and oak ridge exposures. This trail complex is being reworked so that it will lead to the lodge or to the base of the falls without using the paved park road.

The park offers camping for tents and mobile trailers. There are fourteen cottages, which may be reserved. If you are planning to hike all or any extended part of the Appalachian Trail, this park is an appropriate area to practice and break in equipment and clothing.

In July 1992, a torrential five-inch rain fell in the Amicalola Creek watershed and completely wiped out the observation platforms and trail below Amicalola Falls. Repair work began immediately after the storm. Some of the facilities may not be replaced.

32 Leonard E. Foote Hike Inn Trail

General description: Leonard Foote Hike Inn Trail is a new trail with its origin at Amicalola Falls State Park. It follows the Appalachian Approach Trail for only a short distance before it leaves the park. It goes its own way to the unique Leonard Foote Hike Inn. Here one can spend the night in a rustic but adequate and well-designed facility, or return to the park the same day. Meals and lodging are provided for overnight guests. The trail passes through the southern edge of the southern Appalachian highlands.

General location: This trail is in the Chattahoochee National Forest in the northern corner of Dawson County. Its beginning is at Amicalola Falls State Park about twenty miles east of Ellijay and fourteen miles west of Dahlonega on Georgia Highway 52.

Maps: A trail map is available at the park visitor center; Nimblewill USGS quad.

Degree of difficulty: This trail is moderate to strenuous. If hiked from the visitor center at the foot of the falls it is considered strenuous because of the more than 700-foot climb in about one mile. It is less strenuous if you start at the alternate parking area east of the top of the falls. The remainder of the hike has several short steep grades but is generally a moderate hike climbing a total of only about 500 feet in 4.5 miles. One only needs a light daypack for an overnight stay. As a one-day hike up and back by way of Nimblewill Gap on the Appalachian Approach Trail back to the park, a combined total of about fourteen miles, it would be considered strenuous.

Length: This variable hike is 5.5 miles one way from the visitor center to the inn. If you return by way of Nimblewill Gap it is about a 14-mile loop.

Elevations: The trail begins at 1,700 feet at the visitor center or about 2,200 feet at the alternate parking area above the falls and climbs to 3,060 feet at the inn. The highest point along the way is the ridge just before Cochrans Creek, about 3,000 feet.

Special attractions: Spring wildflowers and fall leaf color are always special in the mountains. The hardwood-covered ridges are ideal birding places for spring and fall migrating warblers and other neotropical birds as well as hawks. This trail offers the advantage of the unique overnight lodging at the inn and the grand views of surrounding mountains, especially Springer Mountain, the southern end of the 2,000-mile-long Appalachian Trail. There is a special celestial program planned for visitors to the inn.

Best season: This is truly a year-round hike because of the overnight facilities at the inn. Spring and fall are the best seasons. However, there are many days in winter ideal for hiking. Snow during the winter would make an even more challenging hike as well as a great time to be at the inn overnight.

For more information: Amicalola Falls State Park, 240 Amicalola Falls State Park Road, Dawsonville, GA 30534; (706)265-4703; for overnight reservations and costs at the Leonard Foote Hike Inn, (800)864-7275 or (770)389-7275.

Finding the trailhead: Start at the visitor center at the foot of the falls or, by prior arrangement, at the parking area at the top of the falls. In either case a free permit, which can be obtained at the visitor center, is required to hike this trail.

The hike: The Leonard E. Foote Hike Inn Trail is perhaps the most unique of all the trails in Georgia because of the rustic overnight facility at the end. The trail concept is to provide an overnight experience in the mountains without the necessity of packing in tents, food, and bedding. A simple daypack with personal things is all that is needed. The hike will take three or four hours. The trail winds up and down over ridges and into quiet fern glades in the coves of great yellow-poplars, oaks, buckeyes, and maples; and then through tunnels of mountain laurel and rhododendron thickets. There are several exposed points with grand views in winter when the leaves are off the trees.

To know this trail, as with other trails in the state, you must hike it in each of the seasons. It is much different in spring than in summer, and fall is dramatically different from either, while winter has a charm all its own.

In summer it is almost all under the shade of the thick hardwood-forest canopy. In spring before the leaves are on the trees the early blooming spring flowers are all along the narrow path. In fall the hardwood trees display a grand show of many colors because of the great variety of tree species in the southern Appalachian Mountains. Perhaps the most intriguing time will be in winter when you can hike in cold weather with or without snow and know that at the end there is a warm fireplace, food, and bed that you do not have to carry.

You can start the hike at the visitor center below the falls or arrangements can be made to park above the falls with the advantage of not hiking the strenuous 700-foot climb in one mile. The lower portion of the hike is described as the East Ridge Spring Trail in Hike 31, Amicalola Falls State Park Trails.

From the parking area above the falls follow the Approach Trail to the Appalachian Trail across the paved road where the path at the stone wall directs you into the woods. The Approach Trail is followed about a quarter mile where the Leonard E. Foote Hike Inn Trail branches off to the right and up the ridge. This is a steady climb to the ridge crest.

The forest floor has been relatively clear to this point but now there is, in summer, a thick growth of low vegetation consisting of young trees, grasses, and herbaceous plants. This change in vegetation will continue throughout the hike as you go from west- to east- and south- to north-side ridge exposures.

The more common spring flowers you can expect to see along the path are trailing arbutus, sessile and Vasey's trilliums, both dwarf irises, foam flowers, toothworts, Solomon's seals and false Solomon's seals, jack-in-the-pulpits, pink lady's slippers, wood anemones or windflowers, and white bane berries or doll's eyes—to name a few. Among the trees and shrubs are silverbells, dogwoods, redbuds, buckeyes, yellow-poplars, mountain laurels, and a host of others. Among the many ferns along the way are glades of New York ferns, marginal wood ferns and lady ferns, Christmas ferns, spleenworts, and bracken ferns.

Sassafras seedlings are abundant along the entire path. You might be surprised at the number of seedling and sprouting American chestnuts.

Leonard E. Foote Hike Inn Trail

Unfortunately they will not survive very long because of the chestnut blight. This may be a good place for a resistant strain of American chestnuts to develop.

Mammals in the area include black bears, whitetail deer, foxes, squirrels, chipmunks, raccoons, and opossums along with smaller deer mice, shrews, and moles. Most are only seen as tracks in the soft ground or as feeding signs. Besides the migrant birds there are many resident species like warblers, crows, cardinals, towhees, wrens, hawks, and owls.

Several small brooks and moist areas are crossed until you reach the only moderate-sized stream, Cochrans Creek. In this rhododendron- and mountain laurel–lined stream in a quiet cove hardwood forest you are not far from the end of the trail and unique experience of the Leonard E. Foote Hike Inn.

After your stay at the inn you may backtrack along the same trail to return to the park. Or you can make a loop by going north to Nimblewill Gap, about 1.5 miles, and turning to the south along the AT Approach Trail another six miles for a total loop of about fourteen miles.

33 Vogel State Park Trails

Overview: One of the oldest state parks in Georgia, Vogel is also one of the most scenic. Wolf Creek runs through the park and is impounded to make beautiful Lake Trahlyta. Four trails totaling nineteen miles are administered from this park. Coosa Backcountry Trail is the longest; then there is the Bear Hair Trail and the Byron Reece Nature Trail, with the Trahlyta Lake Trail being the easiest. These trails cover a wide variety of conditions and forest habitat.

Coosa Backcountry Trail is strenuous and more than a day hike. A free permit from the park visitor center is required for hiking this trail and camping overnight.

General description: Four hikes that vary in difficulty and length through this scenic park.

General location: The state park is eleven miles south of Blairsville on U.S. Highway 19 and 129. Coosa Backcountry Trail is crossed by Georgia Highway 180 at Burnett Gap and Wolfpen Gap about 1.5 and 2.5 miles respectively from the park. There is limited off-road parking at these crossings.

Maps: A page-size map of the trail network that originates at Vogel State Park is available from the visitor center; Coosa Bald and Neels Gap USGS quads.

Degree of difficulty: Coosa Backcountry Trail is moderate to strenuous; Bear Hair Trail is moderate to strenuous; Byron Reece Nature Trail and the Trahlyta Lake Trail are easy.

Length: Coosa Backcountry Trail, 12.7 miles with an additional one mile to Coosa Bald; Bear Hair Trail, four miles with additional one mile to the overlook; Byron Reece Nature Trail, 0.6 mile; and Trahlyta Lake Trail one mile; all are loop trails.

Elevations: The elevation at the trailhead where all three hikes begin is 2,290 feet. The highest elevation on Bear Hair Trail is about 3,280 feet. The highest point along the Coosa Backcountry Trail is about 4,200 feet. The elevation change around the Byron Reece Nature Trail is less than 100 feet. There is no change in elevation around the Trahlyta Lake Trail. The lake elevation is about 2,250 feet.

Special attractions: All of the Vogel trails offer excellent scenery, spring wildflower displays, wildlife observation, and birding areas from the lake to the high ridgetop habitat, camping, trout fishing in streams and a lake, and hunting in nearby Cooper Creek Wildlife Management Area; also a sidetrip to Blood Mountain at 4,461 feet, which is a short hike off the Coosa Backcountry Trail.

Best season: The park is open year-round; however, the weather can be severe for short periods in winter. Some flowers begin blooming in late February and March, and some species are in bloom until late October and November. Songbird migrations begin in late March. Warblers, thrushes, tanagers, grosbeaks, and finches will come through the mountains heading north as late as May. Many will end their northward trip in the Georgia mountains and begin nesting in spring. Fall leaf color beginning in October is spectacular because of the many species of deciduous trees.

For more information: Vogel State Park, 7485 Vogel State Park Road, Blairsville, GA 30512; (706)745-2628. U.S. Forest Service, Brasstown Ranger District, 181 Highway 515, P.O. Box 9, Blairsville, GA 30512; (706)745-6928.

Finding the trailhead: A single trailhead that serves three trails is located about 100 yards from the office/visitor center toward the camping areas. The Trahlyta Lake Trail can be reached at several points around the lake.

The hikes: The **Byron Reece Nature Trail** is a short hike with interpretive signs all along the path describing the interesting natural features of the forest. It is a loop off the access trail that begins the other two longer hikes. The trail is named for Byron H. Reece, a mountain farmer and poet, who lived near here before the park was established.

The **Trahlyta Lake Trail** is a comfortable walk around the lakeshore. Canada geese and other water birds, mammals, and amphibians add to the scenic hike.

The **Bear Hair Trail** loop is best hiked in a counterclockwise direction, although it can be hiked either way. Orange blazes point the way. It is a steady climb along tumbling Burnett Branch. One crossing is on a footbridge. Other crossings are by rock hopping and are easy except after a hard rain. You climb through a cove hardwood forest until you get to the level of the laurel and catawba rhododendron. Here the path is slightly steeper and tunnels through the thick shrubs that may be in full bloom in late May and June. The path comes to a gap where the spur trail marked with a green blaze leads to the left to the top of the ridge and the overlook. From the vista clearing at the end of the spur trail, you look right down on Lake Trahlyta in the park. This ridgetop is about 3,280 feet.

Backtracking to the loop trail, you soon follow an old roadbed along a contour. This is a particularly peaceful part of the trail, easy to walk in a fine hardwood forest with yellow-poplars, hemlocks, white pines, oaks, hickories, Fraser magnolias, buckeyes and smaller dogwood, sourwoods, high bush blueberries, and many others. There are some exceptionally large grapevines growing up the taller trees. Wildflowers—dwarf crested iris, wood-lily, showy orchids, pink and yellow lady's slippers, squaw-root, foamflowers, trilliums, jack-in-the-pulpits, bloodroot, and mayapples, just to name a few that bloom in the spring—are abundant along the path.

The trail crosses Wolf Creek and drops quickly through catawba rhododendron and mountain laurel thickets. It passes a boulder field as you look down on the stream. The junction with the yellow blaze of Coosa Backcountry Trail is next. Signs here mark the way to the park, Bear Hair, Coosa Backcountry, and the Appalachian trails. Wolf Creek is crossed again on foot logs and the path with both yellow and orange blazes levels out through tall trees and back to the access trail where the loop is closed. A turn to the right takes you back to the paved road in the park and the trailhead.

Coosa Backcountry Trail is also best hiked counterclockwise. It branches off to the right at the end of the access trail where it and the Bear Hair Trail loops begin. The Coosa Backcountry Trail is blazed yellow and a free permit is required for overnight camping. This is available at the park visitor center. It is not advised to try to hike the 12.7 miles in one day.

Early spring hiking on Coosa Backcountry Trail, Vogel State Park.

Vogel State Park Trails

The path climbs up to Burnett Gap across Georgia Highway 180 and down an old road to the right of Forest Road 107. This road is followed down to West Fork of Wolf Creek and across on a footbridge. Cross FR 107 and begin a steady climb up to Locust Stake Gap. This gap is used frequently as a campsite. The forest up to this point is similar to the Bear Hair Trail. From here you begin to experience the ridgetop hiking so plentiful in the mountains. The forest is more open with oaks and hickories dominant. Virginia pines occur on the dry south- and west-facing slopes. The trail climbs one high, rounded knob after another only to drop between each one down to another gap. The next one is Calf Stomp Gap, which is near 3,200 feet as you cross Forest Road 108. This is about halfway around the loop. The next mile is a climb to the 4,000-foot contour and the junction with Duncan Ridge Trail, which is marked with blue blazes. The ridge top here is open and flat, another area used frequently as a campsite. If you turn sharply to the right and follow the blue blaze for about a quarter mile along Duncan Ridge Trail, you come to Coosa Bald at 4,280 feet. You have now climbed 1,080 feet in about 1.5 miles.

Off the trail to the southwest there is a large rock outcrop. In winter and early spring before the leaves have become fully developed, you have an impressive view of the Cooper River valley and the surrounding mountains. Backtracking to the Coosa Backcountry Trail the yellow and blue blazes run together all the way to Slaughter Gap where Duncan Ridge Trail ends and Coosa Backcountry Trail drops down to Wolf Creek.

From Coosa Bald, the trail passes through Wildcat Gap and up Wildcat Knob. The elevation of the trail here is about 3,800 feet. The path now drops steeply to Wolfpen Gap and crosses Georgia Highway 180 again, elevation 3,320 feet. One of the steepest climbs on the trail now winds up to the next knob at 4,145 feet, drops only slightly into a high gap over 4,000 feet, and then levels out as you go around the east side of Slaughter Mountain. The trail is on an old logging road and is very pleasant with excellent conditions for spring and early summer wildflowers. If you are hiking in April this is also a good place to stop and watch for spring migrating birds. Ravens frequent this high ridge, as they do Blood Mountain and Brasstown Bald areas. A gentle slope down to Slaughter Gap connects you with the Appalachian Trail. But just before you get to the gap, the Coosa Backcountry Trail turns to the left or east and descends rapidly for about a mile before it joins Bear Hair Trail and continues to the park trailhead.

An interesting side hike from the Coosa Backcountry Trail is from Slaughter Gap to Blood Mountain on the Appalachian Trail. From Slaughter Gap it is only a one-mile, one-way hike up the Appalachian Trail to the top of Blood Mountain, the highest point in Georgia on this famous trail. At the mountaintop there is a stone trail shelter and grand views of the surrounding valleys and mountains. The hike up to Blood Mountain is a series of switchbacks along a well worn path through rhododendron and mountain laurel thickets and gnarled oaks. The elevation of Blood Mountain is 4,461 feet, a climb of 580 feet from the gap. This side hike is well worth the effort.

34 Brasstown Valley–Mountain Park Trails

Overview: Brasstown Valley Resort is located on 503-acre Mountain Park in the mountains of north Georgia. It lies under the highest point in the state, Brasstown Bald. The resort was designed to blend into the mountain environment. The cold-water streams on the site were protected from disturbance.

General description: There are four interconnected loop trails with a combined distance of about eight miles. All these loops are connected so that they may be walked in several ways to accommodate the distance and difficulty one chooses.

General location: The entrance to the Brasstown Resort is about one mile north of Young Harris on U.S. Highway 76/Georgia Highway 2 and about seven miles west of Hiawassee on the same highway.

Maps: A page-size map is available from the guest registration desk in the resort and from the Mountain Park office; Hiawassee USGS quad.

Degree of difficulty: The Blue, Orange, and Pink trails are collectively moderate. Brasstown Trek Loop is moderate to strenuous.

Length: Orange Loop two miles; Pink Loop 0.5 mile; Blue Loop one mile; Brasstown Trek Loop 5.5 miles.

Elevations: 1,800 feet to 3,280 feet for a total change of 1,400 feet in all trails.

Special attractions: Exceptional spring flowers and fall leaf color show; mountain hiking associated with a fine resort.

Best season: April to late October is best for the full range of flower blooming times and fall leaf color. Summer temperatures are pleasant and there are many winter days suitable for hiking.

For more information: Mountain Park, P.O. Box 115, Young Harris, GA 30582; (706)379-2040.

Finding the trailheads: The trailheads for the Orange and Blue trails are in the upper parking area for the resort. All other trails are accessed by way of these two trails.

The hikes: The **Orange Loop** trailhead is on the north side of the parking area. It is marked by a brown fiberglass stake with hiking symbols. The path is wide and well graded. It passes down through a hardwood cove of oaks, yellow-poplars, hickories, maples, sourwoods, and dogwoods. In spring expect to see trilliums, foam flowers, Clinton's lilies, Solomon's seals, violets, Christmas ferns, New York ferns, and others. The opening for one of the paved roads can be seen to the right. The edge effect produced along the road will add much variety to the number of birds and mammals possible to see. Interpretive signs are along the way. In about a quarter mile the path crosses a paved golf cart path.

At the lowest level the trail crosses Keys Branch on a footbridge. Large chain and cinnamon ferns, jack-in-the-pulpits, trilliums, and other flowers are here. After crossing the bridge the trail follows up the stream. The golf driving range is visible on the right across the branch. An interpretive sign tells about the trout habitat improvement structure. Many Christmas ferns line the path.

After crossing another footbridge the grade is steeper now as you go up a drier southwest-facing slope. Pincushion moss, huckleberries, and young sourwoods indicate a better-drained soil. At about 0.7 mile the trail crosses the paved park road and continues into a pine-hardwood forest up Keys Branch. The branch now flows over large boulders as a babbling brook. A footbridge crosses the branch. Yellowroot, so very common along all the mountain streams, is here. Many people in the mountains still use the root of the yellowroot plant for medicinal purposes.

After the bridge the path continues up the grade. There will be a number of spring flowers here. Windflowers, false Solomon's seals, and trilliums in spring; and later the wild hydrangea, highbush huckleberry, and others. The Brasstown Trek Loop takes off from the Orange Trail in this quiet cove. As you follow the contour around the steep side of the ridge an old American chestnut stump still stands on the high side of the path.

At about 1.2 miles is the junction of the three trails. The Pink Loop trail goes up the ridge to the left. The Blue Loop trail drops down to the parking area or heads up the ridge to continue on around the cabin area.

The **Pink Loop** is a 0.4-mile climb up the ridge to the crest and back down to the Blue Loop. From the crest of the ridge you can get a nice view of the surroundings in winter and early spring. In summer the foliage precludes much of the view. This is a good place to experience the migration of warblers, vireos, grosbeaks, and even tanagers in spring. These are the neotropical birds referred to on the interpretive sign at the top. These ridgetops are well-drained areas with a mixed pine-hardwood forest made up of pines, oaks, hickories, sourwoods, black gums, and dogwoods; under the trees are highbush and lowbush huckleberries, azaleas, and several of the spring flowers. Squirrels, chipmunks, deer, black bears, and several of the small mice feed on the nuts, acorns, berries, and other foods called soft mast that is most prevalent here. A wildlife opening seen from the trail here adds diversity to the habitat and increases the number of species of animals present. The longer loop trail to Rocky Knob, Brasstown Trek Loop, joins the trail complex on this ridge.

Dropping down the ridge the trail intercepts the **Blue Loop.** To the right leads back to the four-way junction, to the left follows the Blue Loop trail around the cabin area and into a more moist cove hardwood and streamside habitat. There will be many spring flowers here and large ferns in the wet area. During the summer months the cabins are mostly hidden. When the leaves are off the trees the cabins are clearly visible. A footbridge crosses Basin Creek behind the cabins as the path continues through the cabin area and eventually to the paved road. Cross the paved road and follow the path alongside the road to the bridge and road leading to the lodge registration entrance and the parking area. This completes about three miles.

All the trails in this complex are interconnected. A new trail, the **Brasstown Trek Loop,** leads to Rocky Knob and back to the Pink Loop. It

Brasstown Valley–Mountain Park Trails

is a 5.5-mile, moderate to strenuous hike with much greater habitat variety and is more challenging. It will take four or five hours to complete but is well worth the effort in scenery and plant and animal variety. This will be an excellent spring flower hike with good vistas and later for fall leaf colors. There are boggy areas that support an interesting variation in plant and animal life. The larger ferns, jewelweeds, and other water tolerant plants occur here.

A page-size map for the these trails is available at the registration desk at Brasstown Valley Resort and from the Mountain Park office.

35 Unicoi State Park Trails

Overview: Unicoi State Park is one of the most popular parks in the state. The park receives thousands of visitors each year because of attractions such as Smith Creek, a fine trout stream, Unicoi Lake, the mountains, Unicoi Lodge and cabins, campgrounds, and because of its close proximity to the popular resort town of Helen.

Each trail is well marked and information on all trails is readily available from the park office in the lodge. Program people at the park lead scheduled interpretive walks along two of the trails, especially during spring flower periods.

General description: Five trails, in and immediately adjoining the park, provide hikers with about 12.5 miles of diverse habitat and degree of difficulty.

General location: The state park is off Georgia Highway 17/75 near Helen and Robertstown.

Maps: Unicoi State Park page-size trail maps available at the lodge; Helen and Tray Mountain USGS quads.

Degree of difficulty: Easy to moderate.

Length: Unicoi Lake Trail 2.5 miles; Bottoms Loop Trail 2.1 miles; Unicoi to Helen Trail three miles.

Elevations: Unicoi Park elevation is approximately 1,750 feet. The trails change elevation very little.

Special attractions: Wildflowers; wildlife, including whitetail deer, turkeys, songbirds, a variety of small game; waterfalls; camping; trout fishing, and special interpretive programs.

Best season: The park and trails are open year-round. Spring is best for wildflowers and fall for spectacular fall foliage colors. Trout fishing season is from the last Saturday in March to October 31.

For more information: Unicoi State Park, 943 Anna Ruby Falls Road, Helen, GA 30545; (706)878-3983.

Finding the trailheads: From Helen, travel north one mile on Georgia Highway 17/75 to Robertstown. Turn right on Georgia Highway 356 and go one mile to the Unicoi State Park sign. All trailheads are at the upper parking area for the conference center and lodge. The Unicoi to Helen Trail can be hiked from a trailhead at the gazebo in Helen.

The hikes: The **Unicoi Lake Trail** is easiest and most accessible. It is marked by a yellow blaze and can be picked up at several locations. It crosses the highway and continues around the lake, passing the cabins on the east side of the lake. After passing the Trading Post, it returns to the lake shore. A floating footbridge crosses Smith Creek where it enters the lake or the hike can continue up Smith Creek to a picnic area where the creek is crossed on a bridge. Here the trail turns back downstream to the floating bridge. Along the west side of the lake it passes the day-use beach area and along the lake to the information center A-frame and returns to the lodge area by walking along the road crossing the dam. It was finally completed in spring 1999.

Unicoi State Park Trails

To Anna Ruby Falls

Smith Creek

242

Gate

Lake Trail

Information Center

Unicoi Lake

Trading Post

Campground

Smith Creek Trail

Cabins

356

Lodge

P

To Lake Burton

To Unicoi Gap

Smith Creek

Helen Trail

Bottoms Loop Trail

Chattahoochee River

75

Gazebo

Helen

To Cleveland

0   0.5

Miles

N

The **Bottoms Loop Trail** also begins at the upper level parking area for the lodge. This trail consists of a short loop of about 1.3 miles and a longer loop that is 2.1 miles. It is marked by a yellow blaze and turns to the right at the end of the short access trail from the parking area. Signs direct the hiker to both trails, which start at this point. The Bottoms Loop Trail follows a well graded gentle slope through a hardwood cove of yellow-poplars, maples, pines, and several oak species. After passing by a park residence, a small pond can be seen on the left. Wood duck nest boxes have attracted the beautiful duck to the pond, and if you are lucky you may see a pair swimming in the pond. After passing the tennis courts, the trail crosses the road to the maintenance compound and into a quiet woods with mountain laurel and great white rhododendron undergrowth. At the crest of a low ridge, the short loop turns right. The longer loop continues across several low ridge spurs, alternately going from drier ridge sites to more moist valley drainages. Wildflowers, ferns, and mushrooms are abundant. Pink lady's slippers, both dwarf and dwarf crested irises, galax, mayapples, trilliums, jack-in-the-pulpits, several species of ferns and clubmoss grow along the trail.

The trail passes by an old house site with the rocks of the chimney still visible, along with jonquils still blooming after having been abandoned for more than fifty years. Follow a small branch and an old roadbed to the Smith Creek bottoms. Ragwort, bloodroot, jewel weed, yellowroot, and many other moist-soil plants grow here. Two bridges cross the creek as the path leads into a meadow with a dense stand of autumn olive trees planted to attract wildlife. Many species of birds, deer, and even black bears eat the tasty fruits. After the meadow, the trail returns through the maintenance compound and along the same path to the beginning.

The **Unicoi to Helen Trail** follows a portion of the Bottoms Loop Trail and leaves it at the Smith Creek bridges. This three-mile trail is marked with green blazes. Hikers can start at the Unicoi lodge parking area or in Helen at the gazebo near GA 75. The trail is used by many people who join the Volks March activity in Helen or Unicoi State Park.

36 Smithgall Woods–Dukes Creek Conservation Area Trails

General description: The Dukes Creek Conservation Area is one of the newest additions to the areas managed by the Department of Natural Resources. The 5,604 acres of mountain woodlands was acquired as a gift purchase in 1994 from the conservationist, Charles A. Smithgall. It was dedicated to the purpose of protecting existing landscape, maintaining wildlife diversity, providing environmental education, and permitting low-impact recreational activities. Three trails with a combined length of about five miles are regularly open to the public. The visitor center is well worth the time to look around. It is where you may get a map of the Conservation Area and information about the trails and use of the area. Dukes Creek was the center of gold discovery in 1828, the gold rush that began here more than ten years before the California gold rush. Dukes Creek is also a fine trout stream managed as a catch-and-release stream. Trout fishing using artificial lures with barbless hooks is permitted on Wednesday, Saturday, and Sunday. Although the twelve miles of narrow, paved and unpaved roads are not designated as a trail or described here, visitors are invited to walk or mountain bike the roads. Permits for hiking and biking are available at the visitor center. As with all state parks a $2 parking pass is required per vehicle.

General location: The Conservation Area is in northeast Georgia between Helen and Cleveland on Georgia Highway 75 Alternate. From Helen go north on Georgia Highway 75 one mile to Robertstown, then turn left on Georgia Highway 75A and go 2.5 miles to the entrance to Dukes Creek Conservation Area on the left. From Cleveland go north on US Highway 129 for about three miles to Georgia Highway 75 Alternate. Turn right and go 5.7 miles to the entrance on the right. The visitor center and Laurel Ridge Trail is close to the entrance.

Maps: A page-size map of the Conservation Area with trails is available from the visitor center; Cowrock and Helen USGS quads.

Degree of difficulty: Easy to moderate. The Laurel Ridge, Martin's Mine Interpretive, and Cathy Ellis Memorial trails are moderate. The Wetlands Loop Trail is easy.

Length: Laurel Ridge Trail is a 1.5-mile loop; Wetlands Loop Trail is a 0.6-mile loop; Martin's Mine Interpretive Trail is a 1.5-mile loop; Dukes Creek Loop is less than half a mile, and the Cathy Ellis Memorial Trail is one mile one way. About twelve miles of paved and unpaved roads are available for walking.

Elevations: It is 1,570 feet above sea level at the visitor center and 1,841 feet on the Laurel Ridge trail. Other trails are about 1,500 feet to 1,560 feet.

Special attractions: Excellent spring wildflowers; wildlife watching; spring and fall warbler and other neotropical bird migrations with many resident species nesting; dramatic fall leaf color; and year-round trophy trout fishing on Wednesdays, Saturdays, and Sundays. This area provides a unique educational opportunity for students of all ages. Educational programs are designed by the Smithgall Woods Conservation Education Team.

Best season: Spring, summer, and fall; however, there are many days during the winter with ideal hiking weather.

For more information: Smithgall Woods–Dukes Creek Conservation Area, 61 Tsalaki Trail, Helen, GA 30545; (706)878-3087 or (706)878-3520.

Finding the trailheads: Laurel Ridge trailhead is at the visitor center; Wetlands Loop trailhead is 1.1 miles from the visitor center; Martin's Mine Interpretive trailhead is off Shackleford Road 2.2 miles from the visitor center; and the Cathy Ellis Memorial trailhead is about three miles from the visitor center.

The hikes: Only 1.5 miles long, the **Laurel Ridge Trail** is most fascinating because of the variety of habitat types. There are twenty-five marked places on the way interpreted by a leaflet that discusses features at each number. The trail begins at the end of the paved walkway from the visitor center. A large information sign helps to orient you to what you may see.

A well-marked bark-chip pathway leads to the first stop at the footbridge over a small brook that is habitat for trout. Along the streambank is yellowroot, one of the popular medicinal plants of mountain people. From here the path enters a quiet forest of tall yellow-poplars, hemlocks, white pines, maples, sourwoods, and dense thickets of rhododendron and doghobble. In summer New York ferns form a green deep-pile carpet on the moist forest floor, a most attractive fern glade. In spring trilliums, jack-in-the-pulpits, toothworts, foam flowers, violets, robin's plantains, doll's eyes or white baneberries, Solomon's seals, false Solomon's seals, buttercups, and a host of other flowering plants will be here and along the trail.

The path goes up the ridge and into a tunnel of rhododendron and mountain laurel, into another cove, and across another footbridge. The ridge slope here is shaded by white pines, maples, hemlocks, yellow-poplars, and white oaks. Under the canopy the trail is lined with bear-huckleberry and other low shrubs. Ferns and mosses among the leaf-litter cover the porous soil.

Another footbridge crosses a permanent brook. At the end of the bridge is a tree trunk with a patch of resurrection fern. From here to the top of the ridge the trail passes from the moist coves to the higher, drier forests. It does not take much elevation to do this, only a better-drained soil. Oaks, hickories, sourwoods, Virginia pines, thickets of mountain laurel, lowbush blueberries, and daisy-like flowering plants dominate. The nuts, acorns, and berries called soft mast are staple foods for deer, squirrels, opossums, black bears, chipmunks, and many birds. Another interesting plant beside the path is switch cane. It is more frequently growing along river and creek banks. It is a close relative of the giant or river cane.

This ridge area is a great place to watch for fall migrations of hawks and vultures. In spring there will be an increase in the number of warblers, vireos, tanagers, and grosbeaks in the trees as they migrate through.

For about a quarter of a mile the trail goes along the crest of the ridge. There are many blueberry bushes and other thick vegetation. In winter with no leaves on the trees there are great views of the surrounding mountains. In summer the shade from the trees is welcome. A large opening in the trees affords a view of Yonah Mountain to the southeast. Very soon the trail descends a steep slope back into the cove. On the way down the vegetative types change rapidly until you get to the mountain laurel and rhododendron tunnels and back to the New York fern glades and close the loop.

The short **Dukes Creek Loop** can be taken here by going to the left and across the road to the bank of the creek. The Poplar Shelter here is an overlook to the creek. The trail now goes around an open field with the creek on the opposite side. White pines, yellow-poplars, and alders line the bank. At the end is a picnic table well shaded in summer and open to the warm rays of the sun in late fall and winter. From here you go across the lawn to the visitor center. This trail is less than a half mile.

A completely different habitat type is experienced on the **Wetlands Loop Trail** about 1.1 miles down the one-lane road from the visitor center. The

Smithgall Woods–Dukes Creek
Conservation Area Trails

trailhead is at Tower Road. It begins on an old roadbed. This roadbed has grown over with grass and ferns. Scars from the early gold mining are faintly visible. They have been mostly healed by mountain laurels, Christmas ferns, and other plants. Anywhere in the Smithgall Woods–Dukes Creek Conservation Area you may be lucky enough to see a black bear. Wherever there are berries ripening in summer you may see where bears have broken the bushes down to feed on the fruit. Groundpine patches grow along the path.

The path now turns to the reason for its wetland name. A pond has been formed by a beaver dam on the small floodplain stream. Alders have been cut by the large rodents. Wood duck nest boxes have been placed here because of the lack of tree cavities necessary for the tree-nesting duck. Cinnamon ferns and royal ferns are here along with cattails, aquatic grasses, sedges, and rushes. Shrubs including alders, willows, and other water tolerant plants encroach into the water's edge. Red-winged blackbirds will nest in the thick waterside vegetation. The path goes around the wet area and comes to a wildlife opening planted to crops that will attract a number of species of mammals and birds. It is designed to increase the carrying capacity of deer, turkeys, rabbits, quail, and numerous songbirds. Another pond is passed before the trail comes to the paved road. On the opposite side of the road on the bank of Dukes Creek is the Alder Shelter for picnics and maybe just getting out of the rain, which can be frequent anytime of the year. A short walk up the road is the trailhead and the end of the loop.

Two miles from the visitor center the gravel Shackleford Road turns off the main road to the left. There is another ford across Dukes Creek and a parking area about two hundred yards from the ford. This is the trailhead for the **Martin's Mine Interpretive Trail.** The trail follows an old logging/mining roadbed into a cove hardwood forest. Along this road you get to the small branch that is crossed on a short footbridge. There are two options in the trail at this point. One is to the left and through a deep cut in the hillside, now healed by the lush vegetation of the moist cove hardwood forest. The other goes up the branch to a pretty little waterfall and up the hillside to see some of the effects of the hydraulic mining that was carried out to get to the gold-bearing ore. Near the footbridge at the bottom of the hill is where the stamp mill stood. It was used for breaking up the ore before it washed through the sluice boxes or was treated with mercury. Flowing water was a most important element of extracting gold.

The tunnels and vertical shafts that were constructed in the late 1800s are along the trail that passes through the deep cut. Safety fences have been placed around the openings to these shafts, which are today deep pits. Printed leaflets on the gold mining operations are available at the visitor center.

Many interesting and colorful plants are now a part of the natural healing process that has covered the once bare ground. A number of different species of flowers will be blooming here from early spring until late fall. All the common spring flowers are present including foam flowers, toothworts, violets in several colors, pink lady's slippers, Solomon's seals and

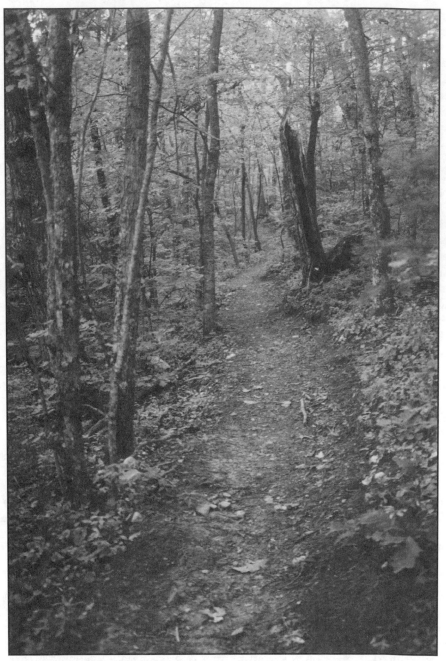

Typical trail on the Laurel Ridge Trail.

false Solomon's seals, windflowers, partridge- or twin-berry vines, trailing arbutus, and if you look closely you may see the tiny pennyworts and parasitic cancer-roots. Ferns are abundant. The early blooming trees are here also; silverbells, serviceberries, dogwoods, redbuds, yellow-poplars, and buckeyes. The shrubs include wild hydrangeas, azaleas, dog-hobbles, mountain laurels, rosebay rhododendrons, huckleberries, and sweet shrubs. Standing at the edge of the deep pit, look for the climbing hydrangea growing up the trunk of one of the larger trees.

Birding in this area can be exciting all year but especially during the warbler and other neotropical bird migrations. The closeness of Dukes Creek adds to the number of species one might see.

The trail continues on toward the creek staying in the hardwood cover. It eventually comes to an old road that follows downstream back to Shackleford Road and the trailhead. On the way you can see the footbridge that crosses Dukes Creek. It provides access to the main road and can be used if the creek flow is so great that passenger cars can not go through the ford across the creek on Shackleford Road. The end of the trail is in the floodplain of Dukes Creek. Water may be standing here in small depressions making excellent breeding areas for toads, frogs, and salamanders. As pointed out earlier the Smithgall Woods - Dukes Creek Conservation Area is very new. It is expected that this trail will be modified during the next few years.

The **Cathy Ellis Memorial Trail** begins about 3 miles from the visitor center. A small parking area is on the left side of the road. An information board here tells of the young Cathy Ellis who lost her life in a tragic accident while hiking in the Chattahoochee National Forest. The trail is about one mile one way. There are plans to extend the trail later to form a longer loop trail.

The path is up a low ridge at the top of which is a picnic shelter. Passing the shelter the trail drops down the other side through a mountain laurel thicket that mountain people used to call an "ivy slick." The term ivy was applied to the laurel because it was found to be poisonous to cattle. It is also poisonous to people. In the more open sites bear-huckleberry grows along the trail. The trench along the downhill side of the trail is called the "Hanby Ditch." It carried water from Dukes Creek to various places where water cannons were used in hydraulic mining. There were as many as fourteen miles of ditches like this that transported water to the various mining operations. As the trail continues down the ridge the laurel gives way to rosebay rhododendron. Christmas and hay-scented ferns are beside the way. Large patches of the ground-hugging partridge-berry vines form a ground cover.

Dukes Creek is now on the left of the trail as it goes downstream under thick overhanging rhododendron. The trail ends at the mouth of Alabama Creek where it flows into Dukes Creek. A few yards up Alabama Creek is an attractive, cascading waterfall completely surrounded by dense rhododendron and mountain laurel. As stated in the information from the visitor center, "Gold mining began in this area with the discovery of a gold nugget in the Alabama Branch of Dukes Creek in 1828 by a slave of Major Frank Logan." A short rest here, contemplating the gold rush, will prepare you for the hike back to the trailhead.

37 Moccasin Creek Wildlife Trail and Hemlock Falls Trail

General description: Moccasin Creek flows into Lake Burton in the northeast Georgia mountains in Rabun County. The Wildlife Trail is a team effort by personnel with the Georgia Department of Natural Resources from the Lake Burton Fish Hatchery, Lake Burton Wildlife Management Area, and the Moccasin Creek State Park. The Hemlock Falls Trail is a newly designated trail on the Tallulah Ranger District of the Chattahoochee National Forest. Although the trails do not have a common trailhead they can be hiked as one trail joined only by a short walk along the unpaved road between the two. The Wildlife Trail is designed to describe some of the wildlife management principles and structures that are beneficial to both game and nongame animals. Hemlock Falls Trail is a pleasant walk along Moccasin Creek, a beautiful, tumbling trout stream. The trail ends at the falls.

General location: About 20 miles north of Clarksville on Georgia Highway 197. Both trails are across Georgia Highway 197 from Moccasin Creek State Park and the Lake Burton Fish Hatchery.

Maps: A page-size map of the Wildlife Trail is available at the Lake Burton Fish Hatchery Office; Lake Burton USGS quad.

Degree of difficulty: Easy.

Length: Wildlife Trail is a 1.2-mile loop; Hemlock Falls Trail is 1.1 miles one way. If hiked together the total distance is about four miles.

Elevations: 1,880 to 2,400 feet.

Special attractions: Wildlife observation, spring flowers, fall leaf color, trout fishing, and primitive camping are only a few of the things that make these trails interesting. Lake Burton, Moccasin Creek State Park, and Lake Burton Fish Hatchery are only a few yards away. Aside from RV and tent camping at Moccasin Creek State Park there is trout fishing in a section of the creek reserved for children under 12 and senior citizens. At the hatchery there is a pond just for children's fishing.

Best season: Spring, summer, and fall, although there are many days during the winter ideal for hiking.

For more information: U.S. Forest Service, Tallulah Ranger District, Highway 41, P.O. Box 438, Clayton, GA 30525; (706)782-3320. Moccasin Creek State Park, Route 1, Box 1634, Clarksville, GA 30523; (706)947-3194. Lake Burton Fish Hatchery, Route 1 Box 1638, Clarksville, GA 30523; (706)947-3112.

Finding the trailheads: The trailhead for the Wildlife Trail is directly across Georgia Highway 197 from the fish hatchery and state park. The trailhead for the Hemlock Falls Trail is at the end of Andersonville Road.

Continue past the parking area for the Wildlife Trail for about three quarters of a mile to the backcountry camping area. The name of the trail has been carved into a large boulder that serves as a barrier to vehicles traveling beyond.

The hikes: The two trails on Moccasin Creek are so close together they can be hiked as one or separately. They are accessed by the same road, Andersonville Road, which turns off Georgia Highway 197. The Wildlife Trail is nearest, only a few yards off the highway. Hemlock Falls Trail is at the end of this road, about three quarters of a mile from the highway. Hiked together it would be about four miles, or separately about three miles.

The well-marked **Wildlife Trail** begins at the small, fenced park with picnic tables. It is on the bank of Moccasin Creek at the water-control dam which supplies water for the fish hatchery. An information board describes the trail and its purpose.

The path is close to the creek as you go upstream. Lush streamside vegetation lines the area between the bank and trail from late spring to early autumn. Among the plants is jewelweed or touch-me-not, a favorite flower of hummingbirds that is common here. The way is marked with stakes, each with a metal disc and arrow showing the way. The stakes have an orange stripe around the top. As you walk the trail the small streams and branches are crossed on sturdy footbridges.

There are interpretive signs about the management practices or devices used in the area. The first of these is a bat box on a yellow-poplar. The next interpretive sign describes a wildlife food plot. Another talks about the watershed. In the wildlife planting is a small four- or five foot fenced-in area called a browse exclosure. It demonstrates how much the plants are eaten by deer, rabbits, and other animals. A weather station is located well off the trail in this opening. The next area illustrates what happens when cleared land is left to lie fallow. An old field succession sign is here. At the far edge of the old field area is a well-established patch of dwarf irises which should be in bloom in late April and early May. The path then passes into a hardwood area. New York, Christmas, and chain ferns are among the ferns growing here and in other places along the path.

At about a half mile you come to a gravel service road. This is Moccasin Creek Road. If you turn right and follow the road (taking the middle dirt road) you come, in about a half mile, to the backcountry campground and end of the road. Here is the Hemlock Falls Trail–engraved boulder, the beginning of this trail.

Continuing across the gravel road the Wildlife Trail comes to a mill pond on the left and the sign telling about the native wood duck. The trail continues through a site with white pines and large patches of New York ferns. The Christmas fern is not as abundant but well represented. Farther along in a drier area blueberry bushes will be in bloom in May and ripe berries present in July. A little farther along you come to the interpretive sign discussing the white-tailed deer and another referring to raptors, or

Moccasin Creek Wildlife Trail and Hemlock Falls Trail

hawks and owls. Before long you come to the gravel road again and cross it. Close by is the check station for the Lake Burton Wildlife Management Area. The last sign describes some of the techniques used to improve the trout-holding capacity of streams.

You are now near the end of the trail, which completes the loop back to the picnic and parking area.

The **Hemlock Falls Trail** is at the end of Andersonville Road, which continues past the parking area for the Wildlife Trail and the check station for the Lake Burton Wildlife Management Area. At the end of the road is a backcountry campsite. A $2 use fee required by the Forest Service is charged here. The large boulder in the road engraved with the trail name is the trailhead. The trail is blazed with a small metal diamond attached to trees along the way.

For the first two or three hundred yards the trail follows an old roadbed that at one time was a railroad bed for hauling timber out of the forest. Along the streamside and well up the bank along the trail rosebay rhododendron, sometimes called great white rhododendron, is the most obvious cover. Dog-hobble, mountain laurel, bear-huckleberry, dogwood, and many other shrubs contribute to the dense trail-side vegetation. In spring before the leaves are on the trees there will be trilliums, jack-in-the-pulpits, foam flowers, Solomon's seals and false Solomon's seals, anemones, and many other flowers blooming. Dogwoods, silverbells, yellow-poplars, buckeyes,

Hemlock Falls on Moccasin Creek.

and other trees will be blooming along with shrubs like dog-hobble and sweet shrub. The predominant fern is the New York fern along with the Christmas fern. White pine, hemlock, yellow-poplar, oak, and maple are the predominant forest trees. Deciduous magnolia, silver bell, black gum, birch, beech, and a host of other tree species compose this cove hardwood forest typical of the southern Appalachian Mountains.

At about 0.5 mile there is an attractive falls on a tributary branch coming into Moccasin Creek on the opposite side from the trail. It may not be flowing during very dry weather. A large rock overhang on the left side of the trail might serve as a shelter should you get caught in one of the frequent spring or summer thundershowers.

About halfway to the falls a footbridge crosses the creek. The trail continues up the right side of the stream. Now the valley through which the stream flows has narrowed, the stream is more turbulent, and you are in dense shade most of the day. The path narrows on this side of the creek until you reach the falls. Hemlock Falls is not very high but it is an attractive cataract with a large pool. Trout fishermen find the pool exciting. It is one of those delightful areas in the mountains where a quiet rest is more rewarding.

The trail above the falls is not marked but it follows Moccasin Creek, which flows down from the highland ridge from Tray Mountain to Addis Gap and the Appalachian Trail.

38 Black Rock Mountain State Park Trails

Overview: Black Rock Mountain State Park is the highest state park in Georgia at 3,640 feet elevation on the crest of Black Rock Mountain. The 1,502 acres lie along the ridgeline of the Eastern Continental Divide. Many scenic overlooks offer views of the surrounding southern Appalachian Mountains.

General description: Three trails totalling about 9.4 miles offers a taste of almost all the varied habitat types in the park.

General location: In the northeast corner of Georgia, three miles north of Clayton on U.S. Highway 441.

Maps: Detailed, page-size map available from visitor center; Dillard USGS quad.

Degree of difficulty: Moderate to difficult. Ada-hi Falls Trail drops 240 feet in 0.2 mile one way. Tennessee Rock Trail loop is moderate throughout. James E. Edmonds Backcountry Trail is a moderate to difficult loop.

Length: Ada-hi Falls Trail is 0.2 miles one way; Tennessee Rock Trail is a 2.0 mile loop; James E. Edmonds Backcountry Trail is a 7.2 mile loop.

Elevations: Black Rock Mountain, at 3,640 feet, is 2,700 feet above the valley at Clayton. The Tennessee Rock Trail and Backcountry Trail begin at 3,280. The Tennessee Rock Trail drops down to 3,200 and climbs to 3,640 feet at crest of Black Rock Mountain. The Backcountry Trail varies between 3,280 and 2,200 feet.

Special attractions: Grand mountain scenery from several high vantage points; variety of mountain environments provide habitat for unusual plant diversity; spring wildflower show; spectacular fall leaf colors; camping; fishing; and a variety of activities for visitors, including wildflower programs, nature walks, and overnight backpacking trips.

Best season: Year-round with spring and early summer best for wildflowers, fall for leaf color. The road to top of mountain may be closed during winter snow and ice.

For more information: Black Rock Mountain State Park, Mountain City, GA 30562; (706)746-2141

Finding the trailheads: Turn west at state park sign and go 2.5 miles to park. The Ada-Hi Falls trailhead is at the concession and trading post area near the campground. The trailhead for the Tennessee Rock Trail and the longer James E. Edmonds Backcountry Trail is at the graveled day-use parking and picnic area on the main access road near a large free-flowing spring and spring house.

The hikes: The **Ada-Hi Falls Trail** takes off from the concession and trading post area. It is only 0.2 miles one way, but in that short walk the trail drops 220 feet. As hikers say "It's 0.2 miles down and 5.2 miles back up." But it is a beautiful hike with nice views in winter when the leaves have fallen. A series of steps made from stone, log, and wood lead down to a small but enchanting falls in a dense rhododendron thicket. Rock ledges and overhangs add variety to the setting. The path ends at a level observation platform, giving the hiker fine views of the stream cascading and sliding down about eighty feet of sheer granite.

The **Tennessee Rock Trail** is a loop designed to pass through a north-facing mountain slope that favors a wide variety of wildflowers and breaks out on top of Black Rock Mountain, following the Eastern Continental Divide. The elevation here is 3,280 feet and shares the same trailhead with the Backcountry Trail. The path, marked with a yellow blaze, starts out at a moderate climb up log steps but then follows the contour wherever possible through a hardwood forest of oaks, hickories, yellow-poplars, sourwoods, dogwoods, and black gums just to name a few. Turning into the north facing slope, the cooler, more moist habitat is marked by moss-covered logs and ferns, including the marginal, Christmas, New York, and wood ferns. Wildflowers blooming in spring include hepatica, bloodroot, anemones, foam flower, halbred-leaved and Canada violets, showy orchids, several species of trilliums, large-flowered bellwort, Solomon's seal and false Solomon's seal, and finally for the sake of ending the list somewhere there are jack-in-the-pulpits, bluets, and parasitic squaw root and one-flowered cancer-root. Later in spring the mountain laurel will bloom, adding fragrance and color to the tunnels of rhododendron through which the trail passes. This trail is designed as a self-guided, nature trail with a leaflet available to explain conditions and species at selected stations along the way. There are about twenty-five stations in the two-mile walk. It leads through several beautiful coves below boulder fields, some with springs.

Black Rock Mountain State Park Trails

Lookoff Mtn. 3162'

Black Rock Lake 2241'

Backcountry Trail

James E. Edmonds

Park Entrance

To Dillard

Mountain City

44

441

To Clayton

Ada-Hi Falls Trail

Campground

Tennessee Rock Trail

P

P

Vistor Center

Black Rock Mountain 3641'

Cottages

0   0.5

Miles

N

The path joins an old roadbed for a short distance. The walking becomes much easier as it enters a white pine stand and climbs on to the ridge crest where a sign indicates that the trail turns sharply to the left. The path then switchbacks to the top of Black Rock Mountain. Here the elevation is 3,640 feet, and during the late fall and winter when the trees are bare, neighboring mountain ranges are visible. The old skeletal remains of American chestnut trees are still easy to recognize along the way. Some are much larger than any of the other living oaks and hickories that have replaced them. Hiking now on the south face of the mountain, the view is straight down to the town of Clayton, about 2,000 feet below. This crest of the ridge is the Eastern Continental Divide. Water on the south side goes into the Atlantic Ocean by way of the Savannah River and the north drainage flows into the Tennessee and Mississippi river systems and into the Gulf of Mexico.

One of the most magnificent views in the north Georgia mountains is from the granite outcrop approached by a set of wooden steps. On a clear day the Great Smoky Mountains in North Carolina can be seen on the far horizon. Walking through a tunnel of rhododendron, the trail comes very close to one of the roads that leads to a cottage area and then back down the mountain to the trailhead, completing the two-mile loop.

Overlook at Black Rock Mountain State Park, highest state park in the state.

The longer **James E. Edmonds Backcountry Trail**, marked with an orange blaze, goes through much the same type of habitat as along the Tennessee Rock Trail but goes lower into the valley and crosses both Greasy and Taylor creeks. These small streams add to the variety of the hike.

The trailhead is the same as Tennessee Rock Trail. Instead of beginning a climb up the mountain, this trail begins a long and gradual descent that is moderately steep in some places until it reaches a fork in the path. The right fork takes the hiker in a counterclockwise direction around a loop that comes back to the fork and then backtracks uphill to the trailhead. As the trail breaks out of the evergreen rhododendron into the hardwood coves one can look down on Black Rock Lake through the trees. Great patches of galax are all along the trail. Galax has a characteristic odor that resembles the scent of skunk. Spring wildflowers are abundant all along the trail. A tributary of Greasy Creek is crossed in another of the many rhododendron thickets that are frequent and beautiful when in bloom. Following along an old roadbed the path comes out in a gap and soon crosses the road from Mountain City to Germany Valley. Crossing the road into another rhododendron tunnel, the trail alternates from open hardwoods to streamside rhododendron as it follows Taylor Creek. The trail crosses the creek on a footbridge and bends back, climbing to a gravel road to Black Rock Lake. Across the road, the path begins the long, steady 600-foot climb up to Scruggs Knob and along the watershed divide through Scruggs Gap. Then it goes along an old roadbed under the crest of Marsen Knob into Gibson Gap. Here the trail turns back down the mountain toward Black Rock Lake or goes up the steeper climb to Lookoff Mountain. The spur trail to Lookoff Mountain is a loop that goes to the granite outcrop that gives the mountain its name. The "lookoff" view from here is spectacular. The edge of the sheer drop is protected by a cable fence with stone-masonry pillars. The north-by-northwest view looks down more than 1,000 feet to the headwater valley of the famous Little Tennessee River.

Returning to Gibson Gap, half of the 7.2 mile hike has been completed. The return trail drops quickly to the head of Black Rock Lake. Cross Taylor Creek on a footbridge at a lower point than before and follow along the south side of the lake to Greasy Creek. Groundpine or clubmoss, a fern relative, grows in the white pine stands along the streams. Greasy Creek is a very pretty, small mountain stream that literally slides down the mountain over the exposed granite that is covered in places with algae. It gives the stream a slick appearance and has been appropriately named. In most places, it slides through a thick cover of rhododendron. The creek is crossed on another footbridge. The trail returns to the end of the loop section and climbs about 700 feet back to the trailhead.

Tallulah Gorge and Tallulah River at low flow.

39 Tallulah Gorge State Park Trails

General description: There are about eight miles of trails in Tallulah Gorge State Park, one of the newest parks in the system. All of about 7.5 miles are more or less horizontal, the other 0.5 mile is vertical. The Hurricane Falls Trail is a series of wonderfully crafted stairs to the bottom of the gorge and the Wallenda Cable Trail is a path down to the bottom farther downstream. A free permit obtained at the Interpretive Center is required for any entry into the gorge.

Tallulah Gorge State Park was the result of a lease from the Georgia Power Company to the Department of Natural Resources in 1963. It has a long history as a scenic area and summer resort place since the mid-1800s. The word Tallulah has its origin in the Cherokee language but cannot be translated. Tallulah Falls, Georgia, is steeped in history from the famous Tallulah Falls School to the building of the Georgia Power Company's Tallulah Falls Dam in 1914 to the highly publicized and exciting crossing of the gorge on a high wire by Karl Wallenda on July 18, 1970.

General location: The state park is easily reached from U.S. Highway 441/23 in northeast Georgia, within the city limits of Tallulah Falls. It is in the corner of both Habersham and Rabun counties.

Maps: Page-size maps of the trails are available at the Jane Hurt Yarn Interpretive Center; Tallulah Falls and Tugaloo Lake USGS quads.

Degree of difficulty: The Stoneplace Trail is moderate to difficult. The rim trails are easy. The Hurricane Falls Trail, a 600-foot, wooden stairway down to the bottom of the gorge, and the Wallenda Cable Trail are strenuous.

Length: The Stoneplace Trail is five miles one way; the rim trails are about one mile each. Hiked together by crossing the bridge the rim trails are about 2.5 miles one way. The Wallenda Cable Trail from Overlook 10 is about one mile one way. A permit is required to use this trail.

Elevations: The Stoneplace Trail varies from 1,700 feet at its highest point to 900 feet at the level of Tugaloo Lake. The rim trails are at about 1,600 feet.

Special attractions: Spectacular scenery of the gorge and waterfalls; unique geological formations of the gorge; outstanding interpretive center that depicts the surrounding area from the mountaintops to the bottom of the gorge; endangered plants and animals, some of which occur only in the gorge.

Best season: This is truly a year-round hiking opportunity. The best time is spring and fall for the wildflower blooming and wildlife watching and fall leaf colors. There are many days in the winter that are suitable for hiking. Summer temperatures are usually comfortable enough for hiking.

For more information: Tallulah Gorge State Park, P.O. Box 248, Tallulah Falls, GA 30573; (706)754-7970.

Finding the trailheads: All trails can be accessed from the interpretive center. The South Rim trails can be reached also from a private parking area off U.S. Highway 441/23.

The hikes: It is most desirable to walk the **North Rim Trail** after experiencing the Jane Hurt Yarn Interpretive Center. The trail is accessed from the rear of the interpretive center. A walkway down from the center to the actual trail is surfaced with material from recycled scrap tires. At the end of this walkway you are directed to the left for Overlook 1 and to the right for Overlooks 2 through 5. The trail is wide and well used. Each of the overlooks on the north side are protected with railings and provide adequate views of the gorge. Each overlook has a different and special, spectacular view. The gorge is about 600 feet deep. Children should be supervised very carefully while visiting the overlooks.

In spring there are many wildflowers in bloom. Mid to late May is the best time for the mountain laurel and catawba rhododendron, also called mountain rosebay. Trailing arbutus, partridge berry, galax, New York fern, and Christmas fern are along the path. Overhead are the white oaks, chestnut oaks, sourwoods, black gums, Virginia pines, and other trees providing shade during the warm months on the way to the different overlooks. All overlooks are well marked and can be visited randomly or by walking to the Wallenda North Tower at Overlook 1 and following around the rim to each overlook in order.

At Overlook 5 the trail continues to the U.S. Highway 441 bridge over Tallulah Dam where steps provide access to cross the bridge to the beginning of the **South Rim Trail.** There is much history associated with this trail since in days past there were hotels, restaurants, and other concessions on this side of the gorge. Much of the trail is an old stone pathway. Overlook 6 still has an old pavilion. Between Overlooks 7 and 8 is the **Hurricane Falls Trail,** which is actually 600 steps down the side of the gorge to the bottom. The steps wind in artful and interesting ways with platforms and rest benches spaced comfortably. This can be a strenuous trip for people who are in poor health or physical condition. It is certainly worth the walk to see the great change in vegetation as you walk from the rim down to the river at the bottom. Species of plants and animals are found in the gorge and nowhere else. For instance, the persistent trillium is an endangered species and the green salamander is very rare. Both occur in the gorge.

Continuing on the South Rim Trail the overlooks end at Overlook 10. This is the beginning of the **Wallenda Cable Trail.** It passes the Wallenda South tower and enters the gorge. This trail is not described here since a permit is required which may be obtained at the interpretive center. A briefing on the trail is obtained with the permit.

The **Stoneplace Trail** is a five-mile hike one way to Tugaloo Lake on the Chattooga River, tributary to the Tallulah River which flows through the gorge. The trailhead is a few yards up the road from the interpretive center at the entrance kiosk. This trail does not pass along the gorge, but uses the old logging roads that traverse the ridges and valleys of the area to the north of the gorge.

Brown posts with the word "trail" and an arrow engraved in the side serve as the markers for the trail. They are located at any intersection of the many places where there is an old road crossing or where the road forks. This is a multi-use trail, which means that mountain bikes may be used. This should pose little problem because the logging roads are wide enough for hikers and bikers to pass without incident.

Tallulah Gorge State Park Trails

Worse Creek

Bad Creek

CHATTAHOOCHEE
NATIONAL FOREST

TUGALOO
LAKE

CHATTOOGA RIVER

GEORGIA

SOUTH CAROLINA

TUGALOO LAKE

RABUN CO., GA

HABERSHAM CO., GA

Tugaloo Dam

157

At first the road goes through a cove with yellow-poplars, pines, sourwoods, and oaks. Grapevines, highbush huckleberries, and an abundance of seedling sourwood trees make a green wall beside the trail. In spring there will be many flowering plants in bloom, especially in the coves where the hillside is steep above and below the trail. The surface of the trail is sandy clay. Impressions of animal tracks are easy to see.

After the cove area the road is more open as it comes to the top of a ridge. More open stands of white oaks, black oaks, black gums, pines and sourwoods, and other smaller trees replace the tall yellow-poplars of the coves. Other roads join the trail road. The signpost indicates the direction to hike.

At about one mile the trail appears to end at a red metal gate. The signpost directs you around to the right of the gate. This land belongs to the Georgia Power Company. Through a lease agreement the Department of Natural Resources now manages the land for various recreational uses, hiking trails being one. Before long the road goes under one of the powerlines that comes from the hydroelectric power substation on the other side of the gorge about a mile away as the crow flies. At this point you enter the Tallulah Gorge Wildlife Management Area. Deer, turkey, black bear, and several species of small game are hunted here in season. A sign gives some of the regulations and seasons.

Near the top of another ridge is a clearcut area where timber has been harvested. The clearcuts, although very unsightly, are beneficial to deer, turkeys, rabbits, and many songbirds. The openings provide an increase in annual seed-producing plants and add the edge between forest and open area useful to many animals. You will usually see more animal tracks in the road beside these areas.

The trail goes in and out of the dry ridge site to the more moist cove areas with rhododendron, yellow-poplar, hemlock, and white pine. The low vegetation will include galaxes, partridge berries, and ferns with dwarf-crested irises, trilliums, and other wildflowers blooming in spring. In summer the daisy-like flowers are in bloom and include whorled-leaf coreopsis, sunflowers, and asters. There are several clearcuts on the trail. Near the last of these is a small patch of running groundpine, one of the clubmosses.

At this point, a little more than halfway, the trail forks and a sign points out that vehicles are prohibited, indicating this section is for walking only. It is one of the prettiest sections of the trail. Here the way is through a shaded moist cove with rhododendron, galax, and spring flowers along the side with white oak, yellow-poplar, dogwood, black gum, and maple trees below the trail. The second powerline crossing is here. The road goes around a more exposed, western slope where bracken ferns grow, with a view of the opposite side of the gorge. In summer this view is partially blocked by tree leaves. In winter with the leaves off it is more scenic.

The vehicle-restricted area ends at a four-way corner. Continue straight ahead. Very shortly the road goes under the same powerline that you crossed earlier, indicating that the trail made a 180 degree direction change. The

Tallulah Gorge Detail Map

road drops down much steeper now as it gets closer to the lake. A spring flows through a culvert under the road. A shelter on the right below the trail is for overnight use or to get out of the weather if caught in a storm. During spring and summer there can be frequent thunderstorms with only rare snowstorms in winter. Except for weather emergencies the shelter can be reserved at the interpretive center for overnight camping. The only convenience available is the shelter.

The last mile of the trail is through the lower, more moist forest with the steep slopes. When you come to the gravel road you know you are at the lake even though you cannot see it in the summer. Turn right, going down the road where a small stream is crossed. Four-wheel-drive vehicles can get to this point by another road, which is used to put canoes or small boats in Tugaloo Lake. This lake is on the Chattooga River which is also the state line between Georgia and South Carolina. The Tallulah River, as it comes out of the gorge, joins the Chattooga River. Georgia Power Company's Tugalo Dam impounds both rivers at this confluence.

The hike back out is the same distance.

40 Victoria Bryant State Park Trails

Overview: This state park is on the northern fringe of the Piedmont in the rolling hills, but the plant and animal species present here are similar to those found in the mountains of Georgia. The park has well kept campgrounds, picnic areas, swimming pool, and a golf course. A short trail along the pond has been developed for wheelchair use. Even the picnic tables are designed to be used in wheelchairs. The wooded area around the pond is a nice place to watch for wildlife.

General description: Two trails totaling a little more than three miles offer pleasant walks along the tumbling Rice Creek and through the surrounding forested hills and valleys.

General location: The park is in Northeast Georgia in Franklin County. It is on Georgia Highway 327 two miles north of U.S. Highway 29 and the small town of Franklin Springs.

Maps: A page-size map is available at the park office; Carnesville USGS quad.

Degree of difficulty: The Victoria Path Nature Trail is easy, while the Perimeter Trail is easy to moderate.

Length: The Victoria Path Nature Trail is slightly more than 0.5 mile; the Perimeter Trail is 2.5 miles.

Elevations: The elevation at the park is about 1,500 feet. The change in elevation along the Perimeter Trail is only about 100 feet.

Special attractions: A very pleasant, forested walk through a mixed hardwood and pine forest. Excellent birding for forest species and those attracted to ponds and fast-flowing Rice Creek.

Best season: This area is accessible year-round. Spring and fall are best for wildflowers, birding, and good weather.

For more information: Victoria Bryant State Park, 1105 Bryant Park Road, Royston, GA 30662; (706)245-6270.

Finding the trailheads: The trailhead for the Victoria Path Nature Trail is the parking area on Rice Creek just below the office and concession building. The trailhead for the Perimeter Trail is at the fish pond only a few yards from the park entrance.

The hikes: The shorter Victoria Path Nature Trail has interpretive stations that are explained in a leaflet. The longer Perimeter Trail includes most of the habitat types in the park typical of the upper Piedmont.

Victoria Path Nature Trail is an attractive loop walk beginning at the parking area on Rice Creek. This trail was constructed by Scout Troop 70 as an Eagle Scout project in 1984. It goes downstream through the mountain laurel and dog-hobble that is thick on both sides of the creek. Sixteen numbered stations described on a pamphlet explain the points of interest along the trail. An overlook platform on the stream side of the trail gives a nice view of the creek and dense laurel thicket. This side of the creek is a north-facing slope where galax, Christmas ferns, robin's plantain, and a number of other shade tolerant plants grow. The forest is mostly hardwoods—white oaks, red oaks, yellow-poplar, sourwoods, maples—with dogwoods growing under the larger trees. You get a good look in the creek at the footbridge that takes the trail up the other side of the creek. Switch cane growing along the river here gives the trail a tropical atmosphere. This walk is especially interesting during early spring when trilliums, foamflowers, toothworts, robin's plantain, and violets are in bloom. The mountain laurel blooms from late April into May along with the dog-hobble. Rock outcrops are crossed with the help of wooden railings. You continue through the laurel to the roadway and up to another bridge and on to the parking area.

This walk gives you a good look at the difference between the plant life on the north-facing slope on the downstream side and the south-facing slope on the opposite side. More ferns, mosses, and shade-tolerant plants live on the north-facing side. The south-facing side is drier and has more open forest floor.

The Perimeter Trail begins at the fish pond on the entrance road. It is paved and barrier free for about 100 yards, offering wheelchair access to an observation deck that overlooks a two-acre pond. This makes an excellent place to view wildlife or to fish. A small island near the deck is used as a nest site by Canada geese. At the end of the pavement, the wide path climbs the side of the small valley. Fiberglass posts with arrows point the way of the trail. The forest here is a second-growth stand of the typical Piedmont hardwoods—oaks and hickories—with dogwoods, redbuds, and other shrubs growing underneath. The flowering trees put on a great show in the spring.

The trail crosses a service road and through a young pine thicket and into another drainage with more hardwood forest. In the bottom of the

Victoria Bryant State Park Trails

To Lavonia

PARK BDY.

GOLF COURSE

PARK BOUNDARY

Perimeter Trail

327

N

Fish Pond

Park Entrance

Pioneer Camp

Tent Trailer Camp

Office

Pioneer Camp

Rice Creek

Picnic Area

Fish Pond

Nature Trail

PARK BOUNDARY

To Franklin

Observation Platform

0   0.5
Miles

sharp valleys with intermittent streams are stands of switch cane. Erosion gullies, now healed, indicate past farming in the area. After crossing two or three low ridges, the trail passes the edge of an impressive stand of American holly and mountain laurel interspersed with switch cane. This evergreen area merges with the vegetation of Rice Creek, which is crossed on a sturdy footbridge. In early spring look for silverbell trees blooming here. The trail follows downstream to the corner of the park property line. This is a fine birding area along with most of the trail, which passes through a wide variety of habitat. Many spring wildflowers grow along the trail.

A barbed wire fence marks the boundary between the park and private land. *Do not hike on the private property.*

The path winds uphill to an open wildlife planting with an elevated observation platform on the crest of the hill. This is a great place to sit quietly and watch for birds and mammals, especially in early morning or at evening twilight. Deer and turkeys use the clearing along with other wildlife. Watch for deer and turkey tracks, which are common in the soft ground along the trail.

From the observation platform the trail goes through recently disturbed areas. In one of the swales there is an especially large patch of groundpine or clubmoss, a fern relative. The barbed wire property line is again evident near the trail before it reaches the dam of a picturesque fish pond, another good wildlife watching area.

From the pond back to the trailhead, the way is marked with footprints painted in the pavement. Use the platform stepway down to the level of Rice Creek, cross the creek on a footbridge, and follow the footprints to the end.

This trail is designed to serve both bicycles and walking. The bike use does not seem to detract from the pleasant 2.5-mile walk.

Broad River Trail

To Check Station and 123

Dicks Creek

Middle Fork Broad River

P

87

Sellers Road

N

0   0.5
Miles

To Nancy Town Lake

Cemetery †

92

Red Root Road

P

41 Broad River Trail–Lake Russell Wildlife Management Area

General description: One of the most pleasant four-mile trails in north Georgia.

General location: In the northeast corner of the state and the Lake Russell Wildlife Management Area, which is a part of the Chattahoochee National Forest in the Chattooga Ranger District.

Maps: Chattahoochee National Forest Map; Ayersville USGS quad.

Degree of difficulty: Easy to moderate.

Length: One way 4.2 miles.

Elevations: The elevation at the Broad River trailhead is 1,100 feet and drops to 900 feet at Broad River Bridge.

Special attractions: Mature forests and mountain laurel thickets along cascading mountain streams with wildflowers, wildlife, good birding and a variety of habitat types. Trout fishing, camping, and hunting are part of the management area activities.

Best season: Spring, summer, and fall for wildflowers and leaf color. It is just as pleasant in winter; however, you should stay on the trail and wear blaze orange cap and/or jacket during November through mid-January when managed deer hunts are in progress.

For more information: U.S. Forest Service, Chattooga Ranger District, 200 Highway 197 N, Clarkesville, GA 30523; (706)754-6221. Georgia Wildlife Resources Division, Game Management, 2150 Dawsonville Highway, Gainesville, GA 30501; (770)535-5700.

Finding the trailhead: The entrance to Lake Russell Wildlife Management Area is about six miles southwest of Toccoa on U.S. Highway 123. From Cornelia it is eleven miles on US 123 to the Ayersville Road. The Ayersville Road is at the large Milliken Plant sign. Go one mile on the Ayersville Road to Forest Road 87, an unpaved road. On the USGS quad maps, FR 87 is named Guard Camp Road. A small sign here points to the "Checking Station." On FR 87, go about 2.9 miles to Dicks Creek, you pass the Checking Station building on the way. The trailhead is about 100 yards beyond Dicks Creek bridge on the right or west side of the road. A large sign, several yards off the road, gives a short history of the Broad River Trail.

The hike: The Broad River Trail follows beautiful cascading Dicks Creek and Broad River. To add variety, the one-way path follows the contour, leaving the stream at times for short distances and winds through mature forests, in dense mountain laurel thickets and back to the stream again. It ends at the bridge crossing near Farmer Bottoms.

The trail can be hiked in either direction. It is easier to hike down from Dicks Creek than up from Farmer Bottoms. By road it is 2.9 miles between the trailheads. Parking at the Broad River Bridge and walking the road up to Dicks Creek and the trail back would make a pleasant loop of about seven miles. The unpaved roads in the Wildlife Management Area are nice quiet places to walk and offer good opportunities to see more wildlife.

This forthright hike is marked with blue blazes and begins about 100 yards from the bridge across Dicks Creek on Guard Camp Road (FR 87). A large sign, several yards from the road, describes when the Civilian Conservation Corps built the trail in 1939 and reopened by the Youth Conservation Corps in 1980. Although the sign says the trail is 3.8 miles long, it is more accurately 4.2 miles. This difference is relatively unimportant since the trail is not strenuous and there are no side trails or old roadbeds that might be confusing.

The first part of the path where the sign is located goes through a briar patch with several young American holly trees scattered about. It enters the woods with typical hardwoods, yellow-poplar, birch, white oak, and others along with tall pines. In early spring, the dog-toothed violets or trout lilies are abundant all along the trail near the creek. You then enter the first of several mountain laurel thickets that will bloom in pinkish-white clusters of flowers in late April and May. Red buckeyes are part of the shrubbery growing under the larger trees and bloom with colorful spikes of red flowers in early spring. These flowers are favorites of early migrating hummingbirds.

Broad River Trail goes between water and rocks because of the steep hillside.

At times the trail follows along very steep-sided slopes with the noise of the rushing water below. Cascades can be heard more than seen in many places. Along these steep slopes, the laurel and other vegetation is so thick it is difficult to see or get to the streamside to photograph the attractive scenes. In other places, the path comes right down to the water's edge. At about a half mile from the trailhead there is a flat area with white pines, hemlocks, and yellow-poplars that would make a nice lunch stop or campsite. Just below this area is the first of the more spectacular cascades on Dicks Creek. The trail leads under several picturesque rock overhangs.

Broad River is reached in about one mile and is recognized by the large open field on the opposite side of the river called Brown Bottoms. At this point, Dicks Creek seems to be larger than Broad River. The path comes right down to the bank of the river and goes through a flat alluvial area for a short distance. Dog-hobble or fetter-bush grows along the bank. In the moist coves, the mayapples erupt in spring with their broad pair of green leaves and single white flower in the crotch. In winter, the green, single leaf of the crane-fly orchid lies on top of dead leaves of the forest floor. The orchid leaves disappear in summer to be replaced by the single stalk of brownish-yellow flowers. Blood-root and yellow and blue violets are very evident along with the heart leaf or wild ginger.

The trail leaves the stream course in places to follow a contour into a deep cove. These deviations into a more open park-like forest add greatly

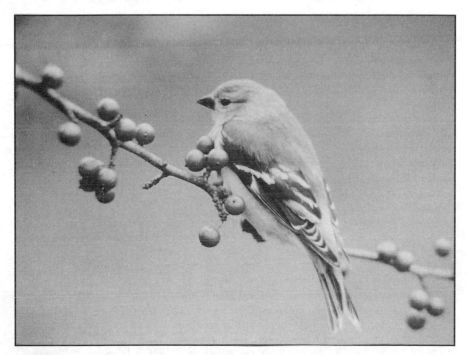

Goldfinch.

to the variety and interest along the path. In places, where intermittent water courses must be crossed footbridges or logs have been installed. In other places, rock ledges are kept moist with spring seeps that support liverworts, ferns, mosses, and flowers such as the saxifrage.

Near the end of the trail, the path comes right to the edge of the river and passes under a low rock ledge making it necessary to rock-hop and step on the sandy bank until you climb back up the bank and away from the water. If the river is up a few feet at this point, it is necessary to climb through the mountain laurel thicket above the rock ledge. From here to the trail's end, you hike through a flat area growing thick with blackberry canes and other tall plants. An unusual number of young American holly trees are growing here, just like at the Dicks Creek trailhead. When you cross Kimbell Creek on a footbridge, you are at the end of the hike and at Forest Road 87, a few yards above the vehicle bridge across Broad River at Farmer Bottoms. Road names here can be confusing. USGS quad maps call this section of the road Sellers Road. Wildlife Management Area map refers to it as Guard Camp Road. This is the intersection of Forest Roads 92 and 87.

42 Oconee River Recreation Area Trails

Overview: The Scull Shoals area of the Oconee River is steeped in history going back to the late 1700s and earlier American Indian mounds. The trails are on and along the river floodplain and the hardwood forests associated with this fertile land. Remains of old buildings and Indian mounds and the relatively unchanged river make this a fine day visit and hiking area.

General description: Slightly more than two miles of easy trails wander through this historic area.

General location: The Oconee River Recreation Area is twelve miles north of Greensboro on Georgia Highway 15 on the southeast side of the Oconee River Bridge.

Maps: Oconee National Forest Map and Trail Guide to the Chattahoochee and Oconee National Forests; Barnett Shoals, Maxeys and Greshamville USGS quads.

Degree of difficulty: Easy.

Length: Scull Shoals Trail is one mile; Boarding House Trail is 0.3 mile; and Indian Mound Trail is about one mile. All are one-way trails.

Elevations: The Oconee River elevation is about 475 feet in the vicinity of Scull Shoals. The elevation of the trails varies only slightly.

Special attractions: History of the Scull Shoals area, wildlife watching, birding, fishing, and hunting are all available. The Oconee River floodplain is a typical Piedmont bottomland hardwood area rich in wildflowers and tree species.

Best season: Year-round hiking is available. However, the Oconee River may be out of its banks during high rainfall periods in winter and early spring. All trails may be partially under water during this time.

Oconee River Recreation Area Trails

For more information: U.S. Forest Service, Oconee Ranger District, 1199 Madison Road, Eatonton, GA 31024; (706)485-7110.

Finding the trailheads: The trailhead for the Scull Shoals Trail is at the boat launching ramp in the recreation area.

For the Boarding House and Indian Mound trails follow GA 15 to Macedonia Road, which is a paved road one mile south of the bridge. Go two miles and turn left on Forest Road 1234, an unpaved road. Travel two miles to Forest Road 1231. Bear left and go one mile to Scull Shoals Historic Area. The trailhead for the Boarding House Trail is at the parking area near the information sign. For the Indian Mound Trail follow FR 1234 from Macedonia Road for two miles to FR 1231 and go 0.5 mile to Forest Road 1231A. Turn right on FR 1231A and go 0.5 mile to the end of the road and parking area. The trailhead is at the parking area marked by a brown fiberglass post marked Trail 102.

The hikes: The **Scull Shoals** path follows the river upstream crossing several small tributaries with steep banks. Water oak, hackberry, sweet gum, red maple, and yellow-poplar are some of the most obvious trees along the trail. Mountain laurel on the moist north-facing banks bloom in late April and many other spring flowers add much color and interest to this easy walk that ends at the historic site of the Skull Shoals Village. The origin of the name Scull Shoals has been lost in antiquity. It may be from Indian skulls washed up after floods or from a family named Scull. It was first recorded in 1788 by Elijah Clarke as "Schel-sholes."

The trails here along the Oconee River are excellent for birding, with both river and upland forest habitat.

Boarding House Trail is a short walk through flat pine woods to the remains of the boarding house. Interpretive signs explain some of the history and identify the building remains. An excellent brochure, available from the Oconee District Ranger's office, provides a good historical account of Scull Shoals Village and the industry that took place here from the late 1700s to the early 1900s. William Bartram, for whom the Bartram Trail is named, may have been one of the first white visitors at this site in 1773. The settlement began in 1784. Indians ceded the area to white settlers about 1790.

Indian Mound Trail begins at the parking area at the end of FR 1231A. The marker post bears Trail 102 and the white blazed path enters a wooded area with a clearing on the left. This trail passes through a fine example of Piedmont floodplain forest. Instead of following close to the river, this trail follows along the base of the low ridges on the east side of Oconee River. Very large water oaks and loblolly pines are along the trail. Red maples, sweet gums, white and red oaks, hackberries, and yellow-poplars are here. A patch of groundpine or clubmoss, a fern relative, grows by the path. A number of wildflowers, including the flame azalea, bloom here in spring. The first of the two Indian mounds is at about 0.6 mile on the trail. A large plaque on a loblolly pine warns visitors not to take artifacts of any kind

Ruins of building at Scull Shoals Village, Oconee River Recreation Area.

from the site. These regulations are designed to protect the archaeological sites on public lands. The mound is about twenty-five feet above the floodplain and completely covered over with trees, indicating that the mound has not been disturbed for many years. The mound site is marked by light blue blazes and rings on selected trees around the site. The second mound is about a quarter mile farther along the white blazed trail. Here the trail passes through a splendid floodplain forest of very large trees. Some of the large loblolly pines have been killed by Southern pine beetles and have become homes for many cavity nesting birds using the hole made by several species of woodpeckers, including the pileated woodpecker.

Twin Bridges Trail

43   Twin Bridges Trail

General description: About two miles in length, Twin Bridges Trail is a fine morning or afternoon hike for campers or day-use visitors.
General location: The trail is in the Oconee National Forest at the Lake Sinclair Recreation Area about fifteen miles east from Monticello on Georgia Highway 212 to Twin Bridges Road.
Maps: Oconee National Forest Map; Resseaus Crossroads USGS quad.
Degree of difficulty: Easy.
Length: 1.8 miles one way.
Elevations: The general elevation of the trail on the Piedmont Plateau is about 550 feet. The low ridges and valleys do not vary more than about 50 feet.
Special attractions: Small streams, lakeshore, wildflowers, and wildlife. Fishing and boating is popular on Lake Sinclair. The recreation area has a well-managed campground. A fine birding area with a variety of wildlife and plants. Family camping is especially pleasant here.
Best season: Although the Lake Sinclair Recreation Area and campground is closed from Labor Day to Memorial Day the trail is open all year. The trail is easily walked any time of the year.
For more information: U.S. Forest Service, Oconee Ranger District, 1199 Madison Road, Eatonton, GA 31024; (706)485-7110.

Finding the trailhead: Go north on Twin Bridges Road 1.1 miles to the recreation area entrance. The trailhead is in the Camp Loop B area about one quarter mile from the entrance.

The hike: The trail winds through a gently rolling countryside of low ridges and valleys in a mixed hardwood-pine forest on the shore of Lake Sinclair. The trail is marked number 119 and drops down a gentle slope from Camp Loop B to a small creek. The blaze is white. The path turns up the creek to the first of two footbridges a short distance from the trailhead. In March, a large patch of small yellow lilies, called dog-tooth-violets, are in full bloom. Beaver cuttings on many of the larger trees are along the stream bank. After crossing the bridges the trail goes through a switch cane thicket, through a stand of young pines, and into a nice hardwood forest. Low rolling ridges and valleys and several small brooks give the trail an interesting character. Lake Sinclair, a Georgia Power Company reservoir, is in sight most of the hike.

There are about twenty interpretive stations along the trail marked by low brown painted, numbered posts. The erosion gullies that you cross are evidence of intensive subsistence farming about fifty years ago. These gullies have healed with mosses, ferns and trees. A short footbridge crosses one of these gullies near a mature yellow-poplar tree that has a large cavity at the base filled with dirt and decayed vegetation. A wild ginger plant has become established in the rich soil. There are a number of large trees with cavities that are used by a wide variety of small mammals, birds, and other animals. Because of the variety of small openings in the forest and

Twin Bridges Trail through a small cane brake.

the adjacent lake, this trail is an exceptionally productive birding area. Also, there are many wildflowers in the moist coves. One of the more interesting is the cranefly orchid that is evident by green three-inch leaves in midwinter. The leaves disappear and in summer the one-foot tall stalk of greenish-yellow blossoms appear. During spring the Piedmont azaleas with pink flowers on four- or five-foot high bushes are in full bloom.

Lake Sinclair is a good fishing lake for largemouth bass and crappie. Several short spur paths worn by fishermen lead away from the blazed trail down to the lakeshore. The tree cover extends right to the edge of the water making a nice shady place to fish from the bank.

The trail ends at a Forest Service primitive campground that is reached by an unpaved road, which leads to Twin Bridges Road about two miles from the entrance to Lake Sinclair Recreation Area. Because of the campground at both ends of the trail, this is one of the only one-way trails with a toilet at both ends. The one at the primitive campground is a privy. The one at the trailhead is a regular campground comfort station.

44 Kinnard Creek Trail

General description: An easy to moderate hike that winds about four miles through abandoned farmland and creek bottoms.

General location: On the Oconee Ranger District of the Oconee National Forest.

Maps: Oconee National Forest Map and Trail Guide Chattahoochee and Oconee National Forests; Lloyd Shoals Dam USGS quad.

Degree of difficulty: Easy to moderate.

Length: 4.1 miles one way.

Elevations: The highest point is about 670 feet and drops to about 540 feet at the south end.

Special attractions: A fine old stand of loblolly pines. Wildlife viewing—wild turkeys, deer, beavers, squirrels, and many songbirds. Wildflowers are abundant in spring and through the summer and fall.

Best season: Year-round; during the deer season from mid-October until January it is strongly recommended that the hikers wear blaze orange coat or vest and cap, and to stay on the trail and hike during midday from about 9 A.M. until about 3:30 P.M. Hunters are more apt to be hunting from daylight until mid-morning and from mid-afternoon until dark. This also is true for the spring turkey season from March through mid-May.

For more information: Oconee National Forest, Oconee Ranger District, 1199 Madison Road, Eatonton, GA 31024; (706)485-7110.

Finding the trailhead: From Monticello, go west 6.3 miles on Georgia Highway 16 to Concord Church Road. Turn south or left and go 1.6 miles to the U.S. Forest Service's Concord Hunt Camp.

The hike: Traveling through abandoned farms from the mid-1930s, this trail stays in the Oconee National Forest that is a patchwork of land acquisition. It passes through recent loblolly pine plantations and much older, but typical Piedmont hardwood stands, especially in the creek bottoms. This is both a walking and horseback trail. Forest Service primitive campgrounds at both ends of the trail with ample parking makes it easy to hike from either end. This is important because two creeks without bridges must be crossed to hike all the way through. There are no stepping stones in these Piedmont streams and they are steep sided. The only way across without wading in sandy mud is to find a tree that has fallen across the creek. Several smaller brooks are easy to cross on exposed rock or small enough to step across. The trail is still very interesting to hike to the creeks and return. The section between the creeks is accessible from an unnamed county road.

The trail begins about 100 yards down Concord Church Road from Concord Hunt Camp at a fiberglass post with Trail 108. After crossing a vehicle barrier, it follows a rutted jeep road through a cleared field to the edge of the Oconee Forest boundary. From here, the white blazed path goes along a young pine plantation and into a mixed hardwood-pine forest.

Kinnard Creek Trail

Concord Church Road

To
Monticello
and
(16)

Concord
Camp

To
Ocmulgee
River

FOREST BOUNDARY

Kinnard Creek

Clay Road

Wise Creek

FOREST BOUNDARY

N

1017

Wise Cr.

Wise Cr.

Rush Creek
Camp

1013

Horse
Camp

FOREST BOUNDARY

To
(83)

0   1

Miles

Erosion gullies are evidence of past farms that were abandoned during the 1930s. This serious erosion of past years has healed with trees, ferns and other plants growing in the scars.

Cross several small brooks through low ridges and valleys into a lush bottom with ferns, wildflowers, and large hardwood trees. Passing along a steep-sided ridge, views extend out over a wet bottomland area with beaver dams. This is a fine birding and wildlife watching area.

The trail drops down beside the small brook, tributary to Kinnard Creek, and runs into a section of the trail that was obliterated by a tornado several years ago. Follow the white blazes to Kinnard Creek, about two miles.

From the south trailhead at Horse Camp on Forest Road 1013, the trail passes alternately through pine and hardwood timber. It goes past Friendship Campground and to Wise Creek where it meets the north end of Wise Creek Trail. There are several small clearings, and the path follows a jeep road at times. Once Wise Creek is reached, crossing is difficult. There is no bridge, the banks are steep and the creek is about thrity to forty feet wide.

Another unnamed county road crosses the trail near its middle between Kinnard and Wise creeks. Space for parking two or three vehicles and trail marker posts with Trail 108 are here. The Forest Service boundary is very narrow here. Look carefully for the blazes. It passes close to the private property to the east and goes through briar patches and young pine plantings to the Wise Creek floodplain.

Walking to the Kinnard Creek side the path is through a more mature pine-hardwood forest and past rock outcrops to the Kinnard Creek floodplain. Beaver cutting activity is clearly visible along the creek. Crossing is virtually impossible without getting wet and muddy. This area along the trail, however, is very attractive and supports a good population of wildflowers. It is another area worth watching for wildlife.

45 Ocmulgee River Trail

General description: About three miles of easy walking through the bottomland hardwoods and pines of the Ocmulgee River.
General location: West of Monticello thirteen miles on Georgia Highway 83, or about three quarters of a mile east of the Ocmulgee River bridge on GA 83.
Maps: Oconee National Forest map and Trail Guide to the Chattahoochee-Oconee National Forests; Berner USGS quad.
Degree of difficulty: Easy.
Length: 2.8 miles one way.
Elevations: About 400 to 450 feet.
Special attractions: Explores the river bank of the historically important Ocmulgee River. Spring wildflowers, birding, wildlife watching, camping, fishing, small and big game hunting in season are all available.

Ocmulgee River Trail

To Wise Creek Trail
(about 3 miles)

FOREST BOUNDARY

To
Monticello

Ocmulgee River

Ⓟ Ocmulgee
Flat
▲ Camp

1099

83

Ⓟ

To
23

N

0   1

Miles

Best season: Year-round, with spring and fall as the best bets for flowers, migrating birds, leaf color, and weather.

For more information: U.S. Forest Service, Oconee Ranger District, 1199 Madison Road, Eatonton, GA 31024; (706)485-7110.

Finding the trailhead: Two access points for this trail give the hiker the choice of walking from the Forest Service's Ocmulgee Flats Hunt Camp on Forest Road 1099 or from the southern trailhead on GA 83. FR 1099 lies to the north of GA 83. The trailhead is on GA 93, but there is very limited parking at this point. The hunt camp on FR 1099 has ample, and relatively safe, parking at the unattended hunt camp. At each trailhead, fiberglass posts bear the number 118 below the hiker figure.

The hike: Horseback riding on this trail is most popular. The trail is marked with white blazes, and the river is in sight throughout most of the route. From the hunt camp there, is a short quarter-mile trail that intercepts the river trail about in the middle. If the turn to the right upstream is taken it is about 1.3 miles to footbridge across a small creek. After crossing the bridge, the path will connect with the Wise Creek Trail in about three miles. If you take the trail downstream, it is 1.2 miles from GA 83.

What this trail lacks in grand scenery, it makes up in interesting wildlife and wildflower habitat. Deer, squirrels, raccoon, and other mammals are evident from the many tracks left in the soft sandy and silty loam of the riverbank. Wild turkeys, wood ducks, hooded mergansers, woodcocks,

Beaver cutting of a large sweetgum tree on the Ocmulgee River Trail.

quail, and other game birds may be seen or heard. A good variety of song birds use the area as residents and during the spring and fall migrations. Beavers, minks, muskrats, and even an otter may be seen along the river's edge with turtles sunning on the logs over the water.

The Ocmulgee River will overflow its banks during flood conditions. The trail may be inundated by as much as three or four feet. The flood water recedes rapidly and the pathway is open again.

The hillsides above the floodplain are excellent areas to explore during the spring for wildflowers. Dogtooth violets, also called trout-lily, grow right on the floodplain as early as late February and early March. Dogwood and redbud trees bloom in abundance in late March and April, about the same time that the turkeys begin to gobble in early morning and the chuck-wills-widows return from their southern winter home and can be heard calling at night.

The Forest Service personnel have plans for much more trail development along the Ocmulgee River. Eventually walking trails are planned to extend from Georgia Highway 16 meandering down to Georgia Highway 83. If this is completed, there will be perhaps twenty or more miles of hiking trails in this interesting Piedmont area.

46 Wise Creek Trail

General description: Like the Ocmulgee River Trail, this footpath goes through pine woods, hardwood bottoms along the river and then up low ridges through mixed pine and hardwoods.
General location: On the Ocmulgee River southwest of Monticello off Georgia Highway 83.
Maps: U.S. Forest Service's Oconee National Forest Map; Trail Guide to the Chattahoochee-Oconee National Forests; Berner USGS quad.
Degree of difficulty: Easy.
Length: 2.5 miles one way.
Elevations: Between 400 and 450 feet.
Special attractions: Fine views of the cascades on the Ocmulgee River, variety of wildflowers, wildlife, excellent birding, camping, fishing, and hunting.
Best season: This is a year-round trail; however, spring and fall are best for wildflowers, fishing, leaf color, and weather.
For more information: U.S. Forest Service, Oconee Ranger District, 1199 Madison Road, Eatonton, GA 31024; (706)485-7110.

Finding the trailhead: At about 6.5 miles from Monticello turn right on Clay Road and go 2.5 miles to McElheney's Crossroads. Turn left on a gravel road and go 1.2 miles and turn right. Go about 0.1 mile and turn left on Forest Road 1019. Stay on this road for 1.8 mile to Forest Road 1098. Follow FR 1098 for 1.3 miles to the Wise Creek Hunt Camp, which is on the bank of Ocmulgee River. The trailhead is at the hunt camp.

Wise Creek Trail

Forty-acre Island

Wise Creek

POWER LINE

1008

1019

To
McElheneys
Crossroads

Ocmulgee River

FOREST BOUNDARY

Long Branch

To 83

N

0   1
Miles

The hike: Beginning at a very scenic place on the Ocmulgee River the trail can be hiked upstream past the beautiful cascades above Forty Acre Island and following the east bank of Wise Creek where it joins Kinnard Creek Trail in a remote section of the forest. The southern section, the most easily hiked in all weather, leaves the Wise Creek Hunt Camp at the fiberglass post with the hiker figure and number 107, the Forest Service's designation for the trail. Although this trail is not designated as a horseback trail, horseback use of the trail is encouraged by the Forest Service, but it has not detracted from the use as a walking trail.

The path follows down the Ocmulgee River for about three quarters of a mile. The forest along the river is typical hardwood bottom trees, water oak, sycamore, hackberry, maple, ironwood and others, with a few large loblolly pines. In very early spring look for the small yellow lilies called dogtooth violets blooming on the river floodplain. Among the boulders, in wet areas, hepatica's bluish-white blossoms will be breaking through the leaf litter as early as February. The path leaves the riverbank and climbs into the pine woods with dogwoods and redbud trees blooming from mid-March into April. The trail winds through the upland area past two very small ponds behind earth dams to catch water for wildlife. The trail joins a jeep road and passes through a thick stand of small loblolly pines and onto a wider, gated service road before reaching the southern end at a gravel road. Here there is a small off-road parking area and the Forest Service trail-marker post. The road at the end of the trail leads out to GA 83 by Mount Olive Church, a distance of about five miles. The road distance between the ends of the trail is 2.8 miles.

This trail follows through two rectangular Forest Service areas that touch each other only at corners. This makes private land very close to the trail at two points. Be respectful of private property and stay on the marked trail, which is only on Forest Service land.

47 Red Top Mountain State Park Trails

Overview: Less than an hour from downtown Atlanta, this state park has about nine miles of excellent trails. They range from a 0.75-mile trail accessible to wheelchairs to a 5.5-mile trail that is a more challenging hike. Situated in the hilly section of the Piedmont, there is a variety of pine-hardwood forests with an abundant white-tailed deer herd, and other wildlife easily and frequently seen.
General description: Five trails with nearly ten miles of easy to moderate hiking through beautiful forests.
General location: North of Atlanta about thirty miles on Interstate 75.
Maps: The park office has a page-size map of the trails; Allatoona Dam USGS quad.

Red Top Mountain State Park Trails

Degree of difficulty: Easy to moderate.

Length: The paved Lake Side Trail is 0.75 mile; the Sweet Gum Nature Trail is 0.6 mile; the Visitor Center/Lodge Trail is one mile; the Campground Trail is one mile; and the Homestead Loop Trail is 5.5 miles.

Elevations: The Allatoona Lake elevation at full pool is 840 feet. The trails vary above this to near the top of Red Top Mountain at 1,100 feet.

Special attractions: Beautiful views of Allatoona Lake, abundant deer population, squirrels, wild turkeys, and other wildlife; fishing; fine lodge, restaurant, and campground; better than average birding, wildflowers, and forest make this a fascinating day-hike area.

Best season: Year-round. Winter hiking is especially pleasant since none of the trails are in situations that would make them to difficult to hike with a light snow. As with all areas at this latitude, spring and fall provide the best animal, wildflower, and leaf color viewing opportunities.

For more information: Red Top Mountain State Park and Lodge, 781 Red Top Mountain Road SE, Cartersville, GA 30120; Park office (770)975-4226; Lodge (770)975-4222.

Finding the trailheads: Leave I-75 to the east at Exit 123 on Red Top Mountain Road for about one mile. The trailhead for all trails except the paved Lake Side Trail is at the visitor center. Trailhead for the Lake Side Trail is at the conference center.

The hikes: The **Lake Side Trail** is a loop that begins at the conference center. It is completely barrier free and wheelchair accessible; however, it is just as interesting for any hikers interested in wildlife. Bird feeders, bird and mammal nest boxes are placed at appropriate places. White-tailed deer come right to the trail and are well conditioned to people and easily seen if one remains quiet. Many birds, including hummingbirds and a variety of songbirds are attracted to the area. Lake Allatoona is visible throughout most of the walk.

Two cross paths make it possible to return to the trailhead without making the entire loop or backtracking. A small field, mixed hardwood-pine forest and lake edge give the walk an interesting mixture of habitat types.

The **Visitor Center Lodge Trail** is a red blazed trail that begins either at the visitor center or Lodge parking lot. It is an undulating path about one mile one way and takes you through stands of almost pure loblolly pine and into a forest of large hardwood trees and beside and across a small stream. Hiking from the lodge a blue blaze trail turns off to the right, picks up the yellow blazed trail and continues for a short distance to the road leading back to the lodge. Two footbridge crossings add charm to the forest walk. The Sweet Gum Nature Trail is a loop off this trail.

The **Sweet Gum Nature Trail** is marked with orange blazes. It makes a loop through a dry ridge of white chestnuts and red oaks with huckleberries, dogwoods, and other shrubs growing underneath. This is a good place to look for spring wildflowers. It overlooks a small quiet valley where two observation decks have been constructed to sit and watch for wildlife. In 0.5 mile you are back to the red blazed trail and can continue on to the visitor center.

Rest benches on paved trail at Red Top Mountain State Park.

The trailhead for the **Homestead Loop Trail** is beside the visitor center building. This 5.5 mile yellow blazed trail is the most varied and interesting of all the trails. It leads you through a wide variety of habitats. Mile-marker posts have been placed along the path, a very handy reference for the beginning hiker. At about two miles you cross the paved road. To the right is the lodge. The trail divides across the road. The loop starts there and goes around counterclockwise, or to the right. The path drops down to one of the arms of Lake Allatoona where the trail crosses higher ridges and provides scenic views of the lake. At about 2.5 miles from the road a blue blazed trail leads down to a point of land overlooking the lake. From a picturesque spot there it is possible see Allatoona Dam to the west. It is a nice place to be just before sunset. Return to the yellow blazed trail and pass near one of the old home sites that was occupied when iron ore and clay was mined from Red Top Mountain. Small clearings in the forest have been planted with grasses for wildlife, especially deer and turkeys.

You can expect to see deer on any of the trails, while the wild turkey is much more wary and difficult to see. Squirrels and many species of birds are sure to be seen.

The path loops back again to the paved road where it is possible to retrace your steps back to the visitor center or walk down the trail to the lodge and return by the red blazed Lodge Trail to the visitor center.

A very interesting **Campground Trail** leads from the campground to the visitor center. It passes an opening in the woods where deer are most apt to be seen. It crosses three bridges and passes the stone ruins of an old homestead. The trail is one way and can be walked from the visitor center or from the campground. The trailhead in the campground is conveniently located near comfort station 2.

48 Fort Yargo State Park Trails

Overview: Although located inside the city limits of Winder, Fort Yargo is a very rural area offering a wide variety of forests, fields, and aquatic environments. The trails lead to the historic blockhouse built in 1792 and through woodlands and open areas around 260-acre Yargo Lake. The Will-A-Way Recreation Area is designed for visitors with disabilities. It includes a special barrier-free trail.
General description: Three easy trails total about three miles.
General location: One mile south of Winder on Georgia Highway 81 in Barrow County.
Maps: A trail map is available in the park office; Winder South USGS quad.
Degree of difficulty: Easy.
Length: The Blockhouse Trail is 0.6 mile one way, the Lake Trail is 2.2 miles one way, and the Will-A-Way trail is 0.4 mile one way. Plans are underway to complete another three miles of the Lake Trail making it a five-mile loop.
Elevations: The trail follows close to lake level, only exceeding it in a few places by thirty or forty feet.
Special attractions: The well preserved historic 1792-era block house, Will-A-Way Recreation Area, fishing, wildflowers, and wildlife watching. An excellent birding area because of the diverse habitat.
Best season: Year-round.
For more information: Fort Yargo State Park, P.O.Box 764, Winder, GA 30680; (770)867-3489.

Fort Yargo State Park Trails

Finding the trailheads: The trailhead is at the parking area for Area B at the end of the footbridge. It is reached by entering the park through the Area B entrance off Georgia Highway 81. The trails begin at the north end of the attractive, long footbridge across the Marbury Creek arm of Yargo Lake. This trailhead serves both the Blockhouse and the Lake trails. The trailhead for Will-A-Way is a short distance from the park office.

The hikes: At the south end of the bridge, the **Blockhouse Trail** to the right leads through a thirty-year-old loblolly pine stand with undergrowth of young yellow-poplar, sassafras, sweet gum, oak, and other hardwood species. It is an easy six-foot wide path. It opens into a powerline right-of-way to the clearing with the fenced yard of the blockhouse. Originally, there were four log stockades or blockhouses built of hand-hewn logs in 1792 by early settlers, the Humphreys brothers, for protection against Creek and Cherokee Indians. The remaining log house is well preserved and photogenic. It is available for historic programs. This trail is 0.6 mile one way.

Returning to the south end of the bridge, the **Lake Trail** leads to the left and goes through remaining stands of pine and hardwoods and the clearing under two powerlines. The infamous kudzu has become well established in the large open field through which the footway passes. This is along the shore of the lake and affords excellent views of the lake and aquatic birds and mammals using it. Deer, rabbits, raccoons, and other small mammals use this area extensively. Persimmon, sassafras, sweet gum, wild plum, sumac, and other sun-loving trees and shrubs have invaded the edges of the field and provide good cover and food for wildlife.

The path crosses a gas-line right-of-way, enters a wooded area and returns to cross the gas line again and through larger loblolly pines to the dam impounding Yargo Lake. The view of the lake from the dam is quite attractive with the reflected tall trees and sky. Leaving the dam, the trail

Footbridge across Marbury Creek arm of lake. Trailhead is here for Blockhouse and Lake trails on the south side of the lake.

follows close to the lake to the parking area and campground. Following the winding roadway back to the trailhead is another 2.5 miles. Eventually the trail will continue through the wooded area on the east side of the lake to make a five-mile loop trail.

The **Will-A-Way Nature Trail** is a 0.5-mile paved trail, completely barrier free for either walking or riding in wheelchairs. It is a very flat walkway close to the lake edge, giving an excellent view of a small marsh and open water. A flat bridge crosses a narrow arm of the lake, and the path loops around a gazebo in a peaceful hardwood cove of maple, sweet gum, hickory, and other trees.

The Will-A-Way Recreation Area was opened in 1971 to serve people with disabilities. It was the first recreation area of its kind to be opened in a state park in this country. Aside from the paved trail, visitors can fish from a bridge and watch birds, squirrels, deer, and other wildlife from numerous benches and other resting areas.

49 Richard B. Russell State Park Trails

Overview: Richard B. Russell State Park is situated on a peninsula of the Richard B. Russell Lake formed by Vans and Coldwater creeks. Several new trails are planned for the park, only two of which are completed at this writing.

General description: A short walking path connects the swimming area with the picnic area. The Blackwell Bridge Trail described below is a 2.2-mile loop.

General location: The park is located about nine miles northeast of Elberton. Take Georgia Highway 77 north from Elberton to Ruckersville Road and Russell State Park Road to the park entrance.

Maps: A trail map is available from the park office; Lowndesville USGS quad.

Degree of difficulty: Easy.

Length: The Blackwell Bridge Trail is 2.2 miles.

Elevations: The elevation varies no more than 100 feet throughout the loop trail.

Special attractions: Birding in spring and fall migrations; spring flowers and fall leaf color; fishing, swimming, and boating in the lake; and camping.

Best season: This trail can be hiked throughout the year; however, fall, winter, and spring are the best seasons for hiking and observing wildlife. Spring flowers and fall leaf color add to these times.

For more information: Richard B. Russell State Park, 2650 Russell State Park Road, Elberton, GA 30635; (706)213-2045.

Finding the trailhead: The trail begins at the corner of the beach parking area.

The hike: The **Blackwell Bridge Trail** begins with a paved path down to a footbridge and an information sign with map. The remainder of the trail is unpaved. The pathway follows around the coves and points of the lake

Richard B. Russell State Park Trails

To Park Entrance
and Ruckersville Rd.

Office

RUSSELL LAKE

Trail
to
beach

P

beach
area

Blackwell Bridge
Trail

Coldwater Creek

Blackwell
Bridge

N

RUSSELL LAKE

0   0.5

Miles

Boat ramp

so that the lake is visible for much of the way. It is much more visible in winter with the leaves off. The trail is under a hardwood forest for most of the way so that even in summer the hike is mostly shaded. The principal trees are several species of oaks, maples, sycamores, sweet gums, black gums, yellow-poplars, and dogwoods; shrub vegetation includes highbush huckleberries, blueberries, and hawthorns. Spring flowers begin to show under the leafless trees in late February and continue until May. Bloodroots, trilliums, dwarf irises, and many others grow in the moist coves. Other common plants seen are Christmas ferns, spleenworts, and patches of the almost white pincushion moss and reindeer-moss, which is a lichen that has a wide geographical distribution from the arctic to north Florida.

The second-growth forest has become good habitat for white-tailed deer, gray and fox squirrels, opossums, raccoons, and other small mammals. It is also a fine birding area with many species of songbirds, hawks, owls, and crows. Near the lake coves you may see such water birds as egrets, herons, ducks, and geese.

Some rock outcrops are apparent along the trail revealing the granite for which Elbert County is world famous.

Less than halfway around the loop you come to the Blackwell Bridge. This structure is the last remaining steel bridge in Elbert County. It was constructed in 1917. A historical marker describes the bridge. Prior to impoundment of Russell Lake several American Indian sites were excavated. One known as Ruckers Bottom yielded artifacts such as clovis points, indicating American Indians using the area as much as 10,000 years ago.

The trail meanders from moist coves to well-drained ridges, giving you a good picture of the habitat of the unique eastern section of the Piedmont physiographic province. A periodic cicada brood emerged here in the late spring of 1998.

The pathway loops back to the starting point and the paved path to the parking area.

50 Bobby Brown State Park Trail

General description: The trail in this state park is about 2.2 miles long and is ideal for family hiking. It is a relatively easy trail with only a few short, steep sections.

Bobby Brown State Park is located on a forested peninsula formed by the Savannah and Broad rivers at the headwaters of Clarks Hill Reservoir. The tip of the peninsula is the site of the Colonial town of Petersburg, the third largest town in the state in 1790. The park is named for Robert T. Brown USN, who lost his life during World War II. Part of the trail follows the path William Bartram trod in 1791 while he was exploring the region for useful plants to be sent back to England for commercial purposes. (See Hike 86, Bartram Trail.) The Savannah River is the state

Bobby Brown State Park Trail

line between Georgia and South Carolina. Clarks Hill Lake is 78,000 acres, one of the largest manmade lakes east of the Mississippi.

General location: The park is located on a beautiful peninsula made by the Savannah and Broad rivers at the headwaters of Clarks Hill Reservoir about twenty-one miles southeast of Elberton off Georgia Highway 72. Follow Bobby Brown State Park Road to the park entrance.

Maps: A page-size map of the park and trail is available from the park office; Chennault USGS quad.

Degree of difficulty: Easy.

Length: 2.2 miles with a short loop at the outer end.

Elevations: The elevation of the reservoir at full pool is about 330 feet above sea level. The trail varies from lake level to about 100 feet above the lakeshore.

Special attractions: Excellent birding and other wildlife watching; spring flowers and fall leaf colors; history of the Colonial town of Petersburg; tent, RV, trailer, and primitive camping; fishing and boating.

Best season: Spring and fall are best; however, this trail can be hiked year-round. There are many winter days ideal for hiking.

For more information: Bobby Brown State Park, 2509 Bobby Brown State Park Road, Elberton, GA 30635; (706)213-2046.

Finding the trailhead: The trail can be entered from the day-use parking area near the swinging bridge and from the loop road past the camping area.

The hike: Leaving the parking area the trail drops down to the end of a small cove of Clarks Hill Reservoir and follows along a contour into the hardwood-pine forest so characteristic of this region of the Piedmont physiographic province. You go around another cove where you may see ducks,

A view of the 78,000-acre Clarks Hill Reservoir at Bobby Brown State Park.

herons and egrets, turtles, and other aquatic animals. Interpretive signs calling attention to wildlife and plants are along the trail. White-tailed deer, raccoons, opossums, gray and fox squirrels, and wild turkeys may be seen and heard along this trail.

All low and wet areas are crossed by well-made footbridges and the trail follows contours as it crosses the low ridges. In about a quarter mile you come to a park road that ends at the opposite side of the swinging bridge from the trailhead. Back into the woods again the path goes around another cove. The lake can be seen through the trees for most of the way. In winter, with the leaves off, the lake is very visible. In about a mile you come to an observation platform at the end of the peninsula. The lake is now around you on three sides. It is here that the information board tells about the colonial town of Petersburg and the Petersburg boat used to take people, cotton, and produce to Augusta during the last years of the 1790s and early 1800. After the Augusta Canal was built these boats off-loaded their wares onto canal boats for the final leg to Augusta (see Hike 67, Augusta Canal Trail).

If you watch carefully while sitting on the observation platform, you may see bald eagles, ospreys, ducks, geese, herons, and other birds associated with Clarks Hill Reservoir.

The trail now turns back in a loop toward the beginning. On this return path you come to a three-sided granite monument describing the site of Fort James. The fort was built in 1773. Also on this monument is a 1776 quote from the naturalist William Bartram describing the fort. The loop is closed going down to one of the longer footbridges crossed earlier. From here it is slightly less than a mile back to the trailhead.

51 Hard Labor Creek State Park Trails

General description: Two interlocking trails provide a pleasant two- or three-hour hike through mixed pine and hardwood forest.

General location: Approximately thirty-five miles east of Atlanta on Interstate 20.

Maps: Trail maps are available at the office/trading post; Rutledge North USGS quad.

Degree of difficulty: Easy to moderate. The moderate portions are only short grades along low ridges.

Length: The Brantley Nature Trail is about one mile and the Beaver Pond Trail is about one mile. With the connecting trails the total length is about 2.5 miles.

Elevations: The trail exceeds the lake elevation by no more than forty or fifty feet.

Special attractions: Spring wildflowers and forest bird migrations. Exceptionally large yellow-poplar and loblolly pine trees. Wildlife watching includes deer, turkeys, squirrels, waterfowl, beavers, and aquatic and other animals attracted by

Hard Labor Creek State Park Trails

Beaver Pond Trail

Beaver Pond

Lake Brantly

Campground

To Fairplay

Fairplay Road

P △

Brantly Nature Trail

Knox Chapel Road

P

Office Trading Post

18 Cottages

Hard Labor Creek

Golf Course

N

0   0.25
Miles

Fairplay Road

To Lake Rutledge

To Camp Daniel Morgan

Old Mill Road

Park Entrance

To Rutledge and 20

To Lake Rutledge

the two lakes and beaver pond.

Best season: Year-round with spring flowers and fall colors as highlights. Weather is more pleasant for hiking at these times.

For more information: Hard Labor Creek State Park, P.O.Box 247, Rutledge, GA 30663; (706)557-3001.

Finding the trailheads: To reach the park take I-20 Exit 49 to Rutledge and continue two miles on Fairplay Road to the park. Two trailheads permit access to the two loop trails from the campgrounds and the office/trading post. Both connected loop trails can be reached from the campgrounds at parking areas along the park road, and across the road from the office/trading post area. These access trails intercept the yellow-blazed Brantley Nature Trail and give access to the red-blazed Beaver Pond Trail. Another short trail connects the loops of Brantley Nature and Beaver Pond trails.

The hikes: The interconnecting trails pass through farmland abandoned in the mid-1930s. Bridges across small eroded ravines built by the Young Adult Conservation Corps during the late 1970s provide crossings over several of the eroded ravines and also offer a different view of the forest floor and vegetation and a nice place to quietly watch birds and other wildlife. Some have rest benches. The trails are such that both loops can be walked so the only repetition is the short access trail between the two loops.

The **Brantley Nature Trail** winds through the rolling ridges and terraces still visible from early farming practices and the mixed pine-hardwood forest with most of the trees less than sixty years old. Loblolly pine, several oak species including very large white oaks, hickories, dogwood, sourwood, yellow-poplar, and beech make up most of the forest species. The undergrowth plants include redbud, goose berries, muscadines, Christmas ferns, and many, many other species. A rare plant, the Piedmont barren strawberry, grows along this trail as well as elsewhere in the park. It is a low plant that spreads by subsurface stems like the cultivated strawberry. It has heart-shaped leaves with three to five lobes extending a few inches above the ground. The flowers, blooming from April to June, are five-petaled and bright yellow. The fruit occurs during the summer.

The **Beaver Pond Trail** is much like the Brantley Nature Trail except that it includes areas of older trees and the beaver pond. One very large yellow-poplar on the inside of the loop about twenty yards from the trail is well over five feet in diameter. Standing water in the beaver pond killed a number of trees that have become excellent trees for cavity nesting birds, including the colorful wood duck. The pond is almost completely covered with vegetation and is a favorite place for quiet birding where pileated and other species of woodpeckers, wading birds, flycatchers, and other forest birds are easily observed.

Both trails, hiked together or separately, are interesting and delightful any time of the year.

52 Watson Mill Bridge State Park Trails

General description: Watson Mill Bridge State Park is named for the 229-foot covered bridge, constructed in 1880, located at its original site across the South Fork Broad River, colloquially known as just South Fork River. The area is characteristic of the Piedmont Plateau physiographic province. The water power from the river at this scenic shoals was used to drive a grist mill for corn and wheat, a cotton gin, a wool factory, and a woodworking shop. In 1905 the hydroelectric powerhouse, raceway canal, and dam were added. The only remains of this era are the canal that was hewn from the granite wall on one side, and the powerhouse ruins and a levee on the other side. One of the trails follows along the top of this levee. The 1,005-acre park has a system of several trails that pass along the river and creeks and over the low ridges. These trails provide a good cross section of the numerous habitat types.

General location: The park is located in northeast Georgia on Watson Mill Park Road off Georgia Highway 22 three miles south of Comer. Comer is about thirteen miles east of Athens on Georgia Highway 72. The park lies in both Oglethorpe and Madison counties. The South Fork Broad River is the county line and flows through the park.

Maps: A small map of the park with the trails shown and a map of the horse trails are available at the park office; Carlton USGS quad.

Degree of difficulty: Each trail is easy.

Length: There is a total of 5.5 miles of trails dedicated to walking and about ten more miles of horse trails that are very satisfactory for hiking. Trails on the south side of the river collectively are about 3.5 miles. On the north side Beaver Creek Loop Trail is 1.5 miles. Ridge Loop Trail is 0.75 mile.

Elevations: The covered bridge is at about 520 feet above sea level. The change in elevation throughout all trails is no more than about 80 feet.

Special attractions: The historical mill, hydroelectric powerhouse ruins, and picturesque 1880 covered bridge; river rapids of the South Fork Broad River; excellent wildflower, bird, and wildlife watching; and picnicking, camping, fishing, and canoeing are all available.

Best season: These trails provide year-round hiking. There will be times of extremely high water when some trails are impassable and a few days in winter when the weather is too cold for hiking; otherwise they can be hiked all year. The best weather is in spring and fall.

For more information: Watson Mill Bridge State Park, 650 Watson Mill Road, Comer, GA 30629; (706)783-5349.

Finding the trailheads: The trailhead for the trails below the covered bridge and along the river is at the small concession building on the south side of the river. The Beaver Creek and Ridge loop trails can be hiked from either parking area on the north side of the covered bridge. The second parking area, a gravel loop off the main road, is the preferred trailhead for both trails.

Watson Mill Bridge State Park Trails

The hikes: From the concession building below the dam the path leads to a footbridge over the canal and is the access to the interconnected system of trails on the south side of the river. Here a large observation platform provides a view of the covered bridge and dam with water flowing over the grand shoals below the bridge.

The **Nature Trail** can be hiked down the canal levee to the powerhouse ruins. As you walk down the levee notice the exposed granite wall on the other side. During the warm months you may see frogs and toads as they hop into the canal waterway. At the end of the levee at the powerhouse you can go down a few steps to the section of the trail that follows up the river with excellent views of the river tumbling over boulders and down the wide, steep shoals. There are numerous ferns and flowers in the moist riverside habitat. Chain ferns, spleenworts, and Christmas ferns grow along with many spring flowers. Dog-hobble and mountain laurel are among the shrubs growing in the moist shade. At times the river may overflow parts of this trail. Large riverine trees, beeches, ironwoods, yellow-poplars, sycamores, water oaks, and others provide shade during the warm months. An exceptionally large loblolly pine is right beside the trail. In early spring, before the leaves are on the trees, the early wildflowers begin to show. Look for tracks of animals in the soft, sandy soil along the path. Tracks of deer, raccoons, squirrels, beavers, otters, and others may be seen. This path leads back to the steps up to the overlook platform.

At the powerhouse ruins you can cross the canal on the footbridge and return on the other side of the canal to the observation platform or you can continue on the **South Fork River Trail** downriver for about a half mile and up Big Clouds Creek for another half mile. This is a one way trail until, on the way back you choose to return by way of the Holly Tree Loop Nature Trail.

The trail is very clear and well used. Following it is easy. There are no blaze marks, only good signs at each intersection. As you go down the river you come to a large observation platform that provides an easy view of the river. If you should have time to sit here for a while you may see a wood duck, other water birds, beavers, turtles, and many kinds of birds using the trees. Some of the trees are beech, ash, hickory, yellow-poplar, sycamore, and water oak, all providing food and nesting sites for the animals. Along the way is a variety of flowering plants. Heart leaf and elephant's-foot are visible most of the year. Trilliums, Solomon's seals, false Solomon's-seals, trout lilies, hepaticas, windflowers, and many others will be blooming in spring.

A footbridge crosses a well-healed erosion gully that affords a nice view of an attractive cove of hardwood trees. Shortly the **Holly Tree Loop Nature Trail** turns off to the right. Here you can walk back to the covered bridge area or continue on to the pioneer campground III only about a hundred yards more.

A rather large and pretty creek, Big Clouds Creek, enters the river at the campground. The trail continues for one-half mile, one way, up this creek past pioneer campsite II and ends at pioneer camp I. The path passes

Watson Mill Bridge and mill dam.

under a piece of history in the form of an old, abandoned steel bridge. Only a few steel bridges of this type are left. The bridge is now covered with vines of muscadine, honeysuckle, and trumpet creeper and provides roosting and nesting places for birds. Big Clouds Creek flows through a typical bottomland hardwood forest, one of the most productive habitats for numbers of individuals and varieties of plants and animals. Thick patches of switch cane grow along the path. In places the creek changes character and tumbles over granite boulders. These are nice places to wade. In the quiet water above and below are good places to fish for small bass, sunfish, and catfish. There are many animal tracks left by deer, squirrels, beavers, wild turkeys, and other birds in the path.

If you choose to return by way of Holly Tree Loop Nature Trail you leave the riverbank habitat and climb up several feet into a drier soil type. Seedling and larger American holly, highbush huckleberries, dogwoods, azaleas, shortleaf and loblolly pines, oaks, and hickories are the dominant larger plants here. Christmas ferns and spleenworts occur with trilliums, windflowers, Solomon's seals, and false Solomon's seals, in the more moist sections.

In about a half mile the trail comes back to the trail near the powerhouse ruins, a short distance from the common trailhead.

The trailheads for both the **Beaver Creek Loop Trail** and **Ridge Loop Trail** are on the north side of the covered bridge. A sign marked "Parking, picnicking and hiking trails" directs you into the ample parking area. The trails begin near the entrance end of the parking area.

200

The Beaver Creek Loop Trail, a wide, well-constructed path, turns to the right and passes through a young pine and seedling hardwood area before it comes to the forks that make the loop. On the right of the trail just before the junction is a large patch of running groundpine, an interesting clubmoss seen most frequently in the mountains.

If you take the right fork the path follows beside a moist drainage area with some old beaver cuttings on some of the sweet gum trees. Flowers blooming here in early spring will be trilliums, windflowers, bloodroots, yellow and blue violets, and others. Later the heartleaf or wild ginger, elephant's-foot, and a variety of mid- and late-summer daisy-like flowers will be blooming. This is an excellent birding area. Walking quietly you can expect to see or hear deer, squirrels, and even wild turkeys.

After about a half mile you cross over a low ridge. In this better-drained area the pincushion moss and reindeer lichen grow under the highbush huckleberries, dogwoods, and a variety of pine and hardwood trees.

The trail drops down into a rich mixed pine-hardwood area with large yellow-poplars, sweet gums, maples, oaks, and hickories. This is the drainage area for Beaver Creek. The path follows this creek for the remainder of the walk. On the one side is the old beaver pond that is now grown over with grasses and cattails and on the other side is the drier forest with exposed granite boulders. Alders border the wet grassy area. Christmas ferns, New York ferns, and chain ferns are common along the way. The trail returns to the forks and continues back to the parking area.

The **Ridge Loop Trail** also begins here. It passes through a very nice picnic area and down to a footbridge across Beaver Creek. Here turn to the right and follow the creek for a short distance before climbing gently up and over the ridge. The habitat is similar to the ridge of the other trail only better drained. Second-growth hardwood trees include oaks, hickories, and black gums with an undergrowth of dogwoods, highbush huckleberries, and a few azaleas. It is very attractive in spring. The loop closes and joins the path back to the footbridge.

Both of these trails are very child friendly. Off-road strollers can be used without much problem, making this a great family hike with small children. The wide path and easy ups and downs make both loops good fitness trails.

If you should like to hike either trail from the parking and picnic area closer to the north end of the covered bridge you must cross over the creek on a footbridge and walk up the creek for a short distance to the next footbridge where a sign directs you to both trails.

Charlie Elliott Wildlife Center Trails

53 Charlie Elliott
Wildlife Center Trails

General description: Several short loop trails through a diverse wildlife management area. The Charlie Elliott Wildlife Center in Jasper and Newton counties is a 6,400-acre area that encompasses the Marben Public Fishing Area, the Clybel Wildlife Management Area, and the Charlie Elliott visitor center. The ideal starting point for most hikes will be the visitor center. The area and the center are named for Charlie Elliott the conservationist, wildlife administrator, and author of many books on outdoor subjects. The visitor center tells his life through the history of the management of fish and wildlife in Georgia and across the nation.

General location: The entrance to the wildlife management center is three miles south of Mansfield or fourteen miles north of Monticello on Georgia Highway 11.

Maps: A page-size map with trails and the wildlife management area is available at the visitor center; Stewart and Farrar USGS quads.

Degree of difficulty: The shorter loops are easy. The Perimeter Loop is moderate because of a few uphill grades and the more than three-mile length.

Length: Rock Outcrop Loop 1.1 miles; Visitor Center Loop one mile; Clubhouse Loop 1.1 miles; Perimeter Loop 3.2 miles; Murder Creek–Margery Connector one mile.

Elevations: Elevations range between 600 and 700 feet above sea level.

Special attractions: White-tailed deer, turkeys, a large array of small mammals, and many species of birds make this an excellent wildlife watching area. The visitor center is designed so that children find much to do with the interactive displays and window viewing of birds and other animals with binoculars provided by the center. The trails encompass a wide variety of habitats from dense woodlands, open fields, and lakeshores to granite outcrops with unique fauna and flora. There are twenty manmade lakes in the area with the trails touching two. Fishing is permitted. One lake is reserved for children ages 12 to 16 years old. The wildlife management area completely surrounds the hiking area and hunting for small game, deer, and turkey is permitted in season. About 300 acres that includes all the trails is closed to hunting. This is an excellent place to bring school-age children because of the displays at the visitor center and the Brooke Ager Discovery Building. The trails are, for the most part, easy with many different options.

Best season: Spring is great for migrating birds, wildflowers, and weather. Fall leaf colors can be spectacular along with wildlife watching. Since the area that includes the trails is a safety zone in which no hunting is permitted, it is safe to hike throughout the year.

For more information: Georgia Department of Natural Resources, Wildlife Resources Division, Charlie Elliott Wildlife Center, 543 Elliott Trail, Mansfield, GA 30055; (770)784-3059.

Finding the trailheads: The visitor center can be the trailhead for all trails since they are all connected. The Rock Outcrop Loop Trail begins on the opposite side of the parking area from the visitor center. The Visitor

Center Loop Trail begins at the porch of the visitor center or from the steps down from the back observation deck. The Clubhouse Loop Trail begins at the porch of the Discovery Building and travels along the dam either to the right or the left.

The hikes: All trails are blazed with a separate color for each trail in the form of a three-inch square decal on a fiberglass stake. Major junctions in the trails are marked by a larger sign with directions. The Rock Outcrop Loop Trail is blazed with blue, the Visitor Center Loop Trail with green, the Clubhouse Loop Trail with red, and the connector trail down Murder Creek and along Margery Lake is yellow.

The **Rock Outcrop Loop Trail** begins at the edge of the parking area opposite the visitor center. The path starts through a dense stand of naturally reseeded loblolly pines and quickly goes into a more mature stand of pines and hardwoods. The path drops down gently into the Murder Creek bottom with large hardwood, maple, sweet gum, yellow-poplar, large water oak and several other species of oak, river birch, and other hardwood trees and shrubs. The large boulders are granite, which you will see occasionally throughout the trails here. Christmas ferns, spleenworts, and woods ferns and many herbaceous plants grow in lush stands in the moist soil along Murder Creek. In the more moist sites you may find chain and cinnamon ferns. Spring wildflowers bloom in abundance before the leaves are on the deciduous trees. Liverworts are on the rocks in the stream and on the streambank. Trout lilies or dogtooth-violets, jack-in-the-pulpits, trilliums, blue and yellow violets, and many other wildflowers make a nice

Clubhouse Lake from the loop trail at Charlie Elliott Wildlife Center.

show in spring. The dogwoods and later the Piedmont azaleas will be in bloom. During the summer and into fall the daisy- and aster-like flowers are blooming along with mints, jewelweeds and stinging nettles. Poison ivy is abundant and is most noticeable as large vines an inch or two in diameter climbing some of the larger trees.

The trail crosses Murder Creek on a footbridge. Take a few minutes to notice the granite boulders over which the creek flows and the several species of small fish—chubs and shiners and dace—that dart about in the pools.

The trail leaves the creek bottom and begins a gentle climb to the area of the several-acre, granite outcrop. Along the path here you will see yucca, reindeer lichen, and other dry-site plants. The unique little plant called the pipsisawa grows along the trail under the loblolly pines and red and post oaks. Red cedar, sumac, and other plants not occurring in the creek bottoms are here. Wild grape or muscadine vines grow on the shrubby vegetation. The trail makes a sharp turn to go around the granite and joins an old roadbed.

When walking this trail one must stay off the exposed granite. The plant life here is very fragile and takes many years to recover from footstep damage.

The trail leaves the old road and goes back down again into a very pleasant cove near Murder Creek. As you go down you cross over one of the terraces that was shaped by an earlier landowner. All of the tillable land was farmed and in row crops about fifty years ago. Notice the blackened bark at the base of many of the young loblolly pines. This was caused by a controlled burn in 1997 as a wildlife management practice. These controlled burns simulate the natural fires that occurred and developed the habitat for species of plants and animals that occurred here naturally many years before land was cleared for farming.

Two exotic plants are favorite browse plants for deer. The Chinese privet and the Japanese honeysuckle are along the trail but have been browsed or eaten by deer until they are stubs or virtually gone. The path drops back down to Murder Creek where you should see many spring flowers from late February through May. They include dogtooth violets, trilliums, jack-in-the-pulpits, heart leaf or wild gingers, hepaticas, robin's plantains, and many others. The shrubs and trees, azaleas, dogwoods, redbuds, dwarf pawpaws, and yellow-poplars begin to bloom in April. Ferns of several species are abundant along the creek in the floodplain and on the inner bank of the stream. Christmas ferns, lady ferns, and spleenworts are the most common.

Just after you cross Murder Creek the second time there is an enormous water oak and the yellow-blazed **Murder Creek Trail** takes off from the Rock Outcrop Loop Trail and follows the creek down to Margery Lake and along the shoreline to Clubhouse Lake. Interesting aquatic and wetland areas are on this trail. Wading birds and evidence of beavers and muskrats can be seen.

Leaving the creek, the way is up a gentle slope to the rather flat ridgetop. Exposed granite boulders are in this more mature hardwood area of oaks, hickories, dogwoods, and a few pines. This area was obviously not farmed as much as other places in the area. Rocks have been piled here. Today spleenwort ferns are growing around them. This area has older trees, indicating that it was probably not farmed as row crops but used as pasture. This is a pretty area when the dogwoods are in bloom.

On the ridge there is a junction of trails. One trail leads down to the alternate beginning of the Rock Outcrop Loop Trail. One leads straight down to the visitor center and the other is the Visitor Center Loop Trail as it continues with the Perimeter Loop Trail to Clubhouse Lake.

The **Visitor Center Loop Trail** begins at the back steps of the center. It is blazed with green. It goes through a nice cove with a permanant stream. In the bottom are many ferns and spring flowers. The path goes around this cove and over a low ridge into another beautiful cove with a tumbling stream. At the bridge the Visitor Center Loop Trail turns right and follows around the upper side of Clubhouse Lake. Beaver cuttings on trees near the lake is evident. Alders line the lakeshore. It then turns uphill and back to the visitor center.

If you cross the bridge you look up into one of the most attractive sites in the woods. The stream here tumbles over granite rocks forming pools and riffles until it enters the lake. Liverworts, mosses, ferns, and many herbaceous plants grow and bloom here. This is now the **Clubhouse Loop Trail**. It is marked by red blazes and is used as a hunter education trail. The true trailhead is at the porch of the "club house" now called the Brooke Ager Discovery Building. It houses classroom facilities and exhibits used in teaching the many aspects of environmental education. The trail completely circles the lake and has a wide variety of habitats from pure pine stands to coves of hardwoods and ridge spurs of mixed pine-hardwoods. It is ideal for watching aquatic birds and other animals. Beavers use the lake and have a lodge against one shore. From the dam there is a bird's-eye view into one of the coves of Margery Lake. The Murder Creek–Margery Connector ends at the west end of the lake. Up the west side of the lake the Perimeter Loop Trail returns to the visitor center in conjunction with the Visitor Center Loop Trail.

54 High Falls State Park Trails

Overview: An area of remarkable natural beauty and historic significance. Multiple-cascading falls that drop almost 100 feet over granite outcrops give the area and the state park its name.

General description: Three trails varying in length and difficulty provide access to the falls as well as historical and natural areas of the park.

General location: About fifty miles south of Atlanta on Interstate 75. The park is located 1.8 miles east of I-75 Exit 65 at High Falls Road.

Maps: Detailed maps of the park and trails are available from the park office; High Falls USGS quad.

Degree of difficulty: Easy to moderate for all three trails.

Length: The longest trail called Non-Game Trail is 2.2 miles; Falls and Nature trail combined are one mile; Historic Ruins Trail 0.5 mile.

Elevations: The Non Game Trail changes a total of about 100 feet in a series of ridges; the Falls and Historic Ruins trails span about 75 to 100 feet of change in elevation.

Special attractions: Scenic beauty of the Towaliga River, cascades and falls; historic powerhouse, grist mill site, iron bridge, and dam; exceptional fishing, camping, and hiking, wildflowers, wildlife, excellent birding along interpretive trails.

Best season: Year-round. There is something of interest throughout the year with spring flowers, fishing, fall colors, and bird migrations being the high points.

For more information: High Falls State Park, 76 High Falls Park Drive, Jackson, GA 30233; (912)994-3053.

Finding the trailhead: Trailheads for the Historic Ruins and Nature trails are at opposite ends of the High Falls Road bridge across Towaliga Creek. The trailhead for the Non-Game Trail is at campground area two.

The hike: The **Historic Ruins Trail** begins right below the dam at the end of the iron bridge, built in 1902. It is a short walk that spans many years in time. The rockwork for the grist mill that was in operation inter- mittently from the mid-1800s until 1960 is still in place. It was burned during the Civil War and was rebuilt in 1866. The pathway crosses High Falls Road and parallels the old stone canal in which river otters, frogs, toads, and other aquatic forms may be seen. Wooden and stone steps lead down the steep riverbank to the old hydro-electric powerhouse. On the way, a platform gives the hiker an excellent view of the falls and Towaliga River as it cascades over the massive granite formation. Winter leaves of the cranefly orchid are very visible along the steep, northeast-facing bank. They disappear in spring and by summer are followed by the slender flower stalk with its pale yellow-brown flowers that frequently go unnoticed.

In about 1890, construction started on the power plant. By 1898 it was in operation and continued in operation until 1958. The dam and the 650-acre lake was completed in 1904. The park office has excellent historical

High Falls State Park Trails

information on the many businesses that flourished on the power supplied by the falling water. Some of the industry in the town of High Falls included a shoe factory, sawmill, carding factory, a broom and mop factory, wooden furniture plants, a cotton mill, blacksmith shop, and grist mill. The town was bypassed by the railroad and none of these are operating today.

On the other side of the river, the **Nature Trail** takes you down the southwest-facing bank of the river with a grand view of the falls. Wooden steps cross over the many boulders and rock formations. The path goes right to the river's edge. Among the rocks on the sandy areas are piles of small mussel shells left by muskrats. They find the mussels on the river bottom and bring them to the bank to eat. The trail leaves the river and meanders through the mixed pine-hardwood where numerous flowering plants bloom from early spring through the summer and fall.

Pay close attention to the warning not to climb on the rock surfaces around the falls. Fatal accidents have occurred.

The **Non-Game Trail** begins on the west side of Area 2 Campground. Crossing a short footbridge, the trail passes through a stand of small loblolly pines. The yellow blaze for this trail is a complete circle around the marked trees. The path merges into a more mature forest of white oak, chestnut oak, southern red oak, black oak, yellow-poplar, red maple, beech, sweet gum and large loblolly and short leaf pines along with a wide variety of flowering trees including dogwoods and redbuds. One very old yellow-poplar has a cavity in the trunk large enough for a large man to hide. The

High Falls from an overlook platform.

trail crosses several low ridges where evidence of past farming is seen in the stone terraces and the more obvious erosion gullies that are now healed with trees and shrubs. Footbridges cross the small brooks and erosion gullies, making that part of the trail easy to negotiate. Spring flowers are abundant with Christmas and spleenwort ferns growing on the moist slopes. One of these gullies is so resplendent with Christmas ferns that children hiking the trail have called it "Fern Gully" reminiscent of the movie with the same name. Wildlife in the area are deer, turkeys, squirrels, foxes, skunks, and many songbirds. With the lake and river nearby, this is an excellent birding hike. The loop ends at the same campground.

55 Mistletoe State Park Trails

Overview: The park is named for Mistletoe Junction, a local area that derived its name from the large growth of mistletoe in the oak trees. Young men and women used to meet here during the holiday season and pick the mistletoe. The forest area is the result of farms abandoned in the mid-1930s and consists of old and young growth pine and hardwoods.

The 10 miles of trails in this Piedmont area leads through a variety of forest habitats, from mixed pine-hardwoods on uplands to creek-bottom hardwoods and the shore of Clarks Hill Lake.

General description: Three easy to moderate trails offer the hiker a variety of habitat and distance.

General location: On the west shore of Clarks Hill Lake about twenty-five miles northwest of Augusta. The park is off Georgia Highway 150, twelve miles north of Interstate 20 at Exit 60.

Maps: Trail maps are available at the park office; Leah and Woodlawn USGS quads.

Degree of difficulty: Easy to moderate.

Length: Twin Oaks Trail 1.9 miles; Turkey Trot Nature Trail 1.2 miles; and Cliatt Creek Trail 1.3 miles. Rock Dam Trail adds another 5.5 miles making a total of 10 miles of hiking trails.

Elevation: Clarks Hill Lake elevation is 330 feet. The trails are no more than 100 feet above this level.

Special attraction: Wildlife, including deer, turkeys, beavers, squirrels, Canada geese, and many other birds abound. Deeply eroded "canyons" and farm terraces are evidence of the early farming. In general the park offers a wide variety of acitivities for the family. Swimming, fishing, canoeing, and camping (both tent and RV) are available to the visitor.

Best season: Spring, fall, and winter are best because of the weather and greater opportunity to see wildlife and spring flowers. The winter season offers many fine days for hiking and with the leaves off the trees you can get better views of the lake and surrounding country.

For more information: Mistletoe State Park, 3723 Mistletoe Road, Appling, GA 30802; (706)541-0321.

Mistletoe State Park Trails

CLARKS HILL LAKE

Loop Trail

Wildlife
Observation
Area

Beach-Camping Trail

Office
Check-in

Cottage
Trail

Turkey Trot Nature Trail

PARK BOUNDARY

Park
Entrance

To 150

Cliatt Creek
Trail

Cliatt Creek

Rock Dam Trail

Bolier Creek

PARK BOUNDARY

N

0   0.5
Miles

Finding the trailheads: Cliatt Creek and Turkey Trot Nature trails share the same trailhead on the entrance road near the maintenance building. Both are loops that begin and end at an information board with map outlines for the well-marked trails. The trailhead for the Twin Oaks Trail is at the park office.

The hikes: The **Cliatt Creek Trail** marked with white blazes passes through a young mixed hardwood and pine forest with a few older trees like the white oak that most frequently marks the site of a former farmhouse. These trees were the best shade trees and not as subject to lightning strikes as pines and taller hardwoods like sweetgum and yellow-poplar. The path passes through terraces constructed on former farmland to stop erosion and spread the water better to the crops. Much of this land was in crops as recent as the early 1950s. It was abandoned because the land was worn out and no longer supported a farm family. The fallow fields gave way to tree species like loblolly pine, sassafras, and persimmon that are now along the trail. From these more recent clearings, the trail leads into an older hardwood forest of sweetgum, beech, maple, yellow-poplar, an occasional large loblolly pine, white oaks, and other oak species, hickories, dogwoods, and many other forest species.

The trail leads to and along Cliatt Creek, flowing over exposed granite rocks before it empties into Clarks Hill Lake. On the shore of the bay and along the creek evidence of beavers is common. A large resident flock of Canada geese from Clarks Hill Lake use the bay and grassy areas of the park. Leaving the lake shore, the trail winds through older hardwoods where many spring flowers grow. Jack-in-the-pulpit, trilliums, bloodroot along with cinnamon fern, Christmas fern and spleenworts grow in abundance here.

The trail then crosses the paved road and into the younger, predominantly pine woods and along a deep erosion gully. The clay soils of the Piedmont quickly erode into deep narrow gullies. One is so large it has a small waterfall beside which an observation platform has been constructed. The age of the gully since the land was farmed is evident from the size of the trees growing in it.

The **Rock Dam Trail** takes off from the Cliatt Creek Trail about one mile down the trail at the junction of an old roadbed and at a large boulder. A signs marks this junction. The trail drops down to the floodplain of Cliatt Creek and goes upstream through a very pleasant hardwood forest of sweet gums, maples, oaks, river birches, yellow-poplars, and a variety of other hardwood species. Dogwoods will be blooming here in spring and all along the trail. Later the Piedmont azaleas will show their soft pink blossoms in the understory before the leaves are fully out on the larger hardwoods. The most common fern is the Christmas fern, with its dark green fronds in clumps lasting well into the winter all along the streambank and the trail, before the young fronds, called fiddleheads, form in early spring. The overflow area supports a variety of spring flowers. Jack-in-the-pulpits, dog-tooth-violets or trout lilies, hepaticas, trilliums, and many more bloom before the leaves are on the overhead trees. Highbush huckleberry, wax myrtle, sumac, young sweet gums, and other trees line the sides of the trail where the canopy is thin or absent. In the dense shade of the larger trees you can see well beyond the trail into the forest.

All along the trail there are large boulders, a part of the erosion-resistant gneiss or granite formations that extend from Augusta diagonally across the state to Columbus. Here at Mistletoe it is most evident by the large boulders protruding above the ground.

Crossing over a low ridge you come to another creek valley. This is Bohler Creek. It is much the same as Cliatt Creek with many wildflowers and large trees in the floodplain. The very large sweet gums, yellow-poplars, water and willow oaks, and river birches form a delightful cove. The same spring flowers occur here as along Cliatt Creek.

Once more the path leaves the moist, shaded creeks and crosses a low ridge following old roadbeds. Grasses grow in the trail and the small, naturally regenerated loblolly pines form thickets beside the wide path.

The trail passes across several old erosion gullies that were formed during the time this area was intensively farmed. These have healed now with little or no erosion today. At one point the path leads right down one of these gullies which ends in a very pleasant open hardwood cove with large loblolly pines, beeches, yellow-poplars, and an impressive rock outcrop. This is particularly beautiful in spring when the trout lilies, hepaticas, trilliums, jack-in-the-pulpits, and other spring flowers begin to show. Azaleas, dogwoods, dwarf pawpaws and other shrubs will be blooming later in spring.

The trail is once again on the bank of Bohler Creek. Here you will cross below a natural dam formed by a single large boulder that extends from bank to bank and forms a small pool above and a pretty waterfall. There is no bridge at this crossing and it may be necessary at times to get your shoes wet to cross over. This natural dam gives the trail its name.

After following along the creek for a short distance the trail again leaves the creek for the drier hillside. The great boulders have weathered into many shapes and sizes. Some elongate boulders have split lengthwise. One has a colony of resurrection fern growing on top.

Barbed wire still attached to some of the trees indicate earlier farming of the area.

The trail now passes around the highest knoll on the way and again comes back to Cliatt Creek. An uncommon vine, called trailing spiny-pod, with light green, heart-shaped leaves and in summer with small clusters of brown and yellow flowers grows near the bank here. It is a relative of the milkweed family. After crossing the creek you are back to the Cliatt Creek Trail. Follow the signs to the right and you are headed back to the common trailhead.

The yellow blazed **Turkey Trot Trail** leads through much the same type habitat for 1.2 miles without a creek or lake shore.

The 1.9 mile one-way **Twin Oaks Trail** marked with yellow blazes leads from the campground to the park office and beach area.

These trails are excellent for birding. Deer, squirrels, chipmunks, foxes, raccoons, and opossums may be seen if the hiker walks quietly in this varied habitat and terrain.

56 Ocmulgee National Monument Trails

Overview: This national monument is under the care of the National Park Service and was established as a memorial to the antiquity of man in this southeast corner of the United States. More than six miles of trails connect all archaeological and natural history features. There is evidence of 12,000 years of human habitation wonderfully interpreted on the ground and in the fine visitor center, which houses a major archaeological museum. Ocmulgee National Monument was established as a memorial to the antiquity of man in this part of Georgia and North America. Between 900 and 1,100 A.D. the people known as

Typical trail through hardwood forests at Ocmulgee National Monument.

Ocmulgee National Monument Trails

Mississippians, skillful at farming, built the mounds so evident at this site.

General description: About six miles of easy trails interconnect to the significant areas within the monument.

General location: The national monument is on the eastern edge of Macon on U.S. Highway 80 East.

Maps: Detailed maps and brochures are available in the visitor center; Macon East USGS quad.

Degree of difficulty: Easy.

Length: Trails total more than six miles.

Elevations: The only significant elevation changes are in various mounds, like the Temple Mound, which is forty-five feet high.

Special attractions: Archaeological interpretation from the Paleo-Indian Pre-9000 B.C. to historic 1690-1715 Creek Indian association with colonial Americans; natural areas providing wildlife observation, including deer and many species of small mammals; plant communities with a variety of woodland types; wildflowers and a fine birding area.

Best season: The park is open year-round. Spring and fall are the best times to walk the trails. However, there is plenty of activity in the wildlife and plant populations in winter and summer to make hikes interesting.

For more information: Ocmulgee National Monument, National Park Service, 1207 Emery Highway, Macon, GA 31201; (912)752-8257.

Finding the trailhead: All trails through the grounds of the monument are connected to the trailhead at the visitor center parking area.

The hikes: The walking trails provide access to the various features of the monument. All pathways of the **Human Cultural Trails** are well marked

Earth Lodge and a wheelchair-accessible trail at the Ocmulgee National Monument.

and easily followed. The main path begins at the visitor center and goes to the earth lodge. The Great Temple Mound is visible in the background. All of the trails around the mounds, village site, trading post, and prehistoric trenches are in open fields. As the hiker walks these paths, wildlife and plant life add to the enjoyment along with the early man-made features. This is a fine place to watch birds. Deer are very evident, along with squirrels and other small mammals.

After walking the human-cultural connecting trails other trails lead to natural features of the monument. From the parking area near the Great Temple Mound, a trail leads around swampy lowland to Walnut Creek.

The **River Trail** takes the hiker on a 0.9-mile walk one way to the Ocmulgee River. This is a very lowland trail and can only be traveled easily during dry weather. It is occasionally flooded by backwater from the river and Walnut Creek. The main vegetation is privet, shrubs of the *Ligustrum* genus with pointed leaves and white flowers, that have become naturalized along many river systems in Georgia. The larger trees are water oaks, hackberries, maples, and sweet gums. Deer use the lowland and feed on the privet. Also, beavers, squirrels, raccoons, and muskrats may be seen. It is a good trail to see birds, especially various water birds such as ducks, kingfishers, and wading birds. The path, which at times may be very muddy, ends at the Ocmulgee River after it passes under I-16 bridge.

The **Opelofa Trail** goes 0.25 mile around the swampy lowland called the clay hole and later joins the Loop Trail that encircles a very wooded knoll of large hardwoods and pine trees.

The **Loop Trail** is 0.3 mile long and is completely away from the mounds and other historical features. The hiker can look down on Walnut Creek bottom, another excellent birding area. Also, watch for deer here.

Another trail leaves from the visitor center to the northwest, called the **Wildflower Trail**. Wildflowers will be seen throughout the park area; however, this trail passes through a beautiful stand of old loblolly pines mixed with water oaks and other hardwoods and is also a fine wildflower area. This path can be followed to the McDougal Mound through woods and a less manicured field. This is 0.4 mile one way and another good birding area. Deer are frequently seen. The residential area of Macon is visibly close beyond the property line of the park.

Ocmulgee National Monument is a well-kept area. All of the trails are shown on a map available in the visitor center. The citizens of Macon are very fortunate to have such a fine interpretive memorial to the human culture and to the unique natural features of the monument readily available for short or long day hikes.

Pink lady's slipper orchids, or moccasin-flower, occur in a variety of moist or dry woodland habitats.

57 Piedmont National Wildlife Refuge Trails

Overview: Piedmont National Wildlife Refuge was established in 1939 to manage the wildlife potential of the exhausted farmland. Natural history and some human history is interpreted in the Allison Lake Nature Trail guide. In addition to the hikes described here, there are several more miles of unmarked trails and a wildlife drive on the refuge.

General description: Three marked trails provide easy walking in an area with a mixture of new and old forest.

General location: The wildlife refuge is in middle Georgia about twenty-five miles northeast of Macon.

Maps: Trail maps are available from the refuge office and visitor center; Oconee National Forest map; Dames Ferry and Hillsboro USGS quads.

Degree of difficulty: Easy.

Length: Allison Lake Trail is one mile; Red-cockaded Woodpecker Trail is 2.9 miles; and the Pine/Creek Trail is 1.3 miles.

Elevations: The elevation along the trails varies from about 450 to 500 feet.

Special attractions: Red-cockaded woodpecker, an endangered species, nesting wood ducks; deer; many other species of wildlife; excellent birding; wide assortment of wildflowers; photography from a permanent blind on Allison Lake; and fishing provide the hiker with many opportunities.

Best season: Year-round.

For more information: Refuge Manager, Piedmont National Wildlife Refuge, Route 1, Box 670, Round Oak, GA 31038; (912)986-5441.

Finding the trailheads: From I-75 take Exit 61 in Forsyth and travel east on Juliette Road eighteen miles to the refuge office and visitor center.

From Monticello take Georgia Highway 11 south about fifteen miles to the refuge sign and turn west on Juliette Road, go three miles to the refuge office. A Georgia State Forestry Department tower is at this intersection.

The trailhead for both the Red-cockaded Woodpecker and Allison Lake trails is at the end of the paved road to the visitor center/office road at an information kiosk and sign.

The hikes: The information kiosk has interesting information about the red-cockaded woodpecker and other wildlife and their needs. Another sign cautions about ticks, warning about this being an area of high tick population. Ticks can transmit diseases, including Lyme disease. For your protection use the following precautions when walking refuge trails: wear protective clothing, tuck pants into footwear, use a strong insect repellent, check for ticks both during and after the hike.

The **Pine/Creek Trail,** the newest hiking trail at the refuge, is interesting because of the variety of habitat through which it passes. It begins at the Refuge Visitor Center parking area as a concrete-paved wheelchair section about 500 feet long. This ends at a backyard wildlife habitat demonstration area with a small pool and appropriate plantings to attract birds,

Piedmont National Wildlife Refuge Trails

butterflies, and other interesting animals. Some of the plants are identified by small labels. Benches are provided to sit quietly and watch.

The trail is first marked as going to Allison Lake. A sign cautions one about the abundance of ticks in the area with the same information as at the trailhead for the Allison and Red-cockaded Woodpecker trails. The admonition should be taken seriously but if prepared with a good repellent and proper clothing you can enjoy the hike with no problem.

A short walk takes you to a T with signs directing you around the loop to the left for the Pine trail or to the right on the Creek trail which we will follow first. Like the other trails the healed erosion scars are very evident here. The path drops down the slope to the creek. The forest changes from a mostly pine overstory to the deciduous hardwoods of the more moist conditions. Red maple, white oak, chesnut oak, red and black oaks, sweet gum, ash, and other hardwoods are the principal trees along with loblolly pine. Muscadine vines climb the trees or trail along the ground. During spring many species of wildflowers bloom before the leaves are formed on the deciduous trees. Very shortly you come to an area of granite rock outcrop. A permanent spring flows from this point into the permanent stream that forms the head of Allison Lake. A bench here invites you to stop and take in the quietness of this pleasant microsystem. This lush, fertile, moist streamside supports a large colony of Christmas ferns, cowslips or bluebells, anemones, jack-in-the-pulpit, trilliums, and many other spring flowers. In late November you can look for the closed gentian to bloom alongside the stream bank.

The trail now follows the creek through the very moist habitat. Soon the backwaters of Allison Lake, which have been dammed by beavers, become a marsh occupied by turtles, fish, wading birds, wood duck throughout the year, and migratory ducks in winter. You may even see the river otter here and along the shore of Allison Lake.

During the warm summer months you are walking in complete shade so that even in warm, humid weather the trail can be a pleasant walk.

The path turns away from the stream and marsh going up a grade to get the higher bank in which the Allison Lake observation deck is located. The rattlesnake plantain (an orchid), pipsissewa, the aromatic heart-leaf, Piedmont azalea, and an abundance of dogwoods form the understory of the hardwood-pine forest. In spring the dogwood's white blossoms put on an impressive display throughout the refuge. From the high bank or bluff you can look down on the backwater where the beavers have dammed sections of the flow. Deciduous magnolia grow near the water along with a number of wet-soil tolerant trees.

The trail to the observation deck, down the slope a little more than 100 yards, is well marked. Here you have an excellent view of the upper end of Allison Lake where beavers have dammed Allison Creek and other tributaries. Wood duck nest boxes are used regularly by these beautiful birds. These boxes imitate the natural tree cavities normally used by wood ducks. The boxes have helped bring the wood duck back from a very low population in the 1950s. Herons, egrets, other ducks, kingfishers, and many other water birds use this area. Visibility is somewhat limited during the summer, but when the leaves are off in winter most of the lake can be seen.

Going back to the loop trail with the signs pointing out the Creek and Pine trails the loop can be completed by following the pine trail which is marked as 0.4 mile to the visitor center. This trail follows through a more open, park-like woods and at times follows along old road beds probably used when this land was under cultivation no more than 60 years ago.

Back at the visitor center you have the opportunity to see the fine displays telling about the management programs and interesting life history information on native species. The hours are Monday through Friday 8 A.M. to 5 P.M. and on weekends 9 A.M. to 5 P.M. except federal holidays.

The **Allison Lake Trail** takes you on a one-mile loop through loblolly pine and bottom-land hardwood forests beside attractive Allison Lake. An interpretive leaflet available at the refuge visitor center tells of the wildlife species that are present and discusses the habitat types and the needs of the wild animals. The photo blind should be approached quietly. It is a quiet place to observe or photograph wildlife. One may see several species of waterfowl, especially during migration times, as well as kingfisher, deer, otter, beaver, and other animals. The covered structure provides protection in all kinds of weather. Leaving the blind, the path leads back to the starting point.

The **Red-cockaded Woodpecker Trail** begins at the same place. The trail follows an unpaved service road across Allison Lake dam. Nest boxes for wood ducks are placed about the lake and are easily seen from the trail. This area was one of the pioneer places for experimental wood duck nest box use to improve the population of this most beautiful of our native ducks. Across the dam the trail continues on the service road for another few yards before it turns into a pine forest on a wide path. Fiberglass posts with hiker symbols mark the wide path throughout the loop.

As the trail enters wetter sites, oak, yellow-poplar, sweet gum, and other hardwood trees replace the pines. Undergrowth of dogwood and occasional redbud trees bloom profusely in early spring. Wildlife along the trail include deer, fox squirrels and gray squirrels, turkeys, and a number of songbirds. At about 0.5 mile, the path divides. The right prong leads to the red-cockaded woodpecker colony, the left is the return path to complete the loop.

Erosion gullies indicate the extent to which this area was farmed during the early 1930s before it became a national wildlife refuge. At slightly more than a mile, you will reach the mature loblolly pines, the focal point of the trail. The towering pines have a white ring painted about eight feet up on selected trees. These are the nest trees of the endangered red-cockaded woodpecker that excavates its nest cavity in an old, live pine tree that has a fungus disease called red-heart. The small woodpeckers chip away at the bark around the nest cavity causing the resin to flow down around the tree. The cavities are fifteen to twenty feet and higher above the ground. A bench has been provided for watching the trees. Quiet observation often results in seeing the 8.5-inch-long woodpecker described as zebra-backed with a black cap and a white cheek. They live in family colonies and use the same nest cavity for several years.

The trail leads away from the nesting colony down to Allison Creek and returns to the junction and back to the trailhead. Along the creek there is evidence of beaver cuttings and slides on the creek bank. Wildflowers, ferns, and other plants that prefer moist soils are abundant along the flood plain. The beautiful Piedmont azalea grows here, blooming in April and May.

58 Sweetwater Creek State Park Trails

Overview: Sweetwater Creek State Park has a wilderness feel, offering many species of wildflowers and wildlife, a beautiful forest, and cascading Sweetwater Creek, all of which are only minutes from downtown Atlanta.

General description: Six miles of trails that pass by the ruins of a Civil War era textile mill and follow along a stream that meanders through beautiful hardwood forests.

General location: The park is about fifteen miles from the heart of Atlanta.

Maps: A detailed trail map is available from the park office; four USGS quad sheets contain sections of the park: Austell, Campbellton, Mableton, and Ben Hill.

Degree of difficulty: Easy to moderate with a few strenuous sections only by virtue of the granite rock boulders that must be negotiated along short sections of the trail near Sweetwater Creek.

Length: Three trails total about six miles. All are loop trails that have a common trailhead.

Elevations: A change from 780 feet at the riverbank level below the falls to the maximum height of 1,050 feet on the surrounding Piedmont Plateau.

Special attractions: A variety of natural and cultural resources, including the ruins of the New Manchester Manufacturing Company and a Civil War era textile mill. Sweetwater Creek is a beautiful, fast flowing stream that wends its way through a granite-boulder streambed in a well-protected wooded valley. Abundance of many species of spring, summer, and fall wildflowers as well as wildlife, including white-tailed deer, turkeys, foxes, beavers, squirrels, and other forest animals.

Best season: Spring with more than 100 species of wildflowers and fall with spectacular tree-leaf colors. The trails are accessible year-round.

For more information: Sweetwater Creek State Park, P.O.Box 816, Lithia Springs, GA 30057; (770)732-5871.

Finding the trailheads: From Atlanta take Interstate 20 west to Exit 12 at Thornton Road; turn left and go 0.25 mile; turn right onto Blairs Bridge Road; turn left on Mount Vernon Road; and the park is on the left. The trailhead for all trails is the parking area at the end of Factory Shoals Road, which turns off Mount Vernon Road about a 0.5 mile from the park entrance.

Sweetwater Creek State Park Trails

To ⑳
and Park Office

GEORGE H. SPARKS
RESERVOIR

Group
Shelter

Mt. Vernon Road

To
㊒

Ⓟ

Picnic Area

Factory
Ruins

Sweetwater Creek

Sweetwater
Falls
Overlook

Pond

N

0   0.5
Miles

The hikes: The shortest trail is the **Factory Ruins Trail**, 0.6 mile one way and marked with red blazes. It leads to the mill ruins along the river. Another 1.2-mile trail marked with blue blazes returns to the trailhead. The longer loop trail with white blazes continues down Sweetwater Creek from the falls overlook, leaves the creek and returns to the trailhead for an additional distance of about five miles.

A tree-covered gravel walkway leaves the parking area through typical Piedmont hardwoods—sweet gum, black oak, red oak, white oak, yellow-poplar, dogwood, sourwood, and others. The trail is well marked and is interpreted by a leaflet available at the park office. The wide, well-used path leads to Sweetwater Creek and downstream to the ruins of New Manchester Manufacturing Company where cloth was made for Confederate troops during the Civil War. This was the undoing of the factory when General Sherman ordered the factory and other buildings to be burned. This happened on July 9, 1864. At the time, mostly women and children were working at the mill. They were told to pack for a long trip, loaded in wagons, and eventually placed in a prison camp at Louisville, Kentucky. The remnants of the brick mill, millrace, and other historical points of interest are seen from this trail along with a wide variety of plants including native azaleas, mountain laurels, and others.

Unfortunately the condition of many of the shrubs close to the path show evidence of much abuse by visitors who pick the flowers when in bloom. The beauty of the creek and valley is just as fetching and interesting as the historical features of the trail. Numbered markers correspond to the interpretive leaflet. Return to the parking area on the same trail or continue downstream to the **Blue-Blazed Trail** or continue around the white blazed loop trail.

Beautiful sights of the Piedmont Georgia are visible downstream from the factory ruins at the falls. The granite cliffs along the bank and outcrops the creek cascades over are spectacular. A well designed set of steps and platform make a grand view of the creek and fall possible.

The rock cliffs support many interesting plants like the rockcap fern, liverworts, and mosses. Returning by the Blue-Blazed Trail, the hiker leaves the creek and follows a gentle contour through several pleasant coves with fern glades and tributary branches rich in wildflowers growing on the forest floor. This trail is about 1.2 miles back to the parking area and trailhead.

Continuing on downstream from the falls the **Long Loop Trail** or **White Blaze Trail** follows the creek for another 0.5 mile or so and turns to the right up a brook flowing over gravel and granite. This setting is within thirty minutes of downtown Atlanta and is similar to the north Georgia mountains. Cascading streams, trees, and flowering plants, and steep hillsides are very reminiscent of the mountains. Large chain ferns, cinnamon ferns, Christmas ferns, and other moist soil plants are abundant along the brook. The trail follows the brook for a short distance and then climbs steadily up the side of the ridge until it opens out on an unpaved road overlooking a long narrow lake frequented by beavers, turtles, wood ducks, herons, and other water birds and mammals. From this point the trail follows the unpaved road through a forested area and into open fields. The fields with young trees like persimmon, sumac, loblolly pine, and oaks add an interesting diversion from the more mature forest. Several service roads are crossed or branch off the trail. It is necessary to keep the white blaze in sight. After going through pine stands and some hardwoods, the trail goes through a campground and to the parking area and trailhead.

Park Ranger Don Scarborough has recorded more than 120 wildflowers in bloom along the trails in Sweetwater Creek Park from early February to mid-June.

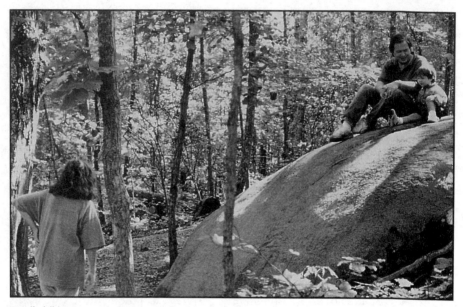

Family hiking on Rock Outcrop Trail at Panola Mountain State Park.

59 Panola Mountain State Park Trails

Overview: Panola Mountain is one of the unique granite domes that occur in the Georgia Piedmont, Stone Mountain being the largest and most famous. Plant and animal life has been protected so that it is possible to see many of the species that are endemic to this massive granite mountain.

The Rock Outcrop and Micro-watershed interpretive trails and a fitness trail are self-guided and provide geological, faunal, floral, and historical information. A fourth trail, about three miles long, leads to the top of Panola Mountain and is available for public use only on Saturday and Sunday afternoon guided hikes led by park personnel. This hike is designed to give a closer look at the undisturbed, 100-acre granite dome. The guided hikes help protect the natural condition of the very fragile plants communities. Only the Rock Outcrop and Micro-watershed trails are described in detail here.

General description: Four trails totaling about six miles offer easy interpretive walks through this unique park.

General location: Eighteen miles southeast of Atlanta on Georgia Highway 155, which is reached from Interstate 20 and Exit 36.

Maps: A page size map of the park and trails is available at the park office and interpretive center; Redan and Stockbridge USGS quads.

Degree of difficulty: Easy.

Length: Rock Outcrop Trail 0.75 mile; Micro-watershed Trail 1.25 miles; and the limited-use Panola Mountain Trail 3.5 miles. The Fitness Trail is one mile.

Elevations: Panola Mountain rises to 940 feet, only 260 feet above South River that flows along its northern edge. There is very little change in elevation along the two self-guided trails.

Special attractions: Unique granite outcrops and the endemic plants and animals that are associated with this peculiar habitat. Panola Mountain is the only undisturbed of the several granite domes in the vicinity. Wildlife including deer, squirrels, rabbits, raccoons, opossums, skunks, and chipmunks may be seen along with interesting lizards and other reptiles. Butterflies abound during the summer months feeding on the wide variety of flowering plants.

Best season: Year-round with spring and fall being the most colorful.

For more information: Panola Mountain State Park, 2600 Highway 155 SW, Stockbridge, GA 30281; (770)389-7801.

Finding the trailhead: All trails share the same trailhead which is at the interpretive center.

The hikes: The **Micro-watershed Trail** leads off to the right behind the interpretive center and passes through a mixed pine-hardwood forest with undergrowth of young sweet gum, sassafras, maple, and yellow-poplar saplings along with dogwood trees and honeysuckle and muscadine vines. Strawberry bush is common with its strikingly colorful fruits in the fall. Ferns are abundant and include bracken, Christmas, wood, cinnamon, and brownstem spleenwort. The first interpretive sign explains, with illustrations, the workings of a watershed. Other signs along the trail point out

Panola Mountain State Park Trails

special features such as the deeply eroded gullies and past farming activities. A platform gives a good perspective of the deepness of the eroded ravines. Dropping into a small creek bottom the forest is almost completely hardwoods with large sweet gums, yellow-poplars, beeches, several oaks and an occasional large loblolly pine. The stream is crossed on a short bridge. Large fern patches of New York ferns grow in the moist alluvial soil along the creek. The loop returns up to the beginning through a much younger growth of pines and deciduous trees, regenerating from a past fire. This is explained on an interpretive sign.

The short but very attractive **Rock Outcrop Trail** makes a loop through a boulder-strewn woods with interesting vistas of large exposures of granite and many colorful plants. During the late summer and fall, the masses of yellow coreopsis, locally known as Confederate daisies, add spectacular color to the otherwise gray rock outcrops. Interpretive stations along the trail provide an educational insight to a naturally interesting trail. The loop is only a mile, but the rock formations and plant and animal life give it a special charm.

Both trails at Panola Mountain Conservation State Park are ideal for family walks. The interpretive center has excellent displays of local geology, plants, and wildlife. The park personnel have frequent nature walks for children and adults. The 617-acre park borders a rapidly growing residential area and provides excellent outdoor activities for its neighbors.

Kennesaw Mountain National Battlefield Park Trails

Old US 41

41

Stillsboro Rd.

P

Visitor Center

P

Mountain Rd.

P

Kennesaw Ave.

Kennesaw Mtn.

Little Kennesaw Mtn.

Pigeon Hill

P

Noses Creek

Burnt Hickory Rd.

Mt. Calvary Rd.

Dallas Highway

Whitlock Ave.

Marietta

John Ward Creek

John Ward Rd.

P

Cheatham Hill

Cheatham Hill Rd.

Powder Springs Road

P

Kolb's Farm

360

N

0 — 0.5
Miles

60 Kennesaw Mountain National Battlefield Park Trails

Overview: This interesting mountain rises abruptly 1,000 feet above the surrounding Piedmont Plateau to the south and the Ridge and Valley area to the north. The national park was established to protect, memorialize, and interpret the Civil War Battle of Kennesaw Mountain that occurred in June 1864. This beautiful wooded, rocky ridge offers much more than just Civil War history. The trails lead through hardwood forests, some of which have been relatively undisturbed for nearly 100 years. The views from the top of Kennesaw and Little Kennesaw mountains are grand, looking southeast to the Atlanta skyline and over the Piedmont Plateau and north to the mountains and ridges.

Hugh Morton, a Georgian who climbed to the summit of Mount Everest, used the steep climbs up Kennesaw and Little Kennesaw mountains as a training ground, carrying a heavy pack to get into shape for his successful Mount Everest ascent. Others have used these trails for training and conditioning for longer hikes like the Appalachian Trail.

General description: About sixteen miles of trails that lead through beautiful wooded country with expansive views of the surrounding mountains.

General location: The park is three miles west of Marietta on Georgia Highway 120.

Maps: Trail maps detailing battle history and trail distances are available from the park visitor center; Ackworth and Kennesaw USGS quads.

Degree of difficulty: The trail across Kennesaw Mountain to Burnt Hickory Road is moderate to strenuous. Other trails segments are easy to moderate.

Length: A number of trail options totaling sixteen miles; several loop trails from sixteen miles to two miles long.

Elevations: The lowest point is near the headquarters area at 850 feet; the highest is the top of Kennesaw Mountain at 1,808 feet.

Special attractions: Civil War history, military research, grand views, mature hardwood forest, rich variety of plant life, and abundant wildlife are available to hikers very near the metropolitan population of Atlanta.

Best season: Year-round for hiking; many of the roads are closed to vehicular traffic during the winter months. The steep trails can be very slippery and dangerous during rare snow and ice conditions. Spring is best for wildflowers and migrating birds; fall for beautiful leaf color.

For more information: National Park Service, Kennesaw Mountain National Battlefield Park, 905 Kennesaw Mountain Drive, Kennesaw, GA 30152; (770)427-4686.

Finding the trailhead: From Exit 116 on Interstate 75 north of Atlanta follow the brown signs to the park. The main trailhead for all trails is behind the visitor center. There are several other access points to other segments of the trails where public roads cross. These are noted on the map.

The hike: The sixteen miles of walking trails can be reached from several points throughout the park. All trails are designed to interpret the many

Cannons on the crest of Kennesaw Mountain, Kennesaw Mountain National Battlefield Park.

points of historical significance associated with the battlefield. Some follow historic battle lines. Others simply connect the important segments of the loop trails.

From the trailhead take a 5.5-mile loop trail or a one-mile, one-way trail that steeply climbs to the main crest of the mountain. A series of switchbacks through an attractive mixed oak-hickory hardwood forest must be negotiated to reach the crest. Grand views of Atlanta to the south and the mountains to the north offer insights as to the military importance of the mountain.

The trail passes through the parking area at the top of the mountain and continues on to Little Kennesaw Mountain. Cannon emplacements along the path point to where the Federal forces approached. Drop down into the gap between Kennesaw and Little Kennesaw mountains, a steep descent, and cross a service road. On Little Kennesaw, the trail crosses gneiss rock outcrops around which are several unique plants. Growing at the edge of the rocks in a few places is a small fern, the wooly lip fern, found only in a few places other than here. Several vantage points give you excellent views of surrounding countryside.

The descent down Little Kennesaw to Pigeon Hill and Burnt Hickory Road is very steep, rocky, and in some places eroded. The trail goes through an area of large boulders. Near the bottom you reach the return trail around the foot and east side of the mountain and by the old CCC camp. This part of the trail is easier and goes through an interesting hardwood forest with many spring flowers. The loop is completed at the visitor center.

If you continue down the south end of the mountain, the trail passes through a mixed hardwood-pine woods and the Confederate entrenchments where General Sherman was repulsed in a severe battle. This section of the trail ends at a roadside-parking area on Burnt Hickory Road.

The Park Service maintains open fields here and in other places in the park much like they were when the Civil War battles were raging. The trail continues south through a pleasant and relatively level forested area. Two loops in the trail between Burnt Hickory and Dallas Road make this an ideal hike without the strenuous climbs of Kennesaw and Little Kennesaw mountains. One loop of about 2.5 miles goes as far as Noses Creek and is an outstanding wildflower and wildlife observation path. The second loop, about two miles, is between Noses Creek and Dallas Road. Both loops are similar in topography and vegetation. This section of the trail system is designated for both foot and horse travel. Hikers are asked to give horses the right-of-way. If you meet a horse simply step to the side of the trail while the horse and rider pass.

From Dallas Road to Kolb's Farm, the trail passes Cheatham Hill where the fiercest fighting of the entire Kennesaw Battle took place. From Dallas Road to Cheatham Hill is 0.7 mile. The very impressive Illinois Monument is here along with many other monuments, markers, and interpretive signs. This is the beginning of a 5.7-mile-loop trail that extends to Kolb's Farm. The loop can be hiked from the parking area at Cheatham Hill or the parking area at Kolb's Farm and restored Kolb's cabin. Union General Hooker used the Kolb house as headquarters during an unsuccessful at-

Den trees provide much needed nesting habitat for many animals. The raccoon makes good use of the holes and cavities.

tack by General Hood's Confederate forces. The hike passes through mixed hardwoods and open fields. The crossings of John Ward Creek are exceptional wildflower areas. The rolling topography, field edges and lowlands makes this section a rewarding birding hike.

Because of its length and varied habitat, Kennesaw Mountain National Battlefield Park is one of the finest hike opportunities in the metro-Atlanta area.

Chattahoochee River National Recreation Area

Hikes 61–66 are in the Chattahoochee RNRA.
The Chattahoochee River begins as a spring in Chattahoochee Gap on the Appalachian Trail high in the North Georgia mountains. It collects water from hundreds of tributaries along its meandering course before it reaches Atlanta to be the largest and most important river and water source for metropolitan Atlanta area. The Chattahoochee River National Recreation Area was established in 1978 to preserve the river corridor and provide recreation under management of the National Park Service. There are eleven tracts of land developed for recreation on the 48 miles of river north and west of Atlanta. Six of these sites with hiking trails are discussed here.

The National Park Service has a very detailed map of the Chattahoochee River from Buford Dam down to Atlanta. It shows all the access roads to the units of land administered by the Park Service.

61 East Palisades Trail

General description: About five miles of winding forest footpaths along the river.
General location: Near a section of the river just inside the Perimeter Highway, Interstate 285 and Interstate 75 on the northwest side of Atlanta. It is directly across the river from West Palisades Unit at river mile 305.
Maps: A page-size map is available from the National Park Service office.
Degree of difficulty: Because of the bluff areas there are short strenuous stretches. But for the most part, the trail is easy.
Length: There are five miles of trails in the unit. One longer loop, a short loop to the overlook, and a one-way walk along the river.
Elevations: The elevation change from the river to the highest point in the unit is about 200 feet.

Special attractions: Wildflowers; ferns; wildlife; history of Native Americans, early white settlers use of the river, and present urban developments. Picnicking, birding, fishing, nature photography, and hiking are common uses of the trail.
Best season: There is something interesting going on in all seasons. Spring flowers begin blooming in March and continue into summer. Fall leaf colors begin in late October. Many winter days are suitable for hiking.
For more information: National Park Service, Chattahoochee River National Recreation Area, 1978 Island Ford Parkway, Atlanta, GA 30350; (770)399-8070.

Finding the trailhead: To reach the trailhead exit I-285 at Northside Drive. Follow this residential road to Indian Trail. Turn right and go 0.5 mile to the parking area. The trailhead is at the parking area. Another trailhead is off Harris Trail, which turns off Northside Drive about a quarter mile beyond Indian Trail. From Harris Trail turn right on Whitewater Creek Road. The parking area is about a quarter mile on Park Service land. The trailhead is at the parking area.

The hike: The East Palisades Unit is 393 acres of hardwood forest with rock outcrops, ravines, and river floodplain. An overlook provides a view of the river shoals. These rapids were called Devils Race Course Shoals by early river boatmen in the eighteenth and nineteenth centuries. They called the granite palisades the "Devil's Stairsteps."

Beginning at the Indian Trail Road parking area, the trail follows an old roadbed for a few yards and drops down in a series of switchbacks to Whitewater Creek and the river. A bridge crosses Whitewater Creek at the lower trailhead. At the river the path is only a few feet from the bank. This is a good place to look for tracks of muskrats, beavers, raccoons, minks, and other mammals using the river's edge. The exposed rocks when the river is down or the whitewater when the river is up makes it easy to see why it received the name "Devil's Race Course Shoals." Large patches of shrubs and switch cane are in the wet areas along the bank. You cross a footbridge and the path begins the climb up along the palisades. One of the largest rock shelters along the river is to the right. This is the steepest way to the overlook. To the left is a much shorter climb over rock outcrops.

For many years, Indians lived along the river, their villages flourishing. But the Indians disappeared with little trace.

From the overlook you get a grand view of the river and appreciate the height of the bluffs. Retracing your steps from the overlook you can return to the trailhead or turn left and go back down to the river through a beautiful, mature hardwood forest of large yellow-poplars, white oaks, chestnut oaks and an occasional deciduous magnolia with exceptionally large leaves. This is an especially good area for spring wildflowers. At the river you can hike upstream along the bank to the end of the Park Service boundary. Private property is close on all sides. Careful hikers will respect the privacy of those who have adjoining property.

Backtrack up the moderate grade to return to the trailhead. The trail comes out on the road about 200 yards from the parking area.

East Palisades Trail

62 West Palisades Trail

General description: The trail follows the riverbank and into the rocky palisades. One spur trail leads up Rottenwood Creek to an old mill ruins.
General location: This trail system is at the junction of Interstate 285 and Interstate 75. The I-75 bridge over the Chattahoochee River crosses over the trail.
Maps: A page-size map is available from the ranger station or from the park office at Island Ford.
Degree of difficulty: The trail passes through difficult rock formations in one short section, but is mostly easy.
Length: There are 4.5 miles of trails in this unit.
Elevations: The elevation change from the river to the highest point is about 100 feet.
Special attractions: A variety of habitats with open fields, dense woods, tumbling streams, and rocky cliffs make this area especially interesting; to this add wildflowers, birding, fishing for trout, nature photography, and the Akers Mill ruins.
Best season: This is a trail for all seasons. Spring wildflowers begin blooming in early March. Migrating warblers and other songbirds pass through in April and May and leaves change colors in October. Trout fishing in this section of the river is year-round.
For more information: National Park Service, Chattahoochee River National Recreation Area, 1978 Island Ford Parkway, Atlanta, GA 30350; (770)399-8070.

Finding the trailhead: There is no direct access from the interstate highways. Access to the parking area is off U.S. Highway 41 called Cobb Parkway. Another access point and parking area is off Akers Drive, which turns of Akers Mill Road. The trailhead at the river is at one end of the open field beyond the Paces Mill Ranger Station in the parking complex. The middle of the unit is at river mile 305.

The hike: The West Palisades has much less mature forest than the East Palisades. It is 302 acres along about 1.5 miles of shoals in the Chattahoochee River. A large picnic area, athletic field, ranger station, restrooms, canoe and raft launching ramp, and telephone are at the Paces Mill parking area and trailhead. The trail begins on the west side of the river across from the toe of Long Island. The first 0.5 mile is a wide trail with fine gravel. This section is wheelchair accessible.

Go under the large I-75 bridge to a high bank overlooking the river. A footbridge crosses Rottenwood Creek and the narrower path continues upriver under typical riverbank trees—sycamore, sweet gum, water oak, river birch, ironwood, boxelder and others. The ridge to the left of the trail supports many wildflowers including azalea, mountain laurel, dogwoods, trillium, Solomon's seal, phlox, violet, and many more. Privet shrubs have invaded the riverbank in places making dense thickets. Large yellow-poplars, loblolly pines, and an occasional deciduous magnolia are in the coves leading away from the river. In October, the hickories, sassafras, dogwoods,

West Palisades Trail

sumacs, red oaks, and other hardwood trees and shrubs put on a beautiful show of color.

Short spur trails used by fishermen lead to the riverbank. Look for the great blue heron feeding in the river and for mammal tracks in the wet areas. Belted kingfishers, wood ducks, and other water birds can be seen along this portion of the trail. Signs of beaver activity are common.

At about one mile, a loop trail leads off to the left. Most of the trail junctions have a map mounted on a post showing where you are. Continue up the riverbank to the steep rocky area with mountain laurel, rhododendron, and several species of ferns. Climb through the rocky bluff, and the trail reaches the ridge with chestnut oaks, white oaks, and hickories. It is easy to imagine yourself in the more remote mountains instead of metropolitan Atlanta. The sound of traffic gives way to the sounds of the river and forest. The next section of trail is difficult because of the rock outcrops. But the river is especially scenic here.

The path drops back down to the river and splits into two paths to the open area with restroom and a helicopter landing pad. A wide sandy beach appears a few more yards ahead at the river's edge. The trail ends at the property line.

Backtracking to the restroom area, the trail follows a steep concrete service road to the ridgetop and to the old road from the Akers Drive trailhead. Stay to the left to return through a pleasant series of ridges and coves with lots of spring flowers. This trail leads back to the bridge at Rottenwood Creek.

Chattahoochee River at East and West Palisades trails.

The trail up Rottenwood Creek is a tedious one-mile, one-way hike. The creek is a rocky-bottomed, cascading stream that looks more like a mountain trout stream than a warm Piedmont stream. It is lined with mountain laurels and rhododendrons, oaks, sweet gums, hickories, yellow-poplars and loblolly pines. The only way to cross Rottenwood Creek is on a large sewer pipe. This is not recommended. At the end of the trail is the old rockworks of the mill dam and the brickwork ruins of the old Akers Mill.

63 Cochran Shoals Trails

Overview: The Cochran Shoals Park is 968 acres, the largest and most popular park along the Chattahoochee River. There are fields, woodlands, wetlands, and the river habitats. Most of the trail system is on jogging, fitness, and bike trails. The fitness trail also is wheelchair accessible. It is a 2.5-mile loop that follows close to the river. This is a good birding and wildlife watching trail. Two other trails lead away from the heavily used areas into forested hiking paths. Ruins of the old Marietta Paper Mill add historic interest to the area.

General description: Several trails offer a variety of natural and historic attractions near a large urban population.

General location: This area is just north of the Interstate 285 bridge across the Chattahoochee River.

Maps: A page-size map is available from the park service office.

Degree of difficulty: Easy to moderate.

Length: There are ten miles of trails in the three sections. The two hiking trails are about 1.5 miles each.

Elevations: Most of the area is in the level floodplain of the river. The two hiking trails lead up low ridges of only about fifty feet.

Special attractions: The two hiking trails are in forested areas with wildflowers and wildlife. Historic ruins, fitness and jogging trails, trout fishing, birding, and wildlife watching.

Best season: Accessible all year, but during the spring and summer be prepared for sudden rain and thundershowers. It is rare that the trails would be impassible because of snow.

For more information: National Park Service, Chattahoochee River National Recreation Area, 1978 Island Ford Parkway, Atlanta, GA 30350; (404)399-8070.

Finding the trailheads: There are two parking areas accessible from the Interstate North Parkway, one on each side of the river. The west side leads to the main trail system. The east side leads to a short path in the Powers Island area. Two other access roads are on the north end in the Sope Creek area. One is at the end of Columns Drive off Johnson Ferry Road, and the other is off Paper Mill Road. Trailheads are at each of these parking areas. All of the trails can be reached on foot from the three parking areas on the west side of the river.

Cochran Shoals Trails

The hikes: The **Grundy Creek Trail** takes off from the fitness trail to the left. It goes through a wet area with wood duck nest boxes. You can expect to see foot prints of raccoons and opossums in the soft soil. Pass an old barn and go up the ridge under a pleasant hardwood canopy that can be colorful in fall. After reaching the top of the ridge go into a powerline right-of-way with views of the large office buildings on the very edge of the park. The path leads down into the Grundy Creek ravine, an area rich in wildflowers. You may see trillium, bloodroot, Solomon's seal, heart-leaf or wild ginger, and other spring blooming plants. Later in July, if you look very close, you may see the foot-high stalk of the cranefly orchid. Follow down the water course across a low ridge and back to the fitness trail upriver from where you entered this hike. Return to the parking area or turn to the left and continue upriver to the **Sope Creek** area and hike along the tumbling Sope Creek to the Marietta Paper Mill Ruins. This hike has even more opportunities to see wildflowers and wildlife. It is possible to hike around the Sibly Pond where waterfowl may be seen in winter months. Wood ducks, belted kingfishers, an assortment of wading and song-birds also frequent the aquatic habitat.

64 Johnson Ferry Trail/ Mulberry Creek Loop Trail

General description: A 2.5-mile loop trail through a unique and extensive wetland area.

General location: This trail is on the west side of the river upstream from Johnson Ferry Road.

Maps: A page-size map is available from the park service office.

Degree of difficulty: Easy.

Length: This is a 2.5-mile loop trail.

Elevations: There is no perceptible change in elevation.

Special attractions: Wildlife—ducks, herons, beavers, muskrats, raccoons, opossums, otters, turtles, frogs, and toads are associated with the wet area and river; the forested area attracts many songbirds. Wildflowers are abundant throughout the growing season.

Best season: This is a trail for all seasons, but be prepared for sudden rains from early spring through the summer.

For more information: National Park Service, Chattahoochee River National Recreation Area, 1978 Island Ford Parkway, Atlanta, GA 30350; (770)399-8070.

Finding the trailhead: It is at river mile 311. The trailhead is at the parking area very close to Johnson Ferry Road.

Johnson Ferry Trail/Mulberry Creek Loop Trail

The hike: The Johnson Ferry Park is 108 acres entirely on the floodplain of the Chattahoochee River. The trail here is an easy but interesting path called the **Mulberry Creek Loop Trail** and goes around a natural wetland area. The remnants of a V-shaped fish trap in the river is visible from the bank during low water. The Chattahoochee Outdoor Center, located at this area, provides canoeing and rafting rental and shuttle services.

From the parking area walk about 0.25 mile across an open field. During the spring and summer, you may see killdeers in the gravel and grassy areas. Past the buildings of the Chattahoochee Outdoor Center cross a short footbridge and enter the wooded walk up the river. Spur trails made by fishermen lead off the trail at irregular intervals. If the water in the river is very clear or low, it is possible to see a V-shaped dark area crossing the channel. This is the remains of a fish trap used by early settlers. It is believed that white settlers learned to build and use these river fish traps from the Indians.

Privet shrubs and switch cane grow in dense thickets along the trail close to the river. The privet is an escaped horticultural plant. The cane is native and in the past extended in great patches along many of the rivers of the Southeast. The large cane brakes of the past were used extensively by wildlife and man.

The north end of the loop comes after crossing two more bridges and passing around deep drainage gullies. Here turn toward the ridge-line and hike back downstream on the opposite side of a wet, and sometimes flooded area. This open brushy area is the pipeline right-of-way. It adds a very important wildlife habitat type called an edge. This is where the wooded area and open area meet. It is particularly important for such birds as cardinals, yellow-breasted chats, brown thrashers, catbirds, and mocking birds. Many other forms of wildlife thrive along this edge, using both the woods and open area as needed.

Wood duck nest boxes have been placed on posts in the natural, shallow pond. In late fall and winter, wood ducks frequently gather here in small flocks. The ridge side of the trail is rich in wildflowers and ferns. There is an endless parade of blooming flowers from early spring to early winter.

The loop is completed back at the bridge; backtrack across the field to the parking area.

65 Island Ford Trail

General description: The Island Ford Trail is a pleasant hike in a mature hardwood forest.

General location: The entrance to Island Ford Park is on Roberts Road just east of Georgia Highway 400 in the Dunwoody community.

Maps: A page-size map is available from the park office.

Degree of difficulty: Easy to moderate.

Length: There are three miles of trails in several loops.

Elevations: From the river to the crest of the low ridges is about fifty feet.

Special attractions: This trail system has river scenery, mature forest, and river environment and the associated wildlife— squirrels, chipmunks, and many birds are in the forested areas; and beavers, muskrats, raccoons, and water birds are along the river. A flock of Canada geese frequent the river here. Wildflowers are abundant with many blooming in spring. The Chattahoochee River supports a fine trout fishery for both wading and bank fishing.

Best season: Year-round.

For more information: National Park Service, Chattahoochee River National Recreation Area, 1978 Island Ford Parkway, Atlanta, GA 30350; (770)399-8070.

Finding the trailhead: The trailhead is in the parking area on the left side of Island Ford Parkway about 100 yards from the entrance off Robert Road at river mile 320.

The hike: The trail is located at the headquarters site for the Chattahoochee River National Recreation Area in gently rolling topography. The river is particularly scenic where it is visible from the path. The trail leads from the parking area into a kudzu patch and soon enters the wooded area as it drops down toward the river through a moist cove with a small stream. This is an especially good place to find spring flowers. A luxurious growth of plants including Christmas ferns, spleenworts, and other ferns line the trail. Redbud and dogwood trees are under the larger yellow-poplar, white oak, American beech, maple, sweet gum, and large loblolly pine trees that form the overhead canopy. A footbridge crosses the little creek. At the river, one of the early-return trails leads back up the hill through lush mature woods. Continue on along the river for splendid views of the shoals as the river divides to form an island.

The flow of the Chattahoochee River is controlled for hydroelectric power production at Buford Dam about thirty miles upstream. Depending on releases from the dam, the river may be very full or quite low with many rocks exposed in the shoals. The water discharged from Buford Dam is cold, fifty-five to sixty degrees, all year. It is managed for rainbow and brown trout and supports a good population of both.

River birch, ironwood, sycamore, red maple, and a number of other water tolerant trees grow right to the river bank. Mosses, liverworts, and

Chattahoochee River at Island Ford Trail.

Island Ford Trail

0 ——————— 1200
Feet

ferns help stabilize the bank. Belted kingfishers, wood ducks, a resident flock of Canada geese, and other water birds are frequently seen along this section of the trail. At the next footbridge, another loop trail returns up the moderately steep ridge and back to the trailhead. In another 0.3 mile cross another footbridge and go to an observation deck that extends out over the river for an excellent view of the river both upstream and down. Retrace your steps to the second bridge and return through alternate stands of pine and hardwoods to the paved road and to the parking area at the trailhead.

The mature hardwood forest at this site is a fine example of what the Piedmont area of Georgia might have looked like before it was cleared and developed.

66 Medlock Bridge Trail

General description: Trails along a forested, narrow floodplain with a variety of trees, shrubs, and vines that attract a variety of mammals and birds.
General location: Access to this site is from Georgia Highway 141 about three miles from Norcross north of Atlanta.
Maps: A page-size map is available from the park service office.
Degree of difficulty: Easy with a short moderate section going up the rocky incline above the floodplain.
Length: The loop trail and the two one-way paths that follow the riverbank above and below the loop combined total 3.1 miles.
Elevations: From the trailhead a few feet above the river to the highest point on the trail is about fifty feet.
Special attractions: Great blue herons use the shallows along the river and are frequently seen. Water temperature is about fifty-five to sixty degrees all summer making this fine trout water and a cool place to avoid the summer heat. Muskrats, beavers, raccoons, squirrels, foxes, skunks, and other mammals use the area.
Best season: This trail can be hiked all year. Trout fishing season is open from the last Saturday in March to the end of October. Birding is good all year. Early spring and fall are special times because of wildflowers and leaf colors. Summer is very popular at this site because of the cool breezes from the cold river.
For more information: National Park Service, Chattahoochee River National Recreation Area, 1978 Island Ford Parkway, Atlanta, GA 30350; (770)399-8070.

Finding the trailhead: Georgia Highway 141 crosses the river at Medlock Bridge just below river mile 331. A paved parking area and boat launching ramp is at this site. The trailhead is at the parking area.

The hike: Medlock Bridge Park is a small forty-three-acre area on a scenic bend in the river that for years was referred to as Gun Club Bend. The river here turns 180 degrees and flows north and northeast for a short distance. The south side of the bend is lined with mountain laurel that

Medlock Bridge Trail

Medlock Bridge

141

Chattahoochee River

P

Medlock Bridge Road

0   1200
       Feet

N

To Atlanta

puts on a floral display in late April. The forested area through which the trail was built has large yellow-poplars, oaks, and hickories. Sweet gum, river birch, and water oaks form a canopy over the laurel. Rock outcrops that cause the river to turn here also produce shoals that are favorite trout fishing areas. Because of vandalism in the past, the parking area has no restroom.

The hike begins at the parking area. Either go to the river's edge and head downstream for about 0.5 mile or go from the south end of the parking area and begin hiking upstream under the mature forest of large trees. There are two loops, both of which leave the river and ascend the low ridge through picturesque granite outcrops. Above the short, but steep climb reach the crest of the low ridge and hike through a forest of white oaks, chestnut oaks, red oaks, hickory, yellow-poplars, and black gums. Dogwoods and redbuds are common under the larger trees. The topography on this higher ground is gently rolling and completely shaded in summer. In the more moist sections of the trail, spring flowers are abundant.

The trail turns back to the river; continue upstream or return to the parking area. The trail upstream goes well above the river over a high steep bank with a mountain laurel thicket. It then crosses a footbridge and several vegetated gullies before ending at the park boundary. Please respect the private property around these very valuable tracts of public land.

It is not unusual to see beaver and muskrat feeding and swimming close to the bank or out in the river, especially at twilight of both morning and evening.

67 Augusta Canal Trail

General description: An easy 8.5-mile walk along the canal and through part of Augusta.
General location: The Augusta Canal extends along the Savannah River from near the community of Martinez downstream to the old Cotton Exchange Visitor Center on the banks of the river in downtown Augusta.
Maps: The Augusta Canal Authority map with canal and Augusta history; Martinez, Augusta West, and Augusta East USGS quads.
Degree of difficulty: Easy.
Length: 8.5 miles one way. About seven miles are along the canal and river and about 1.5 mile along the streets of Augusta
Elevations: There is virtually no elevation change from the dam to Cotton Exchange in Augusta.
Special attractions: History, scenery, birding, and other wildlife watching are a few of the fascinating things waiting for you as you hike this rustic, rural, and urban trail. One of the largest loblolly pine trees you will ever see stands beside the trail. Wildlife includes bald eagles, wood storks, deer, wild turkeys, beavers, muskrats, and even an occasional alligator.

Best season: Year-round. Spring and fall are best for migratory birds, wildflowers, and fall colors. The trail is interesting in both winter and summer.
For more information: Augusta Canal Authority, 801 Broad Street, Room 107, Augusta, GA 30901; (706)722-1071.

Finding the trailhead: The upstream trailhead is at the Savannah Rapids Pavilion and is reached by walking from the pavilion parking area down to the historic lockworks. The downstream trailhead is at the Cotton Exchange Visitor Center, a beautifully developed park on the riverfront.

The hike: This unique trail is upriver from the city of Augusta between the historical Augusta Canal and the Savannah River. It follows the levy and towpath on which the mules traveled to haul boats up the canal. It follows along very beautiful river scenery and many kinds of wildlife and plants associated with the river habitat, ending with a walk along the streets of Augusta to the Cotton Exchange building. Although this is a one-way trail, it can be hiked from either end or from several access points along the way where roads cross the canal. The starting point you use may depend on your interest in urban, historical, or natural settings, or just for exercise.

Beginning at the Savannah Rapids Pavilion upstream from Augusta you get to the towpath by walking down from the parking area to the old lockworks. Cross over the concrete structure, which is the headgate and lock. Here is a spectacular view of the Savannah River and the rapid through which Bull Sluice runs.

Augusta Canal Trail

In his book *Travels of William Bartram*, Bartram said "The village of Augusta is situated on a rich fertile plain, on the Savanna river; the buildings are near its banks, and extend nearly two miles up to the cataracts, or falls, which are formed by the first chain of rocky hills, through which this famous river forces itself, as if impatient to repose on the extensive plain before it invades the ocean. When the river is low, which is during the summer months, the cataracts are four or five feet in height across the river, and the waters continue rapid and broken, rushing over rocks five miles higher up: this river is near five hundred yards broad at Augusta." This was written in 1773 and for the river it is still accurate. But the city of Augusta has grown larger. The Bartram Trail follows the river at Augusta and turns to the west toward Wrightsville as Bartram did more than 200 years ago. The settlement was only about forty years old when Bartram was here.

The river is still a beautiful flowing stream. Even though the canal was constructed many years ago, it does not detract but adds to the history and access to the river.

The trail follows the towpath on which mules pulled barges up and down the canal. There were no trees on the canal banks then to give free passage for the ropes used to pull the barges.

The 3.5-mile walk down to the water pumping station has many features both natural and man-made. Across the canal you can look into the mouth of Reed Creek as it tumbles into the canal looking very much like a mountain trout stream. The forested wetland between the canal and the river is home

251

and resting area for many forms of wildlife. Deer, turkeys, river otters, raccoons, beavers, and squirrels live in this fertile zone. Water birds including gulls, herons, egrets, cormorants, ducks, and even ospreys and bald eagles can be seen along and over the river. A fish ladder has been installed to allow striped bass, white bass, and American shad to continue their spawning migration upriver. A 100-year-old rock quarry operates on the opposite side of the canal. Interstate Highway 20 crosses over the trail before you reach the pumping station that supplies all the domestic water for Augusta. The trail here goes through the fenced parking area and between Goodrich Street and the canal to the bridge just before the 168-foot brick chimney. This chimney is all that is left of the Confederate States Powder Works, which made munitions for the Civil War.

The trail leaves the canal here for a short distance to follow along Pearl Avenue. It turns back to the canal at the Broad Street bridge but does not cross. There are parking spaces and canoe launch sites on both sides of Broad Street. The next crossing is at Fifteenth Street on the Butt Memorial Bridge, which commemorates the heroism of Archibald Butt during the sinking of the Titanic. Follow the canal down to Fenwick Street. Another parking and canoe launch site is here. The trail then leaves the canal and the last of the natural areas. Continue on Fenwick Street to Twelfth Street, down Twelfth to Greene Street, then to Eighth Street, and to the waterfront area at the Cotton Exchange and Riverwalk Park. There is much history along this urban section.

There are many points of interest—including the 1877 Enterprise Textile Mill that produced 10.8 million yards of cloth a year from water powered machinery; an 1848 flour mill; Meadow Garden, the circa 1790 home of George Walton, a Georgia Governor, U.S. Senator, and signer of the Declaration of Independence—for you to stop and visit. At the Riverwalk Park walk through the walkway to the river and see the past high water marks on the brickwork of past floods.

The Augusta Canal Authority is to be commended for developing this fine trail. It can be used for both walking and bicycling. Bicycles must yield to pedestrians. Motor vehicles are not permitted on the towpath between the pumping station and the dam at the upstream trailhead. No gas-powered motor craft are permitted in the canal.

68 Sprewell Bluff State Park Trails

General description: Sprewell Bluff State Park is one of the newest state parks, having been acquired in 1995. All the trails are new. It is located at the eastern end of the Pine Mountain formation, which is the southernmost granite ridge formation in the state. The Flint River twists and turns its way through the ridge, forming an area of grand scenic beauty. The park is about 1,400 acres of forested ridges, bluffs, and river floodplain. A three-mile trail winds along the bank of the Flint River and up the rocky bluffs, providing the hiker with views of the river and surrounding area from overlooks perched on a bluff above the river. Most of the trail is in pine-hardwood forests.

General location: About eight miles west of Thomaston on Georgia Highway 74. Go to Old Alabama Road, turn left, and go about five miles following the signs to the park.

Maps: No map has been prepared for the hiking trails at this writing.

Degree of difficulty: Easy to moderate.

Length: A total of about 3.5 miles.

Elevations: The elevation at the river is about 550 feet above sea level. The highest point in the park on Pine Woods Ridge is 857 feet.

Special attractions: Great scenery from the bluff overlooks over the Flint River; unique geological features at Pine Mountain; the Flint River with fishing, canoeing, kayaking, rafting, and swimming or wading.

Best season: Year-round hiking is in order with spring and fall best for comfortable weather and for bird migrations, spring flowers, and fall leaf color.

For more information: Sprewell Bluff State Park, 740 Sprewell Bluff Road, Thomaston, GA 30286; (706)646-6026.

Finding the trailheads: A trail-use parking area is on Sprewell Bluff Road atop Pine Woods Ridge just before it drops down to the river and day-use area where the other parking area is located. The trailhead nearest the river is located between the children's playground area and public restroom.

The hikes: The Sprewell Bluff trails are a series of interconnected paths with one main trail along the bluff and river. It starts at the day-use area on the Flint River. The day-use area is a long, sandy, pebble and rock beach on the inside of a wide bend in the river. The other trails connect to this trail from the parking area on the ridge. Three pioneer campgrounds are along this trail and are reached by connecting trails that originate in the parking area on the ridge. This interconnection makes it possible to hike any of several loops.

For the longest and most interesting loop you should start at the river day-use area. The trail is marked by a fiberglass stake with the hiking stickman and international marks that exclude vehicles and hunting.

At the start the forest cover includes sweet gums, maples, oaks, and pines. Spring flowers will be along the bank of the trail. Very shortly the path goes by an open right-of-way area with grasses and low vegetation. The area at one time was subject to severe erosion when the soils were

Sprewell Bluff State Park Trails

To Thomaston,
Old Alhambra Rd.

Sprewell Bluff Road

FLINT RIVER

N

0   0.5
Miles

Observation
deck

Day
Use
Area

exposed after logging and other agricultural use. Because of the rainfall and temperate climate these areas healed rapidly. The scars are still present but no longer erode, being protected by the vegetative cover. The trail continues above the river so you can look down on the river. Here the trees are chestnut oaks, black oaks, hickories, sourwoods, dogwoods, and shortleaf pines. Under the trees throughout the trail are red buckeyes, dwarf pawpaws, azaleas, and sparkleberry and huckleberry bushes.

The first trail that comes down from the ridge intercepts this trail and is the point at which the loop is closed to go back to the trailhead. Very soon you reach the well-made platform overlook that gives excellent views of the river and surrounding ridges. It is on the rocky bluff. Leaving the overlook the path continues up and over the bluff. It drops down to the river and gives you the feeling of being in the north Georgia mountains. The trees along the floodplain of the river are white oaks, water oaks, sycamores, black gums, hickories, and other more water tolerant plants. Mayapples, trilliums, dog-tooth-violets or trout lilies, true violets, bloodroots, anemones, and other spring flowers are abundant in season. Mountain laurel grows on the rock bluffs with a northern exposure. Linden, iron wood, river birch, and very large hickories grow in the narrow, fertile floodplain. The trail continues up the river around overflow areas with standing water at times during the year. During flood stage the river may be out of its banks and in the area of the trail.

Animals in the park include white-tailed deer, squirrels, raccoons, skunks, wild turkeys, wood ducks, hooded mergansers, an occasional osprey along the river, and other species. The Flint River corridor with its surrounding ridges is an excellent birding area.

The first campsite you come to going up the river is Number 3. A short path leads off the river trail to each campsite. Each campsite is equipped with a picnic table, fire ring, and privy. As the trail continues up the river it passes the other two campsites. After you pass campsite Number 1 you can continue for another half mile or so up the river. This is a one-way trail. The trail that comes down from the ridge to the campsites can also be used as a return way for a loop up the ridge to the ridgetop parking area. From here the path leads back down the ridge to the overlook platforms and to the trailhead at the river day-use area. This total loop along with the walk past campsite Number 1 is about 3.5 miles.

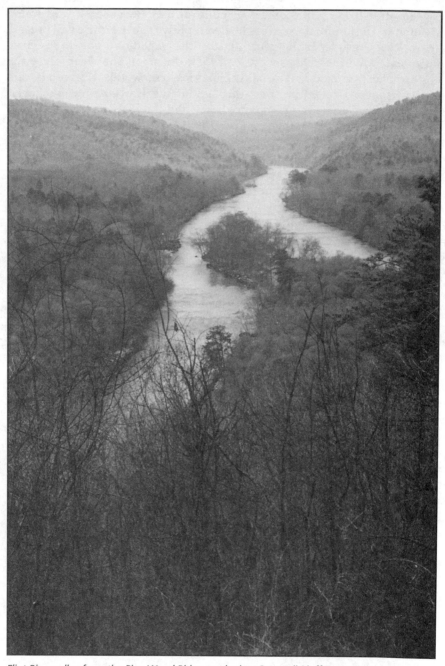

Flint River valley from the Pine Wood Ridge overlook at Sprewell Bluff State Park.

69 Providence Canyon
   State Park Trails

Overview: This park is frequently known as "Georgia's Little Grand Canyon." The soils are very soft and easily eroded. The rolling topography and the geologic location, coupled with clearing the land in the early 1800s for lumber and farming, caused erosion gullies to form. By 1850, the gullies were three to five feet deep. Once the water cut through the erosion-resistant surface layers the softer sandy soils of the "Providence Formation" eroded very rapidly. This has resulted on canyons 150 feet deep with exposed sides that are most colorful. Most of the 1,108 acres of the park have been reforested and are not eroding. These rolling hills are covered with a wide variety of plants from large loblolly and longleaf pines to showy rhododendrons and azaleas.

General description: Two separate loop trails totaling about ten miles offer very pleasant hiking.

General location: The park is about forty miles south of Columbus.

Maps: Good page-size maps are available at the interpretive center; Lumpkin USGS quad.

Degree of difficulty: Easy to moderate with a few very short steep grades.

Length: The Canyon Loop Trail is three miles; the Backpacking Trail is seven miles.

Elevations: The highest point in the park is about 660 feet and the lowest point on the long trail is about 380 feet.

Special attractions: Spectacular views of the colorful canyons, interesting and unusual plants and animals, and an interpretive center that includes a short slide program and displays showing graphically how the canyons were formed.

Best season: The trails are open year-round and are interesting in every season. It is best to hike the canyon floors during dry weather.

For more information: Providence Canyon State Park, Box 158, Route 1, Lumpkin, GA 31815; (912)838-6202.

Finding the trailheads: Take U.S. Highway 27 to Lumpkin. Go west on Georgia Highway 39C seven miles to the park entrance. The canyons, parking, and picnic areas are only a few yards from the highway. The trailhead for both the Canyon Loop and Backpacking trails is at the interpretive center.

The hikes: The three-mile **Canyon Loop Trail** begins at the interpretive center near one of several overlooks. This white blazed trail is on a moderate grade with switchbacks and widely spaced steps between log railings down to the canyon floor. You go from a very dry, well-drained ridge to the moist and shaded canyon floor. The trees on the dry slopes include white oak, southern red oak, blackjack oak, shortleaf pine, loblolly pine, and hickories with dogwoods, blueberries, hawthorns, and a number of wild flowers growing underneath the taller trees. The canyon bottom is a flat alluvial bed of sandy clay that has eroded from the sides of the canyons. The canyons are numbered from west to east. There are nine on this trail, and a

Providence Canyon State Park Trails

map provided by the park office identifies them. Walking up the canyon floor, which is actually the streambed, gives a new perspective to the massiveness of the erosion that has taken place. During wet weather, this sandy streambed is slightly muddy. But the sand makes it surprisingly hard to walk on without sinking into soft mud. Rhododendron and the rare plumleaf azalea grow in the canyons along with thick stands of alders and many other shrubs and trees.

After the optional walk into the canyons and across a boardwalk, the path climbs up the hill on the other side. The trail then follows around the canyon rim just outside a railing. There are a number of overlooks at strategic places around the rim providing excellent views of the colorful canyon walls as you return to the interpretive center.

The complex geological history of the canyons is beautifully interpreted in the center. Each of the colors along the canyon wall represents a different age and composition. Iron ore, manganese, kaolin, mica, and sandy clays are just a few of the substances contributing to the many colors you see.

The **Backpacking Trail** is blazed with red and coincides for a short distance with the shorter trail around the canyon rim, going in a clockwise direction. It is necessary to get a free permit to camp at one of the five different primitive campsites along the trail.

Providence Canyon State Park.

After following the canyon rim and the passing picnic areas, this trail takes off for the backcountry of the park. Privet shrubs that have escaped cultivation grow thick along the path and show much evidence of where deer browse. You will see the devastating effect of the Southern pine beetle. Hundreds of dead pine trees, some lying on the ground, others still standing and serving the local woodpecker population with many nest cavity trees. Other canyons can be viewed along this eastern side of the park before the trail leaves the ravines and alternately passes over the dry, ridge-top forests and down into the moist valleys with larger trees or into openings that were farm fields.

Campsites are merely places along the path with a stone fire ring. Five such sites are more or less evenly placed along the ridges before the trail drops down to the creek that flows from the canyons.

Birding along this trail is limited to forest and small open field habitat. All of Georgia's woodpeckers can be seen, many warblers, turkeys, thrushes, several owls, and other birds using tree-cavities for nesting. Mammals include the white-tailed deer, red and gray foxes, gray and fox squirrels, raccoons, and the very interesting armadillo that has extended its range throughout the Coastal Plain. The diggings seen along the trail are most frequently that of the armadillo searching for insects and other food in the forest leaf litter and sandy soil.

From campsite 2, the trail is an old roadbed. At one point the road forks and the red blaze follows the right fork. Pass campsite 5 and drop down into the creek area. Here the trees are larger, the shrub thickets more dense, and many wildflowers and ferns show up in spring and summer. Cross the creek on a footbridge and start back to the trailhead, walking upstream. Pass a string of large treated timbers that have been placed by Boy Scouts to cross over from their campground on higher ground. Finally, the trail follows the sandy-clay streambed. This continues for about 0.5 mile before you join the Canyon Loop Trail and climb up the ridge along the log-rail path to the interpretive center.

This trail is a good practice hike to test equipment and prepare for longer hikes in the mountains.

70 Reed Bingham State Park Trails

Overview: This Coastal Plain park exhibits just about all the typical habitats of south-central Georgia. The trails are designed to expose you to as many of these as possible. There are bay swamps, flat woods, river swamp, upland pine woods, turkey oak-pine woods on sand ridges, southern mixed hardwoods, old fields, and more. The Little River flows through the park and has been impounded to form a 375-acre lake with fine fishing. Boardwalks through the wetter habitats make it possible to see and be in unique southern swamps.

General description: Four loop trails totaling about 3.5 miles of easy walking through diverse habitats.

General location: Reed Bingham State Park is in south Georgia about midway between the ocean and the Alabama line. It is six miles west of Adel on Georgia Highway 37. Adel is on Interstate 75 at Exit 10.

Maps: A page-size map with descriptions of the habitat types along the trails is available in the park office; Adel USGS quad.

Degree of difficulty: Easy.

Length: There are four loop trails. The Upland Loop is about one mile, the Turkey Oak Trail is about 0.3 mile and the combined Little River and Bird Walk Trail is about 1.6 miles. The Gopher Tortoise Trail is about 0.5 mile.

Elevations: The elevation of the Coastal Plain here is about 100 feet. The trails vary only a few feet from this.

Special attractions: Variety of habitat types, much wildlife, and interesting plants make these trails unique. Both turkey and black vultures winter at the park. As many as 2,000 to 3,000 of these large soaring birds can be seen at one time. The first Saturday in December is designated Buzzard Day with much activity, including boat rides up Little River to see the buzzard roosting areas, clogging, singing and craft exhibits. Wildlife includes the rare gopher tortoise, alligators, deer, armadillos, raccoons, beavers, squirrels, bobcats, foxes, rabbits, and many others. This is an exceptionally fine birding area. The lake provides good fishing for largemouth bass, crappie, bluegill, and redbreast sunfish. Boating and camping also are popular activities.

Best season: Moderate weather makes this a year-round hiking park. Summer months can be hot and humid.

For more information: Reed Bingham State Park, Box 394B-1, Route 2, Adel, GA 31620; (912)896-3551.

Finding the trailheads: The trailhead for the longer trails (The Upland Loop Trail and Little River and Bird Walk Trail) is at the end of the paved park road on the park office side of the lake. The trailhead for the Gopher Tortoise Trail is on this same road just beyond the tent and trailer campground.

The hikes: The Coastal Plains Nature Trails, as the combination of trails is called, leave the parking area at the north end of the paved park road on the east side of the lake. An interpretive shelter at the end of the parking loop is ideally located for a classroom where teachers can orient students

261

Reed Bingham State Park Trails

To
Boat Ramp

Little River Trail

Birdwalk Trail

Boardwalk

To Lake

Boardwalk

Boardwalk

Upland Loop

Turkey Oak Trail

N

P

Class
Shelter

0   0.25

Miles

Gopher
Tortoise
Trail

To
Park Office
and Campground

who are on outdoor education field trips. Two stone pillars mark the trailhead.

The **Turkey Oak Trail** is marked with yellow blazes and takes you through pine flatwoods and back along a turkey oak-pine woods sand ridge. This is the driest of the habitat types with most of the trees, except for the pine, quite small due to the lack of fertility in the well drained sandy soils. Returning to the trailhead again, the path goes through the very interesting pitcher plant savannah. Here the insectivorous plants grow in a very moist, sandy, and acidic soil. Hooded and trumpet pitcher plants trap insects in the long tubular leaves. The tiny sundews, with sticky beads of plant juices on the leaves, also trap insects. Another insectivorous plant called the blatterwort grows in areas with shallow, standing water.

The **Upland Loop Trail** branches off the Turkey Oak Trail and provides a longer walk through upland pine woods. Watch for evidence of digging and scratching marks left by armadillos searching for insects, the major portion of its food. Gopher tortoise and armadillo holes are recognized by the low mound of sand and clay excavated from the holes. This trail leads through old fields. Fires that blackened trunks of the pine trees but did not kill the trees are a very important part of the Coastal Plain ecology, controlling insects and disease that damage trees.

In the spring of 1993, the **Little River and Bird Walk** trails were closed because the boardwalks needed to be repaired. These are the most interesting parts of the hikes, and, hopefully, they will be replaced with wider, safer boardwalks in the near future. These trails take you into the

Boardwalk on Bird Walk Trail, Reed Bingham State Park.

exceptionally interesting wetland habitat of the river swamp, the flood-plain, the creek swamp, and the Southern mixed hardwoods on low ridges locally called "river bluffs." In the wetland areas, the chain ferns, cinnamon ferns, and royal ferns grow in abundance. On the "river bluffs" large southern magnolias and many spring flowers add aroma and color to the hike.

The **Gopher Tortoise Trail**, marked by a large sign on the paved road near the campground, was developed through the nongame program of the Georgia Wildlife Resources Division. This is a well-marked and interpreted trail that passes through wiregrass, turkey oaks, post oaks, and a few live oaks that grow in the sandy soil. The burrows of the large land turtles are made obvious by the mounds of sandy clay at the entrance. The burrows are used by many other animals including rattlesnakes, the large indigo snake, gopher frogs, and insects. As many as thirty-nine invertebrates and forty-two vertebrate animals are known to use the tortoise's burrow. The flat, half-mile trail is well worth the short walk. Take your time and read the interpretive signs.

71 George T. Bagby State Park Trails

General description: The hard packed sand, boardwalk, and accessible gazebo make much of this trail wheelchair accessible with assistance.
General location: The park entrance is three miles north of Fort Gaines on Georgia Highway 39.
Maps: A page-size map is available in the lodge office; Fort Gaines USGS quad.
Degree of difficulty: Easy.
Length: The total length of the four loops and connecting paths is about three miles.
Elevations: The elevation of the lake is 180 feet. The trail is only a few feet above this and varies only slightly throughout its length.
Special attractions: Well-designed trail with four loops; a boardwalk from which alligators are frequently seen during the warm weather; a large gazebo, both of which are wheelchair accessible with assistance, make wildlife watching a special feature. Picnic shelters overlooking the lake and fishing on the 48,000-acre lake are available. The lodge is a fully equipped conference center with restaurant, cottages, swimming pool, and beach.
Best season: Weather in this part of the state makes this a year-round trail. Midsummer is hot and humid while the rest of the year is pleasant.
For more information: George T. Bagby State Park and Lodge, Route 1, Box 201, Fort Gaines, GA 31571; (912)768-2571.

Finding the trailhead: The trailhead for the Chattahoochee Trail is at the end of the parking area for the lodge.

George T. Bagby State Park Trails

To Marina

Group
Shelter

To
Eufaula

(93)

Interpretive
Center

Park
Entrance

Gazebo

Cabins

LAKE
WALTER F.
GEORGE

Pond

Boardwalk

Lodge

P

N

To
Blakely

0   0.25
Miles

The hike: This is a relatively new state park that opened in 1989. The trail, called the **Chattahoochee Trail,** is well marked and passes through several forest conditions. The park is on Lake Walter F. George, an Army Corps of Engineers reservoir on the Chattahoochee River. Numbered interpretive stations along the trail correspond with a map available in the lodge office. This helps identify the many plants and other features on the trail. A boardwalk crossing a pond and along the lakeshore adds greatly to the variety of this interesting hike.

The hike begins at the lodge parking area and forms a series of four small loops. Blue blazes mark the hike throughout. The numbered interpretive stations begin at the outset. The first identifies a large willow oak. Many trees and other plants are identified on the page-size map. At station 19, the trail forks. Take the right fork and go by the beautiful gazebo with a wheelchair ramp. Deer, turkeys, squirrels, and other mammals and birds are attracted to the area near the gazebo, making this a great place to just sit, watch, and listen. The trail goes through alternately dry and moist areas with different plants and animals in each. The gopher tortoise holes are easy to spot by the mound of sand and dirt in front of the burrow opening. Also, armadillo diggings are quite evident along the path. Foxes will modify and use the abandoned tortoise holes. One such modified hole is at station 33.

At about station 27, a spur path turns off to the right and goes to the interpretive center. Hiking on to the left, the first loop is completed at the last

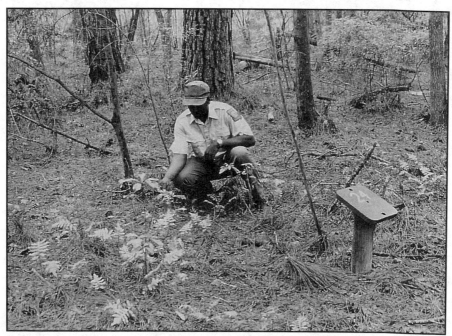

Young beech fern fronds at an interpretive station on nature trail, George T. Bagby State Park.

Boardwalk along pond used by alligators, beavers, and many wading birds in George T. Bagby State Park.

interpretive station 33. Backtrack here for a short distance to a turn to the right where the trail crosses the paved park road. An old whisky still, which was made inoperative years ago, is still standing where it was used near the ever present and necessary branch to provide water for the operation. Across the road, the trail becomes the boardwalk from which alligators, water birds, beavers, frogs, and any number of other interesting wildlife types may be seen. The boardwalk gives a full view of the lake at one point and then turns back into the woods. From here, it is possible to take one of the two short loops that end at the lodge.

Because of the hard sand, wheelchairs can navigate much of the trails and other features with some assistance.

72 George L. Smith State Park Trails

General description: The George L. Smith State Park is located on the Lower Coastal Plain in an area of old dunes that support the dwarf oak forest, characterized by longleaf pines and turkey oaks, wiregrass, and the gopher tortoise and the several species of animals associated with the tortoise's burrows. There are two trails in this unique park. The Deer Run Loop Trail is a three-mile loop and the Squirrel Run Trail is a half-mile path one way along a lake with a boardwalk through a portion of the bald cypress at the lake edge. The historical Watson's Mill and covered bridge used in the past for grinding corn and wheat and sawing lumber is still operable.

General location: The park is about four miles southeast of Twin City off Georgia Highway 23 and at the end of George L. Smith State Park Road. It is in Emanuel County.

Maps: A map of the park with the two trails is available at the park office; Twin City USGS quad.

Degree of difficulty: Easy.

Length: The Deer Run Loop Trail is a three-mile loop. The Squirrel Run Trail is 0.5 mile one way.

Elevations: The elevation is about 150 feet above sea level. There is very little elevation change throughout the trail.

Special attractions: The abundance of gopher tortoise holes; unique habitat of geologically old sand dunes to which many interesting plants and animals have become adapted; historical grist mill and covered bridge; camping, warm-water fishing, canoeing, and scenery in and around the 412-acre lake and Fifteen Mile Creek. Excellent birding, especially during migration in spring and fall.

Best season: An all-season trail system with fall, winter, and spring best. Summer can be hot and humid; however, there are no fewer things of interest to see in summer.

For more information: George L. Smith State Park, 371 George L. Smith State Park Road, Twin City, GA 30471; (912)763-2759.

Finding the trailheads: The parking area for the park office is the beginning point for both trails. To get to the Deer Run Loop Trail, walk through the grist mill/covered bridge. The Squirrel Run Trail starts at the picnic area only a few yards from the office.

The hikes: As you begin either trail take a few moments to enjoy the beauty of the lake with its picturesque cypress trees reflecting in the dark water. The **Deer Run Loop Trail** begins after you walk through the mill house, which is a covered bridge that houses Watson's Mill, to the end of the earthen dam. At this point you will see the sandy road that bisects the loop trail. You can walk the road out and back or use it as a shortcut for only part of the trail. To walk the whole loop take the path to the right past the large information board on which the trail is shown. The blue blazes mark the designated path. However, the trail is so plain there is hardly a need for blazes.

George L. Smith State Park Trails

PERRISH POND

Squirrel
Run Trail

To Twin City
and GA ㉓

Office

P

P

Covered
bridge

Deer Run Trail

PARK BOUNDARY

N

0   0.5

Miles

Watson's Mill covered bridge and mill house. The mill operates much as it did in 1880 when it was constructed.

On the right is the moist soil with the dense vegetation of titis, water oaks, maples, and magnolias; a wide variety of herbs, shrubs, and vines; and at least two species of tupelo. Both the black and water tupelos occur here. On the left are the well-drained, sandy soils of the ancient dunes with the turkey oaks, longleaf pines, sparkleberry bushes, reindeer lichens, bracken ferns, and other shrubs and herbs. In about a quarter mile a short spur trail leads to a small spring branch, a tributary to Fifteen Mile Creek. Beside the dense shrubs and cypress and tupelo trees you can expect to find several ferns, including the royal fern, cinnamon fern, and sensitive fern. The pretty white gordonia or loblolly-bay, a member of the tea family, will bloom in July. Frogs and toads are numerous and one may even see an occasional water snake. This spur ends at a short footbridge over the branch.

Returning to the main path look for the tracks of any of the several mammals occurring here, but rarely seen. The tracks of white-tailed deer, rabbits, gray and fox squirrels, raccoons, opossums, armadillos, bobcats, otters, and foxes may be seen in the sand. During the warm months you may see a number of different butterflies including the giant swallow.

At about a half mile the trail comes to a sandy, two-track road. Do not follow the road but continue on the trail, which turns slightly to the right, away from the road. All along this part of the trail you are following downstream with Fifteen Mile Creek on the right even though it is hardly ever visible because of the dense vegetation.

Just before the one-mile marker there is a bench. If time is not a factor one can sit here and simply enjoy the surroundings. The trail now leaves the dense vegetation and goes through the more open, sandy, drier habitat with dwarf turkey oaks, longleaf pines, an occasional yucca or Spanish bayonet, wiregrass, and a wide variety of plants including one of the hummingbirds' favorites called red mint or scarlet wild basil. This is the typical home of the gopher tortoise that the natives of the area simply call "gophers." This species is on the decline because of loss of habitat. It is truly an anchor species in that the burrows they make are the necessary habitat for a great many species of other animals from insects, spiders, and toads to snakes, including the endangered indigo snake and the eastern diamondback rattlesnake. Researchers have identified more than 350 species of animals that find protection in the burrows. The burrows not only provide protection from heat and cold and furnish needed moisture but, just as important, provide protection from fire.

From the first mile marker to the second you are in the typical sandy ridge habitat of the tortoise characterized by the open turkey oaks and longleaf pine forest. The burrows are easily seen by the large, sandy mound in front of each hole. When walking the trail avoid disturbing the area around the burrows and if you are fortunate enough to see one don't bother it, just let it be. Graduate students at Georgia Southern University are studying the gopher tortoise and its habitat requirements.

The birds you are apt to see include a number of warblers, cardinals, and other songbirds, king birds and other flycatchers, hawks, crows, and vultures. Herons, egrets, ibises, wood ducks, cormorants, and other water birds are associated with the lake and creeks.

At about halfway around the loop you come to another bench near an interesting stand of longleaf pines. The oaks are draped with Spanish moss. Large bracken ferns are present throughout this part of the trail. You may also see in the summer a small white flower called the tread-softly or spurge nettle. Don't try to pick it. The stiff sharp hairs can cause a painful irritation. Fortunately this flower is not very common on the path.

The trail crosses the wide unpaved road that is the extension of the road from the mill. A sign with a map shows where you are.

The path leads toward the lake and some of the more moist areas and eventually along the lake. You pass through a patch of switch cane and across a small footbridge. The dense vegetation gives a jungle-like appearance. After the large sand bank on the left the oaks are more heavily festooned with Spanish moss. The lake is now on the right and when full you can see it through the dense stand of cypress that borders most of the lake. If the lake level is low and dry you can actually walk among the large buttressed cypress trees.

From here to the end of the loop you are walking through a similar habitat to the beginning of the trail but a much more attractive site. The walk ends at the road to the mill house.

The **Squirrel Run Trail** begins at the picnic area on the campground side of the office at a railing. It follows along the lake, the shoreline of which is a picturesque stand of cypress trees. This half-mile path winds through a pleasant stand of pines, water and willow oaks, yellow-poplars, maples, gordonias, and other vines and shrubs. Near the end is a board-walk that takes you through a cypress stand on the edge of the lake. A large platform and benches provide the opportunity to just sit and enjoy this unique, almost subtropical cove. The path ends at the camping area.

73 Magnolia Springs State Park Trails

Overview: Magnolia Springs, and the stream that runs from it, attracts many species of birds, mammals, and reptiles, including alligators. It is home for a wide variety of fish and plant life. The Woodpecker Woods Nature Trail and the longer Upper Loop Trail begin with a short boardwalk and then enter the typical Coastal Plain where tall longleaf pines grow on the drier sites and oaks and other hardwood trees reside in the more moist areas. One portion of the trail borders the attractive Upper Magnolia Springs Lake.

General description: A delightful 3.5-mile hike that begins at the crystal clear pool of the large Magnolia Springs.

General location: Magnolia Springs State Park is located in Jenkins County five miles north of Millen on U.S. Highway 25.

Maps: Trail maps available from the park office; Millen USGS quad.

Degree of difficulty: Easy.

Length: Woodpecker Woods Nature Trail is 0.5 mile one way; the longer Upper Loop Trail is 3.0 miles.

Elevations: The elevation of the Coastal Plain here is about 200 feet above sea level.

Special attractions: Magnolia Springs, a crystal clear running spring that flows an estimated nine million gallons of water per day; nesting colonies of the endangered red-cockaded woodpecker; wildlife including deer, beaver, squirrels, alligators, wading and shore birds, gopher tortoise; remnants of Camp Lawton, a Civil War Confederate prison camp; and the Bo Ginn Aquarium and Aquatic Education Center.

Best season: Year-round; early spring for migrating birds and wildflowers; spring, summer, and fall for alligators, gopher tortoise, and other reptiles.

For more information: Magnolia Springs State Park, 1051 Magnolia Springs Drive, Millen GA 30442; (912)982-1660.

Finding the trailheads: The trailhead for both the nature trail and the longer loop trail begins at the board walk near the main spring pool.

The hikes: The boardwalk leads along a dense shrub bay and into a longleaf pine and oak stand. Here the **Woodpecker Woods Nature Trail**, described in an interpretive pamphlet, loops back to the boardwalk for only

Magnolia Springs State Park Trails

To Waynesboro

21
25

BO GINN
NATIONAL FISH HATCHERY

Upper Lake

Upper Loop Trail

Observation Platform

Dam

Cottages

P
Campground

Woodpecker Nature Trail

Spring

National Aquarium

P

Park Office

Park Entrance

Fort Lawton Ruins

N

0   1000
Feet

To Millen

a half-mile walk. The longer loop trail continues on through the woods to the dam that impounds the upper lake. Crossing the paved road, the path becomes the **Upper Loop Trail** and borders the east side of the lake past the racks where rental boats are stored and goes on to another boardwalk crossing a small wooded swamp of tupelo, cypress, maple, titi, button bush, and other trees and shrubs. As the trail hugs the edge of the lake, watch for great blue herons, little blue herons, egrets, anhingas, and a number of other water birds, especially wood ducks anytime of the year and many other ducks during the winter. Another boardwalk crosses a wet area and the path remains in the woods where dead trees serve as dens for wildlife and attract birds like the large, showy pileated woodpecker. The large longleaf pines provide habitat needed by the endangered red-cockaded woodpecker. A short spur off the main trail turns to the left and to an observation platform, standing well above the water level of the upper end of the lake. This provides an excellent view of the lake habitat and the great number of animals using the lake. Beavers, turtles and frogs of many kinds, ducks, herons, egrets, kingfishers, and an ample variety of other birds. Large fish can be seen splashing for food among the white water lily patches. The overlook will be especially interesting during the winter when the migratory water birds are in.

Returning to the trail, the soil changes to the dry sandy ridge condition that is a remnant of the ancient sand dunes of a former ocean beach. Prickly-pear cactus; the small, twisted turkey oak; a few tall longleaf pines with the enormous cones; holes leading into the burrows of the gopher tortoise; deer and armadillos are characteristic of this sandy area. The trail loops back to the nature trail and to Magnolia Springs again.

Any visit to Magnolia Springs State Park should include a visit to the Bo Ginn National Fish Hatchery and Aquarium located across the footbridge a short distance from the trailhead.

During the Civil War, this site was used as a Confederate prison camp, Camp Lawton. It was located where Magnolia Springs State Park is now because of the ample supply of water from the spring. Remnants of the 40,000-prisoner camp can still be seen on the park.

74 General Coffee State Park Trails

Overview: This is a very fascinating sand ridge and river swamp trail. A boardwalk and several bridges provide access deeper into the river swamp. A variety of rare plants and animals may be seen from the trail. A pioneer homestead of typical buildings depicts early life in this part of the Georgia. The river swamp and sand-ridge wildlife and wildflowers make this trail a most interesting experience.

General description: Four miles of easy trails.

General location: Six miles east of Douglas in Coffee County on Georgia Highway 32.

Maps: Maps of the park and trail are available from the park office and trading post; Douglas North USGS quad.

Degree of difficulty: Easy.

Length: Three miles one way on the River Swamp Trail and one-mile loop Gopher Tortoise Trail.

Elevations: Total elevation change is only about 65 feet from the river swamp and about 165 feet to the sandy ridge, which is about 225 feet above sea level.

Special attractions: Unique and rare plants, including the rare green-fly orchid that grows on the limbs and trunks of oak trees; Spanish moss draped on oaks and pines; the unique gopher tortoise and its burrow plus its co-inhabitants, including snakes, frogs, and insects.

Best season: Year-round.

For more information: General Coffee State Park, 46 John Coffee Road, Nicholls, GA 31554; (912)384-7082.

Finding the trailheads: The trailhead is near the picnic shelters just off the main park access road. A wooden sign at the trail entrance to the wooded area has an outline map of the trail.

The hikes: Orange blazes mark the way as the **River Swamp Trail** penetrates the thick vegetation. The river swamp habitat is best seen from a short spur trail that takes off to the right about 0.25 mile along the trail. The platform provides a vista of a relatively undisturbed swamp that is such an important part of the Coastal Plain river system. This is Seventeen Mile River, which continues on to join the Satilla River and on to the Atlantic Ocean. Trees in this moist soil area include the large buttressed tupelo and cypress, red maple, yellow-poplar, live and water oaks, slash and longleaf pines. Sphagnum moss, chain and royal ferns grow in the very wet areas. Titi and wax myrtle make up most of the shrub vegetation along with an occasional dense thicket of privet hedge that has escaped cultivation.

As the habitat changes from the river swamp to the sandy ridge, palmetto and wax myrtle bushes are more evident along with larger water and live oaks. It is here where the rare green-fly orchids live as an epiphyte on the limbs and trunks of the larger oaks.

General Coffee State Park Trails

Leaving the river swamp, the path moves into the sandy ridge plant and animal community where gopher tortoises and armadillos burrow into the soft, sandy soil. Burrows created by the tortoise to escape heat and cold are used by diamondback rattlesnakes and the endangered indigo snake, frogs, insects, spiders, and a host of other animal species. The tortoise is a native that has been here for many thousands of years, while the armadillo has lived here less than one hundred years, having extended its range only recently eastward from west of the Mississippi River. Here the trail becomes the portion called the **Gopher Tortoise Trail**. Other paths and jeep trails cross the orange blazed trail. Watch for the blazes to stay on the loop that returns to the main trail back to the trailhead. Side trails lead to various campgrounds in the park and to the several small lakes on Seventeen Mile River.

On the ridge, the trees are more stunted, and the soil so well drained that it is dry most of the time. Turkey oaks and scrubby post oaks are the common deciduous trees with the evergreen longleaf pine. One of the more common shrubs is the sparkle berry with the silvery underside of the leaves that seem to sparkle when moved by the wind.

Trees in the swamp are much taller than the trees on the sandy ridge. This difference is so great that from a distance the ridge does not stand out above the swamp.

One should avoid hiking at night without good light because of the nocturnal habits of the rattlesnake and cottonmouth.

75 Little Ocmulgee State Park Trails

Overview: An excellent example of a Coastal Plain sandy ridge habitat with the added interest of a lake. The loop trails pass through towering longleaf pines and stunted scrub oaks.
General description: Nearly five miles of easy trails.
General location: Two miles north of McRae on U.S. Highways 319/441 in Wheeler County.
Maps: Detailed trail map is available at the Pete Phillips Lodge and park office; McRae USGS quad.
Degree of difficulty: Easy.
Length: Three mile Oak Ridge Loop Trail and a shorter return 1.7-mile Magnolia Loop Trail.
Elevations: Very little elevation change on the trail; the lake elevation is 159 feet and the sand ridge is 240 feet above sea level.
Special attractions: Sand ridge habitat with gopher tortoise, indigo snake, water birds, picturesque trees with Spanish moss, a lake with good warm-water fishing, excellent birding area for both land and water birds, the unique pitcher plant, white-tailed deer, both gray and fox squirrels, and other wildlife.
Best season: Year-round, with early spring, late fall, and winter being the best because of biting and other annoying insects.
For more information: Little Ocmulgee State Park, P.O. Drawer 149, McRae, GA 31055; (912)868-7474.

Finding the trailheads: The trailhead is at the edge of the parking area for the lodge and conference center.

The hikes: At one time this area was at the edge of the ocean. As the ocean receded, the beach dunes were left behind and today are the sandy ridges found throughout Georgia's Coastal Plain. It is much like the larger sand ridges described at the Big Hammock Natural Area about fifty air miles east of here.

Both loop trails begin at the parking lot in front of the Pete Phillips Lodge or at the parking area for the group camp. The trail is designed as a short loop called the **Magnolia Loop** and the longer loop referred to as the **Oak Ridge Loop Trail.**

Little Ocmulgee State Park Trails

From the lodge parking area, the trail is a wide, developed path, leading to a boardwalk that crosses a small swampy area. The typical large buttressed tupelo, cypress, and sweet gum trees along with live oaks, maples, and slash pines grow here. Most of the shrubs are loblolly bays, swamp red bays, sweet bays, and titi. Large fern beds of chain ferns, cinnamon ferns, and sensitive ferns occur throughout the wet area. Leaving the boardwalk, the trail crosses a parking lot and continues to the group camp area. At the tennis courts, the trail drops into another small bay swamp and beside a beautiful stand of longleaf pines draped with Spanish moss. Along the sides of the trail a large shrub called yaupon holly grows in tight thickets. This holly has red berries in the fall and provides a winter supply of food to birds and other wildlife. Indians are said to have made a tea of the leaves called "black drink," which caused vomiting, hence the scientific name, *Ilex vomitoria*. The path continues beside the lake where at the shallow edge the insectivorous pitcher plant grows. A boardwalk to an observation platform offers a beautiful view of the Little Ocmulgee Lake. The lake is excellent habitat for wood ducks, gallinules, herons, egrets, anhingas, and many other wading and water birds. Vultures roost in the trees along the lakeshore and may occur in great numbers in the winter. They, like the migratory ducks and moor hens, spend the winter here

Hiking away from the lake, the trail enters the sand ridge that is entirely different from the lakeshore and loamy swamp soils. Here the gopher tortoise digs its burrows, which are very visible because of the small mounds of white sand at the entrance. The scrubby oaks are dwarfed because of the nutrient-starved sand. These trees that are only ten to twenty feet high may be very old and will not get any larger. Lightning fires that occured for thousands of years in the coastal plain produced the wire grass/longleaf pine assocation and the other species of plants and animals found here. This trail area is under a continual "fire ecology" management program to maintain the native species of plants that have evolved from frequent natural fires. Deer, armadillos, raccoons, rabbits, squirrels, and a number of birds and other species of wildlife frequent the area. The trail returns to the group camp and backtracks to the Pete Phillips Lodge. Food service, lodging, and a fine eighteen-hole golf course are available.

Spanish moss hangs from mature longleaf pines at Little Ocmulgee State Park.

76 Skidaway Island State Park Trails

Overview: Skidaway is a barrier island south of historic Savannah. The estuaries and salt marshes bring both salt and fresh water to the area. The two trails have been connected to provide a 5.5-mile walk with excellent birding and wildlife watching. Both trails lead to Civil War earthworks, liquor stills from prohibition days, and shell middens from early American Indians. Spanish moss–draped live oaks and stately longleaf pines with cabbage palms and palmettos gives the trails a subtropical atmosphere. These trails may still be walked individually for a shorter hike around the Sandpiper loop or the longer Big Ferry Trail. A brochure with maps and descriptions of both trails is available at both the main office and the visitor center.

General description: Two trails totaling four miles of easy walking have been developed for access to the uniqueness of this coastal barrier island.

General location: Six miles southeast of Savannah on Diamond Causeway.

Maps: Trail maps and interpretive leaflets are available at park office; Isle of Hope USGS quad.

Degree of difficulty: Easy.

Length: Individually the Sandpiper Trail is one mile and the Big Ferry Nature Trail is three miles. Hiked together the distance is 6.6 miles because of the added section that connects them.

Elevations: Trails are only a few feet above sea level.

Special attractions: Coastal marshes, Civil War earthworks, liquor stills from prohibition days, shell mounds from early American Indians, wildlife—including deer, wild hogs, alligators, other reptiles and amphibians, gray and fox squirrels, and excellent birding; and flowers peculiar to the salt marsh, such as the sea ox-eye, a yellow daisy like flower blooming in late spring to summer. Both trails are wheelchair accessible and are ideal for infant jugging or off-road strollers. I walked the trail with my six-month-old grandson. We used a large-wheeled stroller.

Best season: Year-round.

For more information: Skidaway Island State Park, Savannah, GA 31406; (912) 356-2523 or 356-2524.

Finding the trailheads: From Interstate 16 to Savannah take Exit 34, which runs into DeRenne Avenue; turn right on Waters Avenue and go straight ahead to Diamond Causeway. The park entrance is on the east side of causeway. The trailhead for the Sandpiper Trail is at the visitor center. The trailhead for the Big Ferry Nature Trail is on the park road to the pioneer campground marked by a large wooden sign.

The hikes: The **Sandpiper Trail** begins behind the visitor center and meanders for about one mile along the edge of the salt marsh. Fiddler crabs can be seen scurrying among the clumps of black needle rush and cord grass. After the trail crosses the first bridge, it leads to an island hammock of drier, higher land that supports animals and plants that cannot live in the salty, wet marsh. Deer, raccoons, opossums, both gray and fox squirrels, wild hogs, mice, and a number of different birds use the higher

Skidaway Island State Park Trails

Earthworks

SKIDWAY NARROWS

Big Ferry Trail

Campground

Camping Area

Sandpiper Trail

Visitor Center

PARK BOUNDARY

PARK BOUNDARY

To Savannah

Diamond Causeway

Park Entrance

N

0   2000
Feet

land. Cabbage palms, saw palmettos, large live oaks, and longleaf pines are the dominant trees. Crossing the next bridge the path leads to one of several Confederate earthworks on Skidaway Island. To the right of the trail is the great expanse of the tidal marsh that is so important as a nursery area for fish, shrimp, oysters, and crabs. The salt flats form on the shallower part of the marsh that is covered only during the highest tides. Evaporation leaves the white salt on the mud flats. The trail ends near a swimming pool at the visitor center.

At the back side of this trail you come to a T in the trail. To go back to the visitor center, completing the Sandpiper Trail, you go to the left. To the right takes you along the new portion of the trail into a forested area and then along the edge of the waterway called Skidaway Narrows. This is a section of the Intercoastal Waterway from New York to Miami. It is not unusual to see large pleasure boats under way. This section adds more high ground and a boardwalk over a section that will flood during exceptional tides. From the tidal area it continues to the road with the pioneer campground. At the other end of this road it connects with the Big Ferry Nature Trail.

The longer, three-mile, **Big Ferry Nature Trail** takes off from the park road to the pioneer campground. A sign designates the trailhead. The trail begins along the old road to the abandoned Big Ferry landing. Before the bridges were built, all access to the barrier islands was by private boat or, in some cases like Skidaway, by ferry. Tall longleaf pines and spreading live oaks draped with Spanish moss gives the trail a cathedral like feeling.

Skidaway Island State Park trails are good family hiking trails and are wheelchair accessible.

Cabbage palm, wax myrtle, and bay trees add to the vegetation giving the area a subtropical atmosphere. The well-marked path crosses a freshwater slough with an interpretive marker pointing out the importance of these wetland areas. The first part of the trail loops back along the salt marsh edge for a quick return. Remnants of old liquor or moonshine stills have been left as near intact as possible. They are from the illegal operations carried out during the prohibition years. Another interpretive marker explains their existence. The Civil War earthworks are at the end loop of the figure-eight trail. The low, earthen fortifications are crossed by bridges that protect them from unnecessary wear by hikers and provide a good view of the works.

The trail loops back past the moonshine still. Take the right fork that follows along the coastal marsh. Evidence of early American Indian use of the area is seen in the shell mounds or middens. These were left by the Gaulli Indians. This activity is discussed on an interpretive sign. The significance of the salt marshes is also interpreted by appropriate markers. Patches of bright red on some of the trees is a lichen unique to the barrier islands along the Georgia coast. The resurrection fern grows on the limbs of the live oaks and during the fall the red berries of the yaupon holly are attractive and useful wildlife food. Walking quietly along the marsh edge fiddler and ghost crabs can be seen scurrying along the water's edge and among the many fallen trees that give the shoreline a mystical appearance. The trail loops back to the old ferry access road and to the trailhead.

77 Sapelo Island Trails

General description: Sapelo Island is a 16,500-acre barrier island with grand maritime forests of live oaks festooned with Spanish moss; longleaf and slash pines on the higher ground; pond pines and cypresses at freshwater ponds; salt pans with saltwort; and expansive tidal salt marshes and estuaries. It is managed by the Georgia Department of Natural Resources, Wildlife Resources Division. On the island are the University of Georgia Marine Institute, Sapelo Island National Estuarine Research Reserve (SINERR), R. J. Reynolds Wildlife Management Area, the Sapelo Island Natural Area, and Hog Hammock, a privately owned African-American community. Many of the residents are descendants of slaves of Thomas Spalding who owned the island prior to the Civil War. Several families in Hog Hammock provide overnight accommodations such as bed and breakfasts and other lodging and services. Some also provide guided tours, one of which is in a quaint mule-drawn wagon.

The only access to the island for hiking or staying overnight is by the Department of Natural Resources–operated ferry which leaves the mainland from the dock near the Sapelo Island Visitor Center. The ferry has limited space and reservations for going to the island are necessary. The round trip on the ferry is $10 per person. There is no docking space for private boats at the island. Specific informa-

Sapelo Island Trails

To Chocolate, 4.5 miles
and North end of island, 7 miles

To Raccoon Bluff,
3 miles

Little Sapelo
Island

Duplin River

Airfield

DNR and
SINERR
Office

Hog Hammock

Marsh
Landing

To
Visitor
Center,
6 miles

ferry route

DOBOY
SOUND

Sapelo Island

Reynolds
Mansion

Dean Creek

Nannygoat Beach

ATLANTIC
OCEAN

UGA
Marine
Institute

Interpretive
Trail

N

Lighthouse

Lighthouse Rd.

Beach Rd.

0   1

Miles

tion on visits to the island and lodging can be obtained at the Sapelo Island Visitor Center listed below. The best way to hike and visit Sapelo Island is to make arrangements for lodging or a personal tour through one of the concessionaires in Hog Hammock. Current information about the several people who provide lodging and other arrangements can be obtained from the visitor center or by accessing one of several Sapelo Island websites on the internet. These are listed below.

General location: The Sapelo Island ferry dock and visitor center is located on Sapelo Dock Road in Meridian eight miles northeast of Darien, off Georgia Highway 99, or from Interstate 95 at Exit 11 take Georgia Highway 99 east to Meridian and Sapelo Dock Road.

Maps: University of Georgia Marine Extension Service *Guide to Coastal Fishing* for McIntosh County includes Sapelo Island and surroundings; Doboy Sound, Cabretta Inlet, Shellman Bluff, and Sapelo Sound USGS quads.

Degree of difficulty: All walking on the island is easy.

Length: The Interpretive Nature Trail is 1.25 miles one way; walking the beach at the end may be two or three miles; there are about ten miles of both paved and unpaved roads on the south end of the island that may be walked.

Special attractions: Experience the natural communities of a barrier island through a guided tour; excellent birding for resident and migrating shore birds and waterfowl; wildlife watching; history of early settlement in America; vast expanses of salt marsh; unspoiled beach; visit a restored and functional 1820 lighthouse; experience the African-American community of Hog Hammock; visit the R. J. Reynolds Mansion; deer and small game hunting; saltwater fishing; and the six-mile ferry ride across Doboy Sound during which porpoises and many water birds may be seen.

Best season: Year-round use of the trails and roads is possible. Highest rainfall

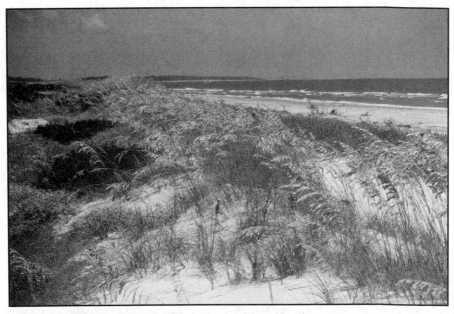

Nannygoat Beach, Sapelo Island's completely undeveloped beach.

is in August and September. Average rainfall is less from October through June. Irritating insects such as mosquitoes, deerflies, and biting gnats called "no-see-ums" are most prevalent from mid-spring to late fall.

For more information: Sapelo Island Visitor Center, Route 1 Box 1500, Darien, GA 31305; (912)437-3224. Visitor center hours: Tuesday–Friday 7:30 A.M.–5:30 P.M., Sat. 8 A.M.–5:30 P.M., Sun. 1:30 P.M.–5 P.M.; closed Monday. Required reservations for transportation to the island on the state ferry are made through the visitor center, which can also provide information on island tours and overnight accommodations and other services operated by residents of Hog Hammock. Websites for more information are: National Oceanographic and Atmospheric Administration; http://inlet.geol.sc.edu/SAP/home.html or Georgia Department of Natural Resources; http://www.dnr.state.ga.us.

Finding the trailhead: The Interpretive Nature Trail begins on the one-lane, paved road from the Reynolds Mansion to Nannygoat Beach. The parking area at the trailhead has a large sign with information about the trail.

The hikes: The **Interpretive Nature Trail** begins in an upland area near the Reynolds Mansion and goes across intertidal marsh, dunes, and interdune areas to Nannygoat Beach. Interpretive signs along the way help you identify some of the plants and points of interest. The boardwalks and bridges are more than just a way to get across the wet areas. They make it possible to stop and get a closer look at the various aquatic environments. There are fresh or brackish wet areas that support alligators, turtles, small fishes, birds, and myriads of insects and other invertebrates. It is an easy way to see some of the tidal influence on the salt marsh.

The boardwalks over both the "ancient" and active dunes protect the dunes from damage by foot traffic and give the visitor to these highly sensitive areas the opportunity to see it up close without damaging it beyond repair. If the dunes are broken down by walking over them it makes them vulnerable to intrusion by the ocean, which would cause even greater damage.

Mammals you are apt to see on the island are white-tailed deer, raccoons, opossums, armadillos, gray squirrels, marsh rabbits, and otters for the larger native species. There are feral cattle left from a dairy and other cattle maintained by R. J. Reynolds. Feral pigs are on the island. The true source of the pigs is not known.

More than 200 species of birds are known to use the island either as residents or migrating through going north or south. One of the most colorful that nests on Sapelo is the painted bunting. The chachalaca is another unusual bird on the island though it is seldom seen. The chachalaca is a relative of the wild turkey that is seen much more often.

From the parking area that is shaded by live oaks you can look out onto a meadow where you might see a painted bunting during the nesting season. The first boardwalk is over a freshwater area and then along the old beach road to the walkway and pavilion out on a salt flat. This highly saline area is only occasionally bathed with tidal water. An interpretive sign tells about the plants in this unique place. Take advantage of the blind placed here to watch or photograph birds and other animals. It is an excellent birding area for wading and shore birds, especially during migration. Along the bank of the salt flat the sea ox-eye, a daisy-like woody plant, blooms with yellow flowers during the summer.

The path now gets to the salt marsh, a sea of green or gold depending on the season. The plants are black rush and cord grass. These great expanses of tidal flats with cord grass provide cover for marsh animals and hold together the soft marsh soils. They are the nursery grounds for many species of saltwater fish and other aquatic animals. They dampen the surge of storms on the coast and filter the entire water cycle of tides and incoming fresh water.

A footbridge crosses Dean Creek, one of the tidal creeks, where you can look down in the water that flows in both directions with the incoming or outgoing tide. After the bridge you will see a grand southern magnolia with its large evergreen leaves and fragrant, large, white blossoms in midspring. The magnolia is with the live oaks and wax myrtles in this pleasant oak hammock. Benches here in the shade invite one to stop and "smell the roses." Resurrection ferns grow in green patches on the live oak limbs along with Spanish moss.

The path is now getting closer to the beach. The first of the dunes are the old, less active dunes. The boardwalk makes it possible to walk over and experience the dune habitat without destroying the fragile plant and animal communities. A low observation tower and platform affords a unique view of this interesting place. From here the walkway passes through the interdune area with a wide variety of plants and animals. This is one of the favorite places for deer and, because of the rabbits and rodents in the interdune area, is a likely place for the eastern diamondback rattlesnake.

Finally the boardwalk climbs the active dune. Here are the graceful sea oats and other salt tolerant plants that provide a picture-postcard scene. Across the dune is the Atlantic Ocean and Nannygoat Beach. The walkway goes right down to the beach. Loggerhead turtles come ashore here to lay their eggs, pelicans glide with wing tips almost touching the waves, and shore birds run up and down the surf finding their kind of food.

The beach pavilion with picnic tables and a comfort station is down the beach about 200 yards. The return to the parking area can be back along the trail or down to the pavilion and back by way of the beach road to the parking area and the Reynolds Mansion.

Another interesting walk is along the unpaved road to the lighthouse. This road is off the beach road going south to the lighthouse about one mile one way.

It is possible to visit Sapelo Island for a half day by scheduling one of the conducted day tours. It is necessary to reserve passage on the ferry and the tour ahead of time. This can be done by calling the visitor center. After the ferry ride to the island you visit a tidal marsh and creek, the Marine Institute, ruins of a sugar mill built before the Civil War, the Hog Hammock community, the Reynolds Mansion, and Nannygoat Beach and return to the mainland for a total of about four hours.

78 Big Hammock Natural Area Trails

Overview: The sandy ridges in the Coastal Plain of Georgia are a pleasant relief to the otherwise flat topography. Big Hammock is one of the largest and least disturbed of these unique areas. A number of species of plants and animals are endemic to these sandy soils. The Big Hammock Natural Area possesses exceptional value for its geological significance and plant and animal populations. This natural area is managed by the Georgia Department of Natural Resources and was acquired with the assistance of The Nature Conservancy. It is part of the Big Hammock Wildlife Management Area.

General description: The two loop trails lead you through the most impressive parts of this distinctive habitat.

General location: In Tattnall County on the northeast bank of the Altamaha River where Georgia Highway 121/144/169 crosses the river about eighteen miles east of Baxley.

Maps: Maps of the Big Hammock Wildlife Management Area are available from the Georgia Department of Natural Resources, Wildlife Resources Division; Altamaha SE USGS quad.

Degree of difficulty: Easy.

Length: Two loop trails of 1.5 and 6.0 miles.

Elevations: The coastal plain is very flat. The only change in elevation is the sandy ridges, remnants of the ancient sand dunes. The dunes are about 100 feet high.

Gopher tortoise at Big Hammock Natural Area.

Big Hammock Natural Area Trails

Special attractions: Ancient sand dunes and the unique vegetation and animals endemic to the dunes. Good population of the rare Georgia plume, a small tree with long many-flowered spikes, plume shaped and quite showy; a clubmoss called sand spikemoss; gopher tortoise; armadillo; an occasional black bear, and other locally common but generally rare species.

Best season: Year-round.

For more information: Georgia Department of Natural Resources, Game Management Section, Fitzgerald, GA 31750; (912)423-2988. Department of Natural Resources, Wildlife Resources Division, 2070 U.S. Highway 278 SE, Social Circle, GA 30279; (770)918-6416.

Finding the trailheads: After crossing the Altamaha River bridge go two miles to the first paved side road on the right. Travel this road 1.3 miles to a stone monument. The trailheads are at this monument, which carries the inscription "Big Hammock Natural Area a Registered Natural Landmark."

The hikes: The trails are marked with short fiberglass trail markers rather than blazes. As you enter the woods from the road the trail leads to the right through the moist base of the sand ridge where bracken ferns, titi, and other moisture-tolerant plant species occur. A boardwalk-spur trail leads into and through a cypress head before making the short climb up the ridge.

Turn up the slope of the ancient sand dune; out of the white sand grow dwarfed trees. Wax myrtle and turkey oaks along the trail are typical of the coastal plain. Watch for mole trails crisscrossing the path in the sandy loam. Also look for signs of foraging armadillos scratching for insects; and occasionally armadillo holes are seen along the trail. Armadillo holes can be distinguished from the gopher tortoise holes by the shape of the entrance. The opening to the tortoise's hole is oval; that of the armadillo is round. The tortoise hole is quickly spotted by the different color of the sand that is at the burrow entrance. Both are found commonly in Big Hammock. The gopher tortoise is a primary inhabitant of the Coastal Plain sandhills. Thirty-nine invertebrates and forty-two vertebrate species are known to use the deep burrows it digs.

Clumps of wire grass and the turkey oaks are indicative of the sandy soils of the ancient dunes. This is also the home of the diamondback rattlesnake and the endangered indigo snake. Prickly-pear cactus, Georgia plume, sand spikemoss, and many other plants tolerant of the dry, sandy soil are abundant. The trail crosses the crest of the sand dune where it becomes obvious that this sandy ridge is a high point and the only change in elevation in otherwise very flat topography. On the ridge crest, the trees—turkey oaks, sand pine, and others—are twisted and stunted. There is very little herbaceous growth on the quickly drained, sandy soil. The path leads down the slope of the dune into another valley between successive dunes or ridges. In the valley, the forest type changes abruptly to tall longleaf pines, white oaks, live oaks with resurrection ferns on the limbs, ironwood, maples, and other plants dependent upon the more moist site. This is the habitat for squirrels, rabbits, and other small mammals and birds.

The loop trail crosses other sandy ridges and returns to the trailhead. Extensive patches of reindeer lichen along with pincushion moss and the fern relative, sand spikemoss, grow throughout the trail. Openings in the tree cover indicate past attempts at farming the sandy ridges.

A gopher tortoise burrow.

79 Laura S. Walker State Park Trail

Overview: This park was a Civilian Conservation Corps camp during the mid-1930s, and some of the earliest history has been preserved. It is only few miles from the famous Okefenokee Swamp.

General description: The easy 1.5-mile trail passes through a large Carolina Bay and pine woods of the Coastal Plain habitat.

General location: In southeast Georgia on Georgia Highway 177, nine miles southeast of Waycross or only a few miles as the egret flies from Okefenokee Swamp.

Maps: The park office has a map of the Nature trail; Winokur USGS quad.

Degree of difficulty: Easy.

Length: 1.5 miles.

Elevations: The pathway is very level. The area is about 125 feet above sea level.

Special attractions: The perfoliate rattleweed found along the trail. The scars from extensive turpentine harvest is evident on the older longleaf pines. Wildlife such as gopher tortoise, indigo snakes, alligators, and white-tailed deer are the more dramatic species along with an abundance of forest and wading birds.

Best season: Although this is a year-round trail, the summer months can be hot and sticky with an abundance of annoying biting flies, mosquitoes, deer flies, and gnats. Winter, spring, and fall are best.

For more information: Laura S. Walker State Park, 5653 Laura S. Walker Road, Waycross, GA 31501; (912)287-4900.

Finding the trailhead: The trailhead is on Highway 177 across the road from the park check-in station and office where ample parking is available.

The hike: The path starts out through a new longleaf pine planting, which today is a large fallow field but in years to come will be a stand of tall pines. Leave the cleared area and enter a typical Coastal Plain pine woods, park-like forest of longleaf pines, palmetto, oaks, and dense shrubs and laurel oaks, sparkle berry, honeysuckle, and other vines. Rest benches have been placed along the trail, making it a great place for early morning birding. The older longleaf pines have large cuts in their trunks where pine resin was harvested to make turpentine. Locally, this was a major industry until the mid-1960s. In this area only a few yards from the trail, the white mounds of sand betray the oval-shaped hole of the gopher tortoise. These large land turtles excavate burrows several feet long ending in an underground chamber that is shared with a surprisingly large number of other animals including the Eastern diamondback rattlesnake, the large indigo snake, a frog, and insects that are endemic to the tortoise's burrow. As the trail enters the wetland area called a "Carolina Bay," a boardwalk stays above the water level and makes it possible to penetrate this fascinating habitat. The stream of dark, tea-colored water is called Big Creek. Sweet gum, tupelo, live oaks, and laurel oaks make up most of the tall forest cover. Shrubs include titi and wax myrtle. Other plants like poorman's soap, cinnamon fern, sphagnum moss, and a variety of others grow under the larger

Laura S. Walker State Park Trail

PARK BOUNDARY

To
82

Group Camp

Office
Check-in
Station
P

Campground

Pioneer
Camp

Boardwalk

Boardwalk

LAKE

Big Creek

PARK BOUNDARY

Dam

177

To
1 23
and
Okefenokee

N

0 — 0.25
Miles

trees and give the area a tropical, jungle atmosphere. Short bridges cross the wet areas and are only long enough to keep your feet on dry ground. The trail leaves the swamp area and returns to the pine woods where clay was dug to build the dam for the Laura S. Walker Lake. One of the pits is now a small pond surrounded by dense vegetation. The trail returns to the trailhead through cut-over pine woods with dogwood, sassafras, and other deciduous trees on which hangs the yellow jasmine vines. The ground cover is very dense along this part of the trail, but the path is wide and easy to follow. The bluejack oak, a small oak endemic to these well-drained sandy soils, along with honeysuckle, bracken ferns, and rattleweed add variety to this pleasant 1.5-mile walk.

80 Crooked River State Park Trails

Overview: There are only a few places along Georgia's coastal marshes and live oak forests where you can hike. One of these is Crooked River State Park. The trails on this small park are short but provide a good cross section of the varied habitat of the Atlantic coastal area. Two trails interlock to give exposure to the mystique of the maritime forest of live oaks and Spanish moss and a walk through more open palmetto-pine land. Although not yet finished, plans are under way to complete a trail for hikers with special needs. It will be accessible for wheelchairs and for the sight impaired.

General description: Two loop trails totaling about two miles of easy hiking.

General location: This park is in the extreme southeast corner of the state near the towns of St. Marys and Kingsland. It is also close to the Kings Bay Naval Submarine Base.

Maps: Crooked River State Park Map; Harrietts Bluff USGS quad.

Degree of difficulty: Easy.

Length: The two loop trails combined are about two miles.

Elevations: The trail is only a few feet above sea level. There is virtually no elevation change in these flat trails.

Special attractions: Local coastal history. Nearby famous tabby "McIntosh Sugar Works" mill built about 1825, used as a starch factory during the Civil War; salt marsh, live oak forest, and palmetto-pine woods; excellent birding for forest and coastal species; wildlife watching; saltwater fishing and camping.

Best season: Year-round with winter, spring, and fall best for birding and to avoid annoying insects. Coastal breezes help moderate the summer heat and humidity. Bird migrations in spring and fall bring many interesting upland, water, and shore birds to the area. Painted buntings are among the most colorful.

For more information: Crooked River State Park, 3092 Spur 40, St. Marys, GA 31558; (912)882-5256.

Finding the trailheads: From Kingsland (on U.S. Highway 17) go east about eight miles on Georgia Highway 40 to Georgia Spur 40. From Interstate 95, it is six miles to GA Spur 40. Go north on GA Spur 40 about seven

Crooked River State Park Trails

miles to the park entrance. The park and trail, about ten miles north of St. Marys, are located on the south bank of Crooked River. The trailhead is in front of cabin 11 at the end of the park road to cabins 6-11. Parking space for several cars is available.

The hikes: Walk down a rather straight sandy road with palmettos on one side and young live oaks, wax myrtles, blueberries, and bracken ferns on both sides. Pass an interpretive sign made by an Eagle Scout that tells about protecting and providing bat habitat. Artificial bat boxes have been placed on trees along this roadway. The white sand, pine needles, and oak leaves in the roadway are easy to walk on. Large southern magnolias are visible from the path. As you enter a mature live oak hammock, a narrow path turns into a scenic and interesting live oak forest where a sign reads "SEMPERVIRENS - THE LIVING TRAIL" with an arrow pointing to the left. Spanish moss, large grapevines, a smattering of palmettos, smaller hollies, wax myrtles, and many other vines and shrubs give the area a tropical atmosphere. Short boardwalks cross the wet areas. Large sweet gum, wild cherry, and hickory trees add to the forest canopy. This maritime forest is characteristic of the land along the tidal rivers and the barrier islands.

A spur trail leads off the main path, and a sign points to the forest edge and the salt marsh. It is possible to walk a short distance into the marsh depending on the tidal level at the time. This point offers a good view of the sharp line separating the trees from the marsh, the great expanse of the marsh grass, and an opportunity to listen and look for such birds as the clapper rail, gallinules, herons, and egrets. Gulls and terns are usually flying over the marsh and river.

Return to the path and continue the loop. At one point you go through a small opening that has gopher tortoise burrows and much evidence of armadillo digging. All along the trail there is scratching made by this hard-shelled mammal, a recent invader of this part of the state.

Along the loop of the forest trail, another trail that is about the same length makes a loop off the roadway at the beginning. The spur loop leads through the thick palmetto and tall pines. This variation in the habitat gives you an entirely different perspective on the coastal plain vegetation. Here the palmetto is very thick, the scattered slash and longleaf pines give more of a park-like appearance. For the birder, it adds to the variety of species. The king birds, mockingbirds, cardinals, thrashers, catbirds, warblers, flycatchers, and other shrub and open-woods inhabiting birds are found here. Butterflies abound along both loops. Look for deer, armadillos, squirrels, lizards, and gopher tortoises.

Prepare for biting flies, mosquitoes, sand flies or "no-see-ums," and ticks when hiking these trails. A good repellent is advised. Hiking in the cooler months will reduce the annoyance of the insects. Ticks are much less of a problem if you stay on the trail.

81   Cumberland Island
National Seashore Trails

Overview: Cumberland Island National Seashore with its maritime forests, dunes, beaches, marshes, and island atmosphere provides an unparalleled escape from the mainland.

Cumberland is the largest of Georgia's barrier islands. Although inhabited by humans for thousands of years, it is still in a near-wilderness state. The island is sixteen miles long and three miles wide at its widest point. One unpaved road, Main Road, runs from Dungeness Ruins on the south end to the northernmost end at Cumberland Wharf. A system of hiking trails laid out on many of the old side roads with connecting paths provides the hiker and camper with many miles of walking trails. The only campground developed with restrooms, cold showers, and drinking water is Sea Camp Beach. Campfires are permitted at Sea Camp. Four primitive campgrounds—Stafford Beach, Hickory Hill, Yankee Paradise, and Brickhill Bluff—are in backcountry sites. None of the backcountry campsites have toilet facilities. Wells with pumps are near the sites; however, the water should be treated chemically or by boiling before drinking. Campfires are not permitted. It is advised that you take portable stoves for cooking and boiling water. Permits are required for all overnight camping on the island. These are obtained at the Sea Camp Visitor Center. Reservations for camping are also required. The National Park Service has excellent brochures describing Cumberland Island National Seashore, how to get there, and the regulations for camping and hiking.

General description: A number of hikes are available that vary in length and difficulty.

General location: Cumberland is the southernmost of Georgia's barrier islands and is located in the extreme southeast corner of the state.

Maps: Cumberland Island National Seashore Wilderness Trail map; other National Park Service maps; Cumberland Island North, Cumberland Island South, and Fernandina Beach USGS quads. These USGS quad maps on waterproof paper can be purchased at the National Park Service office where you board the ferry.

Degree of difficulty: All trails are flat and walking is easy, except for crossing sand dunes at specified places. The 10.6-mile hike to or from the Brickhill Bluff campsite with necessary camping equipment can be considered strenuous in hot weather if it is attempted in one day.

Length: Day hikes from either of the two docks include walks to the beach. From Dungeness Dock to the beach is about one mile; from Sea Camp it is about 0.5 mile. A loop hike including a hike along the beach and the two docks and the river trail between the docks is about 3.5 miles. There are several loop hike options from the Sea Camp Visitor Center to the north along the beach or on interior roads and trails. Remember that the last ferry leaves the island at 4:45 P.M. If the last ferry is missed, a boat must be chartered to return.

From Sea Camp Dock to Stafford Beach Campsite is 3.5 miles; to Hickory Hill Campsite is 5.5 miles; to Yankee Paradise Campsite about 7.4 miles, and to Brickhill Bluff Campsite is 10.6 miles.

Elevations: The island is only a few feet above sea level. The dunes are only twenty to fifty feet high, the highest places on the island.

Special attractions: Island atmosphere and the quietness of the maritime forests; human history from the earliest Indians through the Spanish, British, and French presence to the Carnegie mansions; natural history from seashore and salt marsh to pristine forests and freshwater ponds; outstanding birding, wildlife watching and photography; beach combing; camping; hiking and just being on a relatively undeveloped island.

Best season: Year-round. Spring and fall are best for weather and bird migrations. From October to March the ferry does not operate on Tuesdays and Wednesdays. Biting flies and ticks are most abundant during the summer months.

For more information: Superintendent, Cumberland Island National Seashore, P.O. Box 806, St. Marys, GA 31558; (912)882-4335 for camping and ferry reservations and for literature.

Finding the trailheads: Cumberland Island is reached from the boat landing in St. Marys at the end of Georgia Highway 40. St. Marys is ten miles east of Interstate 95 and is situated on St. Marys River, the Florida-Georgia state line. The ferry trip on the Cumberland Queen or Cumberland Princess from St. Marys to Cumberland Island is about forty-five minutes. Two landings are served, Dungeness Dock and Sea Camp Dock. All trails are reached from either Dungeness or Sea Camp docks.

The hikes: Cumberland Island National Seashore is the most unique camping and hiking experience in the state. The trails system has been developed using the old roads and trails that have been on the island for many years. Since the only access to the island is by boat, the only vehicles on

Camp at Yankee Paradise.

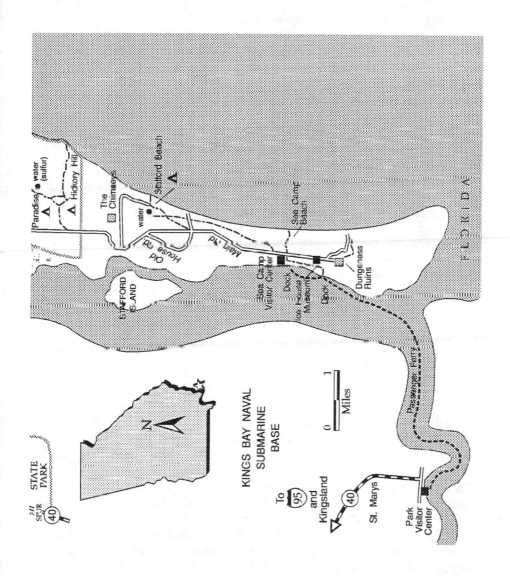

STATE PARK

2/11 SPUR 40

N

KINGS BAY NAVAL SUBMARINE BASE

0   1
Miles

To 95 and Kingsland

40   St. Marys

Park Visitor Center

Passenger Ferry

Paradise water (sulfur)

Hickory Hill

The Chimneys

Stafford Beach

water

STAFFORD ISLAND

Old House rd.

Main rd.

Sea Camp Visitor Center

Dock

Ice House Museum

Dock

Sea Camp Beach

Dungeness Ruins

FLORIDA

the island are those necessary for Park Service maintenance and patrol and the very few private vehicles associated with the small private ownerships still remaining. There are no supplies available on the island. You must bring everything. Drinking water is available at the visitor center and at the Sea Camp Beach campground. All camping is limited to seven days with the option of the developed Sea Camp Beach campground or one of the four primitive backcountry campsites.

Once on the island, all campers must meet in the Sea Camp Visitor Center for orientation and information. A volunteer checks everyone in and provides information on water, human waste disposal, campfires, hiking distances, how to keep raccoons from your food, insects, ticks, snakes, and other information to help make your camping and hiking experience as pleasant as possible. This is especially important for novice campers and first-time visitors to the Cumberland.

If you plan to stay in the Sea Camp Beach campground, the walk is only about 0.5 mile. The Park Service has two-wheeled pushcarts that can be used to transport camping gear to the campsite. Here you are close to the visitor center and to the boat dock and even closer to the beautiful undeveloped beach. The greatest bothers will be the sun, insects, and keeping the raccoons from eating your food. Bring along sun screen for the beach, repellent for the insects, and heed advice from park personnel about safeguarding your food.

For the wilderness campsites, the trail is north. It is possible to hike the Main Road or the **Parallel Trail** to the Stafford Beach campsite. Most hikers prefer the Parallel Trail. On it there will be no vehicles. To hike beyond Stafford Beach, it is necessary to follow the Main Road across an area of private property. After about two miles on the road at **Willow Pond Trail** the wilderness area begins. Follow the trail to the Hickory Hill campsite or just before Hickory Hill turn north on the Yankee Paradise Trail to the Yankee Paradise campsite. In a little more than a 0.5 mile on this trail there is an artesian well flowing sulfur water. Yankee Paradise campsite is on **Duck House Trail.** From here there are several possible routes to Brickhill Bluff campsite. The easiest is to continue past Yankee Paradise camp to the Main Road and follow it for about 3.5 miles to Brickhill.

At each campsite, except Brickhill Bluff, lateral trails lead to the beach. From Hickory Hill the Willow Pond Trail goes east to the dunes and the beach. Duck House Trail crosses the island at Yankee Paradise camp. This trail leads both to Plum Orchard Mansion on the west side and to the beach on the east. On the way to the beach cross a slough that is part of Sweetwater Lake. During very wet seasons this portion of the trail may be flooded. Pond cypress, red maples, black gum trees, and sawgrass grow in this wetland. It is also a good place to see alligators and snakes. Cross the slough to the first dune and then on to the inter-dune area and the dune at the beach. More than 200 wild horses are on the island and the inter-dune area with its grasses is one of their favorite places to graze and loaf.

The Plum Orchard Mansion.

On the west end of Duck House Trail is the grand Plum Orchard Mansion. It was built about 1900. The twenty-room home included an indoor swimming pool, among other amenities. It now serves as a ranger station for the north end of the island. An emergency radio is located here. Its use is described during the orientation session.

82 Harris Neck National Wildlife Refuge and Savannah Coastal Refuge Complex

General description: The Savannah Coastal Refuge Complex is a series of seven national wildlife refuges strung along the entire Georgia coast. Most of the refuges are barrier islands and require personal or chartered boats to get to them. Harris Neck and Savannah refuges are easily accessible by car. At Savannah NWR, walking the dikes that remain from the days of the old rice plantations is permissible during the day. There are no designated trails. At Harris Neck NWR there are a number of roads and trails that are off-limits to motor vehicles and are excellent hiking trails. These are described below. Two island refuges, Blackbeard and Wasaw, are accessible only by boat, have a number of miles of walking roads and only service vehicles are allowed on these

Harris Neck National Wildlife Refuge and Savannah Coastal Refuge Complex

islands. The islands are outstanding areas for wildlife watching and hiking and are well worth the effort to get to them. However, you should get information from the refuge office in Savannah before taking a boat to these islands. There are no lodging or eating establishments on any of the coastal refuges. Recreational camping is not permitted. Hiking is permitted on designated trails and roads daily from sunrise to sunset.

General location: Harris Neck National Wildlife Refuge is eight miles east of Interstate 95 at Exit 12, about eighteen miles north of Darien and thirty miles south of Savannah in McIntosh County. It is located in the tidal zone with salt marshes and tidal creeks and rivers.

Maps: The refuge office has a page-size map of the refuge; University of Georgia Marine Extension Service has *Guide to Coastal Fishing* maps by county (Harris Neck and Blackbeard Island are on the McIntosh County map); Shellmans Bluff USGS quad.

Degree of difficulty: Easy. You are never more than a few feet above sea level. The terrain here is such that a brisk walk or hike just for exercise is just as appropriate as a slow, deliberate wildlife-watching walk.

Length: There are more than fifteen miles of paved roads and walking trails combined, all accessible to hiking.

Elevations: Sea level to ten feet above.

Special attractions: Wildlife watching throughout the year; migratory and nesting birds, especially water birds, in great numbers; endangered and rare species of animals and plants; coastal history from precolonial times to World War II; saltwater fishing and special deer hunts in season. Most of the roads and trails are wheelchair accessible, especially chairs with wide tires. These roads and trails are ideal for taking children in off-road strollers. My grandson, in his stroller, joined me on several roads and trails to the enjoyment of both of us. Care should be taken to protect both children and adults from biting insects. Mosquitoes, deer flies, and gnats can be bad at times.

Best season: Harris Neck as well as all coastal refuges are truly year-round areas. At Harris Neck winter is a pleasant time for hiking. Spring brings on the nesting of many of the wading birds including the endangered wood stork and migrant birds passing through heading north. Wading birds and resident songbirds like the painted bunting continue to nest in summer. Fall is the time for the southward migration of songbirds and shore birds present here in both numbers of individuals and species. Biting insects and ticks are less worrisome during the cooler months of late fall, winter, and early spring.

For more information. Savannah Coastal Refuges, Parkway Business Center, Suite 10, 1000 Business Center Drive, Savannah, GA 31405; (912)652-4415; for Harris Neck, (912)832-4608.

Finding the trailheads: From Interstate 95 take Exit 12 (South Newport), then go south on U.S. Highway 17 one mile to Harris Neck Road (State Highway 131) and east on SR 131 seven miles to the entrance of the Harris Neck NWR and the Harris Neck Creek fishing area. Drive to the sign designating the wildlife drive and box with maps and information brochures. Walking trails along the drive are marked "no motorized vehicles."

The hikes: It is possible to begin all the hikes at the beginning of the wildlife drive. Virtually all of the roads other than the old runways are relatively narrow, one-lane, one-way, paved roads. They are remnants of the earlier use of the area as a residence and later a military air base.

The first section, slightly more than one-quarter mile, is under a closed canopy of live oaks and other oaks and hardwoods all festooned with Spanish moss. This roadway leads to the first two of seven freshwater impoundments constructed to provide habitat for migratory waterfowl, the primary purpose for the federal refuge. Bluebill Pond is on the south or right side of the quarter-mile dike. On the other side is Woody Pond where most of the nesting activity of the endangered wood stork takes place. In 1998 there were more than 100 active nests on the upper end of this pond. The 1.5-mile trail follows over the dike and to the right around Bluebill Pond and back to the roadway, then along the road back to the dike. You are in the woods for all but the dikes on this trail.

About one-half mile farther along the wildlife drive you come to an unmarked, unpaved lane that leads to a runway and the dike for Snipe Pond. This trail passes through mostly old field habitat. You can continue on to the left along the runway and return to the wildlife drive where it passes through the middle of the abandoned air field. Excluding the center runway the remaining abandoned runways comprise more than four miles of ideal hiking and wildlife viewing.

In the late 1930s the Federal Aviation Administration constructed an emergency landing runway for commercial air traffic from Miami to New York. Later the island became a World War II military air base, the run-

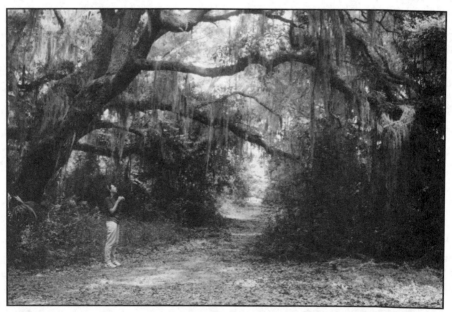

Forests of live oaks and other trees are excellent birding areas, especially during migrations of neotropical birds on Harris Neck National Wildlife Refuge.

ways of which still remain today, although they are almost obliterated by vegetation. Some of the best wildlife watching and birding is done while walking these runways. The fields and shrubby areas are especially good habitat for the painted buntings and other songbirds. Waterfowl, wading birds, and species associated with the aquatic habitat use the four ponds named Snipe, Goose, Greenhead, and Teal. Alligators and otters use these and the other ponds and may be seen almost any time of the year. Since all of these are freshwater ponds they are an added bonus to the salt marsh habitat with the many species living there.

The wildlife drive leads through the runway system and enters a beautiful wooded area of live oaks draped with Spanish moss, palmettos, and many other tree and shrub species. At the T-intersection the wildlife drive goes to the right. This is a good place to park and walk the wooded loop that once contained the barracks and other housing during World War II. It is almost completely covered by an old, impressive live oak canopy. This is also an excellent wildlife area for migrating warblers in early spring.

The road to the left from the T-intersection goes to the site of the Lorillard mansion. The very grand mansion and other buildings were razed because of their unsalvageable condition by the time Harris Neck was obtained by the U.S. Fish and Wildlife Service. The only thing that remains of the mansion's original glory is the elaborate fountain almost completely hidden in the lush vegetation. Several of the ornamental plants used in the gardens of the mansion have remained and continue to reproduce along with the native plants.

The next trail leaving the wildlife drive is about one-quarter mile south from the T-intersection and turns off to the left. This can be hiked as a three-mile loop out to the mansion site, with the return along the paved road. It goes by Widgeon Pond, a good place to see wood ducks and a heron rookery. It passes through both old fields and wooded areas that offer a pleasant variety of habitats for birding and other wildlife watching.

The last of the walking trails is only about 200 yards beyond on the wildlife drive. The walking trails go off either side of the roadway. Both are about one-half mile long one way. The trail to the east leads to Gould's Cemetery and the trail on the other side leads to the runway complex. They pass through old fields and woods. The path to the cemetery comes to the edge of the salt marsh.

The wildlife drive ends at the Harris Neck Road. A turn to the right takes you back to the refuge entrance in one mile.

There are many variations of hikes on Harris Neck. One need only to study the map for a few minutes to choose a place to walk or drive.

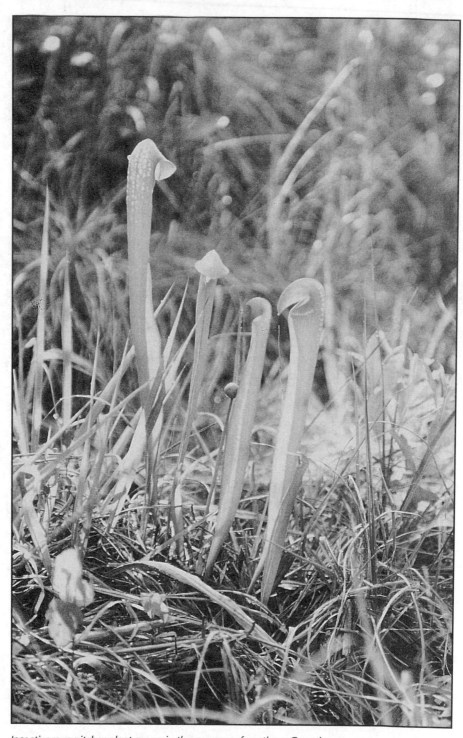

Insectivorous pitcher plant grows in the swamps of southern Georgia.

83 Okefenokee National Wildlife Refuge Trails

Overview: Okefenokee Swamp, more than 400,000 acres, is one of the oldest and best preserved freshwater areas in America. Although the swamp is best seen from a boat, there are several interesting walking trails and a boardwalk that penetrates the swamp for almost a mile.

General description: The 4.5 miles of hiking trails are designed to interpret significant past and present features of the swamp and its surroundings, both human and wildlife.

General location: Located on the Georgia-Florida line in southeast Georgia.

Maps: Maps of the trails and other features of the swamp are available at the visitor center; Chesser Island and Chase Prairie USGS quads.

Degree of difficulty: Easy; boardwalk and parts of earth trails are wheelchair accessible.

Length: Total trails 4.5 miles, including Canal Digger's, Peckerwood Trail, Chesser Island Homestead Trail, Deerstand Trail to tower, and the Boardwalk into the swamp to an observation tower, a 1.5-mile round trip.

Elevations: The topography is very flat with a total elevation change from 120 feet at the swamp edge to 150 feet above sea level along trail ridge east of the swamp.

Special attractions: Okefenokee Swamp and National Wildlife Refuge with grand interpretive displays; unparalleled wildlife watching, including alligators, other reptiles and amphibians, birding and botanical diversity; human and natural history.

Best season: Year-round; winter for migratory waterfowl, beginning osprey nesting, migratory sandhill cranes, many wading birds; spring for wildflowers, alligators begin sunning, wading bird rookeries, migrating warblers in great numbers; summer for green tree, pig, carpenter, chorus, and more than a dozen other species of frogs with their fascinating sounds; flowers and much wildlife; fall brings migratory birds to and through the swamp and beautiful leaf colors.

For more information: Refuge Manager, U.S. Fish and Wildlife Service, Okefenokee National Wildlife Refuge, Route 2, Box 338, Folkston, GA 31537; (912)496-3331 or 496-7836.

Finding the trailhead: Entrance to the Suwannee Canal Recreation Area is eight miles southwest of Folkston on Georgia Highway 121/23. At the main entrance sign turn right and go three miles west to the Suwannee Canal Visitor Center, concessions and boat ramp. All trails are reached from the Swamp Island Drive, a five-mile, paved drive along the swamp's edge.

The hike: The **Canal Digger's Trail** leaves from the visitor center and follows the upland portion of the Suwannee Canal. A pamphlet available in the center describes the history of the attempt to drain the swamp. This is a good trail to walk just to see some of the interesting upland wildlife living at the swamp edge—including gopher tortoises, lizards, and other reptiles, birds, skunks, and armadillos just to name a few.

Okefenokee National Wildlife Refuge Trails

A 4.5-mile wildlife drive from the visitor center to Chesser Island provides access to the other trails. The first is the **Peckerwood Trail** designed to show the endangered red-cockaded woodpecker. This short, 0.2-mile trail is packed with observation opportunities. It circles through an old longleaf pine stand with a number of trees housing the characteristic cavity of the small woodpecker that makes its nest cavity in a live tree. Whitish pine resin flowing from the woodpecker-scored area around the cavity is very visible. The cavity trees have been marked with a white band of paint so they are easy to locate. Other wildlife such as deer, squirrels, and other species of birds are seen frequently on this trail.

On Chesser Island, the **Homestead Trail** is a pleasant walk through a typical Okefenokee homestead farm. The house, outbuildings, and other artifacts of farm life are intact and quite picturesque. This trail is about a 0.5 mile long.

The trail from the homestead takes you through swamp edge trees and shrubs to an observation tower. It is referred to as the **Deerstand Trail**. The observation tower is an ideal place to sit quietly and watch for deer and other wildlife in the clearings nearby. From the tower, the trail continues on to the beginning of the boardwalk.

The **Boardwalk**, only about 2.5 feet off the surface of the swamp, provides an almost unrestricted closeness to the swamp, and still be completely safe from any of the normal hazards associated with wildlife and weather. Alligators, sandhill cranes, herons, egrets, ibises, anhingas, warblers, redwinged black birds, frogs, raccoons, otters, and perhaps a water snake may

Prairie habitat in Okefenokee Swamp, from observation tower at end of boardwalk — Okefenokee National Wildlife Refuge.

be seen along the walk of slightly less than a one-mile penetration into the Okefenokee. It goes from the dense vegetation of the swamp's edge to the open prairie and finally to the observation tower tucked among the cypress trees on the edge of Seagrove Lake. From this height, the swamp presents a primal view with nothing but undisturbed swamp to the horizon in all directions. One almost expects to see a large amphibious dinosaur in the ancient ooze. A spur walkway leads to a blind, completely enclosed with portals for observation or photography. Another shelter about halfway out the boardwalk provides a place to rest and absorb the beauty, get out of the rain, or sit and quietly watch for wildlife. The boardwalk is one of the best ways to see the swamp and not be hampered by a boat or the noise of a motor. The boardwalk is completely wheelchair accessible except for the steps up the tower at the end. Restroom facilities are available at the parking area on Chesser Island.

84 Appalachian Trail in Georgia

Overview: The Appalachian Trail is said to be the longest continually marked trail in the world. It begins at Springer Mountain in Georgia and ends 2,100 miles away at Mount Katahdin in Maine.

The Appalachian Trail grew out of a 1921 proposal by forester and land-use planner Benton MacKaye. For sixteen years, hiking clubs, Civilian Conservation Corps members, and many other volunteers worked to see MacKaye's dream come true. On August 14, 1937, the final two miles were opened in Maine. This completed the 2,054-mile trail from Georgia to Maine. The trail has undergone many changes since 1937. Storms, changes in land use, and other factors have made it necessary to reroute sections of the trail. The original terminus in Georgia was Mount Oglethorpe, twenty miles farther south than today's Springer Mountain.

The Appalachian Trail as we know it today is an excellent example of cooperation between government and private conservation organizations. In Georgia the U.S. Forest Service, the Appalachian Trail Conference, and the Georgia Appalachian Trail Club have worked together diligently to maintain the trail and protect its corridor lands. Congress authorized the Appalachian Trail as the first National Scenic Trail in 1968. The Appalachian Trail Conference now has responsibility for the trail.

There are eleven primitive shelters spaced about a day's hike apart. Most are three-sided and are close to water. The oldest shelter is atop Blood Mountain built by the Civilian Conservation Corps in the 1930s. This is a four-sided stone structure with fireplace and sleeping platform.

The route of the Appalachian Trail is excellent black bear habitat. Because of this it is necessary to take the normal precautions with food at campsites. Hang food from a tree limb at least ten feet off the ground and do not leave food in your tent if you are away from it for several hours. There is little physical danger from bears and they are usually only a problem at heavily used campsites.

Anyone planning to hike long sections of the trail should contact the Georgia Appalachian Trail Club or the Appalachian Trail Conference for current information. (See Appendix A and D).

General description: A wilderness hike along a marked trail for many miles with appropriately spaced shelters, rugged terrain, scenic vistas, seasonal wildflower displays, wildlife, and a variety of hiking adventures and challenges on a world famous trail make the Appalachian one of the most popular of all hiking trails. The Georgia section of the trail is seventy-six miles long, from Springer Mountain to Bly Gap on the North Carolina state line.

General location: The trail lies in the Chattahoochee National Forest meandering through the northeastern portion of the state.

Maps: The Appalachian Trail in Georgia (a map and brochure) prepared by Georgia Appalachian Trail Club, Inc. and *The Guide to the Appalachian Trail in North Carolina and Georgia* prepared by the Appalachian Trail Conference; Appalachian Trail—Chattahoochee National Forest Georgia, printed by U.S.Forest Service; Amicalola, Nimblewill, Noontootla, Suches, Neels Gap, Cowrock, Jacks Gap, Tray Mountain, Macedonia, and Hightower Bald USGS quads.(See Appendix D).

Degree of difficulty: Moderate to strenuous.

Length: Total Appalachian Trail is 2,100 miles long. The Georgia section is about seventy-six miles. Some of the shelters are well off the main trail. Whitly Gap shelter at Wildcat Mountain is 1.1 miles in on a well-marked, blue-blazed trail. Others are as much as 0.3 mile on side trails. Trail relocation to prevent overuse causes variations in mileage from year to year.

Elevations: The trail begins at 3,872 feet on Springer Mountain and drops to about 2,500 feet at Three Forks, the lowest point on the hike. The highest

Two through-hikers on crest of Blood Mountain, highest point on the Appalachian Trail in Georgia.

Appalachian Trail in Georgia

mountain crossed by the trail is Blood Mountain, 4,458 feet. Tray Mountain is 4,430 feet. Most of the ridges crossed are about 3,000 feet.

Special attractions: Wilderness hiking in rugged terrain, scenic vistas, seasonal wildflower displays, and wildlife. Spring and early summer offers displays of azalea, mountain laurel, rhododendron, and many other wildflowers. October is the best fall color month. Mountain scenery that is hidden from view by summer foliage is open in winter with many eye-catching vistas.

Best season: This trail is hiked in all seasons. But sudden and extreme weather changes are the rule. Heavy rainstorms can be expected from late winter through summer. From late fall through early spring be prepared for sudden cold, wet weather with freezing rain and snow.

If you plan to hike the entire Appalachian Trail to Maine from Georgia a March or April start is advised. The Georgia section can be hiked at any time of the year with spring and fall the most popular.

For more information: Georgia Appalachian Trail Club, Inc., P.O. Box 654, Atlanta, GA 30301; Appalachian Trail Conference, P.O. Box 807, Harpers Ferry, W. VA 25425-0807; U.S. Forest Service, Forest Supervisor, Gainesville, GA 30512; (770)532-6366. For specific Ranger Districts see appendix. Georgia Wildlife Resources Division, Game Management Section, 2150 Dawsonville Highway, Gainesville, GA 30501; (770)535-5700.

Finding the trailheads: To get to the southern trailhead at Springer Mountain by road from Ellijay go east on Georgia Highway 52 about six miles to Big Creek Road. Turn left, north, and go thirteen miles to Doublehead Gap. Turn right at Mount Pleasant Baptist Church on unpaved Forest Road 42 and go about 6.5 miles to the Appalachian Trail crossing. The Springer Mountain trailhead is one mile from FR 42. From Dahlonega go west on Georgia Highway 52 about twenty-four miles, pass the entrance to Amicalola Falls State Park, to Roy Road at Stanley's Store. Turn right on Roy Road. It ends at the Big Creek Road in about eight miles. Turn right and follow directions to FR 42 above.

The Springer Mountain access trail from Amicalola Falls State Park is a preferred starting point for long-hikers because of the special parking area and the information available at the visitor center. There are scales available to weigh your pack and a register to record your hike with time, date, and destination. This trailhead is described below under "The Amicalola Falls State Park Approach Trail."

There are a number of ways to get to the trail, including five major paved-road crossings. From south to north: Georgia Highway 60 (Woody Gap), U.S. Highway 19/129 (Neels Gap), Georgia Highway 348 (Richard B. Russell Scenic Highway at Hog Pen and Tesnatee gaps), Georgia Highway 17/75 (Unicoi Gap), and U.S. Highway 76 (Dick's Creek Gap). Also, a number of Forest Roads cross or end at the trail and several Forest Service trails reach the Appalachian Trail. These will be discussed or have been discussed in other hikes.

The hikes: Hikers use the Appalachian Trail in many ways. There are the "through-hikers," those who start at Springer Mountain or the Amicalola Falls State Park approach and plan to hike the entire 2,100 miles to Mount

Katahdin in Maine. It is estimated that about ten percent hike all the way, taking four to six months. The rest discontinue the hike at varying distances up the Blue Ridge. Many others hike only portions of the trail. And there are still others who hike only a few miles to some interesting point, usually using any one of the approach trails or start at one road crossing and go to another. The beauty of the Appalachian Trail is that it seems to accommodate all. This is best described by the plaque on Springer Mountain: "Georgia to Maine - a footpath for those who seek fellowship with the wilderness."

The **Amicalola Falls State Park Approach Trail** is the most popular for through-hikers or for those who want to hike up to Springer Mountain, spend a night in the shelter, and return. This is an 8.5-mile, moderate to strenuous, one-way hike. To reach the park from Dahlonega go fourteen miles west on Georgia Highway 52. From Ellijay go twenty miles east on GA 52. The trailhead is at the visitor center. The park has a special parking area for Appalachian Trail users.

The trail is blazed with blue. From the visitor center at about 1,800 feet hike past the falls at 2,600 feet and into the woods beyond the lodge. Continue to climb along old roads for about four miles to Frosty Mountain (elev. 3,382 feet). Go through Nimblewill gap at 3,049 feet and up to Black

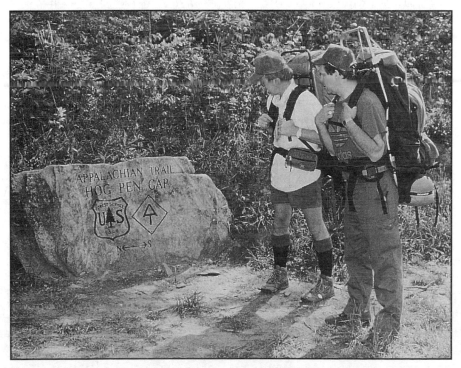

Two Appalachian Trail hikers who have been on the trail four days stop at Hog Pen Gap.

Mountain at 3,600 feet, through another 3,200-foot-high gap where Gilmer, Fannin, and Dawson counties join. The final climb to Springer Mountain (3,782 feet) is 580 feet uphill to the beginning of the Appalachian Trail. The trail then passes through a forest of stunted oaks that will be seen at most of the higher mountain crossings on the way to Bly Gap at the North Carolina line seventy-six miles away.

Jarrard Gap and Slaughter Gap Approach Trails begin at Lake Winfield Scott, 4.5 miles east of Suches on Georgia Highway 180 (see Hike 14).

Byron Reece Picnic and Parking Area is about 0.4 mile north on U.S. Highway 19/129 from Neels Gap. The trailhead for this spur trail at the parking area is about 0.7 mile from the Appalachian Trail, a moderate climb from 3,040 feet to Flatrock Gap at about 3,460 feet. To the right is a stiff climb to the top of Blood Mountain. To the left, the trail drops down one mile to Neels Gap. Another trail, the Freeman Trail, takes off from the Flatrock Gap junction. It is discussed in the following day hikes section. The spur trail and parking area was designed to take pressure away from parking at Neels Gap and the Walasi-Yi Center where hiking and backpacking supplies are available.

Jacks Knob Trail provides access to the Appalachian Trail at Chattahoochee Gap. It is discussed in Hike 13.

Dockery Lake Trail is a 3.4-mile trail from the Dockery Lake Recreation Area. The recreation area is on Georgia Highway 60, twelve miles north of Dahlonega. The trailhead is at the parking lot for the picnic area. This trail climbs about 400 feet to Millers Gap on the Appalachian Trail. This hike goes up Pigeon Root Creek, a tributary to Waters Creek. It is moderate along the creek and becomes strenuous in the last climb to the gap.

Day hikes: There are several excellent day hikes associated with the Appalachian Trail.

• **Springer Mountain** area has two loops that are five and ten miles. The shorter loop is the Benton MacKaye with white diamond blazes from Springer Mountain to Big Stamp Gap and then to Crosstrails and back along the Appalachian Trail to Springer Mountain. The longer loop can be hiked on either the Benton MacKaye or Appalachian Trail to Three Forks and back to Springer Mountain on the other. This trail system is reached on Forest Road 42.

• **Woody Gap to Big Cedar Mountain** is a short two-mile round trip hike to excellent views from the top of Big Cedar. Woody Gap is 3,160 feet elevation. Big Cedar Mountain at the rocky overlook is 3,721 feet.

• **Blood Mountain** is the destination from several points. It can be reached in a strenuous hike from Vogel State Park, using the Coosa Backcountry Trail to Slaughter Gap and up to Blood Mountain (see Hike 33). From Lake Winfield Scott hike up Jarrard Gap Trail to the Appalachian Trail, north on the Appalachian Trail to Slaughter Gap, one mile to Blood Mountain and back to Slaughter Gap and down Slaughter Gap Trail to Lake Winfield Scott (see Hike 14).

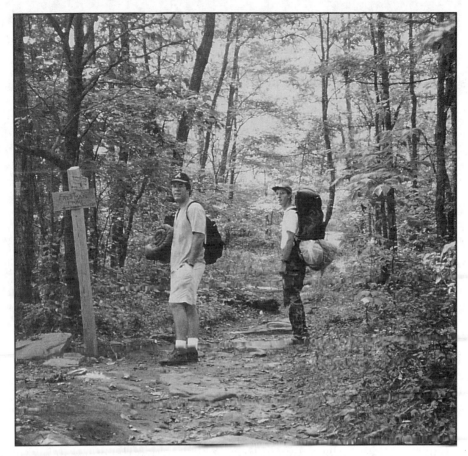

Flatrock Gap on Appalachian Trail at the end of Byron Reece Access Trail.

• **Hog Pen Gap to Wildcat Mountain** takes you into the Raven Cliffs Wilderness Area on a short two-mile, one-way easy to moderate hike. From the parking area at Hogpen Gap (Georgia Highway 346) go south on the Appalachian Trail to the blue-blazed Whitly Gap Trail. Turn south for one mile along the ridge to the overlook and to Whitly Gap shelter.

• **Tray Mountain** is particularly unique in both vegetation and geology. Forest Road 79 reaches the Appalachian Trail east of Indian Grave Gap (see Hike 24). Park here and hike about 1.5 miles to Tray Gap and up the trail to the rocky summit of Tray Mountain, another steep 0.5 mile; or drive on FR 79 to Tray Gap and hike the one-mile, round trip to the Tray Mountain top. A much longer 10.5-mile round-trip hike can be made from Unicoi Gap on Georgia Highway 17/75 along the Appalachian Trail.

The Appalachian Trail is described in detail in *The Guide to the Appalachian Trail in North Carolina and Georgia*. This book and maps contain trail mileages, water and shelter locations, side trails, and other pertinent information necessary to hike in the two states. It can be purchased from many local hiking and backpacking stores or from the Appalachian Trail Conference, P.O. Box 807, Harpers Ferry, W. VA 25425-0807.

A very brief description here will help you plan shorter hikes and orient you for trail and road crossings with distances between roads and location of shelters. It is not intended to be a complete trail description.

The Appalachian Trail from Amicalola Falls State Park Approach Trail to Bly Gap with checkpoint distances and elevations.

Amicalola Falls State Park Approach Trail. From visitor center to Springer Mountain 8.5 miles; elevation, 1,800 feet, parking area, food, and lodging.

0.0 miles - Springer Mountain southern terminus of Appalachian Trail. Begins on white blazed trail to Bly Gap, North Carolina. Elevation 3,782 feet; trail shelter; water; plaque and registration box.

2.5 miles - Stover Creek Shelter; water.

4.0 miles - Three Forks. Elevation 2,500 feet; water; Forest Road 58; limited parking.

7.6 miles - Hawk Mountain trail shelter. Elevation 3,380 feet; water.

8.1 miles - Hightower Gap. Elevation 2,854 feet; Forest Roads 69 and 42.

11.6 miles - Cooper Gap. Elevation 2,820 feet; Forest Roads 80, 42, and 15.

16.4 miles - Gooch Gap trail shelter. Elevation 2,784 feet; water; Forest Road 42.

20.0 miles - Woody Gap. Elevation 3,160 feet; Georgia Highway 60; first paved road, parking area, and trail information sign.

22.9 miles - Miller Gap. Elevation 2,980 feet; Dockery Lake Trail.

25.3 miles - Jarrard Gap. Elevation 3,310 feet; water; Jarrard Gap Trail to Lake Winfield Scott.

27.3 miles - Slaughter Gap. Elevation 3,850 feet; end of Duncan Ridge Trail; Coosa Backcountry Trail to Vogel State Park; information board with detailed discussion of hypothermia; water nearby.

28.3 miles - Blood Mountain. Elevation 4,458 feet; no water; stone building trail shelter; highest point on Appalachian Trail in Georgia.

29.3 miles - Flatrock Gap. Elevation 3,460 feet; Spur Trail to Byron Reece Memorial parking area; Freeman Trail.

30.7 miles - Neels Gap. Elevation 3,125 feet; Walasi-Yi Center with hostel for *through-hikers* only from March to May before Memorial Day. The center also has a hiking and camping outfitting store with books, maps, and snacks.

35.3 miles - Cowrock Mountain. Elevation 3,852; vistas from rock outcrops.

36.2 miles - Tesnatee Gap. Elevation 3,120 feet; Georgia Highway 348 (Russell Scenic Highway); Logan Turnpike Trail, parking.

36.8 miles - Wildcat Mountain. Elevation 3,730 feet; Whitly Gap trail shelter is about a mile south on a blue-blazed trail; water; good views; Ravens Cliff Wilderness.

37.0 miles - Hog Pen Gap. Elevation 3,480 feet; Georgia Highway 348; parking, interpretive signs, and markers.

41.3 miles - Low Gap. Elevation 3,032 feet; trail shelter; water.

46.3 miles - Chattahoochee Gap. Elevation 3,520 feet; water; the beginning of the Chattahoochee River; Jacks Knob Trail to Georgia Highway 180 and Brasstown Bald.

48.53 miles - Blue Mountain. Elevation 4,020 feet; trail shelter; water.

50.7 miles - Unicoi Gap. Elevation 2,949 feet; Georgia Highway 17/75; parking.

53.3 miles - Indian Grave Gap. Elevation 3,120; Forest Road 283; Andrews Cove Trail to Andrews Cove Recreation Area.

54.0 miles - Forest Road 79. Elevation 3,400 feet; Forest Road 79 leads down to Robertstown and Helen.

55.2 miles - Tray Gap. Elevation 3,841; Forest Road 79.

56.2 miles - Tray Mountain. Elevation 4,430; trail shelter; water; rock outcrops and scenic views; only a few feet lower than Blood Mountain; Tray Mountain Wilderness.

61.5 miles - Addis Gap. Elevation 3,300 feet; Forest Road 26; trail shelter; water.

66.8 miles - Dicks Creek Gap. Elevation 2,675, U.S. Highway 76; parking; picnic area.

71.2 miles - Plumorchard Gap. Elevation 3,100 feet; trail shelter; water; this unique shelter was put in place by helicopter.

72.4 miles - Blue Ridge Gap. Elevation 3,020 feet; Forest Road 72.

76.0 miles - Bly Gap. Elevation 3,840 feet; the North Carolina line; no road to this gap as the trail leaves Georgia.

85 Benton MacKaye Trail

Overview: Benton MacKaye (pronounced to rhyme with eye) for whom this trail is named is considered to be the father of the Appalachian Trail. This newest of the long trails in Georgia was conceived in 1979 as a 250-mile hiking trail that would provide an alternative in the southeast to the much-used Appalachian Trail. It now connects with the Appalachian Trail at Springer Mountain and will eventually intersect the Appalachian Trail in the Great Smoky Mountains National Park to form what the Benton MacKaye Association calls a huge figure-eight trail system.

The section through Georgia has been completed to the Tennessee line in the Cohutta Wilderness at Double Springs Gap. The U.S. Forest Service and Benton MacKaye Trail Association members have done a remarkable job in completing the Georgia section of the trail. As with other trail associations all members volunteer their time and energies in building and maintaining these trails on public land and preparing maps. The Benton MacKaye Trail Association welcomes new members.

In Georgia, the trail begins at Springer Mountain with the Appalachian Trail and extends in a sweeping S shape to the north and west. The trail lies mostly in

Benton MacKaye Trail

To Morgantown

To Morgantown

Blue Ridge Lake

Aska

Rich Mtn. Trail

Stanley Creek Rd.

Shallowford Bridge

Rock Creek Rd.

RICH MOUNTAIN WILDERNESS

Big Creek Rd.

Roy Rd.

Doublehead Gap

60

Wilscot Gap

Brawley Mtn.

Skeenah Gap

Rhodes Gap

Duncan Ridge Trail

60

Taccoa River

Bryson Gap

Appalachian Trail

58

42

Three Forks

P

Springer Mtn.

Approach Trail

P

Amicalola Falls State Park

the Chattahoochee National Forest. Although it frequently crosses major roads in the mountains, it has many remote stretches and provides true wilderness hiking. The hike follows rhododendron- and laurel-lined trout streams and crosses one of the longest hiker's suspension bridges in the country. Mountains and ridges with scenic vistas, mature and regenerating forests, and paved and unpaved mountain roads are all part of the trail. This new trail will provide a challenge for any serious hiker.

The trail passes through the Blue Ridge and Cohutta Wildlife Management areas. Firearm deer seasons in the management areas are about four days each in November and December. If hiking during these times stay on the trail, wear a blaze orange vest, and cap or pack cover.

Benton MacKaye would be very proud of what the Trail Association has accomplished in scouting and building this challenging long hike. Hopefully the Tennessee and North Carolina portions will be completed soon. Then a grand loop trail from Springer Mountain to the Great Smoky Mountains National Park on the Benton MacKaye Trail and back on the Appalachian Trail will be possible. It will pass through some of the finest wilderness areas in the East.

General description: Remote wilderness hiking through scenic mountain country with a variety of optional side trips of shorter loop trails along the route.
General location: This long trail lies between Ellijay and Blue Ridge near the Tennessee state line. It crosses U.S. Highway 76, the newly completed parkway between these towns.
Maps: Benton MacKaye Trail in Georgia Map and Guide (a one-page map/ brochure) and eight detailed maps of trail sections are available from the Benton MacKaye Trail Association and most hiker outfitting stores; Chattahoochee National Forest Map; Cohutta Wilderness Area Map; Amicalola, Nimblewill, Noontootla, Wilscot, Blue Ridge, Cashes Valley, Dyer Gap, and Hemp Top USGS quads.
Degree of difficulty: Throughout the seventy-nine-mile trail, sections vary from easy to strenuous. This trail has more moderate sections than the Appalachian, Bartram, or Duncan Ridge trails.
Length: The Benton MacKaye Trail Association reports 78.6 miles as the total trail length in Georgia.
Elevations: Elevations range from about 1,500 feet just north of US 76 to 3,782 feet at Springer Mountain. The trail is a series of ups and downs between these elevations, several reaching 3,500 feet.
Special attractions: Remote wilderness hiking, two waterfalls, scenic views from several mountains and ridges, wildflowers, birding, wildlife, fishing, backpacking, and shorter loops with other trails for dayhikes are all available on this long trail.
Best season: This is a four season trail. As with all long trails you must be prepared for sudden thunderstorms in spring and summer and for sudden cold weather changes from late fall through winter and into early spring. Blooming times for spring flowers may vary as much as a month in the mountains depending on elevations and direction of mountain slopes.
For more information: Benton MacKaye Trail Association, P.O.Box 53271, Atlanta, GA 30355-1271. U.S. Forest Service, Chattahoochee National Forest, Forest Supervisor, 508 Oak Street, Gainesville, GA 30501; (770)536-0541. U.S. Forest Service, Cohutta Ranger District, 401 Old Ellijay Road, Chatsworth, GA,

30705; (706)695-6736. U.S. Forest Service, Taccoa Ranger District, East Main Street, Suite 5, Owenby Building, Blue Ridge, GA 30513; (706)632-3031.

Finding the trailhead: The southern trailhead is the southern terminus of the Appalachian Trail on Springer Mountain.

From Ellijay go east on Georgia Highway 52 about six miles to Big Creek Road. Turn left and go about thirteen miles to Doublehead Gap. Turn right on Forest Road 42 at Mount Pleasant Baptist Church and go about 6.5 miles on this unpaved road to the Appalachian Trail. FR 42 crosses Benton MacKaye Trail in another 1.7 miles. Both trails lead up to Springer Mountain.

From Dahlonega go west on Georgia Highway 52 about twenty-four miles, pass the entrance to Amicalola Falls State Park, and on to Roy road at Stanley's Store. Turn right on Roy Road. It ends at the Big Creek Road in about eight miles. Turn right and follow directions to FR 42, given above. It also is possible to reach Springer Mountain from Amicalola Falls State Park on the 8.5-mile approach to the Appalachian Trail, Hike 84.

There are no roads to the northern end (trailhead) at Double Springs Gap at the Tennessee line.

Other access points to the trail are at road crossings. Georgia Highway 60 is crossed about thirty-five miles north of Dahlonega or 11.8 miles south from Morganton near a grocery store/service station and trout farm. The trail crosses GA 60 again at Wilscot Gap about 7.5 miles south of Morganton. Aska Road is crossed at Shallowford Bridge over Taccoa River. It is 8.4 miles on Aska Road from Blue Ridge to Taccoa River. The next major road is U.S. Highway 76 at Cherrylog Church. Dyer Gap and Watson Gap are the northern most road accesses. From Blue Ridge go north 3.6 miles on Georgia Highway 5 to Old Georgia Highway 2. Turn left on Georgia Highway 2 and go about eleven miles where the pavement ends. Continue on unpaved GA 2 to the top of the mountain at Watson Gap. Turn left on Forest Road 64 and go 3.2 miles to trail crossing a few yards south of Dyer Gap at the old cemetery. There are no roads to the Double Springs Gap on the Tennessee line.

The hike: Benton MacKaye Trail is marked with white diamond-shaped blazes. Trails to water are marked with blue blazes. Some of the side trails are marked with white or blue rectangular blazes. Double blazes indicate significant turns in the trail.

Benton MacKaye Trail leaves Springer Mountain and follows the old Appalachian Trail to Big Stamp Gap. It then crosses over Rich Mountain and down to Three Forks, where Stover, Chester, and Long creeks come together. Between Springer Mountain and Three Forks, the two trails form two loops that are pleasant day-hike trails. The Springer Mountain and Stover Creek trail shelters for the Appalachian Trail are the only shelters near the Benton MacKaye Trail.

From Three Forks to Georgia Highway 60, the blue-blazed Duncan Ridge Trail is contiguous with Benton MacKaye. The Appalachian Trail is the same path for a short distance before it turns up to Hawk Mountain. You cross Bryson Gap and down to the long suspension bridge crossing Taccoa River and on to Georgia Highway 60.

Benton MacKaye continues with Duncan Ridge Trail for the next 4.5 miles to Rhodes Mountain. This is the most strenuous section up Wallalah, Licklog, and Rhodes mountains. Duncan Ridge Trail leaves to the east and Benton MacKaye turns northwest following relatively easy ridgetops to Skeenah Gap. From here follow ridgetops along Wilscot Mountain to Wilscot Gap where the trail crosses GA 60 again.

From GA 60 cross Tipton Mountain and to the lookout tower on Brawley Mountain. From the tower drop down through Garland Gap and across Garland Mountain before the decent to the Taccoa River and Shallowford Bridge. From the bridge hike on unpaved Stanley Creek Road for 3.5 miles. Leave the road to ascend Rocky Mountain. At Stanley Gap, Rich Mountain Trail joins the Benton MacKaye Trail and follows along for about two miles. It is blazed with white rectangles. Beyond Rocky Mountain the Rich Mountain Trail turns off to the right, Benton MacKaye crosses Scoggins Knob and drops down to unpaved Weaver Creek Road.

From Weaver Creek Road to Bush Head Gap, Benton MacKaye follows paved and unpaved roads for 8.4 miles. An off-road trail is being planned here. Stay on Weaver Creek Road to U.S. Highway 76 at Cherrylog Church. Turn south on US 76 for 1.5 miles and turn right on Gilmer County Road 187 to Bush Head Gap.

Fishing on the Chattooga River.

You are now back in the Chattahoochee Forest. From Bush Head Gap to Dyer Gap is a 12.5-mile hike with strenuous climbs. The trail leads southwest to Fowler Mountain and the Tennessee Valley Divide. The trail follows this ridge line more or less through Hallway Gap, past Double Hogpen and Flat Top Mountain before reaching Dyer Gap and Forest Road 64/GA 2.

From Dyer Gap, the trail drops down to the Forest Service's South Fork Jacks River Trail and is contiguous with Benton MacKaye for about two miles where it turns to the right at Rich Cove. Old logging roads are followed up Dyer Mountain. From here it is about a mile along the ridgetops to Watson Gap. From Watson Gap to Dally Gap, Benton MacKaye skirts around private land by following Forest Road 22-1 for a short distance and then turns north and crosses Mill Branch, enters the Cohutta Wilderness Area, passes through Peter Cove and intercepts Jacks River Trail. Turn right and follow both the white diamond and orange blaze of Jacks River Trail to Dally Gap. This is the last parking area on the Georgia section of Benton MacKaye. From here, the trail to Hemp Top and the lookout tower is contiguous with Forest Road 73 (no longer a vehicular road). The last 2 miles is on the Hemp Top Trail (white rectangle blazes) to Double Springs Gap and Tennessee. From the Tennessee line, the Hemp Top Trail continues up the steep climb for about 1.6 miles to Big Frog Mountain on the boundary of Big Frog Wilderness and Cohutta Wilderness areas.

86 Bartram National Recreation Trail

Overview: William Bartram, for whom this trail is named, collected seeds and plants in the northeast Georgia area in the spring of 1776. He was traveling alone, after his Indian guide failed to return, on a trip across the Blue Ridge Mountains to the Overhill towns where he visited the heart of the Cherokee Nation in Tennessee on the Little Tennessee River, now covered by the lake behind the infamous Tellico Dam. One of the plants he first described was the umbrella tree, the deciduous Fraser's magnolia, was on Martins Creek.

The Bartram Trail enters Georgia from North Carolina near Commissioner's Rock and follows the ridge crest that forms the Tennessee Valley Divide down to Warwoman Dell. It crosses the second highest mountain in the state, Rabun Bald, at 4,696 feet. From there it drops down to the Chattooga River and joins the Chattooga River Trail for ten miles.

Bartram traveled extensively in other sections of the state, along the Savannah River near Augusta, along the coast and across Georgia from Augusta to the Ocmulgee River (See Hike 45) near Macon and on to the Chattahoochee River south of Columbus.

The Bartram trail was dedicated a National Recreation Trail on April 22, 1978. This Georgia mountain section is only a short part of a much longer proposed trail.

Bartram National Recreation Trail

General description: This thirty-seven-mile trail goes through a wide variety of habitat types from the high mountain ridges to the banks of the Chattooga River.
General location: This Georgia section of the trail is in Rabun County, the northeast corner of the state.
Maps: Chattahoochee National Forest Map and a page-size map is available at the Tallulah Ranger District office in Clayton; Rabun Bald, Rainy Mountain, Whetstone, and Satoala USGS quads.
Degree of difficulty: Moderate to strenuous.
Length: Total length in Rabun County is thirty-seven miles. It is 17.4 miles from Hales Ridge Road to Warwoman Dell and another 19.5 miles to Georgia Highway 28 on the Chattooga River.
Elevations: The highest point is Rabun Bald at 4,696 feet. Hales Ridge Road crossing is 3,280 feet. Warwoman Road crossing is at 1,920 feet. Chattooga River at Sandy Ford is about 1,400 feet.
Special attractions: Mountain vistas; wildflowers; fishing; hunting; birding; and a trip into the past with William Bartram, botanist, explorer, and artist.
Best season: The northern section of the trail is best in spring, summer, and fall. Winter hiking along the ridge crests can be very windy and cold. The trail is open all winter except during periods of heavy snowfall. Rabun Bald is especially beautiful during the fall leaf change and in early spring when the leaves of the many species of trees are just beginning to show multi-shades of green. Early summer is the time when the masses of rhododendron bloom. The section of the trail below Warwoman is definitely year-round. The Chattooga River is open to year-round fishing and winter trout fishing can be enjoyable.
For more information: U.S. Forest Service, Tallulah Ranger District, 809 Highway 441 S., Clayton, GA 30525; (706)782-3320. Bartram Trail Society, 3823 Lithia Way, Lithia Springs, GA 30057; (770)948-1513.

Finding the trailhead: The north end of the trail crosses Hale Ridge Road, Forest Road 7, about 300 yards from the North Carolina state line. Limited parking space is at this crossing. Because it is downhill most of the way, this is the best trailhead to use if you plan to hike the whole thirty-seven miles to Georgia Highway 28. Another access point is Warwoman Dell Recreation Area on Warwoman Road about three miles east of Clayton. There is good parking here. Sandy Ford Road, a gravel road, leaves Warwoman Road at Antioch Church east of Warwoman Dell and crosses Bartram Trail near Chattooga River and Sandy Ford. Joining the Chattooga River Trail at this point the path goes northeast up the river to West Fork and GA 28 bridge where it leaves Georgia. The Chattooga River trailhead is at a gravel parking lot on the Georgia side of the river.

The hike: Very little of the actual path that Bartram followed during his travels in the 1770s is on public land today. But the great expanse of the Chattahoochee National Forest has made it possible to have this thirty-seven-mile section of his travels on public land. Virtually all of the forests that Bartram saw have been logged over time and again in the nearly 225 years since he rode his horse through the mountains. Although the great cove hardwood forests of yesteryear are gone, the high ridges that separate the Tennessee River Valley from the Savannah River Valley, supporting only stunted oaks and rhododendron thickets, may still look much the same. With the recovery of the forests under the U.S. Forest Service's management it is not hard to imagine the magnificence of the original southern Blue Ridge Mountains as you look out from the truncated tower on Rabun Bald or over the valleys down to Martin Creek toward Warwoman Dell.

Begin the hike where it crosses Hale Ridge Road, Forest Road 7, about 300 yards from the North Carolina line. This trail is marked by a rectangular yellow paint blaze. The elevation is 3,280 feet and the trail remains very near the same elevation to the crossing of Holcomb Creek before the climb to Beegum Gap and the top of Rabun Bald, 4,696 feet. The last 1.5 miles of this climb is through a rhododendron thicket on a well-used rocky trail. The old Forest Service fire lookout was converted into a large observation deck by the Youth Conservation Corps. The 360-degree view from the stone based deck offers a full picture of the many rounded knobs of these very old mountains.

From Rabun Bald, the trail leads to the southwest, dropping rapidly to Flint Gap and to Saltrock Gap. Go to the east and south of 4,142-foot Flat Top. The trail drops quickly through a gap and up again to Wilson Knob and then in more moderate ascents and descents past Double Knob and Wilson Gap. Here the trail intersects a jeep road. The trail stays on the road for about a 0.5 mile and turns to the left and down to Windy Gap. After going around the east of Raven Knob, the path reaches Courthouse Gap, which is about fourteen miles from the beginning of the hike. For the next 3.5 miles, the trail turns to the southeast into the Martin Creek drainage. The trail heads back into thick rhododendron tunnels. The sound of falling water gives way to Martin Creek Falls, which cascades about fifty feet beside the trail before it turns back to the west and goes to Becky Branch. The Becky Branch falls are described in Hike 20—Warwoman Dell Nature Trail and Becky Branch Falls Trail. The trail crosses Warwoman Road and goes into the Warwoman Dell Recreation Area at 17.5 miles.

Bartram Trail now leaves the higher mountains and meanders over lower and more gentle hills and dells for 9.5 miles to Sandy Ford Road, less than a mile from the Chattooga River at Sandy Ford. This is an area of more open mixed hardwoods and pines along the higher, drier ridges with yellow-poplar, beech, hemlock, and rhododendron along the shaded streams. This is a fine wildflower area in spring and like the mountainous section is an interesting birding hike. Wildlife you might see include deer, turkeys, gray squirrels, the rarer fox squirrel, ruffed grouse, woodchucks, and chipmunks. Black bears, foxes, raccoons, and skunks are present but will seldom if ever be seen.

At Sandy Ford, the Bartram Trail joins the Chattooga River Trail about 100 yards beyond Sandy Ford Road. At this junction look for the two-foot diameter, round rock with the trail names and direction arrows carved in the stone. The trail from here to Georgia Highway 28 is described in Hike 87—Chattooga Wild and Scenic River Trail. It is worth mentioning again to take the side trail at Dicks Creek to Dicks Creek Falls and a great view of the river.

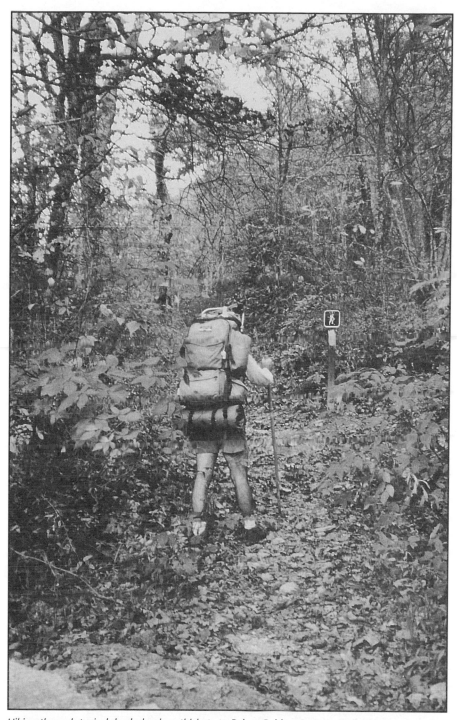

Hiking through typical rhododendron thickets to Rabun Bald on Bartram Trail. This is typical of many miles of trails in the north Georgia mountains.

If you have not already done so, read, at least, chapters III and IV of Part III in *Travels of William Bartram* before hiking the Bartram Trail. And keep in mind that Bartram made his trip alone with only the barest of verbal description of the topography to go on with no previous knowledge of the Southern Blue Ridge Mountains.

87 Chattooga Wild and Scenic River Trail

Overview: The Chattooga River's origin is in North Carolina and ends in Tugaloo Lake fifty miles downstream after dropping more than 2,000 feet. In May 1974, the river corridor was designated a National Wild and Scenic River. It is truly a wild and scenic area of mountainous terrain and beautiful streams. The Georgia portion of the trail coexists for ten miles with the Bartram Trail.

General description: This twenty-mile trail follows the Chattooga River, which forms the state boundary between Georgia and South Carolina.

General location: In Rabun County and the Chattahoochee National Forest on the Tallulah Ranger District.

Maps: The Forest Service has an excellent, large scale, detailed map of the Chattooga Wild and Scenic River with all trails; three USGS quads, Satolah, Whetstone, and Rainy Mountain, cover the Georgia section of the trail.

Degree of difficulty: Easy to moderate.

Length: The Georgia section of the trail from U.S. Highway 76 to Georgia Highway 28 is twenty miles.

Elevations: From 1,582 feet at the GA 28 bridge to 1,208 feet at US 76 bridge, the trail crosses numerous ridge spurs along the river, none of which vary significantly in elevation.

Special attractions: A pleasant trail with good primitive campsites. Excellent wildflower displays in spring and summer. Fishing in the Chattooga River and tributaries at trail crossings. Wildlife including wild turkeys, deer, raccoons, squirrels, and other small mammals. A variety of forest types from old forest habitat to interesting second growth hardwoods and evergreens make this a fine birding area. Access to great canoeing and white-water rafting.

Best season: Year-round with spring and fall best—wildflowers, leaf colors, and bird migration. Fishing in the Chattooga River is year-round. Winter conditions varying from very cold to pleasant walking weather.

For more information: Chattahoochee National Forest, Tallulah Ranger District, 804 Highway 441 South, Clayton, GA 30525; (706)782-3320.

Finding the trailhead: There are three roads providing access to the trail. East of Clayton on US 76 go nine miles to the Chattooga River for the lower trailhead, or east of Clayton for sixteen miles on the Warwoman Road to Georgia Highway 28 and two miles to the river at Russell Bridge for the upstream trailhead and Georgia road access. Another access point is gained from the Sandy Ford Road, a gravel and dirt road, that leads to the Chattooga River five miles from Warwoman Road. It crosses the Chattooga River Trail about 200 yards from the river and is about halfway between the two bridges.

The hike: There are more than fifty miles of trails in the Chattooga Wild and Scenic River corridor in Georgia and North and South Carolina. For the purposes of this discussion we will limit more detailed description to the Georgia section of the Chattooga River Trail.

The upstream portion of the Chattooga River Trail leaves Georgia and goes into South Carolina for 10.4 miles to Burrells Ford and the U.S. Forest Service campground. It continues north through the Ellicott Rock Wilderness for 3.8 miles to the North Carolina state line at Ellicott Rock where the three states join. From there it joins other trails in North Carolina. The total length of the Chattooga River Trail is about thirty-five miles, 20.5 of which are in Georgia.

The hike downstream from GA 28 begins at a brown post with the hiker symbol a few yards from the bridge. Go west down the bank of the river. The blaze is both a metal diamond and yellow paint to indicate it is both the Chattooga River and Bartram trail. The narrow path enters the woods along a steep-sided ridge above the river and quickly joins an old roadbed for about 0.5 mile to the West Fork of Chattooga River. Turn right and go up the West Fork for about 300 yards. At this point, the trail crosses West Fork. Old log steps lead down to the water's edge on both sides and the stream. It is about twenty yards wide and can be forded across a gravel bottom and sand bar. Because the water is swift and cold, a walking or wading staff is recommended for support. During normal flows, it is about knee deep. After heavy rains this crossing would be virtually impossible. An old pair of sneakers or sandals for the crossing will keep your hiking footwear dry. From this point to the south end of the trail there is no further need to wade tributary streams. The larger ones are crossed on short bridges or foot logs. Others can be stepped across. The footbridge across Adline Branch was washed out, but the stream most often can be crossed without getting wet.

On the south side of West Fork, the path winds through a variety of forest types. There are coves with moist-soil plants and large yellow-poplars, oaks, beeches, and sweet gums to mention just a few. The trail crosses drier ridge spurs and goes near stands of pure loblolly pine that were planted by Georgia Power Company following the sale of the land for the wild and scenic river acquisition. An old abandoned hay baler, left from the days when narrow cleared fields along the river bottom were farmed, indicates earlier land uses. There are good views of the river at several places along the trail. For the most part, however, the river is not visible from the path even though the turbulent, white-water rapids can be heard frequently along the trail. For the most part the trail follows at the base of the ridges where they meet the floodplain of the river.

This trail is especially blessed with wildlife populations of wild turkeys, white-tailed deer, grouse, foxes, raccoons, squirrels, chipmunks, and a wide variety of songbirds. This is an excellent birding area.

Chattooga Wild and Scenic River Trail

The first road crossed is unpaved Sandy Ford Road, ten miles into the hike. Just before reaching the road, the Bartram Trail leaves to the right and continues west. A large, round river stone at this junction is engraved with direction arrows for both trails. The river trail continues on to the left and crosses Sandy Ford Road about a 0.5 mile from the forks in the trail. Here there is a nice primitive camping area on Rock Creek. A short walk down the gravel road to the left leads to Sandy Ford where the river is especially scenic with white-water shoals and long pools. There is a clean sandy shore and a primitive campsite here. During the summer months, the river warms up enough for swimming and wading. Because of this, trout fishing is replaced by warmer-water species like the colorful redeye bass, a very sporting member of the black bass family.

Continuing on downstream, the path comes close to several very picturesque points on the river. The going is still easy to moderate for the next ten miles to US 76 and the southern terminus of the Chattooga River Trail.

This trail can, of course, be hiked in either direction. There are a number of good primitive campsites along the way. The twenty miles makes a leisurely three-day, two-night hike and is ideal for the weekend. Since this trail is most often hiked in one direction, it is necessary to arrange for transportation at the end of the hike.

Water is available all along the trail; however, you should only drink it after careful boiling, filtering, or chemical purification. The streams are highly vulnerable to *Giardia* and bacteria causing intestinal diseases.

Plans are in place in the Chattahoochee National Forest to standardize the blazes on both the Bartram and Chattooga River trails. The Bartram Trail is to be marked throughout with a yellow paint blaze while the Chattooga River Trail is marked with a white metal diamond blaze. Where the two trails coincide both blaze marks will be used.

88 Cohutta Wilderness Area Trails

Overview: Steep, rugged, heavily forested mountains, the Cohuttas are true wilderness today. Only sixty-five years ago the area was intensively logged for hardwood timber. Some of the old railroad beds used to haul the timber are still evident. There also were attempts at mining. But these scars have healed over and are not noticeable.

The Cohuttas have rounded and flat-topped ridges and mountaintops. The deep rich soils support distinct plant communities lush with ferns and herbs. This provides a unique botanical experience. Long wilderness hikes and shorter, loop dayhikes are available.

This mountain mass was designated wilderness by Congress in 1975. The Hemp Top section was added in 1987, making it the third-largest mountain wilderness in the east at 37,000 acres. Hiking opportunities are unlimited. Loop

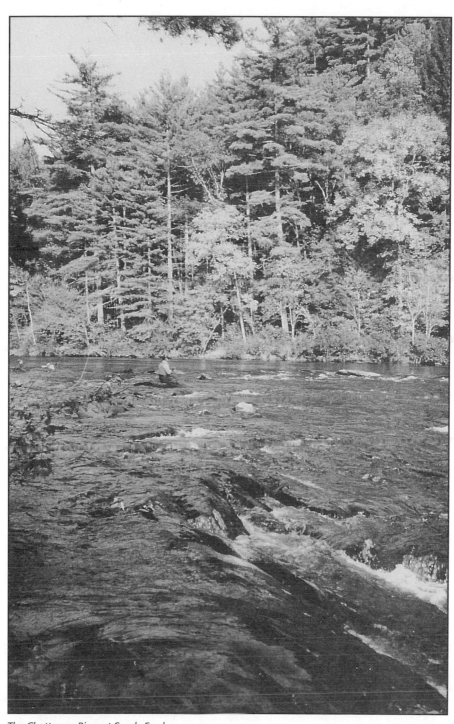

The Chattooga River at Sandy Ford.

Cohutta Wilderness Area Trails

To Blue Ridge

64-A

2

2

2

Three Forks Mountain

N

Rough Ridge (blue)

East Cowpen

Cowpen Mtn. 4149'

East Cowpen

P

Conasauga River (yellow)

Betty Gap

P

64

38

To Ellijay and Eton

Panther Creek (blue)

Falls

Conasauga River (yellow)

Chestnut Lead (blue)

P

68

Tearbritches (orange)

Hickory Creek (white)

P

68

P

17

Lake Conasauga

P

630

To Crandall

0   1   2
Miles

hikes are possible with many combinations of trails and roads. The U.S. Forest Service Roads around the boundary are pleasant to walk along and can make interesting loop trails to get back to a parking area and trailhead.

Geologically, the Cohutta Mountains are more like the mountains to the north—Ocoee, Unicoi, and Great Smokies—than the mountains to the east. Most of the Cohuttas drain into the Alabama river system.

More than forty species of rare and uncommon plants and a variety of game animals—such as black bears, wild boars, turkeys, deer, ruffed grouse, and squirrels—abound in the wilderness. The many cold-water streams support fine trout populations. The native brook trout along with rainbow and brown trout are found in several hundred miles of streams. The redeye bass occurs in the lower, warmer reaches of the larger streams. The redeye bass, a unique member of the black bass family, was first found and described for Sheeds Creek, a tributary of the Conasauga and Jacks River system. This is a fine game fish. Hunting and fishing are permitted in the wilderness area and are regulated by the Georgia Wildlife Resources Division. The small portion of the wilderness area lying in Tennessee is under the supervision of the Tennessee Wildlife Resources Agency.

Use of any motorized vehicles or motorized equipment is not permitted in the wilderness area.

General description: More than seventy-five miles of backcountry trails lead to grand forests, scenic beauty, fishing, hunting, and exploring.

General location: The wilderness area lies on the Georgia-Tennessee state line. Much of the boundary is defined by Forest Roads that are one-lane dirt surfaces wide enough for two cars to pass with care.

Maps: Forest Service Cohutta Wilderness Map printed on a scale of 1:31,680 (serious hikers should purchase this detailed map); the Chattahoochee National Forest Map; Tennga, Hemp Top, Epworth, Crandall, and Dyer Gap USGS quads.

Degree of difficulty: Most trails have strenuous sections, while a few are moderate to easy.

Length: Tearbritches Trail, 3.4 miles; Hickory Creek Trail, 8.4 miles; Conasauga River Trail, 13.2 miles; Rough Ridge Trail, 6.5 miles; Jacks River Trail, 15.6 miles; East Cowpen Trail, 6.6 miles; Penitentiary Branch Trail, 6.0 miles; Hemp Top Trail, 6.0 miles; Hickory Ridge Trail, 3.2 miles; Chestnut Lead Trail, 1.4 miles; Panther Creek Trail, 3.4 miles; Sugar Cove Trail, 2.6 miles; Rice Camp Trail, 3.4 miles; Beech Bottom Trail, 4 miles.

Elevations: Elevations range from 950 feet in Alaculsy Valley in the northwest corner to 4,200 feet at the crest of Big Frog Mountain on the northeast corner of the wilderness in Tennessee. Cowpen Mountain is 4,149 feet. Several of the mountains are above 3,500 feet.

Special attractions: Scenic waterfalls, mountains, and mature forests are ablaze with color in the fall. Birding, wildflower photography, fishing, and hunting for small and big game provides something for everyone.

Best season: Year-round hiking is possible. In spring and summer, sudden heavy rains can cause the streams to become raging torrents that should not be crossed. Winter snows can make the unpaved roads to the area impassible and steep trails dangerous for short periods. Spring wildflowers, spring and fall songbird migrations, and fall leaf color make these seasons the most popular.

For more information: U.S. Forest Service, Cohutta Ranger District, 401 G.I. Maddox Parkway, Chatsworth, GA 30705; (706)695-6736.

Finding the trailheads: Trailheads for most of the trails are at widened, gravel parking areas along these roads. The trail names are clearly marked at the parking areas. Since it is necessary for the Forest Service to close some of the roads during inclement weather, it is recommended to call the district rangers office before your trip, especially during the winter.

Access to the wilderness area is from five small towns around the area. Two are from towns on the east side, Ellijay and Blue Ridge, and three from the west, Eton, Crandall, and Cisco, with directions from Chatsworth.

From Ellijay take Georgia Highway 52 for nine miles to the Lake Conasauga Recreation Area and Cohutta Wildlife Management Area signs. Turn right on the paved road and go about one mile where the pavement ends. Here the road forks. Take the left fork, Forest Road 18. At about 3.5 miles Forest Road 68 turns sharp to the right. Take FR 68 and continue up the mountain for 9.3 miles. Pass the Holly Creek Check Station on the way. Forest Road 64 turns to the right, FR 68 to the left. FR 68 goes to Chestnut Lead and Tearbritches trails and to Lake Conasauga Recreation Area. FR 64 leads to the south end of Conasauga River and East Cowpen trails.

From Blue Ridge go north on Georgia Highway 5 for 3.5 miles to Old Georgia Highway 2. Turn left and continue about eleven miles to the end of the pavement. Continue on the unpaved road until it intercepts Forest Road 22-1 at Watson Gap. Take a sharp turn to the right onto FR 22-1 and go three miles to Dally Gap. This is the west trailhead for the Jacks River Trail. At Watson Gap it is possible to continue on GA 2 to Dyer Gap and follow Forest Road 64 to the right to Three Forks Mountain and the trailhead for East Cowpen Trail.

From Chatsworth there are three alternatives to the Cohuttas. Go north on U.S. Highway 411 about 2.5 miles to Eton and turn right at the traffic light on Fourth Avenue. This paved road becomes CCC Camp Road. The pavement ends in six miles and the dirt road becomes Forest Road 18. In about 3.5 more miles, FR 68 turns off to the left. From here follow the directions for FR 68 as described from Ellijay.

From Chatsworth go north on US 411 for 6.9 miles and turn right on Grassy Street. A sign points to Lake Conasauga Recreation Area. Follow Grassy Street across the railroad track and turn right and then back to the left on Forest Road 630. Follow this road up the mountain for seven miles and cross Forest Road 17 (East Cowpen Road) to the parking area. This is the trailhead for Hickory Creek Trail. At FR 17 turn left and go to the parking area and the north trailhead for Conasauga River Trail or take a right on FR 17 and go to FR 68. Turn left for the trailheads for Tearbritches and Chestnut Lead trails. Continue on FR 68 to Potatopatch Mountain and FR 64 to Betty Gap and the south trailhead for the Conasauga River Trail.

To reach the northern sections of the wilderness area from Chatsworth go north on US 411 to the small community of Cisco where GA 2 crosses US 411 at Greg's General Store. Turn right or east at old GA 2. In about one mile, the pavement ends. In about 0.5 mile, the road forks; take the

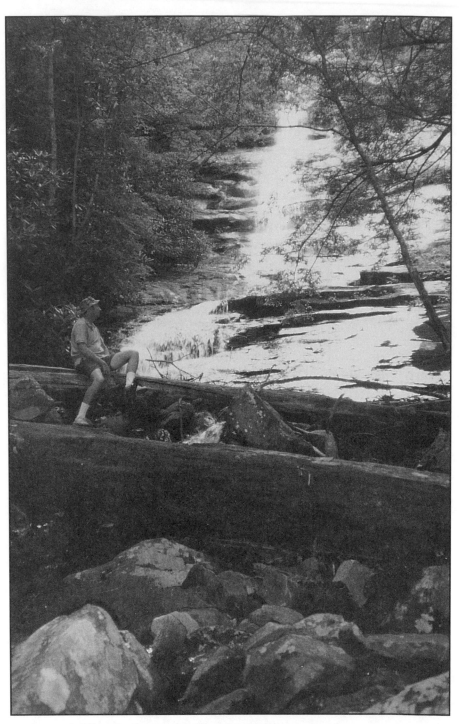

Panther Creek Falls on Panther Creek Trail in Cohutta Wilderness Area.

right fork. In about 1.5 miles, Forest Road 17 is on the right and Forest Road 16 goes to the left. Continue left on FR 16 to the Tennessee line. Just across the Tennessee line is the north trailhead and parking area for the Jacks River Trail. Continue northeast on Forest Road 221-1 to Sheeds Creek and turn sharply to the right on Forest Road 62 and continue to the parking area and trailhead for Beech Bottom Trail. Before reaching the Tennessee state line while on Forest Road 16 pass Forest Road 51. Turn right here and go about two miles and pass the parking area and trailhead for Horseshoe Bend Trail, not in the wilderness area. Continue about another 1.75 miles to the parking area and trailhead for Hickory Creek, East Cowpen, and Rice Camp Creek trails.

The hikes: There are fourteen named trails in the wilderness area. The dendritic drainage pattern of the many mountain streams makes it necessary for the trails to zigzag and switchback from one cove to the next. **Jacks River Trail** is the longest and most arduous. **Chestnut Lead** is a short 1.4-mile trail that connects with the much longer **Conasauga River Trail.** All the trails lead into beautiful mixed hardwood forests and along tumbling streams lined with impenetrable rhododendron thickets. In the summer, visibility is very limited. In the winter the forest is much more open, permitting vistas of surrounding mountains.

Most of the trails have been blazed and color-coded to prevent confusion to the new wilderness user. Because this is a wilderness area the blazes are not as close together as you might expect in other mountain trail systems.

Each of the trails will be described briefly and some of the hazards will be noted to help you plan for the hike.

Hickory Creek Trail is an 8.4-mile trail with a white blaze. The trailhead is at the large parking area at the end of Forest Road 630. The northern trailhead is at the end of Forest Road 51. This is one of the most heavily used trails, especially by fishermen going to Conasauga River. It is about 1.5 miles down an old logging road to the river, then upstream joining the Conasauga River Trail another 1.5 miles to Bray Field where Hickory Creek Trail crosses Conasauga River. From here it leads north for 5.4 miles, crossing Thomas Creek and eventually the headwaters of Hickory Creek before reaching the trailhead on FR 51.

Tearbritches Trail also leads to the Conasauga River. It is blazed with orange. The trailhead is on FR 68. It is a very steep 3.4 miles down to the river, making it a very strenuous hike back up. But for a good loop hike descend to the river and hike up on the yellow blazed Conasauga River Trail 3.2 miles to blue blaze of Chestnut Lead Trail. From here it is only 1.4 miles to FR 68, the trailhead for Chestnut Lead. Hike along FR 68 back to the Tearbritches trailhead.

Conasauga River Trail is a white-blazed trail that crosses the southwestern part of the wilderness area. It is 13.2 miles from the Betty Gap trailhead on FR 64 to the western trailhead on FR 17. It is one of the more popular hikes with Bray Field about midway, a good camping area. This is where Tearbritches and Hickory Creek trails join the Conasauga River Trail. Be prepared to get your shoes wet. The path crosses the river about thirty times. A hiking staff is very useful while wading across the river. Many experienced hikers wear tennis shoes and plan to be wet. Dry camp shoes are carried in the pack. Also be very conscious of the weather on this and Jacks River trails. These streams can become raging torrents after a heavy rain. Do not try to cross the river in high water and be prepared by taking enough food for an extra day should you get stranded and unable to cross the river. The river rises and falls quickly after a heavy thundershower. Conasauga is an excellent trout stream with rainbow and brown trout. No trout are stocked in the wilderness area. This hike can be made from either end.

East Cowpen Trail is not blazed. It is the old roadbed of GA 2. The south trailhead is at Three Forks Mountain parking area, the end of GA 2 for vehicle travel. It is 6.6 miles to FR 51 trailhead. East Cowpen is a high-elevation trail that crosses no water. It provides relatively easy access to other trails. Hiking from south to north the first of these is Rough Ridge Trail that goes to the right and to Jacks River. The next is Panther Creek Trail that leads to the left down to a very scenic overlook above Panther Creek Falls. Farther on 3.8 miles is Hickory Ridge Trail to the right and to Jacks River. From this junction to the north trailhead is 2.3 miles. There are several pleasant campsites on this trail

Jacks River Trail is sixteen miles long and crosses the wilderness area from Dally Gap, the east trailhead, to Alaculsy Valley, the west trailhead. It has orange blazes. This is another very popular trail, especially down to the scenic Jacks River Falls. Just as with the Conasauga River, the path crosses the river many times, some say forty times. One soon loses count and thinks only about wet feet. Here again heavy rains can cause the river to rise rapidly and become very dangerous to cross. Plan for this by taking extra food for an unexpected delay. The falls area is almost the middle of the trail. Downstream about 1.5 miles is Horseshoe Bend with attractive campsites. Except for all the stream crossings this is a moderately difficult hike.

Rice Camp Trail is a relatively short 3.4 miles from the FR 51 trailhead to Jacks River just upstream from Horseshoe Bend and only another 1.5 miles to the Jacks River Falls. You must cross Jacks River to get to the falls. It can be a moderate day hike or a pleasant overnight backpacking hike.

Penitentiary Branch Trail at one time started from Forest Road 73. With the addition of the Hemp Top section to the wilderness area, the trailhead is now Dally Gap. This makes the trail about six miles one way to Jacks River. The hike up the old FR 73 is along the Tennessee Valley Divide and is relatively easy. From the old FR 73 road down to Jacks River is an even, gentle grade for 3.3 miles. This section has yellow blazes. The loop hike to Jacks River on the Penitentiary Branch Trail and then up Jacks River to Dally Gap is about fourteen miles.

Hemp Top Trail, like Penitentiary Branch, has its trailhead at Dally Gap. The hike to the lookout tower is on the old FR 73. This is about 6.5

miles. From the tower to Double Springs Gap and the Tennessee line is another two miles.

Beech Bottom Trail is a pleasant four-mile hike along an old roadbed to Jacks River and is not blazed. It reaches the Jacks River Trail less than a half mile above the falls and is the easiest hike to the falls. It is well marked at the trailhead on Forest Road 62 just across the line in Tennessee. This is the only trail leading from a road into the wilderness on the north boundary.

Rough Ridge Trail is a blue-blazed connecter trail between East Cowpen and Jacks River. From the Cowpen trailhead at Three Forks, it is seven miles to the river. This is a steep up- and downhill trail from the junction of Sugar Cove Trail to the river. It is a strenuous hike back up. There is no water until you reach Rough Creek or Jacks River.

Panther Creek Trail is a blue-blazed connecter trail between Conasauga River Trail about 0.4 mile above Bray Field and East Cowpen Trail. You must cross Conasauga River to begin the rocky climb up to the falls and above to a grand overlook into the Conasauga Valley. There is a much-used campsite above the falls. The trail follows close to Panther Creek and crosses it several times. The hike can be made from the Hickory Creek trailhead, the Tearbritches trailhead, or the East Cowpen trailhead.

Sugar Cove Trail connects Rough Ridge Trail with Jacks River. It is a 2.6 mile white-blazed trail. This is a steep trail down to the river making it strenuous coming back up to Rough Ridge Trail.

Rainbow trout from Cohutta Wilderness are fried over backpack stove near Conasauga River. The native brook trout live in some wilderness area streams.

89 F. D. Roosevelt State Park–Pine Mountain and Mountain Creek Nature Trails

Overview: This state park is on Pine Mountain, a long narrow ridge made up of quartzite rock formations that is the southernmost mountain in the state. The forest is composed of shortleaf pine, hickory, blackjack oak, chestnut oak, and black oak on the drier ridgetop. The undergrowth includes red buckeye, paw paw, Piedmont azalea, sparkleberry, blueberry, and huckleberry. In the coves and more moist sites you can find sweet gum, yellow-poplar, beech, and maple along with loblolly pines. The Pine Mountain Trail goes through all of the habitat types associated with this unique and beautiful mountain. There are thirteen primitive campsites for backpacking hikers. It is necessary for overnight campers to obtain a permit at the park office before camping; campers must use designated campsites. Fires are permitted, unless otherwise indicated.

F. D. Roosevelt State Park's Pine Mountain Trail is very much like many of the trails in the mountains of north Georgia. The views seem to be much more panoramic because everything that surrounds Pine Mountain is flat. It has something for every level of hiking ability. The casual walker can find a quiet one- or two-mile walk in a forested area with grand views. The serious backpacker can test gear and physical ability and spend several days on the trail and never backtrack. The nature trail at the foot of the mountain around the developed campgrounds and Lake Delano offers an entirely different experience along meandering streams in mature forests.

Members of the Pine Mountain Trail Association have cooperated with the Department of Natural Resources in the design and maintenance of the long trail, spending thousands of hours in volunteer work.

General description: Trail system totaling more than 37.6 miles with difficulties varying from easy to moderate.

General location: The park is in the west central part of the state about twenty-five miles north of Columbus.

Maps: The Pine Mountain Trail Association has prepared a very detailed map of the trails. (The 1999 revised edition can be purchased from the Association by mail, see Appendix A. All the funds from the map are used to maintain the Pine Mountain Trail); a page-size map of the park including the trail is available from the park office; Pine Mountain and Warm Springs USGS quads.

Degree of difficulty: The design of the Pine Mountain Trail with numerous switchbacks has eliminated many of the steep climbs so that it is a moderate hike throughout its length. The nature trail is easy with two short moderate sections.

Length: Pine Mountain Trail is twenty-three miles one way. Five connector trails that provide for pleasant day-hike loops add an additional 9.6 miles to the system. The Mountain Creek Nature Trail is a 3.2 mile loop.

Elevations: The elevation at the lowest point on Mountain Creek Nature Trail is about 820 feet. The highest point on Pine Mountain is Dowdell Knob at about

1,420 feet. The west trailhead is at about 1,000 feet and the east trailhead is about 1,300 feet.

Special attractions: Scenic views; history of former president F. D. Roosevelt; nearby Little White House and Warm Springs; spring flowers including native azaleas, dogwood, mountain laurel, and rhododendron; rock outcrops; waterfalls; fall leaf color and excellent birding and wildlife watching make this a desirable hiking area.

Rock cliffs overhang the Pine Mountain Trail at F. D. Roosevelt State Park.

F. D. Roosevelt State Park, Pine Mountain, and Mountain Creek Nature Trails

Best season: Year-round hiking. Occasional snows add interest to winter hikes. Summers can be hot; spring and fall are the best for weather, wildflowers, birding, and scenery.

For more information: F. D. Roosevelt State Park, 2970 Georgia Highway 190, Pine Mountain, GA 31822; (706)663-4858. Pine Mountain Trail Association, Inc., P.O. Box 5, Columbus, GA 31902; or www.pinemountaintrail.org.

Finding the trailheads: The western trailhead for the Pine Mountain Trail is just off US 27 on GA 190 near the Gardens Country Store. The eastern trailhead leads away from the paved parking lot and picnic area at the WJSP-TV tower, just north of GA 190 on US 85W. There are five other accesses to the trail where it crosses GA 190 that runs along the top of Pine Mountain. Three of the five crossings have named off-road parking lots. Paved parking and trail access can be found at Dowdell Knob, the FDR park office, and the FDR park swimming pool on GA 354. The trailhead for the Mountain Creek Nature Trail is near the Trading Post in the RV campground near Lake Delano at the foot of the mountain. The road to the RV campground begins across from the park office on GA 190.

The hikes: The longer **Pine Mountain Trail** can be started from either end or from several points along GA 190. But starting from the television tower on the east end is a good choice.

Enter the picnic area from Georgia Highway 85W. It has space for several vehicles, and a parking fee or Georgia Park Pass is required. The trail is well marked with blue blazes. About 100 yards on the trail, there is a green metal box on a post that houses the register sheets. It is always a good idea to register when starting the hike. A register is also located at the park headquarters. These registers give the park personnel and the Pine Mountain Trail Association a tally on the number of people who use the trail. It is estimated that about 50,000 hikers use the trail annually. They come from many states and foreign countries.

The trail is measured from west to east with stone cairns and signs at each mile. The trail crosses GA 190 at five places, which make it possible to park and walk sections of the trail from one crossing to another and return by road to the parking point. With the approval of the Department of Natural Resources, the Pine Mountain Trail Association members have scouted out and built five connector trails with white blazes that form loops of 3.4, 4.3, 6.7, 6.9, and 7.8 miles. These loop sections make nice day hikes. All of the loops have campsites that give the flexibility for overnight hikes and camping in secluded forest areas. Most of the sites are near ample water sources; however, it is necessary to use standard purification techniques for any drinking water.

The Wolfden loop trail which starts at the WJSP-TV tower, is 6.7 miles long and is particularly interesting because of the plant life, rock formations, streams, and waterfalls. Some of the most interesting rock outcrops and cascades are along Wolfden and Cascade branches. Three primitive campsites—Sasafrass Hill, Old Sawmill, and Bumblebee Ridge—are on this loop.

The 4.3 mile loop that includes Dowdell Knob is especially scenic. The view from the Dowdell Knob overlook is an impressive panorama. This was one of President Roosevelt's favorite places to go for a cookout. Information plaques tell of his visits. There is one campsite, Brown Dog, near mile 16 and Brown Dog Bluff.

The longest of the connector trails (2.7 mile Sawtooth Trail) is between mile markers 6 and 11 south of GA 190. This connector forms the 7.8 mile Big Poplar loop and sports such interesting names as Rattlesnake Bluff, Indian Mountain, and Fox Den Cove. Big Knot, Beech Bottom, and Grindstone Gap campsites are located on the loop.

The Gardens Overlook Loop, the newest addition to the Pine Mountain Trail is a 2.4-mile path on the north side of highway 109 beginning or ending at the Callaway Country Store. Going east on GA 109 for 1.2 miles you come to the Gardens Overlook. If the loop is hiked from the Country Store, I suggest you hike the old trail on the south side of the mountain first and cross over GA 109 at the Gardens Overlook. The east end of this loop takes off from the original trail about 25 yards from the road on the north side. Here you drop down several switchbacks down the steep slope at the bottom of which is a spring seep and a rather dense mountain laurel thicket. The switchbacks make the descent easy and let you see the changes in plant types as you descend into the more moist habitat. The trail is then followed back to the Country Store along a series of undulations over low ridges and into coves more or less along the contours. This is a well designed addition to the total trail and is easy if the descent from the overlook is followed. If you walk up the switchbacks to the overlook I would classify the ascent as moderate, a climb of 240 feet to the road.

The **Mountain Creek Nature Trail** starts near the Trading Post in the RV campground area at Lake Delano. This red blazed hike passes through the moist forest along Mountain Creek. Maples, white oaks, black oaks, and sweet gums form the main canopy with undergrowth of sourwoods and dogwoods. Christmas ferns are very evident in late winter. The honeysuckle has been browsed heavily by deer. Also, watch for the scratch marks of wild turkeys.

The little creek flows under the path as you cross a wooden bridge. This creek bottom has a good number of den trees that will provide housing for many animals—squirrels, raccoons, opossums, and wood ducks among others. Look for tracks of raccoons in the wet areas beside the stream. Alternate hiking trails make it possible to return to the Trading Post after about a one-mile walk. The creek is crossed on a footbridge and the trail follows close to the bank of the deep-sided stream. Mountain laurel and large southern magnolias and loblolly pines grow close to the creek. Leave the creek and pass through an open forest of yellow-poplars, maples, and oaks. A spring flows from the remains of the old Civilian Conservation Corps fish hatchery. The earthwork dams and stone spillway are still very evident. From here the trail crosses a service road that will lead to the **Pine Mountain Trail** not far from the Dead Pine Campground. The path climbs through a dry hillside to the paved road from the campground to GA 190 and the park office. Cross the road and descend into another small stream watershed. The exposed stones under the powerline right-of-way show the quartz crystals typical of the geology of Pine Mountain rock. The bottom of this north-facing cove is dense with mountain laurel. Cross over a footbridge just before the 1.8 mile Pool Trail branches off. From here the path passes an erosion control project on the stream flowing into the lake. The path goes throughout parts of the camping and picnic area before it returns to the Trading Post.

Other State Parks with Hiking Trails

State Park nearest city phone number	Trail name(s)	Miles	Rating	Blaze	Map	Features
New Echota Calhoun (706) 629-8151	Sequoyah Nature	1.2	E	none	yes	Cherokee Indian history
Elijah Clark Lincolnton (706) 359-3458	Hannah Clark	0.7	E	white	no	forest/stream
Tugaloo Lavonia (706) 356-4362	Muscadine Nature Crow Tree Nature	0.3 0.2	E E	signs signs	no no	interpretive sign interpretive sign
Hart Hartwell (706) 376-8756	Hart S.P.	0.7	E	none	no	history, scenic lake
John Tanner Carrolton (706) 832-7545	Nature	0.5	E	none	no	mixed forest
A.H. Stephens Crawfordville (706) 456-2602	Beaver lodge Buncomb Wading pool	1.0 4.0 0.8	E M E	white white white	yes no yes	beaver lodge lake/forest wading pool
Jarrell Plantation Juliette (912) 986-5172	Historical	1.0	M	none	no	1800s Jarrell farm
Indian Springs Indian Springs (770) 775-7241	Nature	1.5	M	none	no	hardwood forest, large trees
Hambburg Mitchell (912) 552-2393	Nature	0.7	E	white	yes	alligator, beaver habitat

(continued)

E = Easy M = Moderate S = Strenuous

State Park nearest city phone number	Trail name(s)	Miles	Rating	Blaze	Map	Features
Kolomoki Mounds **Blakely** **(912) 723-5296**	Wandering Water	1.1	E	yellow	no	gopher tortoise,wiregrass
Seminole **Donalsonville** **(912) 861-3137**	Wiregrass Loop	0.6	E	none	no	wiregrass–longleaf pine
Stephen C. Foster **Fargo** **(912) 637-5274**	Nature	0.5	E	none	no	Okefenokee swamp, boardwalk
Wormsloe **Savannah** **(912) 352-2548**	Tabby Ruins	0.25	E	none	no	grave site, 1730s plantation
Fort McAllister **Richmond Hill** **(912) 727-2339**	Savage Island	0.6	E	none	yes	Coastal forest, marsh views
Sunbury **Midway** **(912) 884-5999**	Historical	0.5	E	none	no	historical,salt marsh, river
Fort King George **Darien** **(912) 437-4774**	Historic Nature	0.3 0.3	E E	signs signs	yes yes	Colonial British ruins sawgrass marsh, wildlife
Hofwyl Plantation **Brunswick** **(912) 364-9263**	Visitor's Path Nature	1.0 0.2	E E	orange none	yes yes	rice culture and plantation old rice fields, marsh

E = Easy M = Moderate S = Strenuous

Appendix A: Local Hiking Clubs and Conservation Organizations

There seems to be a strong awareness in Georgia to take care of the pristine environment suitable for a quiet walk in the woods or a long extended backpacking hike into wilderness areas. This has come about in great measure by members of hiking clubs, conservation organizations and concerned private citizens who are willing to spend time to work on trails and speak out for good land management. Countless hours of volunteer work have been spent by the trail clubs in maintenance of such trails as the Appalachian Trail, Benton MacKaye Trail, Bartram Trail, Pine Mountain Trail, and many other miles of less popular trails. Most of these groups have monthly outings. Also, organizations not specifically involved in hiking trail activities devote many hours working on forest and stream habitat protection. Following is a list of some of these organizations.

Atlanta Audubon Society, P.O. Box 29217, Atlanta, GA 30359; (770) 955-4111

Augusta Canal Authority, 801 Broad Street, Room 507, Augusta, GA 30901

Benton MacKaye Trail Association, P.O. Box 53271, Atlanta, GA 30355-1271

Georgia Appalachian Trail Club, P.O. Box 654, Atlanta, GA 30301

Georgia Botanical Society, 7575 Rico Road, Palmetto, GA 30268

Georgia Conservancy Inc., 781 Marietta Street NM, Suite B100,

Atlanta GA 31410; (404) 876-2900 *Coastal Office* Georgia Conservancy, 711 Sandtown Road, Savannah, GA 31410; (912) 897-6462

Georgia Wildlife Federation, 1936 Iris Drive, Conyers, GA 30207; (770) 929-3350

Pine Mountain Trail Association, Inc, P.O. Box 5, Columbus, GA 31902; www.pinemountaintrail.org

The Nature Conservancy, 1401 Peachtree St. NE, Suite 136, Atlanta, GA 30309; (404) 873-6946

The Sierra Club, Georgia Chapter, P.O. Box 46751, Atlanta, GA 30346; (404) 888-9778

The Wilderness Society, 1819 Peachtree Road NE, Suite 714, Atlanta, GA 30309; (404) 872-9453

Trout Unlimited, Georgia Council, 108 1/2 Sycamore Street, Rome, GA 30165; (706) 234-5310

Appendix B: Federal and State Land Management Agencies

STATE OFFICE AND LAND MANAGEMENT AGENCIES

For information on trails, user fees, overnight accommodations, or special events in state parks and historic sites contact the Department of Natural Resources Atlanta office or any of the regional offices throughout the state. Addresses and phone numbers for individual parks are listed with the discussions for the respective parks. A $2 daily or $25 annual parking pass, called a *ParkPass*, is required of visitors using state park facilities, including trails. The daily parking pass may be obtained at collection boxes at various locations in each park or at the park offices. Senior citizen discounts are available for the annual *ParkPass*.

Georgia Department of Natural Resources State Parks and Historic Sites, 205 Butler Street, Suite 1352, Atlanta, GA 30334; (404) 656-3530. Recreational Trail Info.: www.dnr.state.ga.us

Regional Offices:

Georgia Parks and Historic Sites, P.O.Box 1029, Helen, GA 30545; (706) 878-1590

Georgia Parks and Historic Sites, 2070 U.S. Highway 278 SE, Social Circle, GA 30279; (706) 557-3027

Georgia Parks and Historic Sites, 2024 Newton Road, Albany, GA 31708-5601; (912) 430-4402

Georgia Parks and Historic Sites, One Constitution Way, Brunswick, GA 31523-8605; (912) 262-3180

For information about trails, fishing, and hunting seasons and regulations on Wildlife Management Areas contact the Wildlife Resources Division office in Social Circle or any of the regional offices throughout the state.

Georgia Department of Natural Resources, Wildlife Resources Division, 2070 U.S. Highway 278 SE, Social Circle, GA 30279; (770) 918-6416

Georgia Wildlife Resources Division, Game Management Section, 2592 Floyd Springs Road, Armuchee, GA 30105; (706) 295-6041

Georgia Wildlife Resources, Division Game Management Section, 2150 Dawsonville Highway, Gainesville, GA 30501; (770) 535-5700

Georgia Wildlife Resources, Division Game Management Section, 142 Bob Kirk Road, Thomson, GA 30824; (706) 595-4222

Georgia Wildlife Resources Division, Game Management Section, Route 3, Box 75 Fort Valley, GA 31030-9990; (912) 825-6354

Georgia Wildlife Resources Division, Game Management Section, 2024 Newton Road, Albany, GA 31708; (912) 430-4254

Georgia Wildlife Resources Division, Game Management Section, 1773-A Bowen's Mill Highway, Fitzgerald, GA 31750; (912) 423-2988

Georgia Wildlife Resources Division, Game Management Section, One Conservation Way, Brunswick, GA 31523; (912) 262-31731

FEDERAL LAND MANAGEMENT AGENCIES

U.S. Forest Service

The Chattahoochee and Oconee National Forests have a number of recreation areas. Most of the developed areas are open from late spring to early fall. Some are open all year. These are developed for many different types of outdoor activities. A fee is charged for use of some of the areas. Information about trails, recreation areas, wilderness areas, and other features of the forests is available from the Forest Supervisor's office in Gainesville or from any of the District Ranger's offices.

USDA Forest Service Southern Regional Office 1720 Peachtree Road NW, Atlanta, GA 30367; (404) 347-4191

Chattahoochee National Forest

U.S. Forest Service, Chattahoochee-Oconee National Forest, Forest Supervisor, 1755 Cleveland Hwy., Gainesville, GA 30501; (770) 536-0541. Trail and Recreation Information: www.fs.fed.us/conf/

Ranger Districts

U.S. Forest Service, Armuchee Ranger District, 805 E. Villanow Street, P.O. Box 465, LaFayette, GA 30728; (706) 638-1085

U.S. Forest Service, Brasstown Ranger District, 1881 Highway 515, Blairsville, GA 30512; (706) 745-6928

U.S. Forest Service, Chattooga Ranger District, 200 Highway 197 N., Clarkesville, GA 30523; (706) 754-6221

U.S. Forest Service, Visitor Center, 102 Memorial Drive, Dahlonega, GA 30533; (706) 864-6173

U.S. Forest Service, Cohutta Ranger District, 401 G. I. Maddox Parkway, Chatsworth, GA 30705; (706) 695-6737

U.S. Forest Service, Tallulah Ranger District, 809 Highway 441, Clayton, GA 30525; (706) 782-3320

U.S. Forest Service, Toccoa Ranger District, 6050 Appalachian Highway, Blue Ridge, GA 30513; (706) 632-3031

Oconee National Forest

U.S. Forest Service, Oconee Ranger District, 1199 Madison Road, Eatonton, GA 31024; (706) 485-7110

National Park Service

Southeast Regional Office, National Park Service, 75 Spring Street, S.W., Atlanta, GA 30303; (404) 331-5187

National Parks in Georgia with trails

Superintendent, Chickamauga and Chattanooga National Military Park, P.O. Box 2128, Fort Oglethorpe, GA 30742; (706) 866-2512

Superintendent, Chattahoochee River National Recreation Area, 1978 Island Ford Parkway, Atlanta, GA 30350; (770) 399-8070

Superintendent, Kennesaw Mountain National Battlefield Park, 900 Kennesaw Dr., Kennesaw, GA 30144; (770) 427 4686

Superintendent, Ocmulgee National Monument, 1207 Emery Highway, Macon, GA 31217; (912) 752-8257

Superintendent, Cumberland Island National Sea Shore, P.O. Box 806, St. Marys, GA 31558; (912) 882-4335

U.S. Fish and Wildlife Service

Information about trails, seasonal waterfowl, and other wildlife populations and current wildlife watching opportunities are available from the regional office and from refuge offices.

Southeast Regional Office

U.S. Fish and Wildlife Service, 1875 Century Boulevard S.W., Atlanta, GA 30303; (404) 679-7287. For trail and recreation information: www.fws.gov/r4eao/newspage.html

National Wildlife Refuges in Georgia

Piedmont National Wildlife Refuge, Route 1, Box 670, Round Oak, GA 31038; (912) 986-5441

OKefenokee National Wildlife Refuge, Route 2, Box 3330, Folkston, GA 31537; (912) 496-7366

Savannah Coastal Refuges, P.O. Box 8487, Savannah, GA 31088; (912) 944-4415

Appendix C: Information Sources

Books
Natural history and geographic guides are included but the list is by no means exhaustive. There are many other books dealing with Georgia geography, natural history, and cultural history. They are available in most book stores and in college and larger city libraries.

Appalachian Trail Guide to North Carolina and Georgia, Ninth Edition by the Appalachian Trail Conference and Georgia Appalachian Trail Club, Inc.

The Thru-Hikers Handbook, 1993: A Guide for End-to-End Hikers of the Appalachian Trail by Dan "Wing Foot" Bruce. Appalachian Trail Conference.

The Complete Walker III by Colin Fletcher. Alfred A. Knopf.

Travel Light Handbook by Judy Keene. Contemporary Books Inc.

A Child's Introduction to the Outdoors by David Richey. Pagurian Press Limited.

Finding Your Way in the Outdoors by Robert L. Mooers. Jr. E. P. Hutton Co. Inc.

Camping and Woodcraft by Horace Kephart. The University of Tennessee Press.

Hiking Guide to Georgia's Rabun County by Brian Boyd. Ferncreek Press.

The Chattooga Wild and Scenic River by Brian Boyd. Ferncreek Press.

The Georgia Conservancy's Guide to the North Georgia Mountains. Edited by Fred Brown and Nell Jones with preface by Jimmy Carter.

The Natural Environments of Georgia by Charles H. Whorton. Georgia Department of Natural Resources, Bulletin 114.

The Hiking Trails of North Georgia by Tim Homan. Peachtree Publishers, LTD.

Wild Places of the South by Steve Price. The East Woods Press.

Waterfalls of the Southern Appalachians, A guide to 40 Waterfalls of North Georgia, Western North Carolina & Western South Carolina by Brian Boyd. Ferncreek Press.

Georgia Rivers edited by George Hatcher. University of Georgia Press.

The Travels of William Bartram edited by Mark Van Doren. Dover.

Trees of the Southern United States by Wilbur Duncan and Marion B. Duncan. University of Georgia Press.

The Ferns of Georgia by Rogers McVaugh and Joseph H. Pyron. University of Georgia Press.

Wildflowers of the Southeastern United States by Wilbur H. Duncan and Leonard E. Foote. University of Georgia Press.

Native Trees of Georgia by G. Norman Bishop. Georgia Forestry Commission.

Snakes of the Southeastern United States by Jeffrey J. Jackson. Cooperative Extension Service University of Georgia and U.S. Fish and Wildlife Service.

Butterflies of Georgia by Lucien Harris, Jr. University of Oklahoma Press.

Appalachian Trail Videos

Five Million Steps, The Thru-Hikers Story By Lynne Welden. Lynne Welden Productions.

Amazing Grace, The Story of the Blind Appalachian Trail Thru-Hiker By Bill Irwin. Lynne Welden Productions.

Appendix D: Finding Maps

U.S. Geological Survey 7.5 minute series topographic quadrangles, scale 1:24,000, referred to in the text as USGS quads, are the best and most dependable maps for long hikes and wilderness backpack trip planning. Learn how to read them and then learn to rely on them for keeping oriented on the trail. This is especially important for any cross country hikes, requiring good orienteering techniques. The following is a list of several sources for these maps.

Georgia Geologic Survey, 19 Martin Luther King Jr. Drive Maps and Publications Room, 400 Atlanta, GA 30334; (404) 656-3214

U.S. Geological Survey National Mapping Division, 12201 Sunrise Valley Dr. Mail Stop 809, Reston, VA 22092; (703) 648-7070

Tennessee Valley Authority Maps and Surveys Dept., 101 Haney Bldg. 311 Broad St., Chattanooga, TN 37402-2801; (423) 751-6277

MAPTECH, 655 Portsmouth Avenue, Greenland, NH 03840; (888) 433-8500; has USGS topographic maps for all of Georgia on CD-ROM and a seperate CD-ROM for the Appalachian Trail.

The Georgia Appalachian Trail Club has a small scale map with helpful hints for hiking this famous trail. *The Guide to the Appalachian Trail in North Carolina and Georgia,* which contains maps, trail mileages, water, and shelter locations and side trails can be purchased at hiking and backpacking outfitters and stores or from the Appalachian Trail Conference.

Appalachian Trail Conference, P.O. Box 807 Harpers Ferry, W. VA 25425-0807

A small-scale map and brochure and detailed maps of the trail by sections the Benton MacKaye Trail can be obtained from the Benton MacKaye Trail Association.

Benton MacKaye Trail Association, P.O. Box 53271 Atlanta, GA 30355-1271

The U.S. Forest Service has free recreation maps, a trail guide, and other booklets of the Chattahoochee and Oconee National Forests. Forest Visitors Map, Appalachian Trail Map, Chattooga Wild and Scenic River Map, and the Cohutta Wilderness Map are available for purchase. These can be obtained from the Chattahoochee-Oconee Forest Supervisors Office in Gainesville, or any of the District Rangers Offices or from the Regional Office in Atlanta (see Appendix B).

Page size maps of the trails in most of the State Parks can be obtained free from the respective state park or from the State Parks and Historic Sites Division in Atlanta (see Appendix B).

Some hiking and backpacking outfitters and stores have various trail maps for sale. Some sell the USGS quads.

Back Country Adventures, Route 2, Box 2242-A, Persimmon Rd., Clayton, GA 30525; (706) 782-6489

The History Store, 114 North Park Sty., P.O. Box 358, Dahlonega, GA 30535; (706) 864-7225

Mountain Crossing, 9710 Gainesville Hwy., Blairsville, GA 30512; (706) 745-6095

Mountain Outdoor Expeditions, P.O. Box 86, Ellijay, GA 30540; (706) 635-2524

Outdoor World, 6002 Veterans Parkway, Columbus, GA 31909 (706) 563-2113

Rock Creek Outfitters, 4825 Hixson Pike, Chattanooga, TN 37443; (423) 877-6256

Blue Ridge Mountain Sports, Lenox Square Mall, 3393 Peachtree Road, NE Atlanta, GA 30326; (404) 266 8372

Call Of The Wild, 425 Market Place, Roswell, GA 30075; (770) 992-5400

High Country Outfitters Inc., 595 Piedmont Ave., NE Suite D 201.1, Atlanta, GA 30308; (404) 892-0909

Mountain Ventures, 3040 N. Decatur Rd., Scottdale, GA 3007; (404) 299-5254

Outback Outfitters & Bikes, 1125 Euclid Ave. NE, Atlanta, GA 30307; (404) 688-4878

REI, 1800 NE Expressway, Atlanta, GA 30320; (404) 633-6508

REI, 1165 Perimeter Center West, Suite 200, Atlanta, GA 30346; (770) 901-9200

Geared To Go, 420-B Armour Dr., Atlanta, GA 30324; (404) 875-8828

Appendix E: The Hiker's Checklist

The importance of using a good checklist is most appreciated when you are fifteen miles into your hike and discover that you have forgotten an important item. The thing you forgot may be only an inconvenience or it may be a serious oversight. A good checklist will help you prepare for the best possible hiking experience.

This is only a suggested list. Base your list on the nature of the hike and your own personal needs. Items will vary depending on whether you are camping near your vehicle or backpacking to more remote campsites and staying out one or more nights. Remember, if you are carrying it on your back, select items judiciously. Weight is an important factor.

Make your own checklist; check each item as you pack.

Clothing:

- [ ] dependable rain parka
- [ ] windbreaker
- [ ] thermal underwear
- [ ] shorts
- [ ] long pants
- [ ] cap or hat
- [ ] wool shirt or sweater
- [ ] warm jacket
- [ ] extra socks
- [ ] underwear
- [ ] lightweight shirts
- [ ] T-shirts
- [ ] gloves
- [ ] belt

Footwear:

- [ ] comfortable hiking boots
- [ ] lightweight camp shoes

Bedding:

- [ ] sleeping bag
- [ ] foam pad or air mattress
- [ ] pillow (deflating)
- [ ] ground cloth (plastic or nylon)
- [ ] dependable tent

Cooking:

- [ ] one-quart plastic water container
- [ ] one-gallon collapsible water container for camp use
- [ ] backpack stove w/ extra fuel
- [ ] funnel
- [ ] aluminum foil
- [ ] cooking pot
- [ ] bowl or plate
- [ ] spoon, fork, knife, spatula
- [ ] matches in waterproof container

Food and Drink:

- [ ] cereal
- [ ] bread and/or crackers
- [ ] trail mix
- [ ] margarine
- [ ] powdered soups
- [ ] salt/pepper
- [ ] main course meals
- [ ] snacks
- [ ] coffee, tea
- [ ] hot chocolate
- [ ] powdered milk
- [ ] drink mixes

Photography:

- [ ] camera and film
- [ ] accessories
- [ ] large zip-locked bag

Miscellaneous:

- [ ] maps and compass
- [ ] toilet paper
- [ ] toothbrush
- [ ] water filter or chemical purifier
- [ ] first-aid kit
- [ ] survival kit
- [ ] pocketknife
- [ ] insect repellent
- [ ] flashlight, spare batteries and bulb
- [ ] candles

- [ ] small trowel or shovel
- [ ] extra plastic bags to pack out trash
- [ ] biodegradable soap
- [ ] towel/washcloth
- [ ] waterproof covering for pack
- [ ] binoculars
- [ ] watch
- [ ] sewing kit
- [ ] fishing gear and license

Index

About the Author

A native of Chattanooga, Tennessee, Donald W. Pfitzer retired from the U.S. Fish and Wildlife Service as an assistant regional director of the southeast region after thirty-three years as a fish and wildlife biologist and public affairs officer. He has a master's degree in entomology and botany and has produced thirteen wildlife movies for television for the Tennessee Game and Fish Commission. He originated and hosted the first outdoor television program in the southeast, called *Woods and Waters* in 1955 and has written many technical and popular articles on fish, wildlife, and nature in general.

Don is a member and past president of the Southeastern Outdoor Press Association and the Georgia Outdoor Writers Association. He also is a member of the Outdoor Writers Association of America, charter member of the Georgia Conservancy, and a member of a number of other conservation organizations.

Don continues to be active in environmental education, writing, and photography.

American Hiking Society

American Hiking Society is the only national nonprofit organization dedicated to establishing, protecting and maintaining foot trails in America.

Establishing...

American Hiking Society establishes hiking trails with the AHS National Trails Endowment, providing grants for grassroots organizations to purchase trail lands, construct and maintain trails, and preserve hiking trails' scenic values. The AHS affiliate club program, called the Congress of Hiking Organizations, brings trail clubs together to share information, collaborate on public policy, and advocate legislation and policies that protect hiking trails.

Protecting...

American Hiking Society protects hiking trails through highly focused public policy efforts in the nation's capital. AHS affects federal legislation, shapes public lands policy, collaborates with grassroots trail organizations, and partners with federal land managers to protect the hiking experience. Members become active with letter-writing campaigns and by attending the annual AHS Trails Advocacy Week.

Maintaining...

American Hiking Society maintains hiking trails by sending volunteers to national parks, forests and recreation lands; organizing volunteer teams to help affiliated hiking clubs; and publishing national volunteer directories. AHS members get involved, get dirty and get inspired by participating in AHS programs like National Trails Day, America's largest celebration of the outdoors; and Volunteer Vacations—week-long work trips to beautiful, wild places.

Join American Hiking Society...

Be a part of the organization dedicated to protecting and preserving the nation's footpaths, our footpaths, the ones in our backyards and our backcountry. Visit American Hiking Society's website or call to find out more about membership. When you join, Falcon Publishing will send you a FREE guide as a special thank you for contributing to the efforts of American Hiking Society.

American Hiking Society
1422 Fenwick Lane
Silver Spring, MD 20910
OR CALL: (888) 766-HIKE ext. 1
OR VISIT: www.americanhiking.org

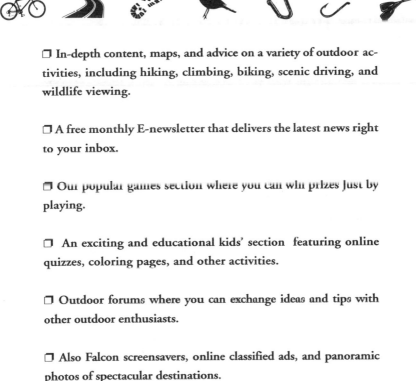

FALCONGUIDES ® Leading the Way™

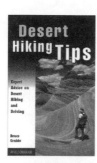

DESERT HIKING TIPS
By Bruce Grubbs
This pocket-sized book explains how to enjoy hiking and exploring the American desert.

HIKING WITH DOGS
by Linda Mullally
This comprehensive hiking guide highlights the benefits of hiking with your dog while helping readers choose, train, condition and care for their canine hiking companions.

ROUTE FINDING
by Gregory Crouch
Explains step-by-step the map reading, land navigation, and route finding techniques crucial to success and safety in the outdoors.

Also Available:
Avalanche Aware, Backpacking Tips, Bear Aware, Hiking With Kids, Mountain Lion Alert, Reading Weather, Using GPS, Wild Country Companion, Wilderness First Aid, Wilderness Survival

To order these titles check with your local bookseller or call The Globe Pequot Press at 1-800-243-0495.
www.Falcon.com